Religion and Modern Society

Religion is now high on the public agenda, with recent events focusing the world's attention on Islam in particular. This book provides a unique historical and comparative analysis of the place of religion in the emergence of modern secular society. Bryan S. Turner considers the problems of multicultural, multi-faith societies and legal pluralism in terms of citizenship and the state, with special emphasis on the problems of defining religion and the sacred in the secularisation debate. He explores a range of issues central to current debates: the secularisation thesis itself, the communications revolution, the rise of youth spirituality, feminism, piety and religious revival. *Religion and Modern Society* contributes to political and ethical controversies through discussions of cosmopolitanism, religion and globalisation. It concludes with a pessimistic analysis of the erosion of the social in modern society and the inability of new religions to provide 'social repair'.

BRYAN S. TURNER is the Presidential Professor of Sociology at the City University of New York (CUNY) Graduate Center and Director of the Committee on Religion, and Director of the Centre for the Study of Contemporary Muslim Societies, University of Western Sydney, Australia. He is a prominent figure in the field of the sociology of religion and editor of *The Cambridge Dictionary of Sociology* (2006).

Religion and Modern Society

Citizenship, Secularisation and the State

BRYAN S. TURNER

CAMBRIDGE
UNIVERSITY PRESS

CAMBRIDGE UNIVERSITY PRESS
Cambridge, New York, Melbourne, Madrid, Cape Town, Singapore,
São Paulo, Delhi, Dubai, Tokyo, Mexico City

Cambridge University Press
The Edinburgh Building, Cambridge CB2 8RU, UK

Published in the United States of America by
Cambridge University Press, New York

www.cambridge.org
Information on this title: www.cambridge.org/9780521675321

First published 2011

Printed in the United Kingdom at the University Press, Cambridge

A catalogue record for this publication is available from the British Library

Library of Congress Cataloguing-in-Publication Data
Turner, Bryan S.
  Religion and modern society : citizenship, secularisation and the state /
Bryan S. Turner.
    p. cm.
  ISBN 978-0-521-85864-9 (Hardback) – ISBN 978-0-521-67532-1 (pbk.)
  1. Religion and sociology. 2. Religion and state. 3. Secularism.
4. Globalization–Religious aspects. I. Title.
  BL60.T85 2011
  306.6–dc22

                                                                2010033391

ISBN 978-0-521-85864-9 Hardback
ISBN 978-0-521-67532-1 Paperback

Contents

Acknowledgements

Various aspects of this volume have appeared elsewhere, but they have also been heavily revised for this publication. The Introduction draws upon a review article on the state of contemporary sociology of religion from *The Sociological Review* (2009, 57(1)). Chapter 1, which sets out a basic definition of religion and the centrality of the body first appeared as two separate entries on the body and religion in *Theory, Culture & Society* (2006, 87(2–3)). Chapter 2 was originally a presentation given at King's College Cambridge in a seminar on social theory, and the argument was later developed as the *Nachwort* to *Die elementaren Formen des religiosen Lebens* (2007, pp. 654–64). Chapter 3 was first published as 'Max Weber on Islam and Confucianism', in Peter Clarke's *The Oxford Handbook of the Sociology of Religion* (2009). A version of Chapter 4 was published in the *Journal of Classical Sociology* (2005, 5(3)) as 'Talcott Parsons's Sociology of Religion and the Expressive Revolution'. Chapter 8 was a seminar in 2009 given at Macquarie University Australia in a series of talks on social inclusion. Chapter 9 was first given as a lecture at a conference on religion and the state which was sponsored by the Australian Academy of the Social Sciences and the University of Western Sydney in 2009. Chapter 10 was originally a lecture given to a conference at Tokyo University in 2007 on Ubiquitous Media, which was organised by *Theory, Culture & Society* and subsequently a version was published in that journal (2008, 25(7–8). Chapter 11 was a conference paper which was delivered to the Asia Research Institute at the National University of Singapore in 2007. Chapter 12 on religion in a global age was first published in the *European Journal of Social Theory* (2001, 17(6)). Chapter 13 was initially a lecture, written with Professor Thomas Cushman, and delivered to the Newhouse Center for the Humanities at Wellesley College. Chapter 14 was a public lecture at the Graduate Center City University of New York in 2009; I wish to thank the participants for valuable criticisms. These various lectures and publications have been systematically rewritten and revised for this volume.

This study in the sociology of religion was finally put together while I was a visiting professor at Wellesley College. I am grateful to the College and to the Newhouse Center for the Humanities for the research opportunity to complete this work. This opportunity to work at Wellesley was initially made possible by Professor Thomas Cushman, to whom I am indebted.

Introduction: the state of the sociology of religion

Defining the field

In this Introduction, I outline some of the major issues in the contemporary sociology of religion and in the process offer a short overview of recent developments in the sub-field. Within this framework, I provide an interpretation of various key issues, such as secularisation, the state and the regulation of religious life, youth cultures and spirituality, the complex relationships between the sacred and the profane, and the nature of religion itself. However, the major issues confronting any understanding of religion in modern societies are all related to globalisation. Two obvious examples are fundamentalism and religious violence. Perhaps the dominant interpretation of these phenomena is that, with the massive disruption to traditional societies and economies, religious cultures provide the raw ideological material of violent protest. The violent secular groups of the 1960s and 1970s – the Red Brigade and the *Baader-Meinhof* – have simply been replaced by the *jihardists* of this century. However, my approach in this volume is to downplay the themes of religious violence and radicalism, looking instead at the development of religious revivalism and piety among diverse urban communities and the consequences of these pious practices for secular societies.

As a consequence of globalisation, modern societies are predominantly multicultural and consequently they are also multi-faith societies in which the state more and more intervenes to organise and regulate religion through diverse policies that I collectively refer to under the notion of 'the management of religions'. In every multicultural society, there are, almost invariably, many typically large diasporic communities that are held together less by the secular ties of citizenship than by a shared religious culture. However, with the creation of these ethnically complex and spatially diasporic communities, religions are also modified by the diverse processes of exclusion, accommodation or integration. In these transformations, the Internet plays a critical role for displaced communities that would otherwise exist without any formal or established religious leadership (Bunt, 2009). Because labour migration typically involves the movement of young people, there has also been an expansion, with the facility of the Internet, of unorthodox, transient religion that is often referred to as 'spirituality'. These expressions of modern subjectivity are not so much religion on line, as on-line religion. The result has been a blossoming of post-institutional, hybrid and post-orthodox religiosity. In the language of Zymunt Bauman (2000), who has been particularly observant of such social forms of post-modernity, we might use the expression 'liquid religion' to capture the flavour of such post-institutional spirituality. This urban milieu of the transient, the underprivileged and the marginalised worker is also a recruiting ground for more radical, oppositional expressions of social resentment expressed in the garment of religion. In Islam, while the Internet facilitates discussion and promotes understanding, apostates can also develop blogs to defend their counter-position, as in the case of Ayaan Hirsi Ali, who maintains a Dutch blog in many languages (Varisco, 2010).

With the contemporary eruption of radical religious movements, religious nationalism and the war on terror, there has also been a transformation of civil society which, with increasing securitisation, may also evolve towards what I have called 'the enclave society' (Turner, 2007a). With the emergence, of enclaves, ghettoes, diasporas and walled communities, society as a whole is divided and fragmented. My argument is that the development of global and mobile societies is therefore producing an 'immobility regime' in which the movement of people is in fact severely restricted by the new demands' for security. One indication of these restrictions is the regulation of borders by the erection of walls and various security installations. Religious diversity, cultural fragmentation, parallel communities and social 'enclavement' pose significant problems for liberalism, democracy and multiculturalism.

The socio-cultural problems of multicultural liberal societies are thus compounded by the growing securitisation of society by the state in response to real or imagined threats to the stability of civil society. There is therefore a serious risk to the continued enjoyment of civil liberties. Within this scenario of growing risk, the state, both liberal and authoritarian, is drawn into the management of religion through diverse policies such as the re-education of religious leaders or the regulation of dress codes or legislation to control marriage and divorce customs. The regulation of female dress codes through restrictions on the veil is the paramount example. Islamic dress codes in particular have become a site for debates not simply about liberalism but about modernity itself (Göle, 1996). In this politically charged environment, the veil – as a shorthand for women, social rights, sexual equality, patriarchy and democratic participation – has become the major point of division between Islam and the West (Lewis, 1993).

These developments often lead to pessimistic and bleak conclusions in the social sciences that predict the erosion of liberty, the breakdown of the public sphere and the growth of urban disorder. There are, however, other developments with globalisation that may give rise to less troublesome outcomes and more optimistic responses. One possibility is the development of various forms of cosmopolitanism that might outweigh the fissiparous tendencies of civil society. Cosmopolitanism, starting with the Stoics, has been associated with secularism and Western elites, but there are other formations such as vernacular and Islamic cosmopolitanism (Iqtidar, 2010). The universalism of the message of Saint Paul in Galatians (3.28) – 'There is neither Jew nor Greek, there is neither slave nor free, there is neither male nor female'– can also be regarded as a foundation of Christian cosmopolitanism that makes Paul our contemporary (Badiou, 2003). As a result, religion – in all its complexity and diversity – stands at the heart of these problematic political and social developments, and therefore the study of religion and religions has achieved an intellectual and political urgency and importance it has not had for decades.

With this eruption of the religious in the public sphere, the notion that modern societies are secular has been seriously challenged and various alternatives to secularisation have been proposed, such as de-secularisation, re-sacralisation and the emergence of a post-secular society. In the modern world, religion, contrary to the conventional understanding of the process of modernisation as necessarily entailing secularisation, continues to play a major role in politics, society and culture. Indeed, that public role appears if anything to be expanding rather than contracting and hence in recent years there has been a flurry of academic activity around such ideas as 'political religion', 'public religions' and 'religious nationalism'. In broad terms, the separation between church and state has become unclear and possibly unworkable, and religion appears to be increasingly an important component of public culture rather than simply a matter of private belief and practice.

Of course, the salience of religion in modern culture depends a great deal on which society we are looking at. While northern Europe has been associated with secularisation in terms of declining participation in church life and with the erosion of orthodox belief, religious vitality has been seen as a consistent aspect of 'American exceptionalism' (Torpey, 2010). It is, in any case, more accurate to talk about the 'de-Christianisation' of Europe rather than its secularisation, and hence about a 'post-Christian Europe' rather than a secular Europe (Davie, 2006; 2010). Outside Europe, Pentecostalism, charismatic movements and religious revivalism are important social developments, and such movements have challenged the historical hegemony of the Catholic Church in Latin America (Lehmann, 1996). In Europe, the growth of diasporic communities with large religious minorities has also changed the cultural map of what were thought to be predominantly secular societies. In Britain, while the Church of England declines, migration from former African colonies has brought African fundamentalism into the predominantly secular culture of British cities, where it facilitates transnational networks and provides a haven for new migrants. The Assemblies of God for migrants from Zimbabwe is one example (Lehmann, 2002). Pentecostalism, having transformed much of African Christianity, is now having an impact on European and American congregations, not only through migration, but also through their evangelical outreach and reverse missionary activity (Adogame, 2010).

There is naturally a temptation to think that, after 9/11 and the terrorist bombings in London, Madrid, Bali and Istanbul, the revival of interest in religion is merely a function of the political importance of understanding radical versions of Islam. The work of Mark Juergensmeyer has been influential in this respect, in such publications as *Terror on the Mind of God* (2000) and *Global Rebellion* (2008). There has been considerable scholarly interest in 'radical Islam', 'political Islam', 'globalised Islam' and so forth (Kepel, 2002; Roy, 1994), but these prejudicial labels can create a false and discriminatory picture of Islamic revivalism as a whole. In the majority of Muslim communities, there is little evidence of political radicalism and even less for naked violence. Comparative research shows that, while Muslims may be critical of American foreign policy, they admire Western-style democracy and want economic development and improvements in education (Hassan, 2002; 2008). The majority of Muslims world-wide condemned the terrorist attack on the Twin Towers, but remained hostile to the Bush administration (Saikal, 2003). Muslims may often be dissatisfied and frustrated, but they are rarely politically hostile to their host environment, and in France, despite the conflict over head-scarves in public schools, the majority of Muslims believe that French democracy is a success (Joppke, 2009).

Scholarly interest in 'public religions' in modernity cannot, and should not, be confined simply to the study of Islam. Scholars have also drawn our attention to the radicalisation of all three Abrahamic religions – Islam, Christianity and Judaism (Kepel, 2004b). The academic study of religion and religions cannot afford to limit its scope to the radicalisation of religious consciousness (Islamic or otherwise) and hence we need to think more carefully about the broader implications of globalisation.

In this volume I will identify various manifestations of the global-isation of religion. These include the rise of fundamentalism in various religious traditions, which is associated in large part with the compe-tition between religions. Secondly, there is a related development in the pietisation of everyday life as more people, but especially women, move into the formal labour market, become urbanised and acquire some education and literacy. Thirdly, there is the growth of post-institutional spirituality in youth cultures and finally there is some resurgence of traditional folk religion, often associated with magical practices and witchcraft (Comaroff and Comaroff, 1999; 2000). The differences within the category of 'global religions' raises an obvious question: Is there any common denominator within the globalisation of religion and religions? In this study, I argue that all forms of religion are now overlaid with consumerism and that many forms of religion have been commodified. The global market has had significant effects on religious life and, as a result, I argue that we are not in a post-secular environment, but on the contrary the separation of the world (the profane) and religion (the sacred) has largely evaporated. Without some significant tensions between the religious and the secular, it is difficult to believe that we are entering a post-secular or re-sacralised civilisation. I explore the further paradox that everywhere we see (worldly) religion flourishing, while the world of the sacred is shrink-ing. My argument therefore hinges in part on a traditional set of distinctions in religious studies which includes faith and religion, the sacred and religion, the religious impulse and the religious institution (Hervieu-Leger, 2000). This argument is laid out more fully in Chapter 1 and underpins many subsequent chapters.

Globalisation studies

Attempts to understand religion in a global context raise interesting conceptual problems about the definition of religion and methodological questions about the nature of global sociology. We can distinguish between global religion (the possibility of a generic religious consciousness) and global religions (the transformation of existing religions by globalising processes). The emergence of global religious cosmopolitanism might be an example of the former and the rise of radical Islam and Christian fundamentalism examples of the latter. Research in globalisation studies has, generally speaking, been concerned to study how existing religions have, for one reason or another, become more global and what consequences that has for belief and practice. Little research in fact has been devoted to the idea of the possible emergence of a new global religion, while more attention has been given to the transformation of an existing culture such as Hinduism into a world-wide religion. In this Introduction I propose to use the contemporary discussion of globalisation as a framework for a more general commentary on religion. Before looking more seriously into the issue of global religion, let us take stock of globalisation as such.

Global sociology is not simply international or comparative sociology. A genuinely global sociology may be difficult to create, but it is not merely the comparative sociology of global processes. It needs to address emergent global phenomena that are specifically aspects of contemporary globalisation (Turner and Khondker, 2010). Secondly, the sociology of religion in the global age has to be more than a macro-sociology of religion in modern societies. The fundamental question is whether globalisation (the increasing interconnectedness of the social world and the shrinkage of time and space) produces new phenomena rather than simply a modification of existing social reality. This argument is somewhat parallel to the position taken by Manuel Castells (1996) and John Urry (2000; 2007), that we need a 'mobile sociology' of global flows and networks to deal with the social changes brought about by globalisation. The specific issue that lies behind this notion of 'mobilities' is whether we can generate a global sociology (a sociology not embedded in local or national paradigms) of global religion (religious phenomena that are not simply the products of the international connectedness of separate and distinct religious cultures). In fact, research into religious globalisation has so far been inclined to suggest that the effect of globalisation has been unsurprisingly to create an interaction between the local and the global. Roland Robertson (1992a: 173–4) coined the phrase 'glocalisation' to describe this phenomenon.

These global processes are inherently contradictory, and hence any general theory of religious globalisation will have to take into account its fundamentally incongruent social character and consequences. The ways in which we explore these processes may require us to transform our underlying philosophy of social science, or more narrowly our epistemological, paradigms. In the jargon of contemporary sociology, in a global world, we will need to become more reflexive about our constitutive presuppositions. The result of this reflexivity about sociology and its understanding of 'globality' is to make the category 'religion' deeply problematical. Is there anything in common between the myriad forms of cultural life about which we, partly for convenience, employ the term 'religion'? To open up this discussion, which preoccupies this study of religion, I shall undertake a somewhat discursive overview of the basic issues.

We can begin a discussion of globalisation with an analysis of the notion of religion as an actual system of belief and practice. Globalisation has been significant in the development of diffuse religious civilisations into formal and specific religious systems. There has been a historical process in which ancient religious cultures have been reconstructed as religious systems. This process of institutional reification has transformed local, diverse and fragmented cultural practices into recognisable systems of religion. Globalisation has had the paradoxical effect of making religions, through their religious intellectuals (their theologians, philosophers and religious leaders), more self-conscious of themselves as 'world religions'. Scholars have often referred to Islam, for example, in the plural ('Islams') to indicate its diversity and complexity, but 'modern conditions have made religions more self-consciously global in character' (Smart 1989: 556) and in the process there is a need to make a religion more coherent. We can trace this development of a global consciousness of a system of religions (Luhmann, 1995) back, for example, to the World's Parliament of Religions in 1893, when religious representatives were suddenly more conscious of the transnational issues of mission and the political significance of being recognised as a religion with world-wide implications. Subsequent parliaments in 1999, 2004 and 2009 sought to promote religious harmony, reconciliation with aboriginal communities and addressed pressing human problems. New media of communication have intensified the interactions between religions, creating a reflexive awareness of religions as separate, differentiated areas of social activity – a development anticipated in Max Weber's discussion of the separate value spheres (religion, economics, politics, aesthetics, the erotic sphere, and intellectual sphere) in the famous 'Religious Rejections of the World and their Directions' (*Zwischenbetrachtung*) (Weber, 2009). The outcome has been the promotion of the idea of 'world religions' as a global system within which the various religions compete for influence on a global stage. Confucianism, Hinduism, Buddhism, Daoism, Jainism and so on have joined the monotheistic Abrahamic traditions as 'world religions' with the creeds, leadership and institutional apparatus that we expect a religion to possess.

To take another example, the growth of religious fundamentalism is often regarded as the principal or indeed the only consequence of globalisation (as the most recent aspect of modernisation). Fundamentalism is a common development in the three Abrahamic religions, but it is also present in various reform movements in Buddhism (Marty and Appleby, 1991). Religious fundamentalism is often mistakenly defined as traditionalism, because it is seen to be anti-modern (Lechner and Boli, 2004). Religious revivalism is thus seen to be a protest against the secular consequences of global consumerism and Westernisation. There is obviously evidence to show how fundamentalism has attempted to constrain and contain the growth of cultural hybridisation, to sustain religious authority and orthodoxy, and in particular to curb the growth of women's movements and to oppose the public recognition of homosexuality. This view is questionable for at least two reasons. First, fundamentalist movements employ the full range of modern means of communication and organisation, and secondly they are specifically anti-traditionalist in rejecting the taken-for-granted assumptions of traditional practice (Antoun, 2001). Fundamentalism is characteristically urban and its target has often been the rural

manifestations of folk religion. In Islam, since the formation of the
Muslim Brothers in the 1920s, fundamentalists have consistently
rejected traditional religion, specifically traditional forms of Sufism. If
we consider fundamentalism as a verb, 'to fundamentalise' a religion
can be seen as a strategy for an alternative modernity, not a traditional
strategy against modernity (Eisenstadt, 2002; 2004).

However, fundamentalism is only one aspect of modern religious
change. It is often claimed that globalisation produces cultural hybridisation, because the interaction of different cultures through migration
and the growth of diasporic communities creates, primarily in global
cities, a new cultural complexity (Appadurai, 2001). With cultural
hybridity, there is also religious experimentation. These hybrid forms
of religion are often constructed self-consciously and they are closely
related to youth movements and to generational change (Edmunds
and Turner, 2002). Global, hybrid religiosity can be interpreted as a
form of religious popular culture. In the United States, for example,
sociologists have identified the emergence of a 'quest culture' that
attempts to find meaning experimentally from different and diverse
traditions. The result is growing religious hybridity. The mechanism
by which these hybrid religious styles emerge is through a 'spiritual
market place' (Roof, 1993; 1999). These quest cultures have been
critically evaluated as forms of expressive individualism, because they
are related to what Talcott Parsons (1974) called the 'expressive
revolution', which gave more emphasis to emotions, individualism
and subjectivity. New Age communities have become a popular topic
of sociological research (Heelas, 1996), but we need to understand
more precisely how the spiritual market-place functions globally
and how its various components are connected through the Internet
(Hadden and Cowan, 2000). Spiritual markets, religious individualism
and hybridisation create problems for traditional forms of authority,
and their individualism is often incompatible with the collective
organisation of traditional religiosity (Bellah, 1964).

There is another common argument in globalisation studies that
connects population growth and the educational revolution of the last
century with religious radicalism. Improvements in diet and public
health in many societies in the second half of the twentieth century
produced a rapid growth of populations. In many developing societies,
these demographic changes often occurred alongside an expansion of
formal education and the growth of literacy. Developing societies

often found themselves with a large cohort of young people who were educated but also unemployed or underemployed. Rapid population growth, expansion in university education, and the inequalities of the neo-liberal economic strategy of the 1980s resulted in disconnected and discontented youthful populations (Stiglitz, 2002). In the West, the post-war growth of universities was able to absorb the socially mobile lower-middle classes and, while the student movements in the late 1960s were troublesome, student radicalism in Western universities only rarely evolved into revolutionary politics. Radical religious movements, in a post-communist environment, have given global expression to waves of young people with high expectations and equally low satisfaction.

Religious radicalism and student political radicalism in general became a feature of campus life. Olivier Roy (1994) in *The Failure of Political Islam* claimed that these circumstances gave rise to the 'new Muslim intellectual' who created an ideological montage of political and religious beliefs, typically blending Marxism and the Qur'an to develop an anti-Western discourse. The Iranian radicals took over traditional notions such as *mustadafin* ('damned of the earth') and relocated them within a Marxist vision of class struggle and the collapse of capitalism. While radicals wanted violent change, the neo-fundamentalist, combining 'popularized scientific information with the strands of a religious sermon' (p. 98) wanted the re-Islamisation of society rather than a revolution, thereby allowing an alliance between neo-fundamentalism and the traditional clergy.

The growth of these student movements has been important in the evolution of 'political religions'. Islamic fundamentalism and political Islam are the classic illustrations. With the decline of communism, radical religion replaced secular politics as the rallying point of those who have experienced disappointment and alienation as a result of the failures of post-colonial nationalism. This argument – religion as an expression of the social disappointment and dislocation of economic change – is now inevitably associated with the clash of civilisations thesis (Huntington, 1993) and with the 'Jihad v. McWorld' dichotomy (Barber, 2001).

The Internet and the construction of global network technology provided the communication apparatus that transformed local student discontent into a world-wide oppositional politics. Simple technology such as the use of cassettes was important in the circulation of radical sermons and played an important role in the early development of fundamentalist movements. The Internet has been generally important in preserving social and cultural connections between minorities, diasporic communities and societies of origin. The Internet now plays a significant role in religious education and missions in the world religions, but paradoxically it has democratic characteristics that are also corrosive of religious authority. The modern Internet is devolved, local and flexible. It permits the growth of alternative religious cultures, providing sites for the organisation of followers and disciples around local charismatic leaders. From a sociological point of view, the Internet poses a radical challenge to authority and legitimacy. How can traditional, text-based and oral authority survive in a post-textual society? How can traditional forms of pedagogy be sustained in a digital culture? Some aspects of these global transformations in religious authority are discussed in Chapters 11 and 12.

In the developing world, religious radicalism is also associated with rapid urbanisation and the destruction of traditional communities and rural occupations. In Iran, this urbanisation produced a floating population of first-generation urban poor. However, in Western societies, these arguments cannot explain religious radicalism. Although there is a plausible argument to connect religious radicalism with social deprivation, some radical movements have also recruited from the lower-middle and middle classes among the children of migrants. Recent arrests in Britain appear to indicate that recruits to radical terrorist organisations can also be drawn from established third-generation Pakistani youth who are British citizens. We need more subtle and complex notions of 'alienation' in order to explain their sense of isolation from mainstream society and their identification with global Islam. In addition there are important differences between migrant alienation, religious identity and citizenship in different European societies and hence it is inappropriate to make hasty generalisations from superficial observations about such Muslim communities.

Although social scientists have examined many dimensions of globalisation, the legal dimensions have often been neglected. There are few general analyses of legal globalisation – an exception is William Twining's (2000) *Globalisation and Legal Theory*. One aspect of Islamic fundamentalism has been the revival of the *Shari'a*, or an attempt to extend the *Shari'a* into the public domain. In practice, the globalisation of Islamic law also involves a modernisation of traditional legal practice – a set of social changes that have been explored by Michael Peletz's (2002) *Islamic Modern*. The revival of Islamic law is a growing source of conflict (in Nigeria, Sudan, France and the Middle East). If the framework for national identity in the nineteenth century was citizenship, then the political framework for political membership in the twenty-first century is unclear. Religious globalisation appears to be closely connected with the national development of what Benedict Anderson (1991) called 'imaginary communities'. As these migrant communities become more established in the West, the question of legal pluralism emerges an important test of the depth of liberal commitment to multicultural and multi-faith societies. This problem of religion, social diversity and legal pluralism is addressed in Chapter 8.

One important aspect of law and globalisation has been the rise of human rights in the twentieth century and what I want to call a human-rights consciousness. The human-rights agenda of this period cannot be easily disconnected from an emerging religious cosmopolitanism which followed the collapse of empires and imperialism. The post-war European settlement saw the destruction of three large multi-ethnic political systems (the Ottoman empire, the Austro-Hungarian empire and the Russian state) and massive displacement of people resulting in cohorts of stateless peoples. The large-scale destruction of civilian populations in the Second World War and the problem of displaced peoples were important factors in the creation of the Universal Declaration of Human Rights by the United Nations in 1948.

Religious assumptions about suffering and healing have played an important role in shaping human-rights institutions, especially the evolution of truth commissions (Wilkinson, 2005). History has become a crucial aspect of human-rights processes, because reparations and justice require adequate records if trials are to take place. Collective memory is not only a condition of bringing criminals to justice, but also an important part of therapy for survivors. History has become a contested part of the legal process of human rights in framing collective memory, especially in relation to National Socialism and the Holocaust. These historical disputes do raise an important ethical and political problem: Is responsibility transmitted across generations indefinitely? Sustaining the idea of intergenerational guilt may be difficult, but without acceptance of responsibility it is difficult to see how forgiveness could have some therapeutic role. Recognition appears to be a precondition of forgiveness. The Truth and Reconciliation Commission in South Africa has been criticised on the grounds that truth-telling often secures an amnesty, but leaves the survivors without a sense of justice. The collective narrative of the African National Congress (ANC) is also under strain with tensions between those who suffered in South Africa and were imprisoned, and those who were exiled and spent their adolescence outside the country; there are tensions between the revolutionary ambitions of the founders and the inevitable normalisation of post-apartheid South Africa. How are collective memories constructed and sustained?

In an important essay *On Cosmopolitanism and Forgiveness*, Jacques Derrida (2001) attempts to unravel the growing importance of forgiveness and repentance in international law that has its origins in the Nuremberg Trials (a series of military tribunals) and the Eichmann trial. Derrida argues that the legal language of forgiveness for crimes against humanity only makes sense within a religious (that is, Christian) framework. Hence this globalisation of a religious language entails a 'globalatinisation' – the spread of Christian values into a global legal framework. Derrida sees an inevitable paradox in the legal quest for forgiveness: forgiveness only forgives the unforgivable. We are searching for the possibility of forgiving unforgivable crimes such as the Holocaust or the genocide of the Armenians. We also expect the criminals to ask for forgiveness, but the unforgivable nature of their crimes normally precludes such motives. Unforgivable crimes are inexpiable and irreparable. Who has the authority to forgive the unforgivable? This question requires a religious answer – only the sovereign has the grace and the right of forgiveness because the sovereign acts on behalf of God. For Derrida, states are always constructed by an act of violence such as the seizure of land or people. But because the sovereignty of the state is typically founded by an act of violence, how can the state distribute the grace of forgiveness? Can we have a notion of 'crimes against humanity' without a notion of evil?

The growth of a human-rights culture with notions of evil, forgiveness, confession and reparations is an example of the creation of a global religious consciousness and not simply the globalisation of an existing legal tradition. Obviously, legal institutions relating to confession and immunity were aspects of medieval Christianity, but the idea that heads of state can be held personally responsible for crimes against their own people before an international court is a product of modern globalisation and, I want to argue, the product of religious globalisation and not just the globalisation of religion. Therefore this process is not just Westernisation, or 'globalatinisation' to use Derrida's expression, because these values also become embedded in local cultures and they call forth indigenous ideas about rights. One interesting example has been the role of Theravada Buddhist values in the reconciliation process in contemporary Cambodia (Ledgerwood and Un, 2003). While Cambodian Buddhist culture had little under-standing of individual rights, Theravada Buddhist values proved to be easily reconciled with a human-rights culture (Luckmann, 1988). Buddhist values of compassion, tolerance and non-violence provided a fertile framework for programmes to promote human-rights values in war-torn Cambodia. Buddhist leaders saw the crisis of the civil war as a consequence of the breakdown of morality, and respect for human rights could only be achieved by the restoration of the basic Buddhist precepts in the community.

The human-rights discourse is a new cosmology that involves a bundle of notions that are profoundly religious: crimes against humanity, forgiveness, reparations, sacrifice and evil. This new culture involves further assumptions about cosmopolitanism and cosmopol-itan virtue – essentially respect for and care of the Other. Following Derrida, Judaeo-Christian religious assumptions have been globalised in the reparations culture. However, notions of vulnerability, human precariousness and dependency are not exclusively Western. Both Buddhism and Jainism have highly developed notions about suffering, impermanence, inter-dependency and care (Turner, 2006). This juridical-culture complex – human rights, truth and reconciliation commissions, international courts of justice, historical memory, genocide and the problem of evil – is one of the most significant, and one of the most neglected, aspects of religious globalisation (Brudholm and Cushman, 2009). The centre stage of scholarly activity has been preoccupied with violence and political religion and has ignored this quiet voice of peace, which currently sits off-stage.

Throughout this volume, I attempt to avoid excessive concentra-tion on religious violence and radicalism. Instead, I look at religion and everyday life and, rather than referring to fundamentalism, I am more concerned to study the growth of piety movements, especially among educated women. In order to understand piety, we need to consider how people try to follow religious rules in their routine encounters with the secular everyday world. At the centre of these piety rules, there is the discipline or management of the body. While the study of violence concentrates obviously on torture and the abuse of the human body, religious practice typically involves a regulation (diet) of the body (Turner, 1992; 1997; 2008a). In the last twenty years, the human body has become increasingly a major focus of modern economy, politics and culture. The importance of the body in modern political debate is a consequence of the bio-technology industry, modern military strategy and techniques, the greying of the populations of the advanced societies, changes in medical technology (such as new reproductive technologies), ethnic cleansing and the globalisation of disease (SARS for example). Perhaps this global consciousness of the body has been enhanced most notably by the HIV/AIDS epidemic. There is a sense of crisis in relation to the human body as signalled by the publication of influential books such as Francis Fukuyama's study of post-humanism in his *Our Posthuman Future* (2002), but what we do not know yet is how these changes are transforming traditional religious cosmologies. These social changes are obvious: new reproductive technologies that have separated sex from reproduction; the transformation of family life by new medical technologies; genetically modified food; the existence of therapeutic cloning and the possibility of human cloning; the applications of neuropharmacology in social control; and the potential for freezing humans by the method of cryonics. When considering the globalisation of religion, we should also think about the globalisation of the body.

Comparative religious studies and the construction of Buddhism

Throughout this study, the distinction between religion and the sacred becomes both a useful tool and a foil for defending aspects of the original secularisation thesis. If we can sustain a distinction between religion and the sacred, then one version of the secularisation thesis can recognise the modern growth of institutional religions and the concurrent decline of the sacred. This distinction emerged in traditional comparative sociology of religion. Religious studies should be in particular concerned with the social setting and historical origins of religion, its social and political consequences, and its impact on civilisations. In short, it should be sociological. This distinction is useful in evaluating most theories of secularisation which can often be parochial observations on local developments.

In part, I agree with the critical response of Steve Bruce (2001), who has consistently argued that there is little empirical support for the idea of a 're-sacralisation' of society. As sociologists, we do not need to recant our earlier views about the growth of secular societies. However, I depart from Bruce's defence of the secularisation thesis only in the sense that he concentrates too much on religion in Europe and North America. The picture is very different in Africa, Asia and Latin America. It follows that one cannot confront the secularisation thesis without undertaking comparative research seriously and increasingly, I would argue, globalisation research. It is in this context that the value of a distinction between the sacred and the religious becomes obvious.

Of course, this distinction takes us back to classical sociology. The consistent question in the background of this debate – from Émile Durkheim onwards – has been whether Buddhism is a religion at all. The beliefs and practices of Buddhism on the surface appear to be so different from the Abrahamic faiths that it consistently presents itself as the litmus test of both generic and particular definitions of religion. This issue provides one reason for some attention to the work of Trevor Ling, who was professor of comparative religion at the University of Manchester in the United Kingdom. He wrote extensively on Buddhism (Ling, 1973) and also produced an influential textbook on comparative religion (Ling, 1968). Because Ling wanted to understand religions from a historical perspective, he also thought that we should not study religions separately, but simultaneously, in order to examine how they interact with each other, including how they borrow from and influence each other. He looked at the historical origins of the great 'world religions' and explored how they were interrelated in time and space. The argument here is that we should not impose our contemporary and historically specific understanding of 'religion' on a range of civilisations and social movements that may have very different characteristics.

Within a religious studies framework, we cannot take 'religion' for granted as though it referred to a discrete, distinct and unchanging set of phenomena. Ling approached this issue from several dimensions. Like other scholars of his period, he distinguished between religion (generic) and 'religions' (specific historical manifestations). He explored the differences between the human quest for the sacred (or faith) and the particular institutionalisation of these human endeavours. In this respect he followed Max Weber's idea about charismatic change and the institutionalisation of charismatic figures, or Rudolf Otto's concept of the holy ([1923] 2003). This approach was to some extent dependent on Wilfred Cantwell Smith's influential *The Meaning and End of Religion* (1962). The argument in summary is that 'religious inspiration' is historically transformed into 'religious institutions'; this formulation opens up the possibility that the latter is a corruption of the former. Because Ling wanted to treat the history of religions very seriously and drew a distinction between 'the religious impulse' and 'the religious system', he wanted to pay special attention to the founders and founding of religion.

Ling's approach was to claim that religion in the modern period (from the middle of the seventeenth century) had in the West been transformed into a private conscience of the individual, involving a separation of church and state, and the decline of public rituals and a religious calendar. Ling argued that outside Christianity things had been very different. In *The Buddha* (1973) he argued that Buddha Gautama had not been interested in founding a 'religion' in the Western sense, but wanted to combat individualism through a reform of society. Buddhism was a social philosophy that assumed a close involvement between state and religious community (the *sangha*). The Buddha sought not a new religion but a new society. With respect to the foundations of early Islam, Ling also concluded that the Prophet also sought a new society which was, for example, expressed through the Constitution of Medina. Similar arguments can be developed in terms of Confucianism. The philosophy of Confucius was not meant to create a personalised, individual form of religion, but on the contrary to develop a blueprint for the proper ordering of society and government.

Another special feature therefore of Ling's approach in this critical exploration of religious institutions was to draw out a paradoxical parallel between Marxism and Buddhism. Karl Marx had been a nineteenth-century critic of organised Christianity, which had been an aspect of the alienation of the working class. Marx wanted to reject the Christian view of the world in order to create a new society based on equality, and in which private property and individualism would be destroyed. In Germany Marx saw an alliance between the repressive

Prussian state and Protestantism. In books such as *Karl Marx and Religion* (1980) and *Buddha, Marx and God* (1966), Ling drew a parallel between Marx's criticisms of excessive individualism in capitalism and the Buddha's criticisms of excessive individualism in the emerging cities of north-eastern India in his own day.

Ling, in these historical, comparative and sociological studies, had been profoundly influenced by Max Weber, especially the series in the *Archiv für Sozialwissenschaft und Sozialforschung* and subsequently published as *The Religion of India* (1958a), *The Religion of China* (1951) and *Ancient Judaism* ([1921] 1952). However, he profoundly disagreed with Weber's characterisation of 'ancient Buddhism' in *The Religion of India*, where Weber said 'it is a specifically unpolitical and anti-political status religion, more precisely a religious "technology" of wandering and of intellectually-schooled mendicant monks ... it is a "salvation religion" if one is to use the name "religion" for an ethical movement without a deity and without a cult' (Weber, [1921] 1952: 206). Ling disagreed completely, arguing that Buddhism had very clear political concerns for the reform of society, and it was not simply a movement of isolated monks, but had to build a *sangha* to carry out the reform of society. Ling did agree that the atheistic framework of Buddhism made the use of the word 'religion' problematic in this context.

Ling's work brings out, therefore, many of the issues associated with the comparative study of religion in which Buddhism, with its antipathy to the monotheistic, prophetic traditions, cannot be easily classified. Ling's solution was to treat Buddhism as a civilisation with a particular conception of the collective life of the individual. Ling's approach does, however, bring out yet another problem, which is that it is very difficult for contemporary considerations of Buddhism not to see Buddhism through the lens of Buddhist studies. In thinking about Buddhism it is difficult to avoid its prior interpretation in religious studies as a result of its interaction with, among other influences, Christian missions and Western colonialism (Newell, 2010).

Western Buddhist scholarship took shape in the 1850s, when academic scholars were relatively uninterested in Buddhism as it was actually practised in British Ceylon and Burma or in French Indo-China. Instead, they favoured the study of the classical Buddhist texts. This preference for ancient texts was partly driven by the impact of Protestantism on European cultures, because Protestantism also emphasised the importance of textual research in Biblical criticism and regarded the survival of ritual in Roman Catholicism as an aberration. Catholicism was seen by its Reformed critics as a corruption of the primitive church, and Protestant missionaries saw nineteenth-century folk Buddhism as a corruption of the lofty ideals of the original Buddhist community. Buddhist scholars as a result preferred Theravada Buddhism over Mahayana and Tantric Buddhism, and treated Tibetan Buddhism with its rich ritual life and pantheon of gods and goddesses as 'Lamaism', which they equated with Catholicism (Lopez, 2002). Early Buddhist studies were also fascinated with the problem of recreating the life of the Buddha, just as biblical scholars were at the time in search of 'the historical Jesus'. The historical Buddha was implicitly placed alongside Martin Luther, because they were both seen to be religious reformers. The Buddha's criticisms of the caste system were seen to place him in the role of an Asian social reformer. Against this legacy, modern Buddhist studies are more influenced by anthropological and sociological research that examines the actuality, not the 'textuality', of Buddhism (Schopen, 1997), and as a consequence there has been a re-evaluation of the status of Tibetan Buddhism.

Although Ling's account of Buddhism was also influenced by this legacy, in that for him Buddha was a social reformer, he recognised that one cannot interpret Buddhism via Weber as a socially withdrawn, soteriological community of intellectuals. There is finally one further aspect of Ling's career that raises an issue that remains somewhat submerged in this volume – apart from resurfacing briefly in my discussion of Pierre Bourdieu in Chapter 6. Ling was a critic of 'religions', while being himself profoundly religious. That is, he was conscious of the problems associated with the exclusionary claims of religion as it became institutionalised as a religious system. His encounter with Indian spirituality had opened a depth of personal experience that could no longer be comfortably housed within his own Christian identity. In this respect he saw himself as more Buddhist than Christian, indeed he followed the philosophy of Rabindranath Tagore in arguing that the way of the Buddha is the elimination of all limits of love. His life and work raised in an acute form the enduring question of the relationship between faith and knowledge. Can a scientific scholar of religion also be religious? For Ling, in taking a broad and comparative definition of religion as civilisation, the combination of faith and reason was not an insuperable problem. He was able to manage sociology and theology simultaneously and so believing and knowing were not separate realms.

Conclusion: the end of the social?

My approach to the sociology of religion, and to sociology more generally, has been deeply influenced by the intellectual contributions of Alasdair MacIntyre, who was both sociologist and philosopher, and combined historical insight with political criticism. In this study, my approach to the definition of religion and the sacred, and to the broad processes of secularisation and de-secularisation, can be regarded as an attempt to combine the sociological legacy of Durkheim with the philosophical brilliance of MacIntyre. For both Durkheim and MacIntyre, secularisation involved the dilution of the collective and emotional character of religious practices alongside the erosion of community by modernisation. In modernity, there is an inevitable erosion of the authority of collective religious belief and a greater indeterminacy about religious practice, as individuals become more reflexive about underlying classificatory principles. The social roots of belief are slowly destroyed by the growth of modern individualism and by the technologies of communication that bypass embedded social relationships.

Why has there been a revival of religion in the public sphere? Why have forms of religious nationalism become so prevalent? One answer is that religious cosmologies and symbolisation have a collective force that was not fully available to the ideological systems of humanism, communism and nationalism. By contrast, religion allows a national community to express its history in deep-rooted myths or sacred time as if that national history had a universal significance, namely to express the mythical history of a nation in terms of a story of suffering and survival about humanity as a whole. The implication is that social life can never be an entirely secular arrangement.

PART I

Theoretical frameworks: the problem of religion in sociology

1 | *Religion, religions and the body*

Introduction: etymological roots

The definition of religion has for a long time confounded the sociology of religion. The basic issue is common to sociology as a whole and it concerns the problem of the cultural specificity of our basic concepts. Our understanding of religion may have only small relevance to other societies. In part because Christianity was in the nineteenth century associated, rightly or wrongly, with Western colonialism, there is the suspicion that the definition of religion in the social sciences will be heavily coloured by Christian assumptions. This issue comes out very clearly in Max Weber's comparative sociology of religion, in which, for example, it is not clear that Confucianism is a religion at all. Belief in a High God is largely absent from Asian religious cultures and Confucianism is perhaps best regarded as a state ideology relating to social order and respect for authority. Similarly, Buddhism may be understood as 'the Righteous Way' (*Dharma*) that develops meditation practices to regulate human passions. Daoism is typically a system of beliefs and practices promoting health and longevity through exercises such as breathing techniques. Syncretism is also a notable characteristic of China, especially between Buddhism and Daoism, and hence these religious traditions often overlap and borrow from each other. There was also a cultural division of functions in which Confucianism was important in family concerns, Buddhism for funeral services and Daoism for psychological and health matters.

Weber and Durkheim had very different strategies in trying to define religion. Durkheim, in search of a generic definition in *The Elementary Forms of Religious Life* ([1912] 2001), treated religion as simply one aspect of a more general question of classification. For him, religion involved the classification of phenomena into the sacred and profane, that is, things that are set aside and forbidden. However, Durkheim was less concerned with beliefs and more interested as a sociologist in how religious practices demarcate the classificatory boundaries and further how collective experiences constituted communities. Scattered Australian aboriginal groups are brought together periodically by their common religious practices with the result that their sense of belonging is regularly re-invigorated during episodes of collective emotional euphoria. Durkheim was concerned to understand religion as such rather than the different manifestations of the sacred in world religions.

By contrast, in *The Sociology of Religion* Weber (1966) was probably less concerned with these anthropological questions and more interested, from the perspective of historical and comparative sociology, in how religious orientations contribute to general patterns of social change. His most famous work in the sociology of religion – *The Protestant Ethic and the Spirit of Capitalism* (2002) – was a study of the social and economic role of the Protestant sects in the rise of rational capitalism. Consequently Weber was interested in the study of religions in all of their complexity and diversity in the comparative study of human civilisations. Whereas Durkheim had begun his work on aboriginal religion with a long and complicated analysis of the sacred, with the scientific goal of providing a generic definition of religion, Weber argued that a satisfactory definition of religion could only be attempted as the conclusion to scholarly research.

One consequence of these definitional problems is that we must remain sensitive to the actual meaning and origins of the words we use to describe religion and the sacred. Derrida, in 'Faith and Knowledge' (1998: 34) notes, following Émile Benveniste's (1973) *Indo-European Language and Society*, that the word 'religion' (*religio*) has two distinctive roots. Firstly, *relegere* means to bring together or to harvest. Secondly, *religare* means to tie or to bind together. The first meaning indicates the religious foundations of any social group that is gathered together, while the second points to the disciplines that are necessary for controlling human beings and creating a regulated and disciplined life. The first meaning indicates the role of the cult in forming human membership, while the second meaning points to the regulatory practices of religion as the discipline of passions. This distinction formed the basis of Kant's philosophical analysis of religion and morality. In *Religion within the Boundaries of Mere Reason* ([1763] 1998), Kant distinguished between religion as cult, which seeks favours from God through prayer and offerings to bring healing and wealth to its followers, and religion as moral action that commands human beings to change their behaviour in order to lead a better life. Kant further elaborated this point by an examination of 'reflecting faith' that compels humans to strive for salvation through faith rather than the possession of religious knowledge. The implication of Kant's distinction was that Protestant Christianity was the only true 'reflecting faith', and in a sense therefore the model of all authentic religions. Kant's distinction was fundamentally about those religious injunctions that call men – I use this gendered form deliberately – to moral action and hence demand that humans assert their autonomy and responsibility. In order to have autonomy, human beings need to act independently of God. In a paradoxical fashion, Christianity implies the 'death of God' because it calls people to personal freedom and autonomy without any divine assistance. Hence the Christian faith is ultimately self-defeating, because human maturity implies that an autonomous individual would no longer need the support provided by institutionalised religion. The paradoxical consequence, which has been observed by many philosophers after Kant, is that the very success of Christianity in creating human independence is the secularisation of society.

These Kantian principles were almost certainly influential in the sociology of Max Weber. In *The Sociology of Religion* (1966), Weber distinguished between the religion of the masses and the religion of the virtuosi. While the masses seek comforts from religion, especially healing, the virtuosi fulfil the ethical demands of religion in search of spiritual salvation or personal enlightenment. The religion of the masses requires saints and holy men to satisfy their needs, and hence charisma is corrupted by the demand for miracles and spectacles. More importantly, Weber distinguished between those religions that reject the world by challenging its traditions (such as inner-worldly asceticism) and those religions that seek to escape from the world through mystical flight (such as other-worldly mysticism). The former religions (primarily the Calvinistic radical sects) have had revolutionary consequences for human society in the formation of rational capitalism. The implication of this tradition is paradoxical. First, Christianity (or at least Puritanism) is the only true religion (as a reflecting faith), and secondly Christianity gives rise to a process of secularisation that spells out its own self-overcoming (*Aufhebung*).

The history of the sciences of religion and religions

The emergence of a science of religion and religions in which the sacred became a topic of disinterested, objective inquiry was itself an important statement about the general character of social change. Indeed, such a science of religion might itself be taken as an index of secularisation. The very development of the sciences of religion implies an important level of critical self-reflexive scrutiny in a society. In the Western world, the study of 'religion' as a topic of independent inquiry was initially undertaken by religious men (typically theologians) who wanted to understand how Christianity as a revealed religion could be or was differentiated from other religions. The need to study religious diversity arose as an inevitable consequence of colonial contact with other religious traditions (such as Buddhism) and with phenomena that shared a distant family resemblance with religion, such as fetishism, animism and magic. Because the science of religion implies a capacity for self-reflection and criticism, it is often claimed that other religions that have not achieved this level of introspection do not possess a science of religion. While different cultures give religion a different content, Christianity was a world religion. For G. W. F. Hegel, religion and philosophy were both modes of access to understanding the Absolute (or God), and the philosophy of religion differed from theology in that it was the study of religion as such. In Hegel's dialectical scheme, the increasing self-awareness of the Spirit was a consequence of the historical development of Christianity. The philosophical study of religion was an important stage in the historical development of human understanding.

There is an important tension between religion and philosophy in terms of their claims to truth. This tension is between revelation and reason as different modes of understanding. The Enlightenment was significant in the development of classifications of religion, since the Enlightenment philosophers typically treated religion as a form of false knowledge. The Enlightenment philosophers emphasised the importance of rational self-inspection as a source of dependable understanding against revelatory experiences. For Hume, Voltaire and Diderot, Christianity was a form of irrational or mistaken knowledge of the world, and hence the Enlightenment sharpened the distinction between revelation and reason as the modes of apprehension of reality. The sciences of religion are a product of the Enlightenment in which knowledge of religion was important in the liberation of human beings from the false consciousness of revealed religion. Diderot was specifically critical of Christian institutions, and Hume, who was critical of the claims made by revealed religion for miracles, wrote somewhat ironically of the differences between monotheistic and polytheistic religions. The former religions are more likely to support authoritarian states, while the polytheistic traditions are more conducive to pluralism. The Enlightenment associated political intolerance with monotheism in general and Catholicism in particular, and advocated the separation of church and state as a necessary condition of individual liberties.

While Enlightenment philosophy was overtly hostile to religious institutions, the Enlightenment itself had an important impact on religious thought. The Jewish Enlightenment, or Haskalah, emphasised the rational individual, natural law, natural rights and religious toleration. The Jewish Enlightenment sought to make Jews equal citizens with their Christian and secular counterparts in European societies. Moses Mendelssohn played an important part in presenting Judaism as a rational religion, and these European developments partly paved the way towards Zionism. The problem of religion as a form of rational knowledge also preoccupied the young Marx, who in 'the Jewish Question' argued that the 'solution' to the Jewish problem was their movement into the urban proletariat and adoption of secular socialism, but the final emancipation of the Jewish worker could not be achieved by political emancipation alone without a total transformation of capitalism. The point of Marx's argument was that the final demise of religion as a form of consciousness could only be achieved through a transformation of the actual structure of society.

In other societies similar developments took place. In Russia, Peter the Great was responsible for imposing many of the ideas of the Enlightenment on a society that was historically backward. The building of St Petersburgh was to demonstrate architecturally the importance of Western reform and Enlightenment values. Russian Orthodoxy was held to be a particularly barbaric form of Christian religion. Peter's contact with German Enlightenment resulted in a combination of German Pietism and the rationalism of Leibniz. In this form of benevolent despotism, modernisation and the Enlightenment ensured that opposition to these foreign cultural standards involved a combination of Russian nationalism and Russian Orthodoxy.

In fact, the relationship between the Enlightenment and religion was a good deal more complex than this introductory note might suggest. One might argue more accurately that the Enlightenment philosophers were hostile to institutionalised Christianity, specifically the Roman Catholic Church, rather than to religion *per se*. If we set the Enlightenment within a broader historical framework, it is clear that the eighteenth-century philosophers were drawing inspiration from the Reformation of the sixteenth century and the Renaissance humanism of the fifteenth century. The Renaissance involved a rediscovery of the humanistic literature of Greek and Roman antiquity. The Renaissance placed Man at the centre of learning and knowledge, emphasising human perfection through education, rather than human sinfulness and depravity. This humanistic philosophy was spread by the invention of printing in the mid fifteenth century, and printing in turn facilitated the growth of the Reformation in the sixteenth century. Both Christianity and humanism were influenced by the European discovery of the Americas in 1492 and by new routes to China and Japan. Colonialism and the discovery of aboriginal cultures presented a significant challenge to the biblical notion of the unity of humankind. The Enlightenment philosophers had much in common with the Cambridge Platonists and the latitudinarian movement of the seventeenth century, which sought to reject what it saw as the fanaticism of the English Civil War and attempted to present Christian practice and belief as reasonable. The English notion of reasonableness was not quite what Marx and Hegel had in mind by the historical march of rational knowledge and the spirit, but it was a long way from the experiential intensity of the conversionist sects. This broader historical sketch indicates a greater philosophical (indeed theological) continuity between the Christian humanism of Erasmus, the rationalism of Diderot and the dialectical idealism of Hegel; it also explains why their contemporaries suspected a political plot between freemasonry and the Enlightenment to attack the Roman Catholic Church.

While we commonly refer to the Enlightenment as if the Enlightenment philosophers shared the same ideas, there was, for example, a substantial difference between Rousseau and Voltaire over the question of religion. In Rousseau's famous letter to d'Alembert, in which he complained about the ways in which the modern theatre could corrupt the citizens of Geneva, the real target of Rousseau's argument was Voltaire, because in the debate about the theatre Rousseau demonstrated that he had clearly abandoned the underlying secular principle of the Enlightenment. The context of their dispute was the Lisbon earthquake of 1755, which had all but levelled the city. Rousseau had responded to that disaster as a social rather than a natural crisis; if people had not been living in large cities, these earthquakes would not have had such disastrous consequences. While the event was catastrophic, the universe as a whole was good. Voltaire satirised Rousseau's position, which was based on Rousseau's need to believe in a just world and a living God. Rousseau replied that he had suffered too much in this world not to believe in a better world. As a result, Rousseau resented Voltaire's optimistic secularism. Voltaire, who was rich and famous, could not stop complaining about the world, while Rousseau, poor, obscure and sick, took pleasure in his own situation. In attacking the Parisian theatre, Rousseau was defending the lifestyle of the artisans of Geneva against the wealthy families of the Genevan upper class 'who were building ostentatious mansions, adopting a lavish lifestyle, and looking to Paris for culture' (Damrosch, 2005: 300). In this exchange, it became clear that Rousseau was defending a version of Deism in which he rejected the idea of the corruption and depravity of the human soul, arguing on the contrary in *Emile* ([1762] 1979) that it is society that corrupts the natural goodness of the child who must be protected from the immortality and shallowness of the modern world, as was amply illustrated in the Parisian theatre. Rousseau did, of course, argue that Christianity, which divides the world into the spiritual and the physical, is inappropriate as a public religion in setting up the division between church and state. In *The Social Contract* of 1762, Rousseau (1973) recommended adherence to a 'civil religion' that would unite the citizenry behind the state. Such a religion should be tolerant and not exclusive, that is, no longer simply a national religion.

Secularisation

In the 1970s and 1980s, religion ceased to be a topic of central importance in sociology, and the sociology of religion was increasingly confined to the study of sects and cults. With the dominance of modernisation theory, it was assumed that religion would not play a large part in social organisation. At best it would be relegated to the private sphere. In short, secularisation, which was assumed to be a necessary component of modernisation, proved to be enormously difficult to define. Out of convenience I follow James Beckford's discussion in *Social Theory and Religion* (2003) and my own *Religion and Social Theory* (1991) in claiming that secularisation involves the following:

(1) There is the social differentiation of society into specialised spheres in which religion becomes simply one institution to provide various services to its followers or to the community; secularisation is the decline of the scope of authority structures; fundamentalism is the attempt to halt this differentiation.

(2) Rationalisation involves the corrosion of the power of religious beliefs and the authority of religious specialists (such as priests). This argument is associated with Weber's notion of 'disenchantment'. While this argument acknowledges the impact of science on public explanations of phenomena and the conduct of public life, social survey research shows that belief in magic and superstition remains very high in advanced societies. Eschatology can also have a potent role in secular society. In the United States, Christian fictional literature depicting the return of Christ in the publishing series *Left Behind* has sold over seventy million copies. These stories are loosely based on the book of Revelation and this literary genre gives expression to what evangelicals call 'the Rapture', which is a contemporary account of the disappearance of Christians from the earth and their entry into heaven, leaving behind sinners and unbelievers. The series combines a traditional apocalyptic religion with conservative political attitudes. For example, in the struggle with evil forces, the UN appears as the anti-Christ on earth. Around eight million American Christians believe that the Rapture is coming soon, and this transformation of the world is indicated by, for example, the crisis in the Middle East.

(3) Modernisation (often a combination of differentiation and rationalisation) is a cluster of processes emphasising individualism, democratic politics, liberal values, and norms of efficiency and economic growth. Because modernisation undermines tradition, it cuts off the communal and social foundations that supported religion as a traditional institution. However, religion continues to play a role in supporting national, regional or class identities in

industrial capitalism, for example in Northern Ireland, Catholic France, the Solidarity movement in Poland or the Orthodox revival in Russia.

(4) Secularisation may simply be the transformation (metamorphosis) of religion as it adjusts to new conditions. There are many versions of this argument. Sociologists have argued that the social is essentially religious, and what counts as 'religion' does not decline; it just keeps transforming. Thomas Luckmann (1967) has argued that modern societies have an 'invisible religion' that characterises the transcendence of the everyday world. There is an 'implicit religion' of beliefs about spiritual phenomena that are not necessarily Christian or components of formal religion. In modern societies there is 'believing without belonging', because religious membership and attendance decline, but belief in the Christian faith is still prevalent.

Over the last two centuries, secularisation in the narrow meaning (decline in church membership and attendance, marginalisation of the church from public life, dominance of scientific explanations of the world) has been characteristic of Europe (especially northern, Protestant Europe) and its former colonies (Australia, New Zealand, Canada), but not characteristic of the United States, where religion remains powerful, or in many Catholic societies, especially in Latin America and Africa. In these societies, Pentecostalism and charismatic movements have been growing. In Islam, Christianity and Judaism there have been powerful movements of fundamentalist revival. In many societies, with the growth of youth cultures and popular culture generally there have been important hybrid forms of religiosity, often employing the Net to disseminate their services and beliefs. In post-communist societies, there is clear evidence of a revival of Orthodoxy (Russia and Eastern Europe) and Islam (in China), and Buddhist movements and 'schools' have millions of followers in Japan. Shamanism thrives in Okinawa. In some respects, this conclusion is compatible with Weber's sociology of virtuoso–mass religion in that rational and individualistic Protestantism (Kant's moralising faith) appears to be self-destructive, and there is also an ongoing demand for mass religious services (Kant's cultic form of religion) in most human societies. There is one difference here. In the past, the educated and disciplined virtuosi determined the official form of religion. Periodically religion gets 'cleaned up' as the virtuosi expel the magical, popular, cultic accretions: the Buddhist monks, often with the help of a righteous monarch, reject the magic of their followers; Christian reformers – from the desert fathers to John Wesley – condemned the corrupt practices of the laity; in Islam according to Ibn Khaldun, prophets enter the city to reform the House of Faith. In the modern world, the laity have some degree of literacy and they can access radio, the Net, TV, travel and mass consumerism. The globalisation of popular religion makes it increasingly difficult for the virtuosi to regulate the masses. In Thailand, popular Buddhist charismatics sell magical charms and amulets over the Internet; on Muslim websites, popular American mullahs offer *fatwas* on every aspect of daily life. The growth of global spiritual market-places means that 'religion' constantly transforms itself becoming increasingly hybrid and reflexive. Fundamentalism is in this sense an attempt to control the consumerist spiritual market-place, but this growing hybridity may only be a problem from the perspective of those religious traditions that represent the Kantian moralising faith. Syncretism has been historically the norm.

Religion and political violence

One reason for sociological scepticism about the secularisation thesis from a comparative perspective has been the modern association between religion and political violence (Vries, 2002). Given the contemporary relationship between terrorism and political Islam, it is difficult to avoid the popular question: Is there any relationship between Islam as a religious system, violence and authoritarian rule? The traditional answer of mainstream political science has been to argue that, because Islamic culture does not differentiate between religion and politics, it assumes an undemocratic and typically an authoritarian complexion. This conventional answer follows Weber's thesis of caesaropapism and liberal political philosophy.

A more promising argument might be that no religious system has a deep relationship to democracy. Charisma is hierarchical, and religious communities (churches, temples and monasteries) do not democratically elect their leaders. Prophets receive revelations that are not tested by popular assent. In this respect, the principle of authority in

Islam might be an exception. Whereas Shi'ite Islam saw authority descending from the Prophet, Sunni Islam accepted the idea of communal consensus for the first four Rightly Guided Caliphs. In Christianity, there is the argument that the Protestant sects embraced the idea of a 'priesthood of all believers', a politics of No King, No Bishops, popular assembly, Presbyterianism and the rule of local chapels, and female ministries, but the openness to debate also led to antinomianism and the quest for 'godly rule'. There is also the view that Confucianism is essentially a philosophy of good governance and good order rather than a religion as such. In Buddhism, there is a tradition of powerful and just (but undemocratic) monarchs who periodically purify the monastery (*sangha*) and the kingdom to establish a just society and personal merit – a tradition that has its origin in King Asoka's rule over the Magadhan Empire. Any religion whose system of authority claims to be the result of revelation (hence of prophecy, ecstatic visions, charisma) does not support the idea of truth as the outcome of communal consensus. Holy war, crusade and just war have been used to illustrate the relationship between violence, monotheism and hostility to the outside world. In these political struggles, *jihad* has become a popular description of violent confrontation. Sympathetic interpretations of Islam normally argue that *jihad* means 'spiritual struggle' but has been corrupted to mean 'armed struggle'. William Watt's account of the origins of *jihad* in the intertribal raids (*razzia*) that were common in Arabia is important for understanding the greater *jihad* (war against external enemies) and the lesser *jihad* against polytheism. In *Islamic Political Thought* (1999), he argues that *jihad* ('striving' or 'expenditure of effort') had entirely secular economic origins, namely camel raids. In the great expansion of Islam in its first century, there was little intention of spreading the religion of Islam 'apart from other considerations that would have meant sharing their privileges of booty and stipends with many neo-Muslims' (p. 18). In subsequent generations, it 'has roused ordinary men to military activity', whereas later mystics have described it as 'self-discipline' (p. 19).

In sociological terms, twentieth-century, political Islam is a product of the social frustrations of those social strata (unpaid civil servants, overworked teachers, underemployed engineers and marginalised college teachers) whose interests have not been well served by either the secular nationalism of Nasser, Muhammad Reza Shah, Suharto or

Saddam Hussein, or the neo-liberal 'open-door' policies of Anwar Saddat or Chadli Benjedid in Algeria. The social dislocations created by the global economy produced ideal conditions for external Western support of those secular elites in the Arab world who benefit significantly from oil revenues; bureaucratic authoritarianism has been the political result. In summary, Islamism is a product of a religious crisis of authority, the failures of authoritarian nationalist governments, and the socio-economic divisions that have been exacerbated by neo-liberal globalisation.

Olivier Roy and Giles Kepel have developed an influential interpretation of the failure of political Islam. Their account of the radicalisation of Islam starts with the Algerian crisis, the October riots of 1988, the coup of 1992 and the increasing violence between the state, the GIA (*Groupements Islamiques Armes*) and the FIS (*Fronte Islamique du Salut*). The failure of radical Islam to establish itself in confrontation with the Algerian state resulted in the export of political Islam to Central Asia, Afghanistan and Pakistan, but these revolutionary Islamic movements have failed to establish fundamentalist Islamic states. Political Islam is the consequence of social frustrations, articulated around the social divisions of class and generation, following from the economic crises of the global neo-liberal experiments of the 1970s and 1980s. The demographic revolution produced large cohorts of young Muslims, who, while often well educated to college level, could not find opportunities to satisfy the aspirations that had been inflamed by nationalist governments. Kepel's thesis is simply that the last twenty-five years have witnessed the spectacular rise of Islamism and its failure. In the 1970s, when sociologists assumed that modernisation meant secularisation, the sudden irruption of political Islam, especially the importance of Shi'ite theology in popular protests in Iran, appeared to challenge dominant paradigms of modernity. These religious movements, especially when they forced women to wear the *chador* and excluded them from public space, were originally defined by leftist intellectuals as a form of religious fascism. Over time, however, Marxists came to recognise that Islamism had a popular base and was a powerful force against colonialism. Western governments were initially willing to support both Sunni and Shi'a resistance groups against the Russian involvement in Afghanistan after 1979, despite their connections with radical groups in Pakistan and Iran.

These religious movements largely cancelled out the legacy of Arab nationalism that had dominated anti-Western politics since the Suez Crisis of 1956. The ideological basis of Islamism was devised in the late 1960s by three men: Maududi in Pakistan, Qutb in Egypt and Khomeini in Iran. For Kepel, Islamism is the product of both generational pressures and class structure. First, it has been embraced by the youthful generations of the cities that were created by the post-war demographic explosion of the Third World and the resulting mass exodus from the countryside. This generation was poverty-stricken, despite its relatively high literacy and access to secondary education. Secondly, Islamism recruited among the middle classes – the descendants of the merchant families from the bazaars and *souks* who had been pushed aside by decolonisation, and from the doctors, engineers and businessmen, who, while enjoying the salaries made possible by booming oil prices, were excluded from political power. The ideological carriers of Islamism at the local level were the 'young intellectuals, freshly graduated from technical and science departments, who had themselves been inspired by the ideologues of the 1960s' (Kepel, 2002: 6). Islamic themes of justice and equality were mobilised against those regimes that were corrupt, bankrupt and authoritarian, and often supported by the West in the Cold War confrontation with the Soviet Empire.

Enlightenment and cosmopolitanism

In the last decade, Huntington's analysis of 'the clash of civilisations' (1993; 1997) has orchestrated much of the academic discussion about inter-cultural understanding. While Edward Said's criticisms of Orientalism offered some hope that intellectuals could cross cultural boundaries and establish a road towards mutual respect and understanding, in the post 9/11 environment, Huntington's pessimistic vision of the development of micro fault line conflicts and macro core state conflicts has more precisely captured the mood of Western foreign policy in the era of global terrorism. Huntington, of course, believes that the major cultural division is between the Christian West and the Muslim world. Given Huntington's description of 'the age of Muslim Wars', any attempt to engage with Islamic civilisation is now seen as a 'war for Muslim minds' (Kepel, 2004a).

Although the Enlightenment has been much criticised by post-modern philosophy, this criticism is somewhat misleading when applied to Leibniz, the German founder of the (predominantly French) Enlightenment. He is best known as a mathematician, but Franklin Perkins (2004) shows a rather different, but equally important, side to Leibniz's philosophy, which appears extraordinarily pertinent to modern times. Leibniz lived in a period of intense trade and commerce with the outside world and, alongside this emerging capitalist enterprise, Leibniz advocated a 'commerce of light' or mutual enlightenment. Contrary to Spinoza's view that there is only one substance, Leibniz argued that the world is characterised by an infinite diversity, richness and completeness. This world is teaming with diverse entities that exist in a state of harmony, and in the *Discourse on Metaphysics* ([1686] 1992), he claimed that God had created the best of all possible worlds (a theodicy), which is 'the simplest in hypotheses and the richest in phenomena'.

Recognition of the diversity of cultures and civilisations leads us to recognise the inherent value of difference. Leibniz advocated a tolerance of diverse views, but went beyond the philosophers of his day to establish a moral imperative to learn from cultural diversity. He applied this ethic to himself, committing much of his life to studying China from the reports of missionaries and merchants. Differences between entities or monads require exchange, but it also establishes a commonality of culture. Leibniz was not, in modern terms, a cultural relativist – if all cultures are equal (in value), why bother to learn from any one of them? While all knowledge of the outside world is relativistic, Leibniz argued that, because we are embodied, there are enough innate ideas to make an exchange of enlightenment possible. According to Perkins, from the doctrine of blind monads Leibniz developed a hermeneutics of generosity that regarded inter-cultural understanding as not merely a useful anthropological field method, but as an ethical imperative. Leibniz, in short, developed a cosmopolitan virtue in his attempt to establish an exchange with China that offers us a guideline for understanding our own times, especially a cosmopolitan exchange with Islam. Leibniz is a sort of rational and moral antidote to Huntington.

How might we illustrate cosmopolitan or Leibnizian historiography? I suggest we examine the work of Marshall G. S. Hodgson in his monumental *The Venture of Islam* (1974). Hodgson, formerly a professor of history at the University of Chicago, set himself the task of *Rethinking World History* (1993). His thesis was that Islam was an integral part of Mediterranean civilisation, which can in turn only be understood from the standpoint of world history. He shifted the central point of European historical geographical imagination eastwards and southwards, giving Cairo, Damascus and Baghdad greater prominence in European civilisation. His work embraced a cosmopolitan virtue in that he was a Quaker, attempting to understand Islam hermeneutically. From a sympathetic, pacifist stance, he criticised the militaristic evolution of imperial Islam as a social system. These imperial systems were alien to the inner religious tradition of Islam. Hodgson showed hermeneutic generosity to both Christian and Islamic faiths, demonstrating, for example, how a sense of justice was crucial to Islamic theology. Hodgson's world history was an attack on Western provincialism, but it also contained a critical assessment of the relationship between faith and political empire. From Hodgson we might conclude that the recognition of cultural difference does not mean uncritically accepting those differences. On the contrary, we need a critical recognition theory in which there is a place for dialogical critical understanding. I call this perspective a 'critical recognition ethics' that is at the heart of cosmopolitan virtue, in which caring for the differences of the other does not rule out critical judgement of other cultures.

Religion and the body

One problem with the cosmopolitanism debate is that it is often focused only on what people believe. Do they entertain positive beliefs towards strangers and outsiders? It might, however, be more useful to focus on practices rather than beliefs (Holton, 2009). This criticism raises a much larger issue, which is the tendency of sociology, but less so of anthropology, to concentrate generally on attitudes, beliefs and values and to neglect practices. Throughout this study I draw attention to the body, practice and habitus, thereby drawing on the work of Pierre Bourdieu, whose work is discussed more closely in Chapter 6.

In common-sense terms, one might think that religion is crucially about the training of the soul for its union with the divine, and hence the human body has to be subordinated to this higher purpose. In the classical tradition of the sociology of religion, there was as a result little attention given to the role of the human body in the history of religions. There is little or no reference to the human body and embodiment in the work of Max Weber, Émile Durkheim or Georg Simmel. In more recent developments in the sociology of religion, there has been a growing concern to understand the central place of the body in religious belief and practice. As we will see in subsequent chapters, the sociology of the body has played a seminal part in the revival of interest in religion and society (Turner, 1997; 2008a; 2009e). In this chapter on the problem of defining religion, we can turn now to a consideration of human embodiment in religious belief and practice.

Because the human body is the most readily available 'instrument' by which to convey meaning, for example by gesture, the body plays a critical role as the expression of society as a whole. It has an immediate capacity to express sacred values, human sexuality and social power. For example, the distinction between right-handed and left-handed people has been a basic form of classification, in which the left hand points to phenomena that are handicapped, or evil (sinister: the English word 'sinister' is derived from the Latin for 'left side', which is always associated, for example, with evil). The right-handed side are things that are handsome. In Heaven, the virtuous will sit at Christ's right hand. Traditional societies harnessed the body to express the sacred authority of the group or society, and hence there is a close relationship between the body, the sovereignty of a king and the notion of sacredness (Agamben, 1998).

There is always a necessary relationship between the sovereign power of the state, power over the body and the control of life. Since the body expresses both sacred and sexual power, this control involves sovereignty over both sexual and religious expressivity. The power of the body – its sexual potency – is often expressed through performance in dance. Formal, stylised dance typically occurred within the court, where the carefully trained and manicured body expressed, not its own power, but the power and authority of the sovereign. The dancing body was an expression of the order of society as orchestrated in the sacred body of the king, while popular dances were noteworthy for their coarseness and vulgarity. Bruegel the Elder's paintings of peasant dancers at a wedding feast show the strong but uncouth bodies of ordinary peasants that are fuelled with alcohol. There is always a social division between the regulated sexuality of classical dance such as ballet – the dance *par excellence* of the court and the elite – and the grotesque, vulgar dances of the ordinary people. This division in dance performance is parallel to the division between the sacred and the profane, which defines the nature of religion.

Scruples

The body is typically subject to our social scruples. The distinction which we have already noted between *relegere*, meaning to bind together, and *religare*, to tie together or to discipline, has important implications for how we might study the body and religion. First, the body is important in religious practices that are directed at healing, and therefore an important aspect of all religious rituals is related to the maintenance of the body. One central role for all forms of charismatic religious power (such as saintship) is to bring good health to the bodies of disciples. Secondly, the function of religion is to control or regulate the body for religious ends. This control can be achieved either through ascetic practices such as diet which monitor the body, or by mystical means such as dance which enhance bodily powers. We might think about these two functions by considering the verbs 'to salve' and 'to save'. Thus, religion is concerned with salving the body and saving the soul, but these two functions are often diametrically opposed. The salving of the body through therapeutic techniques was often related to reproduction and the enhancement of human sexuality, while saving the soul involved ascetic practices to suppress or deny sexuality through exercise, diet and meditation. There is therefore a crucial distinction in religious systems as to whether the body is regarded as a source of positive or of negative power. In an Orientalist paradigm, the 'religions of Asia' were assumed to use the body as a positive source of (sexual) power. In Weber's *The Sociology of Religion* (1966), there was a basic assumption that Christianity (especially Protestantism) emphasised inner-worldly asceticism, while the Asian religions emphasised mystical practices to enhance the body.

In Weber's view, religion is oriented to the practical needs of the everyday and we might argue that religion exists simply because human beings are vulnerable and they face existential problems relating to birth, ageing and death. Although, for example, ancient Mayan and Egyptian mortuary and funeral practices were very different, they have one thing in common: they express a perplexity about the world in which death turns the living body into a putrefied mess and eventually into a 'not-body'. Egyptian and Mayan visions of the afterlife were different, but they both addressed the problem of human death and the conundrum of non-existence (Meskell and Joyce, 2003). Although the Mayans may have contemplated the 'not-body' with less existential horror than the Egyptians, who went to extraordinary lengths to develop mummification, death in both cultures exposed the vulnerability of our being-in-the-world and the precariousness of human institutions.

In Western Christianity, the body also played a major part in understanding evil and holiness. Theologians solved the paradox of Christ's perfect humanity and his divinity by developing the doctrine of his immaculate birth by a virgin whose womb was not penetrated. In the Annunciation, we might say that Mary was a not-wounded immaculate mother. The problem of death and decay was resolved through the resurrection stories of Lazarus and Jesus in the New Testament, in which the wounding and death of Christ on the Cross was merely a prelude to his resurrection and entry into Paradise. Our embodiment in the world is characterised by its precariousness, and religions are cultural modes that seek to address our vulnerability by mythology and by bodily practices that attempt, for example, to disguise our death by giving our face a mask or through the mummification of the corpse. Doctrines of resurrection and practices of mummification are both cultural institutions that address our experiences of the incompleteness of embodied lives in the everyday world.

The concept of vulnerability is derived from the Latin *vulnus* or 'wound' (Turner, 2006). It is instructive that 'vulnerability' should have such an obviously corporeal origin. In the seventeenth century, vulnerability had both a passive and active significance, namely to be wounded and to wound. In medieval religious practice, veneration of the Passion was associated with meditation on the Seven Wounds of Christ. These wounds were evidence of the humanity and suffering of Christ and these human attributes came to emphasise his vulnerability (Woolf, 1968). These meditation themes of Christ's suffering evolved eventually into the cult of the Sacred Heart. To vulnerate is thus to wound, but in its modern usage it has come to signify the human capacity to be open to wounds. Vulnerability has become, in one sense, more abstract: it refers to the human capacity to be exposed to psychological or moral damage. It refers increasingly to our ability to suffer (morally and spiritually) rather than to a physical capacity for pain from our exposure or openness to the world. This openness to wounding is part of what Arnold Gehlen (1988) has called our 'world openness', namely that we do not live in a biologically determined or species-specific environment. The very survival of humankind requires self-discipline, training and self-correction. In order to manage their world openness (*Weltoffenheit*), human beings have to create a cultural world to replace or to supplement their instinctual legacy. Ontological incompleteness provides an anthropological explanation for the human origins of religious institutions. Because we are vulnerable we need to build a 'sacred canopy' (Berger, 1969) to protect us from our ontological insecurity.

There have been in the history of human societies a number of important and permanent connections between religion, reproduction and the body. The core to these mythological, cosmological and theological connections is the principle of generation, regeneration and resurrection (Coakley, 1997). Social struggles over the control of human reproduction have been reflected in controversies between matriarchy and patriarchy as forms of authority, and these political controversies can be discerned even in the historical origins of the tradition of a High God. The body has thus played a pivotal role in the Abrahamic religions (Christianity, Judaism and Islam) where notions of family, generation and reproduction dominated their core theology and cosmology. These religions were profoundly patriarchal, and hence sexuality, the sexual division of labour and the status of women were major considerations of religious practice and belief.

There is obviously much disagreement about the origins of human mythologies with respect to the question of motherhood. For Mircea Eliade (1961), with the development of agriculture the symbolism and cults of Mother Earth and human fertility became dominant. An alternative view is that with the rise of agriculture, the plough breaks up the earth and makes it fertile. The plough is a phallic symbol that points to men taking gardening away from women, and in Sumerian mythology Enki, the male god of water (semen), became the Great Father. However, the development of a High God that replaced many of these fertility cults occurred simultaneously in a number of regions of the world. This creative religious period, from approximately 800 to 200 BC, has been defined as an 'axial age', because it was the crucial turning point in the formation of civilisations. Confucius, Buddha, Socrates, Zoroaster and Isaiah, whose cosmological views had important common features, shaped the axial age of the emerging agrarian civilisations, within which city life began to emerge. It was the cultural basis from which sprang the ethical, prophetic leaders of monotheism, which resulted eventually in the so-called 'religions of the book'. The prophets of the axial age addressed human beings in the name of a supreme, moral being who could not be represented by an image and who could not be easily constrained or cajoled by ritual or magic. In Judaism, this contractual relationship came eventually to include rituals to achieve the purity of the body, such as *kosher* food and circumcision.

Thus, the interconnection between divinity, body and fertility was historically ancient, but when God as the Creator began to acquire the status of a Person, then He began to be conceptualised as a Father, specifically a Father to those tribes and communities that remained loyal. There is therefore an important mythical role for a Father who is the patriarch of nations. In the Old Testament, 'Jacob' and 'Israel' are used interchangeably. There is in the Old Testament an important division between the idea of creation in Genesis and the narrative account of the covenant between God as Father and the nation. This differentiation is important in understanding the division between God as the Creator of Nature and God as the Father of a nation, between an impersonal force and a personal God, between natural history and salvation history. Because Yahweh was a jealous God, there was a sacred covenant between God and the tribes of Israel, which excluded those who worshipped idols and false gods. Those who were faithful to the God of Israel marked their bodies as a sign of their communal membership. In Christianity, a universalistic orientation that recognised the Other was contained in Paul's letters to the Galatians and Romans, which rejected circumcision as a condition of salvation.

With the evolution of the idea of sacred fatherhood, there developed a range of problems about the body. How are bodies produced and reproduced? If bodies fragment and decay, then redemption and resurrection are problematic. There have been (and continue to be) major political and social issues about the ownership of bodies and authority over them. Matriarchy and patriarchy can be regarded as social principles for deciding the legitimacy and ownership of bodies, especially parental ownership and control of children. Patriarchy has specific and important connections with religion as a principle of reproductive legitimacy. The rites and rituals that surround birth and rebirth are fundamental to all religions, and the notion of regeneration has been crucial to ancient cosmologies. In these cosmological schemes, there were common homologies between the reproductive work of a creator God, the creative force of nature and reproduction with human families. Mythologies are typically constructed upon these generative homologies to form systems of dichotomous classification between red menstrual blood as a symbol of transmission between generations, and white semen and milk as symbols of food, sustenance and reproduction.

It is, however, necessary to recognise the diversity of views about women, sexuality and the body in different religious traditions. While the early Judaeo-Christian teaching about women was not uniform, its legacy included a deeply negative understanding of women and sexuality. In the Genesis story, the original co-operative and companionate relationship between man and woman is replaced after the Fall by a relationship of domination in which man becomes the ruler of woman. The Mosaic Law was addressed to a society in which women were components of household property and could not take decisions for themselves (Biale, 1992). The wife was the property of the husband and an adulterous wife was punished with death. A wife who did not produce children was not fulfilling her duty and infertility was a legal ground for divorce. Barrenness in the Old Testament was a sign of divine disapproval. Because menstruation and childbirth were ritually unclean, women were frequently precluded from participating in cultic activities. Israelite marriage was a contract between separate families, and thus wives were dangerous to men, not only because they could manipulate men with their sexual charms, but because they were recruited from outside the husband's family. These negative images of women in the Old and New Testaments have proved to be remarkably resilient historically.

The underlying principles of Christianity were inevitably patriarchal in the sense that the structure of Christian theology required the concept of Jesus as the Son of God in order to make sense of 'salvation history' as a redemptive act of sacrifice. God so loved the world that He gave His only Son that human beings could be saved from sin. The body and blood of Christ are fundamental to the Christian theology of salvation. If Christianity is in this sense patriarchal, then we need to pay some attention to the ambiguous status of Mary (Rubin, 2009; Warner, 1983). In theological terms, the virginity of Mary was necessary in order for Christ to be without sin, but Christ also had to be of woman born in order to achieve human status, and thus to experience our world. Over time, Mary herself was removed from the possibility of any connection with sin, and became detached from an association with the Fall of Adam and Eve. The doctrine of Immaculate Conception was declared in 1854, and she was exempt from original sin.

Mary was ambiguous in other ways. Mary became, in a patriarchal world, the great medieval symbol of motherhood. In the fourteenth century, the visions of St Bridget of Sweden pictured the Virgin, following the birth of Christ, on her knees in worshipful adoration of the Child, and by the fifteenth century paintings of the adoration of the mother were common. But the Virgin was also in her own right a vehicle of worship and adoration. The more she was exempt from sin, the more her status approximated that of Christ. In oppositional theology, she was often regarded as equal to Christ in the concept of co-redemption. Because she was spared from sin, she was also exempt from the physical experiences of the typical female – sexual inter-course, labour and childbirth. She was removed from basic physical activities except for one – the suckling of the infant Jesus. As a result, a cult emerged around the breast of the Virgin and the milk that nur-tured baby Jesus. The theme of the nursing Virgin (the *Maria Lactans*) became an important part of medieval cultic belief and practice. In the absence of a powerful female figure in the Gospels, medieval Chris-tianity elevated the spiritual status of Mary, who became the great champion of procreation and family life. This theological legacy con-tinues to underpin much of the Catholic Church's teaching on procre-ation, contraception, abortion and family life.

Because the dominant political concerns and anxieties of society tend to be translated into disrupted and disturbed images of the body, we can talk about the 'somatic society' (Turner, 1992). The 'dance macabre' gave gruesome expression to the devastation of the medieval social order that had been brought about by the ravages of the Black Death, and in modern society the scourge of cancer and AIDS have often been imagined in military metaphors of invading armies. Social disturbances are grasped in the metaphors by which we understand mental and physical health. Body metaphors have been important in moral debate about these social disruptions. Our sense of social order is spoken of in terms of the balance or imbalance of the body.

In the eighteenth century, when doctors turned to mathematics to produce a Newtonian map of the body, the medical metaphor of hydraulic pumps was used to express human digestion and blood circulation. The therapeutic bleeding of patients by knife or leech was to assist this hydraulic mechanism, and to relieve morbid pressures on the mind. Severe disturbances in society were often imagined as poor social digestion. These assumptions about social unrest producing disorder in the gut are reflected in the basic idea of the need for a government of the body. Dietary management of the body was translated into fiscal constraint, reduction in government expenditure and the downsizing of public functions. In the discourse of modern management, a lean and mean corporation requires a healthy management team. In neo-liberal ideology, central government is an excess – a sort of political obesity. The modern idea of government is taken from these diverse meanings of diet that stands for a political regime, a regimentation of society and a government of the body. Regulating the body, disciplining the soul and governing society were merged in political theories of social contract and the state.

Human fluids are potent, and they can have both negative and positive effects. Fluids exist in a transient world, and disrupt the stability of categories. The secretions of saintly bodies were collected by the faithful, and their healing properties were used by mothers to protect their children. The Sufi saints of North Africa offered protection from the evil eye through the fluids that flowed from their bodies in religious festivals. Christ's blood is also a charismatic transfer of sacred power to humankind, and the Christian community is constituted by the Eucharist in which Christ's body becomes available symbolically to the faithful. Mary's milk was a symbol of wealth and health, but blood and milk can also contaminate and disrupt social relations. Red symbolised danger; white, as in Mary's milk, brought comfort and sustenance. There has been a universal fear among men of female menstruation, because the leaking bodies of women are sources of pollution. In early colonial times, speculation about the reproductive processes of native peoples conjured up strange women who could avoid menstruation by having their bodies sliced from the armpit to the knee. The Puritan Cotton Mather in his sermons on Uncleanness located filth with sexual functions and the lower parts of the body, while the soul and the mind were in the upper secretions. These classificatory principles that are based on bodily functions were an important aspect of the classification of clean and unclean, namely in the classification of polluting substances.

The body also provides an important nexus between the state and the individual, and so the body has become in modern times a site of political conflicts. This connection can be illustrated by the life of Gandhi, who used control of the body as a weapon against British imperial rule in the struggle for independence. Gandhi's preoccupation with sex, diet and health reform illustrates the connections between the body politic and the individual organism and its management (Alter, 2000). Gandhi was receptive to Western health 'fads' such as vegetarianism and nature cure, and he was dogmatically opposed to allopathic medicine, because it provided violent cures of the symptoms of specific diseases rather than a holistic approach. Gandhi conceptualised colonial rule as the subjection of Indian bodies, and hence political liberation required a transformation of the subject body. The treatment of the disease in the body politic required first the healing of the subordinated, colonial body. One technique that was central to Gandhi's politics was therefore the religious practice of celibacy (*brahmacharya*) in Hinduism. Gandhi's experiments with diet, clothing, and sexual abstinence were in many respects consistent with traditional Hindu theories of government that the role of the righteous king was to restore the moral balance of society, in part by the ritual regulation of his own body.

In contemporary society there is the commercialisation of the body for a new medical economy in which, in addition to the harvesting of body parts, there is a transformation of disease categories by genetic science. The body is being converted into an information system whose genetic code can be manipulated and sold as a commercial product in the new biotech economy. In global terms, the disorders and diseases of the human body have become productive in a post-industrial economy (Fukuyama, 2002). In terms of media debate, the new reproductive technologies, cloning, and genetic screening are important illustrations of public concern about the social consequences of the new genetics. Improvements in scientific understanding of genetics have already had major consequences for the circumstances under which people reproduce, and genetic surveillance and forensic genetics may also transform criminal investigation and the policing of societies. The code of the body becomes a major tool of criminal investigations.

These technological and scientific developments in medical sciences have three negative consequences: they have undermined the directness and comfortableness of our relationship to the natural environment and to the body; they have multiplied the environmental and social risks of modern society, especially those associated with globalisation; and they have transformed the possibilities of human embodiment through bio-technology and the emerging use of cyborgs. In short, technological modernisation has raised significant problems for the body, religion and the self. As we have seen, the body has been crucial to the development of religious metaphors of sociability. These corporeal metaphors were fundamental to the evolution of the theologies and rituals of the world religions. Central to these cosmologies was the notion of the transfer of charisma (or grace) between human beings through the conduit of bodily fluids: blood, water, sweat, milk and sperm. In the New Testament, the account of God's action in history involved the sacrifice of the body of Christ for the sake of human salvation. Once human beings had been turned out of the Garden, early metaphors of property employed the notion of an investment of sweat or labour in the earth. But these corporeal metaphors of the sacred are increasingly obsolete and irrelevant in a high-technology and post-modern cultural environment. For example, there is an archaic cosmology common to many religions in which the body is the metaphor of a house and a house is the metaphor of a cosmos. In this homology of house–body–cosmos, 'man cosmicizes himself; in other words, he reproduces on the human scale the system of rhythmic and reciprocal conditioning influences that characterises and constitutes a world, that, in short, defines any universe' (Eliade, 1961: 173). The intimacy between self, body and cosmos has been shattered by the globalisation of electronic information, the reconstitution of human biology into informational systems and the cultural displacement of the self as central to experience. We have lost the relevance and immediacy of effective and relevant religious metaphors.

Religious metaphors were obviously set within a specific culture and mode of production. The metaphors of Jewish and Christian cosmology were orchestrated around a theme of pastoral relationships – *Agnus Dei*, the Great Shepherd, the Flock, the Black Sheep and the Pastor. These metaphors of pastoral and agrarian societies were able to articulate a set of common experiences and a common language of responsibility, stewardship, care and dependency, namely a common language of vulnerability. The wounds of Christ became a fundamental symbol of human suffering and frailty. These symbolic wounds of suffering came to express the power of vulnerability. Such metaphorical devices are increasingly remote from the modern imagination, because they have lost their metaphorical force. The possibilities of therapeutic cloning through the application of stem-cell research do not fit easily within traditional religious cosmologies, which assumed a 'natural life' for human beings in this world.

The endless cycle of agrarian activity, of sowing and harvesting, produced another set of metaphors of dependence and obligation that expressed social responsibility and dependency. The gathering of the harvest became a basic metaphor of human salvation. In modern societies, global corporations harvest human organs or tissue in order to make a profit from human frailty. With industrialisation, there has been no significant evolution of a set of shared metaphors to express the human condition and the communal links that are important for the renewal of sociability. As a result 'the religious sense of urban populations is gravely impoverished. The cosmic liturgy, the mystery of nature's participation in the Christological drama, have become inaccessible to Christians living in a modern city' (Eliade, 1961: 179). There is a contemporary exhaustion of adequate metaphors necessary to a shared language of community, because the relationship between body and society has been fundamentally transformed. The metaphors of the global village attempt to express thin and fragile networks (webs) or individualised journeys through virtual reality (surfing), but they are not collective metaphors of community that connect body, self and society.

Conclusion

Religion as an expression of the social forms of human communities inevitably changes with major changes in society. In this study of religion and the making of modernity, I want to examine how the growth of modern consumerism has influenced the form and content of religion. One example of this influence is the commodification of religious objects and practices. Another change has been the impact of democratisation on religious ideas. In general terms, these changes have been described in terms of a secularisation thesis. However, with the growth of radical religions such as 'political Islam', it has been argued that the secularisation thesis is no longer valid. There has been, it is claimed, a significant growth of public religions including the Iranian Revolution, the rise of the Christian Right and the Sandinista movement. While I accept the view that there has been a change in the place of religion in the public sphere in some societies, especially with the decline of communism, there has nevertheless been a secularisation of religion at the social level. This study is therefore conducted at two levels. The first is the role of religion in the practical mundane world, namely at the social level. The second is the institutional role of religion in relation to the state and the public sphere, namely at the political level. Throughout this volume, I attempt to weave these two levels together to provide a comprehensive sociology of religion. At both levels, I consider the arguments for and against the secularisation thesis. While there has been some erosion of the conventional liberal view of the separation in the public domain of religion and state, the secularisation of everyday life is all too clear when we think about the body and religion. Medical technology has led some gerontologists to predict that human beings can enjoy extended life expectancy free from the tribulations of sickness and infirmity. In short, it is claimed that human beings can live forever (Turner, 2009g). The implications of this promise of immortality and human physical perfection for traditional religions are very profound. With the promise of eternity in this life, will human beings need the comforts of religion?

2 | *Émile Durkheim and the classification of religion*

Introduction: the social and the sacred

Why read Émile Durkheim, and in particular why immerse ourselves in a study ostensibly about Australian Aboriginals from material that had been gathered at the end of the nineteenth century by British colonial administrators? Although Aboriginal religious practices may appear to have only curiosity value, a century later interest in Durkheim's sociology of religion appears to be growing. While the secularisation paradigm was dominant in sociological theory in the 1960s, Durkheim's fortunes in professional sociology were relatively low. The contemporary revival of the sociology of religion and the apparent influence of religion globally, especially in the political sphere, has restored the idea that religion is somehow critical to the actual constitution of the social world. The current political crises around the state and religion have made Durkheim's *Elementary Forms* ([1912] 2001) once more a salient topic of social and political theory. As a result, contemporary philosophers such as Charles Taylor, when seeking to analyse contemporary societies in his *Varieties of Religion Today* (2002), constantly invoke Durkheim as a source of inspiration and as a paradigm for understanding the public role of religion. There has also been a return to the question of the sacred in modernity in Massimo Rosati's *Ritual and the Sacred* (2009), and a special issue of the Scandinavian journal *Distinktion* on the sacred has been recently published (Arppe and Borch, 2009). The general relevance of Durkheim to cultural sociology has been presented by Jeffrey Alexander (1988b) in *Durkheimian Sociology* and in the *Cambridge Companion to Durkheim* (Alexander and Smith, 2005). The list of such references is fairly elastic.

In this volume on the sociology of religion, I argue that the social and the religious are necessarily connected and hence changes in social life produce changes in religion and vice versa. Furthermore, in modern societies, partly because of excessive individual consumerism after several decades of the deregulation of the economy and the privatisation of public utilities, the social has been steadily eroded and the social ties that bind people into communities are becoming thinner and weaker. There is a general sense that national identities are being decomposed and that national attachments are declining as the mass media feed us with artificial globalised forms of self-reference. Modern societies are therefore anomic in the sense that we no longer possess a normative framework or, to borrow a phrase from Peter Berger (1967), a 'sacred canopy' within which to conduct social life. Durkheim is central to this debate, because he so clearly articulated the notion that the ultimate roots of the social are religious.

In this chapter, I want to give a somewhat different interpretation of Durkheim to say that we can detect a parallel set of relations between the sacred and the religious on the one hand and the social and society on the other. The sacred is the original wellspring of the religious and hence religion is the institutionalised outer framework or institutional casement of the sacred. In modern societies, we have as a result the paradox that religion is flourishing while the sacred is in a state of decay. In my terms, secularisation is the modern development of the religious as the empty shell of the sacred. Religion has become a set of institutions that function to support the secular world rather than a set of institutions that shapes and directs the world. In tandem, the social has been eroded, while society as its institutional superstructure continues on its precarious way. The implication of the argument is that neither religion nor society can survive indefinitely without some regeneration of the creative impulse of the sacred and the social. In short, the religion–society complex is only parasitic on the sacred–social foundation. This proposition is the core of Durkheim's later sociology and the reason he remains of perennial interest.

The origins of Durkheim's sociology of religion

Religion became the dominant interest of Durkheim's sociology towards the end of his intellectual development. In his early work he sought to develop a 'positive science of morals' or a sociology of *la morale*. In *The Division of Labor in Society* ([1893] 1960), this interest in 'moral statistics' was important in his attempt to analyse individualism and the crisis in French society from the perspective of a positivist epistemology in which he treated 'social facts' as things. In *Suicide* ([1897] 1951) this focus on morals was evident in his analysis of social isolation as a cause of rising suicide rates. The development of sociology was thus closely connected to Durkheim's general attempt to understand 'the social' as an object of empirical inquiry. The methodological principles for the study of social facts were laid out in *The Rules of Sociological Method* ([1895] 1958), namely that sociology studies institutions and social trends that exist independently of the individual. In more precise terms, the *locus classicus* of this tradition was initially presented in *Primitive Classification* ([1903] 1997), where Durkheim and Mauss attempted to understand the general schema of logical classification as manifestations of social structure. Classical sociological explanations are therefore sociological in the strong sense of the term, because they do not refer to individual dispositions as causes of action and seek instead to understand how social structures determine the social life of the individual. Insofar as sociological explanations do not employ references to social structure or social facts in Durkheim's sense, they are not examples of what I have called the strong programme of classical sociology (Turner, 1999a). Within a weak programme of sociology, where the focus is on the meanings which individuals attach to the social, there can nevertheless be explanations that are valuable and sociologically significant.

Classical sociology should also be understood to be a critical discipline, because it specifically represented an attack on the ideology of industrial capitalist society, namely the ideology of utilitarian liberalism. This critical tradition is conventionally associated with Marxism and Marxist sociology, but here again Durkheim offered the definitive critique of the amoral notion of the market and the individual in the economic doctrines of the Manchester School. Both *Suicide* and *Professional Ethics and Civic Morals* (1992) represent political attacks on English economic individualism and the sociology of Herbert Spencer, and thus Durkheim's professional or academic sociology was directed often implicitly towards a critical evaluation of a trend in society – the celebration of egoistic individualism over collective life – that was destructive of the social. Durkheim's attack on the corrosive consequences of the ideology of egoistic individualism is in this respect the precursor of much of French sociology as illustrated by the critical writing of Pierre Bourdieu and Luc Boltanski.

Durkheim's focus on religion took shape after he had already created a distinctive Durkheimian approach to sociology as the positive science of *la morale*. His analysis of religion was influenced by a variety of sources. Durkheim's approach to the study of religion was influenced by connections with socialism and the legacies of Claude H. Saint-Simon and Auguste Comte, as illustrated by his arguments in the posthumously published *Le Socialisme* in 1928, translated into English in 1958 as *Socialism and Saint-Simon* ([1928] 1958). Durkheim's emphasis on solidarity and collective representations was in part the legacy of Comte's notion of 'the religion of humanity' and of French socialism (Wernick, 2001).

However, his approach to religion was also connected with the biographical fact that Durkheim, while no longer a practising Jew, came from a rabbinical family. Durkheim as a French citizen lived as an intellectual in the secular world of republican France and in a political context where 'cosmopolitanism' was often used as an 'anti-Semitic code word for Jews' (Richman, 2002: 83). For Durkheim, French anti-Semitism was deeply involved in the Dreyfus Affair, when a young French officer, who happened to be Jewish, was accused of betraying military secrets. Durkheim's involvement in the Dreyfus crisis was also bound up with struggles in the educational field between the study of classical literature and the French language against the emergence of a new curriculum, including sociology itself.

While Durkheim and his followers operated within this world of secular political struggles, it makes good sense to assume that Durkheim's view of religion was influenced by his Jewish background (Scharf, 1970; Strenski, 1997). Durkheim's father, grandfather and great-grandfather were rabbis. He was as a result well aware of the importance of religious rituals in maintaining the social solidarity of such a marginal religious community in Catholic France (Lukes, 1973: 40). With its dietary practices and everyday rituals of purity, Orthodox Judaism can be understood as a primary example of Durkheim's argument about religion as a classificatory scheme that divides the world into the sacred and the profane. Durkheim's sense of the profound or elementary relationship between fundamental categories of knowledge, the sacred and social solidarity was inspired as much by Judaism as by his academic criticisms of Spencer's sociology.

In this volume, I argue that there is a tendency in modern social thought to neglect rituals and religious practice in favour of a concentration on belief. Durkheim's sociology is attractive because it has an emphasis on the importance of religious practice in the maintenance of social groups. Durkheim derived much of his analysis of ritual practices from the work of the Scottish theologian-cum-anthropologist William Robertson Smith. In his *Lectures on the Religion of the Semites* ([1889] 1997) at Marischal College in Aberdeen, Scotland, Smith had shifted the focus of scholarly attention towards rituals or practices rather than religion as a system of (particularly unscientific) beliefs about reality, arguing that festivals bound the religious community into a social group. Smith's lingering commitment to orthodox Protestant theology led him to see the Protestant churches as institutions that had evolved beyond these 'elementary forms'. One significant problem for Protestant intellectuals was how to explain the differences between primitive rituals such as a communal meal and Christian practice such as the Eucharist. One solution was to appeal to evolutionary theory itself in order to argue that Protestantism was the most highly evolved religion, and that its rituals and beliefs were essentially abstract propositions that could be justified by rational argument. Protestant theology attempted to express religious truths through metaphors that have replaced ideas about actual relationships. Protestantism was therefore sharply contrasted with the Catholic doctrine of the transubstantiation of the bread and wine in the Eucharist. In his second lecture, Smith notes that with 'Christianity, and already in the spiritual religion of the Hebrews, the idea of divine fatherhood is entirely dissociated from the physical basis of natural fatherhood. ... God-sonship is not a thing of nature but a thing of grace' (p. 42). Smith can in many respects be taken as a representative figure of Victorian Christianity in its underlying drift towards a secular understanding of religious belief. Alasdair MacIntyre in *The Religious Significance of Atheism* (MacIntyre and Ricoeur, 1969) interpreted Mrs Humphrey Ward's novel *Robert Elsemere* (1914) as an account of the intellectual climate of this late Victorian world in which there was a transformation of nineteenth-century Protestantism from an evangelical faith to a secular justification of religious practice and eventually to humanism and socialism. In England, liberal Protestantism was a road into secular liberalism and Smith's work was influential in changing the understanding of religion, because Smith, in claiming that religion was entirely social, saw religion as a collection of institutions and practices.

It is against a background of individualistic, rationalist and psychological theories of religion in the work of E. B. Tylor, Max Müller and James Frazer that Durkheim's generic definition of religion was intellectually a new departure. According to his famous definition in *The Elementary Forms* ([1912] 2001), religion is not a belief in a High God or gods, but rather a unified system of beliefs and practices based upon a classification of social reality into sacred and profane things, and furthermore these beliefs and practices unite its adherents in a single moral community. Durkheim redirected attention away from individuals to social groups, or what he called a 'moral community'. Religion as a classificatory system that is grounded in the dichotomy between the sacred and profane is thus set apart from magic, which was seen by Durkheim to be an individual activity; there is no church of magic for Durkheim. Religion survives because it satisfies a basic social function, not a psychological one. Thus Durkheim argued that 'No society can exist that does not feel the need at regular intervals to sustain and reaffirm the collective feelings and ideas that constitute its unity and its personality' (p. 322). In this sense there are no false or irrational religions, because religion is the self-representation of society that is its collective representation. In these arguments Durkheim was influenced by pragmatism, specifically *The Varieties of Religious Experience* ([1902] 1963) by William James. From a pragmatist position, the truth or falsity of religion is not the most relevant issue. Religion as practice is only more or less useful in helping us to cope with reality, and its practicality is more important than the veracity of its beliefs in explaining reality. Religion is above all else a collective activity based on the classification of things into the sacred (set apart and forbidden) and profane (part of the everyday world). Because religion is social, it is experienced as obligatory on the life of the individual. In this sense, it is in Durkheim's terms a 'social fact' – a phenomenon outside the individual, existing independently and exercising moral force over the life of the individual. Finally, Durkheim's theory is not an evolutionary view of religion. In modern society, while the collective sense of the sacred may be less vivid and less compelling, the same functions can be detected. The notion of 'elementary forms' does not necessarily imply any evolutionary framework, because it carries the meaning of 'foundational' rather than 'primitive'.

Rational encyclopedic knowledge and religion

Although in many respects sociology is a product of Enlightenment rationalism, the problems of classification that lay behind the Encyclopedia of Diderot have not been central to debates in modern sociological theory. In retrospect we can see the Encyclopedia as the epitome of the modernisation project, of which the social sciences are a manifestation. The encyclopedic project proclaimed the possibility of complete knowledge and the triumph of reason over competing systems, especially over religion and mythology. The Encyclopedia celebrated the triumph of reason and assumed the irrelevance of revelation. It became a central element of the notion that modernisation produced, if not required, secularisation. Generally speaking, contemporary social theory has been much less optimistic, confident and assertive. Knowledge in modern societies is seen to be infinite, fragmentary, contextual, reflexive, contested and diffuse. More importantly, a variety of social and intellectual movements (feminism, post-colonial theory, critical ethnography, post-modernism, deconstructionism, and so forth) have made the idea of classification essentially problematic. Michel Foucault's *The Order of Things* (1974) and Richard Rorty's *Philosophy and the Mirror of Nature* (1979) have exposed, among other things, the conventionalism of any classificatory system as unavoidable. Classificatory schemes as conventions are always waiting to fall over.

My argument is that Durkheim's sociology of religion has to be understood alongside his study of classification. *Primitive Classification* first appeared in *L'Année Sociologique* volume vi (1901–1902) in 1903. Durkheim and Mauss's argument is complex and much contested (Durkheim and Mauss, [1903] 1997). Rodney Needham's introduction to the work treats their argument sceptically. He complains that 'This tendency to argument by *petitio principii* is more seriously expressed elsewhere in the essay ... they do not merely assert an evolutionary development in social organisation from the simple to the complex which makes their argument more plausible, but they expressly presuppose the very thesis of the argument itself' (pp. xiv–xv). The scale of the ambition of Durkheim and Mauss was considerable, namely to examine Kant's moral philosophy from a sociological point of view. What is the obligatory nature of the moral imperative? It can only be social.

We can see Durkheim's sociology of knowledge as a whole as a critical response to Kant. For Durkheim and his school, classificatory principles are not individualistic, a priori and rational. Their authority and effectiveness come from the fact that they are collective, that they remain vivid as a result of social rituals, that they remain forceful because they draw upon collective emotions, and finally their reality is underpinned by the fact that they represent social structures. Classification works because it is a collective representation. These notions were brilliantly reinforced by social anthropologists such as Robert Hertz who, in *Death and the Right Hand* (1960) showed that the classification of evil by the left hand was not a function of the physiological structure of the body or the division of the brain, but of the sacred/profane dichotomy. The conclusion was that the logical force of a classificatory system was rooted in a collective experience of the sacred. Left-sidedness in human societies is sinister because of its classificatory opposition to the right side, not because of a physiological disposition.

A crucial step in the argument was his rejection of the idea that religion can be based on false belief – otherwise how could it survive? Religion survives because it satisfies a basic social function, not a psychological one. Following Rousseau in these matters, he claimed that in this sense there are no false religions. Religion is the self-representation of society, its collective representation.

We can now turn in more detail to the development of his argument about the sociology of knowledge by looking at three key texts – 'Individual and collective representations' in 1898 in the *Revue de metaphysique et de morale*, *Primitive Classification* (with Marcel Mauss; [1903] 1997) and *The Elementary Forms* of 1912. As an exercise in the development of sociological theory, it is therefore worth having a detailed examination of Durkheim and Mauss's *Primitive Classification*. Their arguments have been either neglected by philosophers or treated as unsupportable, but from the perspective of sociology one can learn a lot about the general problem of classification from their work, and they raise difficulties that are still relevant to the sociology of classification. I take their underlying question to be: How are classifications made authoritative? More specifically, if classification is essentially arbitrary, how can classification in general have any authoritative force? *Primitive Classification* clearly anticipated the more complex and complete presentation of *The Elementary Forms*. Both publications attempt to understand sociologically forms of classification, especially forms of religious classification that divide the world into the sacred and the profane.

In *The Elementary Forms* there is a double meaning to Durkheim's notion of the 'elementary'. At one level it does mean 'primitive' and hence Durkheim's sociology on a reflection on the early fieldwork that had been carried out in Australia by the British anthropologists and administrators Spencer and Gillén. But Durkheim's intention was also to give a sociological account of the fundamental and form of national structures of consciousness. In the French title of *Primitive Classification* (*De Quelques formes primitives de classification*), the *formes primitives* are the elementary principle or forms of classification. The basic argument of the book is a piece of classic Durkheim. We cannot understand forms of consciousness by a study of the consciousness of separate individuals. More specifically, we cannot grasp the nature of thought through a psychological study of the contents of human minds. The social comes before the individual, and thus to understand both consciousness and classification, we need to study its social forms. Durkheim and Mauss argue that 'It is enough to examine the very idea of classification to understand that man could not have found it, essential elements in himself ... Every classification implies a hierarchical order for which neither the tangible world nor our minds' can provide a satisfactory and adequate model ([1903] 1997: 7–8). The explicit thesis of their study is that it is society itself that presents the mind with the 'primitive forms' of classification.

Durkheim's work is often profoundly contradictory. As Talcott Parsons recognised in *The Structure of Social Action* (1937), Durkheim sets out in *The Elementary Forms* to argue that it is society that produces religion, but what the book actually shows is that it is religion that produces society. In *Primitive Classification*, Durkheim and Mauss wanted to demonstrate that it is the organisation of society that produces the same categories of classification upon which individual consciousness is constructed. The basic philosophical target of *Primitive Classification* was the epistemology of Immanuel Kant, because the basis of their sociology was that consciousness is not the product of the constructive capacities of the isolated individual contemplating nature. The capacity of an individual to think is made possible by the pre-existence of systems of classification that are collectively held.

This argument is intrinsically interesting but it is not quite the argument that Durkheim and Mauss developed in *Primitive Classification*. What they actually argued was that the force of social classification derives its power from shared emotions. In the conclusion, they asserted categorically that 'Society was not simply a model which classificatory thought followed; it was its own divisions which served as divisions for the system of classification. The first logical categories were social categories; the first classes of things were classes of men, into which these things were integrated' (Durkheim and Mauss, [1903] 1997: 82). Several pages later we find the following argument: 'for those who are called primitives, a species of things is not a simple object of knowledge, but corresponds above all to certain sentimental attitude. All kinds of affective elements combine in the representation made of it. Religious emotions, notably, not only give out a special tinge but alternate to get the most essential properties of which it is constituted. Things are above all sacred or profane, pure or supreme, friends or enemies, favourable or unfavourable, i.e. their most fundamental characteristics are only expressions of the way in which they affect social sensibility. ... it is this emotional value of notions which plays the true preponderant part in the manner in which ideas are connected or separated, it is the dominant characteristic in classification' (p. 85). The emotions of the individual find their source in the collective practices of the group, just as for Rousseau the individual will is ultimately simply a particular manifestation of the general will.

We may legitimately restate their argument as saying that the political authority or social legitimacy of a classification system receives its force from arrangements that are collective, and which are sustained by a shared emotional life – a form of life that is arising periodically out of such collective rituals. The argument then suggests that the obligatory collective rituals produce shared emotions and it is through the shared effervescence of these occasions that collective classifications gain their social force and political authority. In the hunter–gatherer societies of central Northern Australia, the social groups that constituted tribal life were dispersed because the harsh and arid environment could not easily sustain large collectivities, and in these circumstances social life was sustained by the fact that social groups periodically came together to celebrate these common festivals. The rituals produce, to employ the phrase of Benedict Anderson (1991), an 'imagined community'.

This argument raises the obvious question about modern society, namely: What happens to the authority of classificatory systems and belief systems generally where the force of collective emotions are diminished by the secularisation of religious systems? Do we have any collective rituals to overcome the fragmented nature of modern, complex, multicultural societies? Durkheim and Mauss anticipated this question very directly, when they claimed that 'the history of scientific classification is, in the last analysis, the history of the stages by which this element of social affectivity has progressively weakened, leaving more and more room for the reflective thought of individuals' ([1903] 1997: 58). However, Durkheim and Mauss believed that this element of shared affectivity could never be entirely absent. These shared or collective emotions are 'the ensemble of mental habits by virtue of which we conceive things and facts in the form of co-ordinated or hierarchized groups' (p. 88).

For Durkheim, the collective and emotional character of classificatory practices in modern societies has broken down and, as a result, with modernity there is more indeterminacy of belief. Individuals can become more reflexive about classificatory principles, because they are subject to a process of individualisation. We can reconstruct Durkheim's argument to think about two abstract types of society. In pre-modern societies, the social world is thick and sticky; it is difficult to join social groups without rites of passage and considerable ritualistic effort, such as entering a sweat lodge and having visions. Sticky societies are even more difficult to leave than to join; attempts to leave the society (such as apostasy) may be punished by the threat of violence, if not death. In modern societies, membership of social groups in a civil society tends to be voluntary and people come and go according to their own preferences. Membership is fluid rather than fixed. Social movement between groups tends to be fluid, while movement between states is heavily regulated by state bureaucracies. Correspondingly, in pre-modern societies, beliefs are not held on an individual but on a collective basis, and individuals can neither exercise choice when it comes to endorsing collective beliefs nor can they easily change membership of their social group, which is normally determined by gender and age. This contrast is my interpretation of Durkheim's notion of mechanical and organic societies in *The Division of Labor in Society* ([1893] 1960).

Durkheim's account of classification is not in my view evolutionary, but his entire sociological work is based on the problems presented by modern (organic) society as opposed to traditional (mechanical) societies. In *The Division of Labor,* he had made the now famous distinction between mechanical solidarity (low individualism, low differentiation, strong social cohesion, and shared beliefs and rituals) and modern societies based on organic solidarity (high individualism, low social cohesion, high social differentiation, and minimal agreements about beliefs and rituals). In traditional societies, simple forms of classification are possible. Totemism employs elementary classification to associate kinship divisions with concrete signs or representations. The process of classification is elementary, and supported by an overarching framework of shared culture.

The utilitarian dilemma

There are at least three important tensions or contradictions in Durkheim's work. Firstly, religion is a collective representation of society, but in some sense it is the religious that produces the social. Secondly, while Durkheim was critical of the rationalist dismissal of religion on the basis of an appeal to positivist science, his own theories are positivist in the sense that social facts are things. Thirdly, Durkheim thinks that the sacred world of primitive society cannot survive in modernity, but he is not clear about what, if anything, can replace religion. He is tempted to answer that it is a new form of 'institutionalised individualism' and he was also in the period leading up to the First World War only too aware of the force of nationalism as a collective representation of society. These contradictions, as we have seen, were the topic of Parsons's criticisms of Durkheim in *The Structure of Social Action* (1937). What is at stake here is the problem of social solidarity in modern societies: Can a modern civil religion solve the problem of social order? To go deeper into this problem, we need to consider Parsons's views on religion and how Parsons's sociology came to depend in certain key aspects on the philosophy of Alfred North Whitehead.

Whitehead was, along with Bertrand Russell and Ludwig Wittgenstein, one of the most influential British philosophers of his generation. All three had close connections with Cambridge, especially with Trinity College. Whitehead, however, did not get a professorship at Cambridge but, after a period at the University of London, finished his career as professor of philosophy at Harvard. Whitehead's work is currently enjoying a revival, which is associated with changes in the epistemological framework of science, a revival of vitalism and the legacy of Henri Bergson, and an appreciation of Whitehead's contribution to the study of both science and religion. One other reason may be the recognition of certain parallels between Whitehead's *Process and Reality* ([1929] 1978) and Martin Heidegger's *Being and Time* ([1927] 1962). Both were concerned with the temporal dimensions of being (Cooper, 1993).

There are obviously major differences between Whitehead's philosophy and Parsons's sociology, so why attempt a comparison? There are at least three reasons why such a comparison is worthwhile. Firstly, Parsons, especially in *Structure*, gave ample recognition of Whitehead's influence on his thought. I shall argue, however, that Parsons actually appears to have misunderstood Whitehead's philosophy. Secondly, both men rejected rationalist criticisms of religion, and shared a sense of the importance of the sacred in society. They both accepted the distinction between the sacred and the profane, in which the latter is represented by the world of utilitarian rationality. Thirdly, Parsons's concept of social action has close affinities with Whitehead's ideas, but Whitehead's understanding of human embodiment in the experience of the everyday world is superior to Parsons's relatively shallow appreciation of the embodiment of the social actor. This comparison is therefore organised around these three aspects.

Parsons saw his encounter with the philosophy of Whitehead as an important aspect of his intellectual development, as he freely recognised in 'On Building Social System Theory: A Personal History' in *Social Systems and the Evolution of Action Theory* (1977). Throughout the twentieth century, American sociology was dominated primarily by a positivist philosophy of social science and embraced large-scale quantitative surveys as its preferred method of research. There are, of course, exceptions – the presence of the exiled Frankfurt School in America, the qualitative research of the Chicago School, the critical work of C. Wright Mills, and the radical theories of the New York intellectuals – but the prevailing mood of American sociology was practical, applied, reformist and empiricist. Parsons was therefore something of a maverick figure. Having undertaken research as a young scholar at the London School of Economics and Heidelberg University, Parsons was primarily influenced by European sociology, specifically Max Weber, Émile Durkheim and, to a lesser extent, Georg Simmel. In a technical sense, Parsons did not undertake empirical research, least of all engage in survey research and data analysis. The attraction of Whitehead for Parsons was that Whitehead's view of what constitutes science was highly relevant to Parsons's rejection of the legacy of positivist science.

Parsons wanted an analytical strategy to defend his view of the centrality of theory to sociological research, and an epistemology to reject naive confidence in the collection of empirical facts as the hallmark of a valid empirical science of society. For Parsons, there are no theory-neutral data in sociology (or any other science) which scientists can collect and read without interpretation. All data are produced within a pre-existing theoretical paradigm, and hence theoretical development and elaboration are not idle or trivial exercises. To treat social science data as if they were 'things' was to commit what Whitehead had called in *Science and the Modern World* 'the fallacy of misplaced concreteness' ([1925] 1967: 75). Whitehead's view of science provided a sophisticated justification for Parsons's own commitment to the development of 'theory' in sociology, or to what he called in the preface to *Structure* the 'systematisation of theory'.

Whitehead's epistemology proved useful in Parsons's discussion of the alleged reification of concepts in Durkheim's *The Rules of Sociological Method* ([1895] 1958). Parsons wanted to regard Durkheim as a positivist who defined the phenomena of sociological investigation as 'social facts'. By this term Durkheim meant social structures or processes that exist independently of individuals and which exercise social or moral force over them. For example, according to Durkheim a system of laws is a social fact; it exercises moral constraint over the individual and it is not dependent on the subjective whim of individuals. It is an independent and autonomous social force in society. For Parsons, this theoretical strategy involves the fallacy of misplaced concreteness. Of course defining 'the social' in sociology has been a persistent problem, but Parsons wanted to avoid what he regarded as Durkheim's positivism. 'Society' is not an 'observable reality' because it is not part of nature. It belongs to what Whitehead called the world of 'eternal objects' (Parsons, 1937: 444).

Parsons probably somewhat misunderstood the radical character of Whitehead's claims. Whitehead was a process theorist rather than a social constructionist, and as a result Parsons somewhat distorts Whitehead in order to use him to justify the systematisation of theory. Whitehead's metaphysics were concerned with the difference between what is (concrete actuality) and what could be (potentiality), and his view of 'nature' was concerned with the endless concretisations of potentialities into the actual, and with their constant process of perishing and disappearing. This is a position shared with Nietzsche, who in *Ecce Homo* (1979: 66–7) argued that modern metaphysics was based on the substitution of becoming by being by philosophers who despised the body and the 'little things' relating to nutrition, place, climate, recreation and so forth (Stauth and Turner, 1988: 25).

Whitehead was critical of instrumental rationality or the performance principle for reasons that he shared with Parsons, namely that this perspective provided little understanding of art and religion. Unlike the performance principle, aesthetics and religion involved fantasy and imagination, and hence forms of consciousness that could transcend the mundane norms of the everyday world. Whitehead's 'eternal objects' are occasions that question the world as it is and hold out the hope of an alternative. These objects stand against the performance principle and hence the 'truth that some proposition respecting an actual occasion is untrue may express the vital truth as to the aesthetic achievement. It expresses the "great refusal" which is its primary characteristic' (Whitehead, [1925] 1967: 158).

Although Parsons probably did not fully grasp the radical nature of Whitehead's views on science, religion and aesthetics, there was at least one valid point of convergence. American sociologists embraced a positivist epistemology because it was a neat validation of their commitment to a neutral, value-free science of society. Positivist or behavioural social science was fond of quoting Max Weber's arguments about value judgement, neutrality and value clarification. This professional idea was to present sociology as a useful but not judgmental tool of public policy in the service of public bureaucracies. Parsons was a liberal not a radical, but he understood the limitations of positivism, and he upheld the legacy of classical European sociology as requiring a tradition of theoretical analysis. Ironically, Parsons's employment of Whitehead to attack the idea of a-theoretical, unbiased, judgement-free observation had a parallel in Herbert Marcuse, who, also heavily influenced by Whitehead, wrote that empirical sociology 'freed from all theoretical guidance except a methodological one, succumbs to the fallacies of misplaced concreteness, thus performing an ideological service while proclaiming the elimination of value judgements' (Marcuse, 1964: 254).

Although I believe that Parsons oversimplified Whitehead's philosophy in under to provide some authoritative warrant for his own elaboration of theoretical sociology, Whitehead would have been sympathetic to Parsons's critique of utilitarianism. *Structure* is a sustained critique of utilitarian theories of action in the social sciences, and an attempt to build the foundations for an autonomous discipline of sociology, interconnected closely with economics and politics. For Parsons, classical economic theory has to assume the randomness of the ends of action because it remains silent about values. What people choose and value is simply a function of consumer wants as constrained by scarcity. The theory of marginal utility is not an explanation of the role of values in action and choice; it can only tell us about consumer preferences between available commodities. Furthermore, the concept of instrumental rationality in economic theory cannot preclude the use of force and fraud in human societies as rational solutions to scarcity, and thus the instrumental assumptions about action cannot provide a satisfactory account of how social order is created and maintained. If during a thunderstorm I want your umbrella, it is rational for me to use deception to get it off you, but the consequences for social order and our friendship are as a result not promising.

There is therefore a systemic problem in classical utilitarianism which was resolved by a set of assumptions which is not explicable within the original domain assumptions: Alfred Marshall's questioning of the hedonistic assumptions in the notion of need in his discussion of real and artificial wants; Pareto's difficulties in explaining 'non-rational' action in his distinction between residues and ideology; Durkheim's problems with the theory of happiness with respect to the division of labour and the definition of values as social facts; or the persistent problems of defining rational and irrational action in Weber in relation to behaviour versus action. In general, classical economics solved the problem of order by ad hoc, random and arbitrary theoretical solutions which involved famous appeals to the 'hidden hand of history', shared 'sentiments' and common wants, and the self-correcting changes that produce micro-equilibrium. In short, Parsons rejected the classical arguments of economists such as

Bernard Mandeville that, if we all vigorously pursue our private vices (such as greed), the unintended consequences will be beneficial (wealth, economic growth and happiness).

The solution to these difficulties in utilitarianism was located in various forms of radical positivism. These solutions either explained action by reference to 'environmental' features or to the hereditary legacy of genetics. In fact, utilitarianism had great difficulty in explaining rationality at all. If rational men are driven by hedonistic desires to satisfy their wants in a context of scarcity, why do they act irrationally at all? Given inadequate means, why will some people allocate scarce resources to luxuries or choose short-term measures while squandering their future? Some aspects of these problems of irrationality are outlined in the section on 'taste' towards the conclusion of *Structure*, where Parsons provides a discussion of the problem of habitual action. Irrationality within a paradigm of radical positivism has to be explained either in terms of the faulty psychology of the individual, or lack of consumer sovereignty, or inadequate information about the market. Some set of circumstances – beyond the rational control of the individual and outside the 'natural' exercise of egoistic reason – has to explain why interest does not rationally determine the selection of means.

This 'Hobbesian problem of order' was the centrepiece of *Structure*. In Hobbes's *Leviathan* ([1651] 1962), rational actors are driven to agree to a social contract to remove the state of nature in order to bring about stability and order, but fraud and force still remain viable options, given the competitive nature of Hobbesian society. A social contract skates on the thin ice of human competitiveness. A social contract is in the collective interest of society as a whole, but individuals or social groups may well turn to criminal behaviour to achieve personal advantage, which undermines collective benefits. Parsons's use of the fraud/force couple offered a powerful criticism of radical positivistic utilitarianism in the 1930s, but also raises important problems for contemporary economic rationalism, because Mafia-type organisations are effective means of social redistribution in societies where state organisations are corrupt and ineffectual.

His own theory of *voluntaristic* action recognised that the theory of action in utilitarianism could not solve the problem of order without recognising the existence of an independent and autonomous realm of values without which ends would be random and action would be deterministic. Hence, a voluntaristic theory of action requires a social component and we might reasonably argue that 'the social element' involves the creation and maintenance of the cultural system wherein lie ultimate values which in turn provide norms for the selection of means.

For Parsons, the Hobbesian problem of order has to be resolved by reference to shared values which control the fraud/force problem by regulating contracts in a normative and collective fashion. Society is possible because there are shared values which each new generation acquires through training ('socialisation'). Adherence to these values and conformity to social norms are rewarded by psychological reinforcement and by more straightforward material rewards.

Thus, in *Structure*, one of the critical tests for sociology was the explanation of religion. In fact the sociology of religion, as a special field of sociology, remained an ongoing preoccupation of Parsons throughout his academic career. The complex place of religion in the process of modernisation could not be resolved by some simple theory of secularisation, which meant that Parsons embraced neither a naive notion of disenchantment nor a nostalgic view of value-harmony in traditional societies (Robertson and Turner, 1991). Parsons's rejection of nostalgia allowed him to see the United States as a society within which Protestantism had shaped the values of individualism and activism in a manner which made secular, liberal capitalism the fulfilment, not the denial, of the Protestant Reformation.

Religion as the refusal of utility

The implication of the Durkheimian theory of social change is that the problem for modern society is the decline of these collective events and festivals which help a society to enforce its collective memory through shared emotions. Our classificatory systems tend to lack the force and authority of traditional patterns, and hence our classificatory principles are reflexive, contingent and arbitrary. With the decline of these religious systems of classification, secular systems do not have the collective force of such ritualised patterns. There is a sense, therefore, that in Durkheim's sociology the religious is the social, and the social is the religious. The end of the social in the modern world coincides with the decline of the authority of the religious paradigm. The end of the social releases the individual to become the carrier of the purely subjective self. The critical problem of modern society, as in Durkheim's personal life, is the problem of uprootedness or *deracinement* – a state of society that becomes manifest in the high rates of egoistical suicide in the contemporary world (Seigel, 2005: 484).

Whitehead also in his own way turned the rationalist account of religion on its head. Holding to an evolutionary view of religion, Whitehead identified its three stages (Crosby, 1983). In these three stages, God appears as the void, then the enemy and finally the companion. In the first stage of communal religion, there is blind emotion, and religion, having no object, is void. In the second, religion evolves into myth and God is a dangerous, avenging God, namely the God of the Old Testament. Finally God emerges as a trustworthy companion. While Whitehead recognised the social dimension of religion, he was more concerned with religion in relation to the solitariness of the individual, and actually defined religion in *Religion in the Making* as 'what the individual does with his own solitariness' (Whitehead, 1926: 16). For Whitehead, the religion that is forged out of solitariness is a 'purified religion' or 'rational religion', while 'communal religion' is merely a stage in the evolution of religion. In the early stages of its development, religion assumes an authoritarian form, and seeks to suppress the individual, thereby protecting the fragile relationship with God. Early religion is provincial, whereas a developed religion involves the emergence of a 'world consciousness'. This view of religion, we might note in passing, is consistent with Jacob Taubes's account of Marcion and Saint Paul, for whom the avenging God of the Old Testament has been overthrown by the God of love in the New Testament (Taubes, 2004).

Whitehead's view of religion was perhaps best expressed in *Science and the Modern World* ([1925] 1967), where he argued that interest in religion was fading since religious leaders adhered to ideas and values that were incompatible with the modern world, namely that they held on to the authoritarian model. Religion is presented as useful in creating an orderly society by imposing rigid moral constraint on individuals. But Whitehead was far from being critical of the religious vision, especially when it is associated with the great refusal. Religion is a living and vital experience when the worship of God is no longer a rule of safety, but can be an adventure of the free spirit or a quest after the unattainable. The death of religion comes with the final suppression of 'the high hope of adventure'.

Institutionalised individualism is a Kantian theory of the social agent as a moral being faced by inevitable choices, whose behaviour can become socially responsible. Parsons's treatment of the social actor as a form of institutionalised individualism is a sociological attempt to combine an economic theory of action with a Kantian theory of moral action. Parsons followed Durkheim in attacking English egoistical theories of the individual, especially in the work of Herbert Spencer. Whereas the economic individual of classical economics was a hedonist, both Durkheim and Parsons embraced an altruistic (Kantian) model of the individual. To act morally is to act in terms of the categorical imperative – behave as you would wish others to behave towards you.

There is a persistent conceptual problem with this solution to the question of the autonomous individual in liberal capitalism. Parsons's account of the individual in the consumer revolution may be part of the legacy of European individualism, but the emphasis on affective and emotional components of action against the rational and the cognitive is hardly Kantian (Parsons, 1974). The consumer or expressive revolution is associated with an affective expressivity that is not part of the legacy of a Kantian 'reflecting faith'. American society was the modern cradle of individualism, which writers such as Alexis de Tocqueville recognised as a unique product of the American Revolution. The expressive revolution as it became articulated in the student rebellions of the 1960s was a new cultural movement that may have been part of the legacy of the American Protestant settlers but was also a significant departure from the asceticism that Weber had detected in the 'spirit of capitalism'. The expressive revolution celebrated hedonism, self-expression and hostility to conventional norms and social institutions.

The body and the organism

An adequate theory of ritual and emotions in any sociology of action needs to take a position on the character of the agent, namely to take a position on the mind–body problem (Turner, 2009a). With few exceptions, classical sociology had little to say about human embodiment. In Weber's sociology, the body is implicitly located in the concept of 'behaviour' rather than action, because the primary feature of action is the rational selection of means to ends. Parsons adopted a similar strategy in treating the body as part of the environmental conditions of action. Durkheim engaged in an interesting set of reflections on the mind–body dichotomy in his account of the soul in *The Elementary Forms* ([1912] 2001). As one might anticipate, Durkheim approached issues relating to the body, the soul and the self within the analysis of classification. He observed that the ethnographic data from Australia demonstrated that an Aboriginal made a direct equation between the totem and the person: 'Each individual thus has a double nature: two beings coexist in him, a man and an animal' (p. 104). Aboriginal religion recognised a sharp distinction between body and soul, but that distinction was not absolute. In many cases, the soul and the body are mingled. The soul is the breath and 'When blood is spilled, the soul escapes with it' (p. 185). This binary opposition between soul and body is yet another example of the division between the sacred and the profane, which Durkheim believed was a universal form of classification. While we may share in the same collective consciousness, we will see those collective features from a specific angle. Durkheim observed that 'there must be a factor of individuation. It is the body that plays this role. Since they are distinct from one another and occupy different points in time and space, each of them constitutes a special setting in which collective representations are refracted and coloured in different ways' (pp. 199–200). Durkheim's discussion of the body is important, but he characteristically conceptualised the body within the framework of sacred–profane classification. Durkheim did not approach the body from the perspective of performance and action, and did not adopt a phenomenology of the body. In his classificatory scheme, body (profane) and soul (sacred) were ultimately separate.

Perhaps the obvious thing to say about Whitehead's position is that, in his theory of the organic body, the biological is active not passive; it does not appear as simply a condition of action. There is an important parallel between Heidegger's *Dasein* and Whitehead's organic, and indeed for Whitehead our worldly involvement is through the feelings of the human body, but these are not merely passive encounters. Whereas objects in the Cartesian world are passive, inert phenomena, Whitehead wanted to create a picture of the world as a dynamic plurality of interacting objects in an ever-renewing process. In this regard, Whitehead's picture of reality is very similar to Heidegger's *Verweisungszusammenhang* (or referential togetherness) (Schrag, 1970). In Whitehead's philosophy, the constant emerging and perishing of events expresses the intentionality behind this together-ness of events. For Whitehead, therefore, the human body can never be merely the condition of action as an external and stationary phenomenon.

Heidegger famously described our relationship to the body and technology through the illustration of the hammer that so perfectly fits the hand in the action of striking a nail. This relationship was paradigmatic of the notion of the ready-to-hand relationship of body and world. In Whitehead ([1929] 1978: 81), this relationship involves the body as 'the starting point for knowledge of the circumambient world'. Our most fundamental experiences of worldliness come through the functioning of our own bodies. Thus, 'the feeling *of* the stone is in the *hand*; the feeling *of* the food is the ache *in the stomach*' (p. 118). Our perception and appropriation of these sense data are made possible by what Whitehead called, in a manner that resembles Heidegger's ready-to-handedness of existence, 'the *withness* of the body' (p. 64).

Parsons accepted implicitly a division of mind and body that Whitehead ([1929] 1978: 246) regarded as a 'disastrous separation'. What both men shared, however, was recognition of the significance of religion as a perspective on reality that could not be explained away by reference to a narrow, positivist version of reason. Parsons's failure to fully grasp the dynamic nature of Whitehead's view of the bio-logical meant that the early sociology of action lacked an adequate account of embodiment in relation to knowledge and action.

Conclusion

Durkheim's sociology remains relevant because it raised fundamental questions about the relationships between religion, society and self. He approached these issues through a sociology of knowledge that created an important role for shared emotions and shared beliefs in constituting the foundations of authority behind any system of classi-fication. The problem is: How does religion survive, if at all, in a society with a high division of labour and a culture that is profoundly individualistic? Modern writers, but especially Talcott Parsons and Robert Bellah, have struggled with the idea of civil religion as the social glue of modern society. Behind these questions of substance, there were other epistemological questions about the actual status of religious knowledge in relation to science. Parsons in particular confronted the tendency of any positivist theory of science to treat religion as either false or ephemeral. The paradoxical stance of Durkheim was to argue there are no false religions and they support society, while arguing that religious symbols do not in fact represent the sacred totemic world but society itself. In grasping the actual nature of religion, Whitehead's philosophy of religion is valuable in treating religion as a refusal of the limited world of utility. Finally, these theories – indeed any theory of religion – requires some minimal understanding of human embodiment to understand religious symbolism, but above all we need to ground the theory of religious practice on some notion of embodiment.

3 | *Max Weber and comparative religion*

Introduction: religion as a 'moralising faith'

There has been much academic debate about the coherence or otherwise of Max Weber's sociology as a whole. Much of the analysis has focused on the notion of rationalisation as the master theme of his sociological work. By rationalisation, Weber referred to a set of interrelated social processes by which the modern world had been systematically transformed into a rational system. Among these various processes, rationalisation included the systematic application of scientific reason to the everyday world and the intellectualisation of mundane activities through the application of systematic knowledge to practice. Rationalisation was also associated with the disenchantment of reality that is the secularisation of values and attitudes. The sociology of religion was therefore a central aspect of Weber's sociological interests as a whole. An influential interpretation of this theme of religion and rationalisation was developed by Friedrich Tenbruck (1975; 1980) in his essays on the thematic unity of Weber's work.

Tenbruck questioned Marianne Weber's description of the posthumous *Economy and Society* (1978) as Weber's principal work (*Hauptwerk*). By directing attention away from *Economy and Society*, he focused on Weber's various contributions to the study of religion. For Tenbruck, there is no particular key to the interpretation of *Economy and Society*, precisely because that text is a posthumous conglomerate of disparate elements which do not constitute a recognisable major work. Tenbruck identified the underlying anthropological dimension of Weber's sociology, namely his account of humans as 'cultural beings'. This cultural activity involved the issue of the meaningfulness of the everyday world, especially the brute need to satisfy economic needs. Tenbruck thus emphasised the central role of 'the Economic Ethics of World Religions', namely Weber's interest in the sociology of religion with respect to the rationalisation process. The various studies of Judaism ([1921] 1952), Confucianism and Daoism (1951), Hinduism and Buddhism (1958a) and the incomplete studies of Islam and Islamic law or *Shari'a* (Turner, 1978; [1974] 1998) are a series of empirical applications of the theme of religious prescriptions for economic behaviour. These works on the economic ethics of world religions represent the principal consolidation of the initial argument of the essays on the Protestant ethic. The Protestant ethic thesis was simply a component of the central analysis of religion and economics which occupied the *Gesammelte Aufsätze zur Religions soziologie* (Weber, 1921). Tenbruck also underlined the special importance of the 'Authors Introduction' (*Vorbemerkung*) to the sociology of religion as a whole, which was included by Talcott Parsons in his 1930 translation of *The Protestant Ethic and the Spirit of Capitalism* (2002). Weber also wrote an additional introduction in 1913, which was published in 1915 with the title 'Intermediate Reflections' (*Zwischenbetrachtung*), which was conceived after the 'Authors Introduction' was already in print. The *Zwischenbetrachtung* was translated by Hans Gerth and C. Wright Mills in *From Max Weber* (Gerth and Mills, 2009: 323–62) as 'religious rejections of the world and their directions'. Tenbruck's argument is therefore that the analysis of 'the Economic Ethics of the World Religions' dominated Weber's intellectual activities from around 1904 to 1920. Because his publications on religion occupied this creative period of Weber's life, we should regard these texts on religion and economics as his principal work, rather than *Economy and Society*.

In this exegetical framework, the thematic unity of these texts in the comparative sociology of religion is the study of the ways in which religious orientations towards the world did or did not lead to an ethic of world mastery, that is to a process of rationalisation. In the 'Introduction', the 'Intermediate Reflections' and the 'Author's Introduction', Weber developed a universalistic and historical conceptualisation of these rationalisation processes. This development is wholly compatible with Weber's interpretative sociology, because it was these meaning systems within religion that generated specific world-views that acted as the motivations for action. This interpretation is also consistent with the idea of the fatefulness of world images in Weber's meta-theory, because it was paradoxically the irrational quest for salvation which generated a rational solution to being in the world (Turner, 1996).

Weber's interest in the religious quest for salvation resulted in an anthropology of the rules which govern the practical conduct of life (*Lebensführung*). In this anthropology of conduct, Weber distinguished between a theodicy of good fortune (*Glück*) and a theodicy of suffering (*Leid*). In coming to terms with fortune and suffering, human beings extend their conception of their personal experience beyond the everyday material world. It is these experiences of fortune and suffering which destroy the rational or purposive categories of pragmatic orientation to reality. However, it was only within the monotheistic and ascetic religions that the rationalisation of the question of theodicy reached its ultimate fruition. The development of the concept of a universalistic God in a framework of history and salvation, demanding a human quest for salvation, produced a rational theodicy of reality as such. In short, it was the legacy of the Judaeo-Christian world, which included the notions of ethical prophecy and monotheism, which were crucial to the development of a radical solution to the question of theodicy in terms of highly intellectual, rational soteriologies. For example, the intellectual rationalism of the Protestant sects was critical in pushing European civilisation towards a pattern of religious individualism based on life regulation and personal salvation. In short, Weber was in the process of developing a comprehensive sociology of piety as the core issue of his sociology of religion.

Many of these issues have been taken up and further elaborated by Wilhelm Hennis (1988) in his important study of Weber in his essays in reconstruction. For Hennis, the central question in Weber's sociology is to do with the issues of personality and life orders. Hennis argued that it was the development of *Menschentum* which was the central question of Weber's sociology, namely how certain cultural developments produced a particular type of personality and a particular rational conduct of life (*Lebenführung*), particularly in the idea of calling as part of the constitutive question of modern culture (Stauth and Turner, 1986). In more precise terms, Weber's sociology was concerned with the historical origins of life regulation as a rational conduct of personal behaviour in the development of modern vocations in the social world. Weber's analysis of the Protestant ascetic organisation of life is therefore simply one dimension of this analysis of *Lebenführung*, or the study of the personality effects of particular kinds of religious activity. The rationalisation theme to which Weber

draws attention in the Protestant ethic thesis involved a transformation of patterns of discipline and methodology relevant to particular
forms of economic life regulation. Weber's analysis of capitalism was
not so much concerned with the understanding of its economic structure and functions, but with the ways in which a capitalist economy
had an 'elective affinity' with certain forms of personality and life
order. By 'personality' Weber did not have in mind what we would
now understand in academic circles as an empirical social psychology,
but rather what kind of ontology would be produced by different life
orders. That is, Weber asked an ontological question from the standpoint of German cultural values.

One aspect of the intellectual motivation behind the exegesis of
Hennis (and Keith Tribe, 1989) was to re-establish Weber as a figure
in classical political philosophy, thereby emphasising his concern to
understand the political order of society as the foundation of ethics
and ontology. In this regard Weber belongs to a tradition of political
philosophy that started with Aristotle, in the sense that Weber's sociology of religion sought to contrast the virtues and habitus behind the
various world religions, since from different personality constructs
evolved the virtues (or piety) of different religions.

These exegetical issues, particularly as they impinge upon questions of liberalism and democracy, have dominated much of the
philosophical debate about the implications of Weber's work in
contemporary Germany (Gneuss and Kocka, 1988). This critical
(re)interpretation of Weber is specifically directed against Talcott
Parsons's interpretation of Weber as one of the founding fathers of
the sociology of action. Hennis has been explicit in his view of
Weber as contributing to a German tradition of political and philosophical enquiry. According to Hennis, Weber's central question
was about the ethical character of human existence and not about
the narrow question of the cultural foundations of Western capitalism in the theology of the Protestant sects. As a result, we can better
understand 'Weber was a *German* thinker, from the land of
"Dr Faustus"' (Hennis, 1988: 195). The tragic problem of Weber's
sociology is that the heroic personality of Protestant asceticism is no
longer compatible with the secular world of capitalism – 'Today its
spirit has fled from this shell –whether for all time, who knows?
Certainly victorious capitalism has no further need for this support
now that it rests on the foundation of the machine. Even the

optimistic mood of its laughing heir, the Enlightenment, seems destined to fade away, and the idea of the "duty in a calling" haunts our lives like the ghost of once-held religious beliefs' as he concludes in *The Protestant Ethic and the Spirit of Capitalism* (Weber, 2002: 121). The shell of capitalism is the famous 'iron cage' in which our behaviour no longer has the sustaining framework of religious belief and where the principles of utility are dominant but devoid of any ultimate significance.

This interpretation of Weber is in fact compatible with an article by Karl Löwith that first appeared in the *Archiv für Sozialwissenschaft und Sozialpolitik* in 1932, and was translated in 1982 as *Max Weber and Karl Marx* and was recently reprinted as a new edition ([1932] 1993). Löwith sought to demonstrate that, regardless of the very important differences between Karl Marx and Weber, their sociological perspectives were joined by a common philosophical anthropology. There was as a result an important convergence in their attitudes towards the destructive features of bourgeois civilisation which Marx developed through the idea of alienation and Weber through the theme of rationalisation. From the perspective of this ontology, both Weber and Marx saw capitalism as a destructive economic system, but one which also opened up new possibilities through the transformation of traditional systems.

The common theme in these accounts is the recognition of the profoundly ethical character of Weber's social theory and its underpinning in a particular anthropology of personality and life orders. Both Tenbruck and Löwith share this interest in the religious theme within Weber's life and work, particularly the focus on questions relating to theodicy in which the rationalisation theme was a product of the existential question of meaning in Weber's sociological framework. My conclusion is firstly that the differences between Tenbruck and Hennis (or between seeing Weber as a sociologist or as a political philosopher) are not significant. They insist on the ethical character of Weber's work. We can argue that Weber was working towards a sociology of piety, namely the rules of pious activity in the everyday world. Piety eventually produces character as a result of such training. Secondly, we can in fact better understand Weber's concern for the interconnections between piety and ethics by recognising the long-lasting impact of Immanuel Kant's philosophy of religion on Weber's sociology as a whole.

In his comparative studies, Weber sought to preserve the view that the radical message of Protestant Christianity involves a heroic struggle for self-mastery or piety, the consequence of which is the radical transformation of the traditional world. For Weber there were two related issues here. In order for the radical ethic of Christianity to function, religion had to be clearly separated from the state otherwise the religious ethic was subordinated to the secular interests of power. This fusion of religion and politics was the problem of 'caesaropapism', the authoritarian domination of society by the confusion of sacred and secular power. Weber's view of the necessary separation of religion and politics is a core aspect of liberal philosophy, but in the German case it also reflected Weber's experience of the political legacy of Bismarck and the *kulturcampf* in which the 'iron chancellor' had successfully manipulated anti-Catholic sentiment to political advantage. Weber's views on political power reflected his experiences of Bismarck's statecraft, which had destroyed many of the institutions that could have kept the state accountable to parliament. Bismarck had destroyed liberalism and reinforced political passivity in Germany. That was also the legacy of Lutheranism, which defended law and order over liberty of conscience.

As a liberal Weber was not sympathetic to Catholicism and he was in any case deeply influenced by his mother's Protestant piety and specifically by the moral teaching of William Ellery Channing, who emphasised rational control over the instincts rather than emotional experiences of divinity (Mitzman, 1971: 29). Catholicism remained an issue in Weber's sociology of religion. While he did not devote much explicit attention to the social consequences of Catholicism in Europe, devoting most of his intellectual energies to Protestantism, we can assume that Catholic piety was regarded as a conservative social force.

Furthermore, religion as an ethical activity of self-creation had to be distinct from popular religion as merely a set of rituals for bringing good fortune and good health. Religion as a radical faith of transformation had to be concerned not with *Gluck* but with *Leid*. This was the problem of routinisation in which a radical religion of inner conviction became merely a therapeutic practice of folk religiosity. In adopting these moral issues from Kant, Weber also had to, as it were, look over his shoulder to Friedrich Nietzsche, and especially to the questions: Are these Christian morals in fact merely driven by resentment, in which case they are not a self-reflexive moral world-view, and secondly is a warrior religion somehow 'healthier' than the religion of slaves, namely early Christianity? To what extent is Islam, which does not privilege suffering and repentance, a healthier (life-affirming) doctrine than the religion of the crucified Jesus?

Given Weber's ethical concerns, both Islam and Confucianism offered him two useful case studies since, as far as Weber was concerned, neither wholly rejected caesaropapism. Firstly, Weber's treatment of Confucianism is somewhat ambiguous because, while he classified it as a world religion, in practice he interpreted it as the ethics of the literati within the Chinese court system. Secondly, while Weber was forced to recognise Islam as a member of the monotheistic, Abrahamic tradition, in practice he interpreted it as a warrior religion in which there was no fundamental separation of secular and sacred power. Confucianism was simply a court ethics whose principal value was filial piety. For Weber, Islam was a warrior religion whose soteriological doctrines were transformed by a history of imperial power. Christian ethics were also corrupted by the history of the medieval Catholic Church, but the radical message of the primitive church was constantly revived by the Protestant sects whose ethical demands produced a reformation of personality.

The Kantian legacy

As we have seen in Chapter 1, Kant, in *Religion within the Boundaries of Mere Reason* ([1763] 1998), distinguished between religion as a cult which seeks favours from God and religion as moral action. Kant further elaborated this argument through an examination of 'reflecting faith' that compels human beings to strive for salvation through inner reflection. These authentic moral demands in true religions contrast sharply with those folk practices that are essentially magical in creating a technology to manipulate the world. In order to have autonomy, human beings need to act independently of God. True religion involves a technology of the self; false religions are merely magical technologies of manipulation. The real psychological tension in radical Christian soteriology was that the faithful could not influence God by prayer or ritual, and hence divinity tragically assumed the form of a 'hidden God' (Goldmann, [1956] 1964). In a paradoxical fashion, Christianity implies the tragic 'death of God' because it calls people to freedom, and hence the Christian faith is ultimately self-defeating.

Alongside these Kantian-inspired concepts of life orders and personality, Weber developed the idea of various spheres of life into which the world is divided. These different spheres make demands on both the individual and social levels, and can combine or conflict with each other. This analysis of the spheres of life in the two lectures on 'politics as a vocation' and 'science as a vocation' found a more elaborate classification in the 'Intermediate Reflections', where Weber identified a wider range of life spheres or value spheres: economics, politics, aesthetics, the erotic, the intellectual and the religious. The different world religions represent different resolutions of the various levels of contradiction between religion and 'the world'. One central question for Weber is whether religion is simply a sphere of values or in fact the principle that guarantees or determines the other spheres. Is religion a component of the life spheres of the world or that source of values that determines the diverse activities of society? If religion is in tension with the other spheres (as in the notion of religious orientations and their rejection of the world), then Weber's sociology implies a special status for religion. If religion is simply one institution, then there is no essential conflict. Secularisation in terms of the differentiation of the spheres of life meant that religion had simply become a separate institution alongside the other life spheres of activity. Furthermore, the differentiation of the spheres meant that no single coherent meaningful life was possible, and hence this polytheism of values was the 'fate' of modern people (Gerth and Mills, 2009: 357). The attempt to preserve charisma through the cultivation of 'a cosmic brotherhood', as illustrated by the discipleship around Stefan George (Norton, 2002), could only be an aristocratic religious response and unlikely to succeed in an age of mass democracies and the rationalised bureaucratisation of politics. In this Weberian sense, therefore, religious studies are a product of the differentiation of the life spheres, the disenchantment of reality and the assimilation of religion by culture.

The most influential account of this 'moralising faith', of course, was presented in Weber's *The Protestant Ethic and the Spirit of Capitalism* (2002), in which he argued that the religious practices of the virtuosi had been taken out of the monastery and into the ordinary household, and from there piety or 'this-worldly asceticism' had undertaken to penetrate the daily routines of the household in the regulation of ordinary life. Perhaps the most celebrated version of this penetration of the world in Britain was undertaken by John

Wesley and the Methodist chapels. The Wesleyan sect took its name 'Methodism' from the methods by which the laity came to regulate their lives, such as modesty in dress, regularity of prayer and acts of charity towards the poor. The sociological consequences are well known (Thompson, 1963). Pious practice and biblical study produced a disciplined and literate Methodist laity which came to exercise some degree of political and cultural leadership in the British working class. As a result, Methodists came to be predominantly a comfortable bourgeoisie, moving gradually away from their original piety. The experience of Methodists came to be identified by sociologists of religion as a key feature of a more general process of secularisation.

Weber's schema of religious orientations implied a hierarchy of religions in terms of their inner consistency to a radical this-worldly asceticism. Weber may therefore have accepted a hierarchy of values mapped onto a hierarchy of religions, with Calvinism and Lutherism at the top of this chain of radical engagement with the world through the emotional and pietist sects (such as Wesleyan Methodism) to the Old Testament prophets of Judaism. The Islam of the Muslim Empires and post-prophetic Judaism fall below the religious orientations of Protestant Christianity, but the Abrahamic religions were more radical than the religions of the Orient, namely Confucianism, Daoism and Buddhism. Thus Weber's study of the economic ethics of the world religions implied a hierarchical order in terms of the radical character of their ethics and their social consequences. These assumptions have been frequently criticised and any such hierarchical arrangement of religion has in recent scholarship been condemned as a species of Orientalism (Said, 1978). The notion of a clear hierarchy of religious orientations does not fit easily into a modern context, where religions are globalised and when religious leaders attempt to promote ecumenical dialogue in multicultural societies. Weber's attempts to create a value-free science of society left him poorly equipped to offer specific advice or guidance with respect to desirable ends of action, and the values that underpin the idea of a secular vocation appear to be arbitrary. Weber's secular science of society has been rejected by philosophers such as Leo Strauss (1950) and Eric Voegelin (1952), who did not accept Weber's sociology as an adequate grounding for politics, or the modern study of religions. In defence of Weber, although his views may be unfashionable, it can be said that they raise a number of challenging questions that continue to influence modern analysis: Is something equivalent to the ascetic piety of Puritanism necessary as a challenge to the secular spheres, especially the spheres of politics and economics?

The sociology of Islam

Weber did not produce a complete study of Islam and his view of Islam has to be reconstructed from a variety of sources, most notably his sociology of law and his classification of types of prophecy. By comparison with his work on Protestantism and the 'religions of Asia', Weber's sociology of Islam has been somewhat neglected. The principal exceptions have been Maxime Rodinson's *Islam et capitalisme* ([1966] 1978), my own *Weber and Islam* ([1974] 1998) and Wolfgang Schluchter's edition on Islam (1987), which has been translated as *Max Weber and Islam* (Huff and Schluchter, 1999). These works interpreted Weber's commentary on Islam as an aspect of his more general project, namely to show why modern, rational capitalism appeared uniquely in the Christian West.

Let us start with his more general set of questions. Firstly, Weber sought to understand the status of Muhammad as an ethical prophet and how the Prophet articulated a set of revelations in the Qur'an to challenge the traditional values of Arab society. In this respect, we can see the commentary on early Islam as a contribution to the more general study of authority, of which charismatic authority was a major dimension. Weber's view of the Prophet by comparison with his analysis of the Old Testament prophets in *Ancient Judaism* ([1921] 1952) was not complimentary, and Weber was more impressed by the Prophet as a military leader who created a state. On this basis, Weber developed a set of significant contrasts between Christianity and Islam. For example, Islam has no Church as such and no sacerdotal priesthood. The *ulama* (the religious leadership of Islam that functions mainly at a local rather than national or institutional level) do not exercise authority over institutionalised grace and their authority is not derived directly from the Prophet but from their training and the consensual recognition they receive from the community. Whereas in the Roman Catholic Church, religious authority is ultimately inscribed in papal authority and the bishops, such that the 'keys of grace' are located in a centralised, hierarchical and ultimately bureaucratic structure.

In the case of Islam, Weber was aware of an important difference between Shi'ism and Sunni Islam. While the Shi'ites identified authority with the descendants of the Prophet and anticipated the eventual return of a spiritual leader (the *imam*), the Sunni tradition recognised the caliphate as the legitimate system of authority. The pre-Islamic Iranian priestly model of despotism was imitated by later Islamic regimes, whose aristocratic power was legitimised by the *ulama*. For example, the works of al-Mawardi (974–1058) described a rigid social world composed of aristocratic horsemen, priests, peasants and merchants. The model was both functional and hierarchical. In response to these despotic institutions, political conflict in Islam has been subsequently organised around utopian criticism of the urban hierarchy, a utopian opposition that often appeals nostalgically to the egalitarian solidarity (*asabiyya*) of the foundation community. For example, in the Iranian Revolution of 1977–9, Ayatollah Khomeini mobilised the oppressed and the innocent in the name of a radical Islamic state against the urban elite, who were the principal agents of the Shah's authoritarian programme of economic modernisation. The revolution involved a successful alliance between the clergy behind Khomeini, sections of the urban working class and the dispossessed (*Mostaz'afin*), who were typically landless rural migrants. In radical Islamism, the voice of the people became an expression of divine will against the inequalities of the secular state. Authority in Sunni Islam is communal, devolved and localised, and hence there is considerable dispute over the correct interpretation of law and tradition in a religious system where legal decisions (*fatwas*) can be posted on the Internet by any teacher who claims to represent a religious community. In this respect, the *ulama* have sociologically a much closer relationship to the Jewish rabbinical institutions as a devolved and competitive assembly of religious teachers and scholars. Neither Judaism nor Islam have a social role that approximates to the sacerdotal priesthood of Western Christendom.

Secondly, Weber was interested in a related set of relationships between state and Church, which we can summarise under the sociological concept that was implicit in the structure of *Economy and Society* (1978), namely the issue of caesaropapism. As prophetic, Abrahamic religions of revelation, both Christianity and Islam stand in opposition to the empirical world where violence, inequality and cruelty reign supreme. The problem with all revealed religions is the establishment of religious authority over secular processes of political power, economics and social structures (Arkoun, 1994: 59). This endless struggle between the ideal world of the brotherly community of love and the brutal reality of everyday life has been the principal religious leverage towards social change in human societies (Parsons, 1966: xlvii). The core components of worldliness in the Abrahamic religions have been sexuality and money that represent the corruption of power and selfishness. The religious orientations of asceticism, mysticism and 'legal-mindedness' represent the historically dominant religious rejections of the fallen world. This sacred–profane dynamic is particularly important in Islam. Its first theological premise is the affirmation in the Qur'an (the *sura* of unity, cxii): He is God alone, God the Eternal. Islamic doctrine is radically egalitarian, because its monotheistic fundamentalism precludes any ontological hierarchy in either human society or nature, but there is a permanent contradiction between theology and the history of hierarchy and inequality in actual societies (Marlow, 1997). While the divine purpose is to establish peace between human beings, the early history of the Islamic caliphs was violent: 'Umar, 'Uthman and 'Ali, the successors or caliphs of the Prophet, were assassinated.

Thirdly, Weber provided a comprehensive analysis of Islamic law which contributed an additional illustration of his study of charismatic authority (in the form of revelation) and rationalisation. Islam is a revealed religion that came to mankind through the prophetic agency of Muhammad. This revelation is contained within a sacred text or Qur'an that was assembled after the death of the Prophet. Once this process of collection was complete, the Qur'an as the word of God was closed and transformed into a canon of revelation (*mushaf*). This closure of orthodoxy was known as the closing of the gate of *ijtihad* (the closure of any significant intellectual re-evaluation or legal judgment). Western sociologists including Weber argued subsequently that the rigidity of Islamic cultures was a consequence of the attempt to contain legal and theological speculation within a narrow framework (Turner, [1974] 1998). In addition to the Qur'an, Muslims have the tradition (*sunna*) of the Prophet known through a chain of authority of witnesses (*isnad*). This tradition is the *hadith* (customary teaching). We might say, therefore, that the law, the book and the Prophet constitute Islam. More precisely, Islam as a religion is the beaten path (*sunna*) of the Prophet.

Fourthly, Weber was interested in the sociology of the city as either a military camp or a site of democratic institutions. In *The City* (1958b) Weber had argued that in the West the city had distinctive features that promoted the rise of citizenship and democratic civil institutions (Turner, 1993a; 1986). The European city was not based on tribal affiliation; it was not simply a military base; and finally it was relatively autonomous as a self-governing set of institutions. Christianity had contributed to these developments by creating a social bond that was based on a religious fellowship rather than on blood. By contrast, Weber argued that the city in the Middle East was essentially a military camp and that tribal and familial allegiance had never been totally broken down by the idea of religious belonging. The city in the history of Islam had not emerged as a basis for civil institutions to limit the power of the state.

At its inception, Islam was an egalitarian brotherhood that assumed the equality of free (male) believers, developing neither church nor priesthood. Muhammad's 'constitution of Medina' was a political contract between various tribes to form a state, not a church. In this new arrangement, Jews, for example, retained their identity but swore loyalty to the Prophet. This religious egalitarian monotheism was reinforced by Arabic tribalism that also had an egalitarian ethic (Watt, 1953). These early religious doctrines were, however, compromised by the success of Islamic military expansion, which encouraged the growth of a more status-conscious and hierarchical social order. The prominent religious role that was played by the wives of the Prophet (in particular Khadija the first wife and 'Aisha the third wife) was eventually overshadowed by the patriarchal cultures of the Islamicate societies in which women, outside the elite, became socially invisible. These tendencies were increasingly legitimised by the Islamic incorporation of Greek political thought, which conceptualised the city as a hierarchical political formation. In the new polis, social order required the harmony that was produced by a wise but despotic leader (Watt, 1999). In Iraq and Iran in the Sassanian period, social inequality became progressively hereditary, and the dominant class was recruited from the landed nobility.

Finally, Weber's more narrow concern was with piety. This concern suggests that sociology should examine fundamental differences between religious traditions in terms of the emergence of the self. At the core of Christianity was a world-view based on the notions of personal responsiveness to the redemptive love and historical actions of a personal God, operating in a corrupt world through a series of sacrificial acts (Hodgson, 1960). The crucifixion of Jesus was the foundational event in this cosmic history of salvation. By contrast, the core of Islam was the demand for personal responsibility towards God, who has established a framework for moral order through the revelation of the law. The ethical concerns of Irano-Semitic monotheism, as expressed through its ethical prophets, were embodied in the law, on the one hand, and by the quest for mystical understanding of God, on the other. The unity of Islamicate culture was developed through 'Sharia-mindedness' – a moral code which constituted the inner conscience of Islam, and which expressed an opposition to the hierarchical and despotic systems of power that often characterised the Mughal, Safavi and Ottoman empires (Hodgson, 1974, I: 238). The community of the pious and learned (*ulama*) developed the religious activities that cultivated this Sharia-mindedness as a major religious orientation in Islam.

Sharia-mindedness, which was carried down the centuries by *ulama* and Sufis, was founded on a sense of justice and thus stood in opposition to the culture of the emerging military states of Islamicate empires. The practices that developed Sharia-mindedness are an equivalent religious orientation to what Weber had in mind by his distinction between ascetic inner-worldly religion and mystical other-worldly orientations in *The Sociology of Religion* (1966: 166). It is also the equivalent of the idea of a 'technology of the self' (Foucault, 1997: 224), since Sharia-mindedness requires discipline to produce a special type of personality; Sharia-consciousness is a technology of self-understanding. The notion that Sharia-conscience functioned as a religious critique of traditional pre-Islamic society is important in order to emphasise the idea of Islam in opposition to folk religions, to the Sufi orders of ordinary society. This puritanical view of religious consciousness was thus sharply contrasted with the magical practices and popular rituals of the Sufi brotherhoods. Sharia-mindedness was the core of the Islamicate legal tradition, and a major issue in the resurgence of Islam in the modern world.

The critical literature on Weber's sociology of religion is considerable. Suffice it to say that Weber's vision of 'Asian religions' has been condemned as an example of Orientalism in which a dynamic West is contrasted with a stagnant East. Looking more closely at the substantive features of Weber's analysis of Islam, contemporary research suggests that the city was a context within which civil institutions such as charitable associations (*waqf*) flourished and that in many Islamic urban centres civil society flourished around the mosque and the *madrasa*. There is also the argument that Weber overstated the impact of imperial military institutions and values on Islam and at the same time neglected the role of the Sufi brotherhoods as conduits of trade, especially between the Middle East and Southeast Asia (Reid, 1988). Although these criticisms are substantial, Weber's sociological perspective continues to influence debates, often implicitly, around the compatibility between Islam and democratic institutions (Sadiki, 2004). Indeed the 'clash of civilisations' (Huntington, 1993; 1997) can be regarded as a revival of Weber's own civilisational analysis.

The sociology of Confucianism

Weber's study of Confucianism and Daoism has also received considerable scholarly attention and his analysis of Chinese society is relatively well known (Bellah, 1963; Eisenstadt, 1985; Schluchter, 1983; Sprenkel, 1964). In Weber's typology of religious orientations to the world, Islam and Confucianism stand at opposite ends. In fact it is not clear that Confucianism is a religion at all in Weber's terms. He observed: 'Confucianism, like Buddhism, consisted only of ethics and in this *Tao* corresponds to the Indian *dharma* ... Confucianism meant adjustment to the world, to its orders and conventions. Ultimately it represented just a tremendous code of political maxims and rules of social propriety for the cultured men of the world' (1951: 152).

Weber also took note of the fact that Confucianism tolerated a range of popular cults and did not attempt to systematise them into a coherent religious doctrine. Confucianism did not represent an inner-worldly attack or a challenge to the world, being content to teach an adjustment to the secular sphere. The morally superior man of the educated literati would stay away from any pursuit of wealth in this world and as a consequence the educated bureaucrat of the imperial civil service was honoured far more than the businessman.

Confucianism was more precisely a theory of the family as the basis of social order and it taught obedience within the household and civil society. The widespread belief in both Confucianism and Daoism of *yin* (female) and *yang* (male) sustained an ideology in which men and women had ontologically separate natures. Although in early Confucianism *yin* and *yang* were complementary, when Confucianism became the dominant official state ideology of the Han dynasty (206 BCE to AD 220), these principles were hierarchically organised. Women were defined as weak, cold and passive, being associated with the moon, while men were associated with warmth, strength and the sun. Unsurprisingly, recent feminist criticism has been directed in the main against Confucianism, which is associated with foot-binding and the cult of chastity that were dominant themes in the Ming (1368–1644) and Qing Dynasties (1644–1911). In the *Classic of Filial Piety*, Confucius established norms of respect for elders, but also defined the virtuous wife as a submissive and respectful member of the household. Widows were to remain chaste and dedicated to their parents-in-law and to the memory of their dead husbands. These norms affirmed the authority of the husband and gave a distinctive preference for male offspring.

From Weber's perspective, Confucianism also taught contentment and happiness in this life and shared with Daoism a commitment to practices that promoted longevity. It is often argued that Daoism and Buddhism were popular in Asia because they offered a refuge from Confucianism, because their religious practices and values were less harsh and rigid. The Daoist classical texts (*Daodejing*) of Laozi are said to give expression to more feminine virtues. *Dao* – the mystical source of being – entailed the idea of *wu wei* or non-action in which people can become free from desire. The values of Confucianism and Daoism can be said to be the opposite of ascetic Protestantism and anathema to Weber's personal values. In general, Weber did not believe that happiness was a genuine goal of ethics and hence he attacked the utilitarian promise of satisfaction through the market. He was equally scornful of Freudianism, which he regarded as a form of mental hygiene which sought to make people happy. In this respect Weber may have followed Nietzsche, who had condemned what he called the 'Happiness of the Last Man'. This may in part explain his criticism of Confucianism, in which the deities of the Chinese heavens 'obviously desired only the happiness of the world and especially the happiness of man' (Weber, 1951: 153).

By comparison with the Abrahamic religions, is Confucianism a religion at all? Chinese civilisation has no tradition of prophecy and did not develop a sacerdotal stratum of priests with control over sacraments. In one sense, the emperor was the high priest of the state religion. The worship of deities was a matter of state business, while ancestor worship was required by all social classes. There was no soteriology as such and the 'Confucian had no desire to be "saved" either from the migration of souls or from punishment in the beyond' (Weber, 1951: 156). In this sense Confucianism was a state theory which institutionalised filial piety as the core duty of religious activity. Confucianism tolerated both magic and mysticism, provided that they were useful instruments for controlling the masses. From the perspective of the elite, 'magic was powerless in the face of virtue. He who loved the classical way of life need not fear the spirits; only lack of virtue in high places gave power to the spirits' (p. 155). Both Buddhism and Christianity were opposed at various stages by the emperor because they were a threat to social order and devotion to the emperor cult. We can reasonably regard Confucianism as the state religion of the literati and Daoism as the popular religion of the masses.

In Weber's sociology of religion, Confucianism and Puritanism both represent significant but alternative types of rationalisation, in that they offered pious frameworks for the regulation of the everyday world. Both promoted self-regulation and restraint, but Confucianism sought to preserve and defend a status hierarchy based on the ideal of the educated gentleman, filial piety and civilised behaviour as conservative life orientations. Puritanism promoted piety as a technique for a 'revolution of the saints'. Paradoxically, Puritan vocations also contributed to the fashioning of rational capitalism in the West. By contrast, Weber identified a variety of conditions that inhibited capitalism in China. These included the fact that many technical innovations were opposed by conservative religious groups. The very strength of the kinship system and ancestor worship protected its members from adversity and discouraged a work discipline and the rationalisation of work processes. These same kinship groups prevented the development of modern legal institutions, the codification of laws and the rise of a class of professional lawyers.

Weber's analysis of Confucianism has of course been much disputed. He did not consider the widespread influence of Confucianism outside China, for example in Vietnam and Japan. In the Japanese case, Confucianism often played a more radical political role in opposition to Shinto. Despite these criticisms, Weber's view of Chinese capitalism continues to influence research, for example with respect to the entrepreneurial role of overseas Chinese communities in the global economy (Redding, 1993).

Conclusion: religion, economics and politics

Weber's analysis of Christian radicalism in relation to Islam has become an implicit dimension of the clash of civilisations thesis and his analysis of Christian dynamism in relation to Confucianism continues to form the principal foundation of theories of the rise of capitalism in modern Asia (Bellah, 1963). Whereas sociologists have often neglected the social role of religion in advanced capitalism, accepting the secularisation thesis, Weber placed religion at the centre of the social world. Indeed, religion was a core defining sphere of meaning. Although social scientists have been critical of the Huntington thesis, from a Weberian perspective the struggle between religions must be an inevitable outcome of the process of globalisation. Weber's vision of world cultures presupposes a Darwinian struggle for survival, or 'elbow room' as he claimed in his inaugural professorial lecture. Despite their normative commitment to the principles of 'brotherly love', even Islam and Christianity must participate in this global struggle. At the same time, Confucianism as the ethic of civic stability has been drawn into the ideological justification of the Asian capitalist tigers.

4 | *Talcott Parsons and the expressive revolution*

Introduction: the expressive revolution

Talcott Parsons's sociology of religion remains distinctive in the sense that he did not subscribe to the secularisation thesis, but instead saw American liberal democracy as the fulfilment of Protestant individualism and congregationalism. In addition, his notion of the 'expressive revolution' remains an essential tool for the analysis of modern spirituality (Parsons, 1974). The rise of romantic love as a theme of popular culture in modern society can be interpreted as a feature of the expressive revolution, but it is also a legacy of the emphasis on emotional conversion and attachment to the person of Jesus in pietism. The expressive revolution is the modern framework for the legacy of Protestant emotional piety, but at the same time romantic love is an essential component of the contemporary consumer ethic. In this regard, religiosity survives in the context of consumerism as an aspect of what Robert Bellah (1967; Bellah and Tipton, 2006) called 'civil religion in America'. However, another dimension of this development has been what Alasdair MacIntyre (1984) called 'emotivism', that is the breakdown of a shared moral framework in which a moral life could be lived on common grounds. We can regard emotivism as a further extension of the individualism inherent in expressive cultures, in which feeling good is equivalent to being good. If the emerging capitalist society of the late seventeenth century began to embrace 'possessive individualism' as illustrated by John Locke's theory of property, then we might say that late capitalism cultivates a form of 'expressive individualism', namely a subjective individualism emerging out of the evolution of modern consumerism, but with roots in Protestantism. The negative side of expressive individualism is the incremental erosion of the communal foundations of both moral coherence and religious practice.

Parsons's sociology of religion

Parsons's early sociology was obviously directed towards a debate with economics, and hence towards Max Weber's sociology of social action. Parsons, who had been initially trained in the study of institutional economics, became interested in the anthropological and sociological debates about religion and magic, because these phenomena raised interesting questions that challenged the underlying assumptions of conventional economic theory, namely rational action and utilitarian explanations of choice. Religion appeared in Parsons's sociological agenda in the famous argument in *The Structure of Social Action* (1937), because religious action was a clear illustration of the importance of the non-rational in human society. The narrow notion of rational and irrational behaviour with respect to scarcity did not offer a valid paradigm for understanding religious rituals. The focus on instrumental rationality in micro-economics could not explain the existence of social solidarity based on common values. Parsons was drawn to Weber's economic sociology, partly because Weber's analysis of the Protestant ethic thesis was in many respects an important challenge to this conventional economic wisdom. Weber's sociology of religion showed the limitations of rational models of social action and social order in classical economics. This early engagement with Weber led Parsons to consider more widely the history of the economic ethics of the world religions.

In the process of this intellectual encounter with Weber, Parsons translated *The Protestant Ethic and the Spirit of Capitalism* in 1930 and wrote a highly influential introduction to Weber's *The Sociology of Religion* (1966), in which Parsons interpreted Weber as arguing that the ascetic calling was the critical lever to push societies down the path of modernisation. In the process of interpretation and translation, Parsons was largely responsible for introducing Weber to an American sociological audience. While overtly the theme of his early engagement with Weber's sociology was the limitations of economics in providing an adequate account of social life, much of the deeper significance of the early Parsons was his implicit relationship to Kantian philosophy, because Kant's emphasis on free will and responsibility was attractive to Parsons's own moral beliefs and consistent with his own idea of the importance of the notion of voluntary action in his general account of the sociology of action.

While the early Parsons was Kantian, the later sociology was clearly more profoundly inspired by the work of Émile Durkheim, but Durkheim's project in his sociology of knowledge and morals was also Kantian. Durkheim was also concerned with the problem of the individual that lay at the heart of Kant's ethical theory, and with Kant's notion of a categorical imperative, namely that we should not treat human beings merely as means to the satisfaction of our own needs. Durkheim asked a Kantian question (What gives moral injunctions their force?), but he gave it a sociological answer (the collective effervescence that emerges from common rituals as the basis of collective life). While Durkheim's sociology had been a major issue in Parsons's *The Structure of Social Action* (1937), his evaluation of Durkheim was further developed in his 1973 article on 'Durkheim on Religion Revisited'. By departing from the Kant–Weber view of secularisation and rationalisation, Parsons avoided one of the pitfalls of modern sociology, namely the assumption that secularisation is uniform and an inevitable feature of modernity. For various reasons that I shall explore, the secularisation thesis has proved to be a problematic component of the sociological theory of modernisation. Parsons did not accept the secularisation thesis that became the hallmark of much European sociology. Parsons, by contrast came, especially in the essay on 'Christianity' (1968b) and 'Religion in Postindustrial America' (1974), to argue that American denominational pluralism and the American value system were an institutional and cultural realisation of (Protestant) Christianity. In retrospect we can see secularisation not as a necessary consequence of modernisation, but more narrowly as a feature of European history. Parsons saw Protestant Christianity as an aspect of American modernisation and began to develop a view of different pathways to modernity that did not exclude, but in fact depended on, religion. He was deeply interested in societies such as Japan where religion and modernisation also appeared to be complementary and not antagonistic. Parsons departed from the Kant–Weber interpretation of Christianity as a moral faith and as the precursor of contemporary secularisation, and returned to the problem of the individual and society through a reappraisal of Durkheim. The conclusion of this intellectual trajectory was that the expressive revolution produced modern individualism as a component of the modernisation of culture. The cognitive rationalism of the Protestant Revolution was being replaced by an affective and expressive orientation to life in the cultural revolutions of the 1960s.

In defending Parsons's vision of modernisation as an upgrading of the basic evolutionary potential of Western Christianity, I argue therefore that sociologists have often neglected one of the more interesting and important features of Parsons's analysis of modern American history, namely the concept of the 'expressive revolution'. Parsons became interested from a critical perspective in the student protests of the 1960s, which severely disrupted universities in North America and Europe. This analysis was developed in Parsons and Platt's *The American University* (1973). Parsons saw student culture as a symptom of a more general social movement away from the cognitive rationalism and instrumentalism of early capitalism to an affective–expressive culture. The prominence of themes relating to love and emotion in contemporary popular culture is evidence of this expressive revolution, but a revolution that is in some respects the offspring of the subjectivity of pietism and at the same time a corrosion of ascetic Protestantism. The expressive revolution is thus the contemporary manifestation of the Western subjective self, whose authenticity is exhibited in terms of emotional responsiveness (Seigel, 2005).

David Martin was one of the few sociologists to adopt this notion in his study of Pentecostalism. Noting a 'consonance' between Pentecostalism, global liberal capitalism and the expressive revolution, Martin argued that some versions of 'Pentecostalism not only resemble consumer culture but overlap the modes of the modern media' and claimed that religion is 'remade in the image of business with buildings more like cinemas than churches' (2002: 15). There is, one might add, an elective affinity between consumer culture, religious revivalism and expressive individualism. The association between religion and consumer culture that we can detect in the 1960s gained momentum in the United States with financial deregulation in the 1970s, and matured along with the evolution of the Baby Boomer generation (Edmunds and Turner, 2002; Roof, 1993; 1999). These issues are considered in more depth in Chapter 14 in the discussion of religious responses to economic crises in recent American history.

Parsons died in 1979. By the 1980s, religion had ceased to be a topic of central importance to sociology. Commitment to the comparative analysis of religion faded away, and the sociology of religion came to be increasingly confined to the study of denominations and sects in

American society and to secularisation in Europe. With the dominance of modernisation theory, it was assumed that religion would not play a large part in social and economic development. At best it would be confined to the private sphere. However, secularisation, which was assumed to be a necessary component of modernisation, proved to be enormously difficult to define.

Sociologists such as Kingsley Davis (1949) and Bryan Wilson (1959), who confidently predicted the erosion of religion with the spread of secularism and scientific cultures, would find it difficult to explain adequately the great post-communism resurgence of religion. Parsons, by contrast, did not accept the secularisation thesis. He saw the secular success of post-war America in the 1950s and 1960s as the triumph of liberal Protestantism. The history of America, with its separation of religion and politics, religious pluralism and individualism was the fulfilment of religious individualism and Protestant piety. The Cold War tended to reinforce this picture of the triumph of American culture against secular totalitarianism and atheist communism. The contrast between religion in America and militant atheism in China could not have been more stark or profound. While the Red Guards under Mao Zedong's leadership during the Cultural Revolution (1966–7) were busy destroying Buddhist pagodas, Catholic churches and Daoist temples, the Christian Right was equally busy condemning communists. In the same period, liberal politics was influenced by theologians such as Reinhold Niebuhr, who sought to steer a course between the political left, who were blind to the excesses of communism, and the political right, who instituted a witch hunt against reds in Hollywood and Harvard. In this context, Parsons came to appreciate liberal Protestantism as an illustration of the adaptive upgrading of American society. This view of American civilisation was eventually challenged by the Vietnam War, against which the expressive revolution was a political and aesthetic response of youth. A 'disobedient generation' emerged to call into question many of the underlying assumptions of post-war American society and the values that had steered America through much of the first half of the twentieth century (Sica and Turner, 2006).

There was therefore in Parsons's mid career a convergence between his analysis of American liberal Protestantism and Robert Bellah's concept of 'civil religion in America'. Their politics and values were certainly different, but there is some convergence between the idea of civil religion and Parsons's view of the continuing relevance of Christianity as a public religion in the twentieth century. Bellah's article first appeared in *Daedalus* (1967) and was reprinted in *Beyond Belief* (1970). This analysis of American civil culture was also an application of the argument in 'Religious evolution' (1964), which was first given as a lecture in 1963 from ideas that Bellah had developed with Parsons and S. N. Eisenstadt at Harvard University in their seminar on social evolution. In this lecture, Bellah argued that the 'historic religions discovered the self ... modern religion is beginning to understand the laws of the self's own existence and so help man take responsibility for his own fate' (Bellah, 1970: 42). Because of this emphasis on self-knowledge and understanding, the traditional authority of the Church would be shaken, but Bellah, like Parsons, did not subscribe to the secularisation thesis. In a comparative perspective, Bellah recognised the persistent strength of religion in Japanese society in *Tokugawa Religion* (1957), and the religious motifs that constituted 'civil religion' in the United States.

Bellah, like many historians of American life, recognised the religious symbolism and significance that were attached to the War of Independence, the Constitution, the Civil War and the emancipation of slaves in the American South. These collective symbols were part of a sacred history that Bellah described tragically in *The Broken Covenant* (1975). American civil religion existed alongside Christianity, and was not a sect of the Christian religion. This religion was not 'religion in general' but had various specific components and beliefs. As a result of the Civil War, it had a tragic vision of history with a strong emphasis on death and sacrifice. Bellah, following the lead of Reinhold Niebuhr, argued that Abraham Lincoln was the epitome of civil religion, which was activist, individualistic and moral.

Although there is considerable overlap between Parsons's view of American Protestantism as an 'upgrading' of activist values in an evolutionary scheme of social development and Bellah's concept of 'civil religion', Parsons was much influenced by and critical of the student protests of the 1960s, and hence he saw a change of values taking place that gave greater emphasis to emotions. Was this recognition of the emotional life the end of the Protestant ethic or the development of the concept of the self in Western Christianity?

The expressive revolution: the romantic love complex and Christian fundamentalism

While there is much to support the secularisation thesis as a description of modern European history, it is important not to confuse the decline of Christian institutions with the decline of religion. In other words, we must not equate 'de-Christianisation' with the decline of religious sentiments and world-views. The importance of values of intimacy (individual emotional attachment and loyalty in intimate relationships) in a secular age can be taken as an indication of the continuity of religion in Western societies. From Protestantism, Western societies have acquired an emphasis on the individual and individualism through such phenomena as conversion, a personal relationship to Jesus, private devotion and Bible study. Conversion experiences emphasised the importance of experiencing a loving relationship with Jesus, where emotional intensity became a measure of spiritual intensity.

Individualism in secular society has also become increasingly emotional and erotic. Ulrich Beck and Elizabeth Gernsheim-Beck (1995: 179) argue that love is now our 'secular religion', and claim that as 'religion loses its hold, people seek solace in private sanctuaries', but this interpretation fails to recognise that modern erotic, sentimental love is itself part of the legacy of Protestant pietism. This emotional component of religious experience entered Protestantism in eighteenth-century England through Wesleyan Methodism, specifically from the evangelical field preaching of John Wesley and the evocative hymns of Charles Wesley. Hymn singing and extemporary prayer preserved a tradition of emotional expressivity. However, it is in German pietism that one finds the specific origins of this modern emotional trend in Christian spirituality. Friedrich Schleiermacher (1768–1834) defended religion against the rationalist criticisms of the Enlightenment, asserting that religious feelings of dependency are the foundation of religious faith. Schleiermacher's 'anthropology' recognised a common humanity that was articulated through feeling. From this religious tradition, one can derive the modern notion that private and intimate experiences are fundamental to the authentic self, and that marriage is primarily about establishing satisfactory relations of companionship and intimacy. These ideas have been especially potent in the United States in the New Age Movement

(Heelas, 1996) and more generally in American approaches to marriage and divorce. Happiness in a secular society depends crucially on successful, that is intimate, relations in marriage, while separation and divorce are closely related to unhappiness.

Modern sociology has given special attention to the contemporary themes of romance and intimacy (Beck and Gernsheim-Beck, 1995; Giddens, 1992; Luhmann, 1986). Romantic love in modern societies is equally contradictory because it requires or at least celebrates erotic, intense, fleeting and contingent relationships, and at the same time values enduring, permanent and faithful relations of love. These social changes in our personal lives include the secularisation of love, the growing prominence of love in film and advertising, the celebration of love in popular culture and its equation with personal happiness, the association of love with consumption and the insertion of 'fun' and 'excitement' into the practices of marriage and domesticity. If courtly love poetry expressed a feudalisation of love in the Middle Ages, the secularisation of modern society is expressed in the commercialisation and democratisation of love. In America, emotional commitment had since the eighteenth century been regarded as a necessary aspect of a successful marriage, but it was not until the development of a mass market and advertising, especially in the 1930s, that a new emphasis on expressivity, romantic attachments and erotic adventure emerged in the market-place. In particular, romantic couples are involved in lifestyle and the consumption of leisure, of which romantic love is an important ingredient. Romantic holidays in exotic locations have become an essential feature of a loving but exciting relationship.

In the first half of the twentieth century, sexual love, in advertising and film, emerged as a utopian ideal, wherein marriage could also be exciting and romantic, especially if the couple had sufficient income to participate fully in leisure and consumption. The use of close-ups in film and photography and the employment of movie stars to advertise commodities created a social cosmology, in which consumer icons represented the new lifestyle. This romantic marital state in marriage does not necessarily include children, who reduce a couple's income and leisure time.

In *Consuming the Romantic Utopia* (1997), Eva Illouz shows how the love utopia was based on the democratisation of love and the possibility of mass consumption. 'Love for everyone' was combined with 'consumption for all'. However, social reality constantly brought this utopia into question. In the early decades of the twentieth century, marriage as an institution was in a profound crisis. The underlying factors were changes in matrimonial legislation, the entry of women into the labour force, unrealistic expectations about the romantic character of marriage and conflicts over domestic expenditure. Marriage-guidance experts began to devise a battery of practical solutions to inject fun into marriages, because it was assumed that the companionate marriage was no longer adequate unless it could find space for erotic love and sexual pleasure. The rise of the 'dating system' also illustrates the new emphasis on youth culture, the cultural importance of intimacy and the private sphere, and the focus on 'going out' and 'dining out' as norms of both courtship and marriage. The commodification of love has become part of the American Dream. For example, romanticised advertisements rarely picture the couple at home with children, but emphasise instead the couple as tourists in a landscape, at a romantic restaurant or in a luxury hotel. Parsons's writing on the nuclear family and youth recognised the social tensions and personal conflicts within this social evolution of marriage and love in American society (Parsons, Bales, Olds, Zelditch and Slater, 1955).

The paradigm of romantic love, sexual satisfaction and youthfulness is now sufficiently powerful in popular culture to influence older generations, who either expect to enjoy love and romantic attachment into old age, or that they can avoid growing old in order to maintain their romantic attachments. These assumptions underpin popular commentaries on love and the ageing woman. While the elderly are encouraged to sustain romantic love, there has been what we might call an 'infantilisation' of romance by which teenagers have been drawn into the complex of consumption and romance through popular music. These changes in expressiveness, romance and youthfulness constitute what Parsons called the 'expressive revolution', a social change that he regarded as a new religious movement of significance (Parsons, 1974). This concept of a revolution in emotions was not fully developed in Parsons's later sociology, but it is an important insight into changes in Western societies in the late twentieth century.

The expressive revolution was closely related to subjective individualism in popular culture and the importance of choice in lifestyles and values. We need to understand more precisely how these spiritual market-places function globally and how they are connected electronically through the Net. This American religious revolution involved a shift from the cognitive–instrumental values of early capitalism to an affective–expressive culture. In support of Parsons's argument about expressivity, one could refer to the example of the pop star Madonna, whose popular songs 'Like a Prayer' and 'Open Your Heart' have been interpreted as aspects of popular religion, whose themes are often compatible with liberation theology. Her recent transformation into Rachel as a committed follower of Kabbalah mysticism is a further illustration of the idea that the individual should be free to choose any religion or combination of religions to feel good. Individuals are free to reinvent themselves and refashion themselves constantly and self-consciously.

A major feature of many fundamentalist movements is the desire to restore family values, improve Christian education and protect children from lifestyles that are simultaneously anti-American and anti-Christian. We can see the development of the Christian Right as a delayed response to the failure of the Vietnam War and a critique of the values of the radical student movements of the 1960s. This perception of the erosion of American values was at the heart of the Moral Majority that was formed in 1979 under the leadership of Jerry Falwell. The original inspiration for this movement came from political groups that were frustrated with the Republican Party, and it included Protestants, but also Roman Catholics, Mormons and Pentecostalists. American domestic and foreign policy had to be based on the Bible, and in order to restore America to its true mission it was necessary to struggle against the 'moral minority' that exercised power over the government. The New Christian Right, as they came to be known, was against abortion, against gay rights and against drug liberalisation. In fact, there was a significant emphasis on problems relating to sexuality. More recently they have led campaigns against gay marriage and the ordination of gay clergy. Fundamentalists regarded feminism as a 'disease' and equated homosexuality with pederasty. It was 'secular humanism', a catch-all phrase that included feminism and liberalism, that had emasculated American men. In this respect, fundamentalism was able to address a range of popular anxieties about male impotence, high divorce rates, female self-assertion and low birth rates.

American fundamentalism responded to this cultural and political crisis in a number of ways. From the late 1980s there were aggressive, and occasionally violent, campaigns against abortion clinics by so-called moral 'rescuers'. On the educational system, Christian creationists led an attack on evolutionary science and Darwinism in an effort to assert the literal truth of Genesis. In terms of family life, fundamentalists reasserted what they thought to be the biblical view of marriage, namely the importance of male headship. For example, the Southern Baptist Convention meeting in 1988 amended its Baptist Faith and Message Statement to declare that a woman should 'submit herself graciously' to the leadership of her husband. The result of the amendment by the largest American Protestant denomination was to jettison the principle of an egalitarian family. This assertion of male leadership was seen to be a necessary step in restoring the family that is in turn seen to be fundamental to the continuity of Christianity and to the health of the nation. In practice, Christian interpretations of what leadership actually means in day-to-day terms are variable and pragmatic, but the influence of these fundamentalist ideas has been significant, as illustrated by President Clinton's eventual confession of sinfulness to a breakfast meeting of Christian leaders.

While American fundamentalism has been predominantly a Protestant religious movement of the southern states, there has also been a remarkable convergence of opinion between fundamentalism, the political right, Catholic conservatives and, ironically, components of the women's movement around pro-natalism. These diverse movements have in various ways rejected liberal America in favour of the regulation of pornography, anti-abortion legislation, the criminalisation of homosexuality and the virtues of faithfulness and loyalty in permanent sexual partnerships. In short, these values confirmed a religious view of sexual and marital relationships that transcended denominational affiliation. Fundamentalism can be interpreted in this respect as a sustained struggle against the expressive revolution; it is a struggle between two conceptions of the self – the Kantian ascetic and disciplined self, and the expressive–affective mobile self. The first is the direct descendant of Protestant asceticism and the second is a distortion of the expressive self of the conversionist sects of the eighteenth and nineteenth centuries.

Durkheim and individualism

Towards the end of his life, Parsons returned to a close textual reading of Durkheim. It is important to recognise the close relationship between Durkheim's analysis of classification systems and his sociology of religion. Durkheim's theory of religion was a theory of classification, that is, the study of religion was located within the larger project of a sociology of knowledge, and should be read as an application of his sociology of classification. Durkheim's *The Elementary Forms* ([1912] 2001) is a specification of the project with Marcel Mauss on *Primitive Classification* ([1903] 1997). The emotional effects of collective rituals were especially important for enforcing their collective or objective authority. Durkheim and Mauss developed the sociology of emotions as objective elements of the social structure. The force of such collective emotions is derived from their effervescence that is produced by the collective effect of social rituals. The implication of the Durkheimian theory of social change is that the problem for modern society is the decline of these collective events and festivals which help a society to enforce its collective memory through shared emotions.

In his essay on Durkheim, Parsons returned towards the end of his life to the significance of Durkheim and recognised the strong affinity between his own theory of social action and Durkheim's project. Durkheim was, of course, also working within a Kantian problematic. His theory of classification and his sociology of knowledge were a critique of Kant's idea of the individual. For Durkheim, the individual was the product of the collective, and morals have a force because they are social facts – they have the moral authority of the collective. The tension between Parsons's early voluntaristic theory of social action and his work on the media of social interchange was finally resolved in his idea of 'institutionalised individualism', a theory that shows the continuing importance of Kant in Parsons's work (Bourricaud, 1981).

Conclusion: from the expressive to the emotive culture

There may be some general agreement in modern society that marriages based on expressive commitment, erotic ties and mutual respect are morally desirable and that marriage on the basis of mutual attraction is to be preferred over arranged marriages. This argument could be developed further to claim that 'no-fault divorce' is a better solution to an unhappy marriage than protracted conflicts in court, where partners have to demonstrate in public some unseemly aspect of their marital history. Although the expressive revolution may have had many negative features – such as a loss of respect for authority – and while sexual permissiveness may have been in some circumstances a thin disguise for male sexual exploitation of women, one legacy of the 1960s has been a greater tolerance for difference and diversity. In retrospect, Parsons was one of the few sociologists to capture this epoch in his notion of the expressive revolution. Equally remarkable was the insight that the revolution was an unintended consequence of the legacy of American piety.

One additional feature of the expressive revolution has been a greater emphasis on emotion as an arbiter of the good life and as an index of personal authenticity. My view of secularisation has been inspired by Alasdair Macintyre's criticism of emotivism as the characteristic framework of modern ethical debate. Emotivism is an expression of the decay rather than the survival of a shared moral framework. In a modern fragmented society, it is not that we are confused about particular moral questions, but rather that we have lost the shared moral framework within which we can have an understanding of what a coherent moral position is. Our moral framework is fragmented and we no longer share a meaningful moral scheme.

The cultural and philosophical response to this situation is what MacIntyre calls 'emotivist ethics', in which moral arguments about values are treated as if they were simply individual preferences. Arguments tend to be construed as nothing more than a rhetorical device which conveys a person's feelings about social reality. For MacIntyre, emotivism is the philosophical doctrine that evaluative judgements are only expressions of preference, or expressions of feeling, and that we employ such moral judgements not only to express our own attitudes but also to evoke such effects in others. Although MacIntyre associated emotivism with particular late-nineteenth-century philosophical developments in his *A Short History of Ethics* (1998), emotivism has been deeply institutionalised in our own consumer culture. The contrast with Parsons could not be more complete. For MacIntyre, individualistic and evangelical Protestantism has been, especially in America, the conduit of emotivism in popular culture. Secularisation in MacIntyre's terms is very much the triumph of Protestantism as institutionalised emotivism.

5 | Mary Douglas and Modern Primitives

Introduction

The work of Mary Douglas provides a framework for thinking about modern culture, the changing nature of social solidarity, the decline in the social functions of religious rituals and the quest for personal authenticity through corporeal regulation. Douglas can be relatively easily interpreted as a modern exponent of Émile Durkheim's sociology, especially of his sociology of knowledge and religion. Durkheim's core sociological ideas are well known, and hence I shall merely sketch some of the salient issues in this 'Introduction'. In *The Elementary Forms of Religious Life* ([1912] 2001), Durkheim argued that the separate components of a culture can only be understood within a system, and thus the idea of the profane only makes sense in the context of its opposite, namely the sacred. We can therefore study religion as a classificatory system that divides the world into people, objects or spaces that are either sacred or profane. From a sociological perspective, this system is important because such religious rituals have the function of creating cohesive social groups and rituals that give rise to collective emotions which in turn reinforce group cohesion. In terms of Durkheim's typology of societies, we have evolved from a social world in which the individual was submerged in the social group (mechanical solidarity) to a society based on separate individuals held together by such institutions as the law, the division of labour and nationalist ideologies (organic solidarity); and finally we are in a transitional stage between the old and the new – the old gods are dead and new ones have yet to arrive. While Durkheim was what we may call a 'moral socialist' in his view of the state and property, as outlined in his *Professional Ethics and Civic Morals* (1992), his cultural doctrines had conservative implications – human beings need rituals, but modern society has lost them (or most of the ones that matter). The implication of Durkheim's sociology, for example in his concept of anomie, is that the modern world is less stable and less secure than traditional societies. In particular, the identities of young people who have not yet secured full-time employment and have not yet entered into stable marriages may be more dislocated than their parents and hence more subject to the anomic pressures of modernity. The young, the unattached, the unmarried and those who are dislodged from their religious tradition are more exposed to suicidal pressures than those individuals who are embraced by more traditional social roles and communities (Durkheim, [1897] 1951). How do these youthful generations in modernity gain some sense of social identity and membership? One obvious answer in urban settings is that they enter, albeit briefly, gangs which play a crucial role in adolescent socialisation, where gang membership and personal identity can be defined by a global youth culture and in some instances literally fixed by the urban culture of tattoos and piercing. The paradox of much popular culture in youth groups is that, while it is often socially deviant, group life offers some possible protection from anomic uncertainty and social isolation. Gang identity and membership, however socially deviant, may connect young people to some forms of social solidarity, no matter how fleeting.

One connection between Durkheim and Douglas can therefore be established through a consideration of the sociology of the body. Religious rituals in a society based on mechanical solidarity typically require the scarification and modification of the body through painting, tattooing, piercing and so forth. It is difficult to read Baldwin Spencer and F. J. Gillen's *The Northern Tribes of Central Australia* ([1904] 1997), which formed the ethnographic basis of *The Elementary Forms*, without being struck by the centrality of the human body in ritual performance in Aboriginal Australia. The painted body became a major vehicle for the enactment of tribal myths and customs, especially through dance performance. We can view the body as a cultural medium that indicates a person's social status within the social group and it is through the process of ritual tattooing and piercing that classifications of sacred and profane are marked on the body. One might imagine that body modifications were an important part of traditional tribal religion, but relatively unimportant in the social life of modern society based on individualism and organic bases of solidarity. What then might be the role of body modification in modernity within the paradigm of the sociology of Durkheim and Douglas?

Douglas's anthropology of classification

In *Purity and Danger* (1966), which was based in her African field-work in *The Lele of the Kasai* (1963), Douglas built on Durkheim's perspective by observing that the world is classified and divided into things that are prohibited and things that are not. The sacred is typically protected from unclean things, but at the same time the sacred is dangerous and can destroy just as profoundly as profane objects. The sacred carries with it the meaning of restriction, and hence it is set apart and human access is restricted. Nothing is essentially in itself either sacred/profane or clean/unclean, but these differences are the product of a system of classification which sorts things into such categories. We should pause briefly to consider the word *sacer* at this point, for it is in this Latin notion that the distinction between the sacred and the profane world is most clear. However, it is also at this point that we discover the ambiguity of the sacred which is 'consecrated to god and affected with an ineradicable pollution, august and accursed, worthy of veneration and evoking horror' (Benveniste, 1973: 452).

The central idea of *Purity and Danger* is that primitive ideas about pollution have nothing to do with hygiene. The ban on the consumption of pork is not because pork meat was thought to go off quickly or to be inedible. In this respect Douglas drew considerable inspiration from the list of restrictions in Leviticus. Both Leviticus and Deuteronomy contain long inventories of things that can be eaten or not eaten. Douglas argued that Leviticus exhibits a complex classificatory system that has nothing to do with primitive ideas of cleanliness and hygiene. For example, Leviticus sets up a scheme (based on Genesis) in which two-legged fowls fly with wings, while in the water scaly fish swim with fins. On earth four-legged animals hop, jump or walk. Any creature whose method of locomotion defies or contradicts this classification is unholy and unclean, because it causes confusion through combinations that break the underlying classificatory principles. Animals that appear to have hands but go on all fours are unclean, such as the mouse, the crocodile, the shrew, some lizards and the mole. Eels and worms that can swim in water are unclean, because they have no fins. Some insects fly but have no wings or feathers. Pigs have cloven feet but they do not chew the cud – so they are dirty. But prohibitions on the mixing of things and activities also apply to human beings. Thus Leviticus 18 instructs both men and women not to have sexual relationships with beasts, because such relationships would clearly constitute a serious perversion.

Throughout her anthropology Douglas was anxious to reject the idea that whereas primitive people have bizarre rules about pollution, we have modern ideas about hygiene and we do not confuse ideas about religion and personal cleanliness. For Douglas, there is no difference in regard to ideas about pollution between modern and primitive with respect to classificatory schemes. We also have taken-for-granted rules about food, dirt and imperfection which are not related to hygiene. Why are dogs not on the menu of Western restaurants? Why don't we eat hot pickles with our Scottish porridge? It follows that we also have taken-for-granted rules about things in proper places. We typically tell children not to place shoes on a table or to leave bedroom equipment and clothing in the living room. Modern Islam and Judaism have quite extensive rules about eating and cleanliness – kosher foods in Judaism and the *halal/haram* categorisation in Islam. One can argue that there is a '*halal* consciousness' that allows Muslims to negotiate everyday problems about dining in public restaurants where there is the risk of religious contamination from pork (Kamaludeen, Pereira and Turner, 2009). In short, we organise our social world in terms of norms about what should be where. Generally speaking, we do not like ambiguity or anomaly, and classificatory schemes avoid or resolve potential uncertainty about the confusion of objects, places or people. Classification rules help human societies to manage risk and uncertainty by creating rules that provide a cultural map to allocate all phenomena within frameworks.

This aspect of Douglas's argument is not overwhelmingly convincing. The transgression of pollution taboos in traditional societies evoked a sense of horror and disgust. Transgressions brought with them a threat of catastrophe for the individual or group. While the breaking of the dietary rules of the major religions (such as Judaism and Islam) may still cause dismay, when a child breaks a taken-for-granted rule (such as 'Do not leave your shoes on the table'), it is regarded as an inconvenience or a nuisance, but not a moral catastrophe. Eating pickles with porridge might be regarded as merely eccentric. We probably distinguish between things that are simply superstitious ('do not open an umbrella indoors') and things that are simply common sense ('do not walk under a ladder'). The main difference between the past and the present is that we are self-reflexive about such norms and they are open to debate. In a modern society, we are, probably influenced by the psycho-analytical theories of Sigmund Freud, inclined to treat excessive scrupulosity – washing hands – not as the avoidance of some pollution but as neurotic behaviour. In all societies, when a woman gives birth to twins, especially conjoined twins, it is regarded as both an anomaly and a crisis. In traditional societies, twins could often survive and live normal lives, but they might also be regarded as monsters. Twins as monsters showed or indicated some impending natural crisis, but in a modern society, while conjoined twins may still be regarded as anomalies, parents are more likely to turn to surgery than to ritual classification for a solution. The continuity between traditional societies based on a definite classification of clean and unclean and modern societies is limited and it is the discontinuity not the continuity that appears important.

Group and grid

In conjunction with her theory of classification, Douglas developed a theory of social solidarity. In *Natural Symbols* (1973) she claims that all societies can be compared along two dimensions: group and grid. Group is the degree of division between the outsiders and insiders of a society. Grid refers to whether individuals share a common system of classification and group refers to the social pressures that regulate the behaviour of individuals. By combining weak and strong group and grid, she identified four ideal types to examine the rules that relate individuals to one another. Thus where there is 'high classification, piety and sacralized institutions, strong boundaries between impurity and purity; this is the prototype original Durkheimian system in which God is Society and Society is God' (p. 91). Such a system minimises conflict and tends to survive over time. Societies with weak group and weak grid have an emphasis on the individual, who is seen to be separate from the group, and the classificatory scheme is weak and private. Because of the lack of group mentality, all social classifications are negotiable in modern societies, where social integration is diminished by the growing pluralism of values. Because social norms are unstable and shifting, political institutions are required to exercise social control.

The classificatory schemes Douglas discussed in *Purity and Danger* do not really hold in modern societies with the same degree of authority and coherence, and where there is greater cultural fluidity around norms and social membership. In most traditional societies, there is a strong connection between ethics and prohibitions. This is very clear in anthropological research on the Nuer, where prohibitions on various categories of people whom one can marry are enforced by notions of pollution. These prohibitions, combining ideas about both pollution and morality, are in fact necessary in maintaining the whole social structure and avoiding social conflicts, but in modern societies where the social structure is less rigid, such prohibitions become confused and uncertain. In traditional societies, religion can be said to be constituted by 'a double set of accounts: it enables people to hold each other accountable to a common commitment to rituals that testify to their right-mindedness; it also provides a balance sheet on which their relation to God can be assessed' (Douglas, 1980).

Douglas looked at many forms of religious behaviour. For example, she regarded ritual sacrifice as ultimately bringing about further social integration and coherence. Sacrifice is interesting because it often sanctions a taboo or the breaking of a strong prohibition such as killing human beings, eating their flesh, killing sacred animals and so forth. Douglas thought of sacrifice in a metaphorical way as 'letting off steam' or releasing strains in a social system in order to allow for new patterns of integration or renewal. Abraham and his son Isaac, on the one hand, and Christ as the Lamb of God, on the other, were sacrificial persons or events within a cultural system that was finally reintegrated – for example by Christ's resurrection. Can sacrifice always be comfortably contained within the cultural system or are there transgressions that confound and confuse such classification? Are there events or processes or people who cannot be safely classified or held within the system? Is Douglas's approach so logically sound that nothing can fall outside it?

Douglas's anthropology of the body

Mary Douglas addressed the anthropology of the body directly in her *Natural Symbols* (1973). Her account of bodily symbolism has been somewhat neglected in the emergence of a sociology of the body in contemporary sociology. Her approach started with Marcel Mauss's essay on body techniques (Mauss, 1979) and revolved around the idea of two bodies – the social and the natural. She interpreted Mauss as saying that there is no natural body since all body techniques have to be acquired through learning and practice. By contrast, Douglas was concerned to preserve some notion of a natural body in order to look at parallel relations between social and natural hierarchies. In her search for binary relations between open and closed systems and informal and formal ones, she produced a number of 'rules' with regard to the management of the body in human affairs.

The first rule is that there is a drive towards consonance and coherence between experience, culture and aesthetic appreciation. In this respect, nature and culture converge, because there is a 'natural tendency to express situations of a certain kind in an appropriate bodily style' (1973: 97). Her second rule is that the social controls of a society place certain limits on the employment of the body as a medium of expression. The control of the body is always an expression of social control. The absence of such controls may be required in circumstances where powerful emotions, such as may occur in forms of religious ecstasy, may erupt. By contrast, where highly formal social relations are in operation, then obviously there will be excessive attention to bodily regulation. The socialisation of children is very concerned to achieve control over bodily functions in order to avoid embarrassment and disruption to social life. The third rule, therefore, is that formal systems of social control require a corresponding pattern of physical regulation. The final rule is a purity rule in which societies progressively seek to disembody all forms of expression; in short, there is a tendency for the natural body to disappear from social attention once it has been regulated and controlled. As the social body becomes more elaborate, the natural body is associated with animal life and a strong opposition between mind and body, and between culture and nature emerges. The more a society values refinement, the less noise is permitted to emanate from the body. Smacking lips, yawning or farting are regarded as coarse, vulgar and disrespectful.

In some respects modern life has become less controlled by formal ritual systems and this would suggest that bodily regulation has also been somewhat relaxed. Douglas's fourth rule or purity rule might apply to modern Western societies. One example illustrates Douglas's conservative response to modern de-ritualisation. She was critical in the chapter on 'The Bog Irish' in her *Natural Symbols* of the tendency to understate the importance of ritual in modern Roman Catholic practice and doctrine. In particular, she noted that the Roman Catholic 'hierarchy in England today are under pressure to underestimate the expressive function of ritual. Catholics are exhorted to invent individual acts of almsgiving as a more meaningful celebration of Friday' (1973: 60). In the eyes of the people who want to modernise Roman Catholic practice, avoidance of meat on Friday is now merely an empty ritual. The explanation offered by the clergy who want to remove such practices, she argued, was derived from a 'Teilhardist evolutionism' which claims that 'a rational verbally explicit personal commitment to God is self-evidently more evolved and better than its alleged contrary, formal, ritualistic commitment' (p. 22). For Douglas, the logical conclusion of these arguments against ritual would be the divorce of the Church from its own history, namely 'the mystical body, the communion of saints, death, resurrection, immortality and speaking in tongues' (p. 201). This view of the Church and modern society raises interesting sociological questions about how we might regard the social solidarity of youth gangs and their rituals of membership including tattoos and bodily piercing.

Body piercing and tattoos

Evidence of tattooing and related practices comes to us from the earliest societies. Egyptian mummies from the period of the Middle Kingdom have revealed an extensive culture of body marking. In a religious cosmology, the inalienable tattoos of this world may be bartered for spiritual privileges in the next. Tattoos generally functioned to guarantee good health and to ward off evil. Throughout the Mediterranean and Middle East, even after the spread of puritanical Islam, tattoos and amulets protected the individual from the evil eye. In Hawaii, tattoos were also employed to memorialise deceased relatives, and in Indonesia they were indicative of important accomplishments. Despite the potential for transgression, both piercing and tattooing have been customary practices from ancient times. Tattooing can be traced back to the Upper Palaeolithic era and has been common in Eurasia since Neolithic times. For example, Otzi the Iceman dated circa 3300 BC had fifty-seven tattoos on his body. Some tattoos are thought to have had therapeutic value in the treatment of arthritis and rheumatism. Tattooing was especially widespread in the Philippines,

Japan and Polynesia and the word 'tattoo' or 'tatau' comes from Tahiti. Captain Cook's Science Officer acquired a tattoo and many sailors returning with Cook had adopted tattoos in the Pacific Islands, and this early naval practice was the origin of a long custom for British sailors to have tattoos. These body marks were typically permanent, collective and largely obligatory. They were set within a shared culture of collective meaning and hence the significance of a tattoo could be read unambiguously.

Following Douglas's orientation to the principles of social member-ship as expressed through bodily modifications, body marks (which I use as a short-hand for tattooing, piercing, cicatrisation, painting and so forth) indicate social membership through the metaphor of the human body as a space where we think about and constitute the body politic. In particular, body marks designate political (specifically gender) identity at certain points in the life-cycle. The ritual mutilation of the penis in Australian Aboriginal societies was a famous illustra-tion, which designated male identity at a point in the life-cycle where boys cross over into adulthood. Changes in the nature and purpose of tattoos indicate changes in the nature and purpose of social life. The contemporary interest in tattoos is no longer confined, as in earlier periods of Western industrialisation, to the working class, youth cul-ture or criminal communities, but extends through the social scale as tattoos are used to produce an aesthetic enhancement of the body. Tattooing is now more closely related to the theme of sexual pleasure in popular culture than to specific life-cycle transitions. Elderly Baby Boomers may adopt ear-rings and tattoos just as readily as their children. Body piercing and marking have evolved into body art as decoration. However, the need to imitate the body markings of other and earlier cultures in contemporary primitivism can be taken as further evidence in post-modern cultures of what we might fruitfully term 'the exhaustion of idiom' (Turner, 2001a). In modern culture, we have difficulty creating shared and endurable symbols and myths from our urban world and may therefore seek to adopt our symbolism from earlier times in which symbolic meaning was richer and more highly defined. In modern cultures, these borrowed symbols are components of a culture of simulation that does not easily recognise or sustain 'authenticity'. Popular idioms are necessarily clichés. As a result, cultural globalisation has produced a melange of tattoos which are both ironic and self-referential.

We can now begin to use Douglas's framework as a way of thinking about body piercing and tattoos or body modification in general. Her anthropological ideas are relevant to piercing; because it involves an entry into the body and because there is normally the possibility that blood may be spilt, it is an abomination from a traditional framework in the sense that blood should remain in the body as an envelope. Blood on the outside is a disruption or a breaking of the cultural integrity of body. There are, of course, many forms of tattoos. Criminal tattoos are common in Japan, Russia and Vietnam, where they are signs of identification and membership and they often carry information about the status or skills of the criminal person. Celebrity tattoos have in modern times somewhat reversed the stigma of the criminal tattoo with the fashion for tattoos reaching its zenith with David Beckham. The tattoo expert Louis Malloy flew from Britain to the USA to give Beckham the winged cross on the back of his neck. While Beckham's tattoo represents a passing fashion, in pre-modern societies tattoos were permanent and they carried specific ritual information about the individual. Some tattoos and body piercing were also obligatory. We might say that in pre-modern societies body modifications were involuntary and irreversible. In modern societies tattoos have become voluntary and temporary (Turner, 1999b).

From Douglas's perspective, body piercing is an interesting issue. It clearly raises the problem of contagion and contamination in breaking the skin of the body. In the Abrahamic religions in varying degrees, numerous cultural barriers are constructed to proscribe and condemn tattooing. In Christianity, the King James Version of the Bible contained the Leviticus prohibition on tattoos. Leviticus 19:28 states that: 'You shall not make any cuttings in your flesh on account of the dead or tattoo any marks upon you.' Similarly, Orthodox Jewish belief prohibits the use of tattooing because the human body is assumed to be perfect and not in need of any decoration that might be associated with vanity. The Torah clearly states 'Do not make gashes in your skin for the dead. Do not make any marks on your skin. I am God.' Maimonides clearly bans tattoos (Mishneh Torah, Laws of Idolatry 12:11). In addition, modern Jews also remember the fact that Jews were forced to wear tattoos during the Holocaust and hence in Judaism the removal of a tattoo by a laser can count as an act of repentance.

Christians believe that the New Testament supersedes the Old Testament and therefore the prescriptions in Judaism do not automatically apply in Christian practice. The obvious example is circumcision; Paul declared that Christians had to be circumcised in their hearts in order to belong to the Universal Church. However, Christianity opposed body piercing, referring to the Bible citing 1 Corinthians, and therefore evangelical Christians, rejecting tattoos as an ornament designed to draw attention to oneself, treat body modification as an example of self love or pride. While the majority of Christians reject piercing and tattooing on strictly religious grounds, the Church of Latter-Day Saints has also banned piercing on medical grounds. Muslims also reject tattooing for similar religious and moral reasons. According to the *hadith* (customary teaching), God has made human beings perfect and therefore it is a blasphemy to change the human form. Islam is, however, divided between two dominant traditions – Sunni and Shi'ite Islam. While Sunni Islam abides by the prohibition on tattooing, the Shi'a scholars (Ayatollah Sistani and Khamenei), who do not necessarily accept the traditional *hadith*, think that there is no authoritative prohibition on tattoos.

Body piercing as transgression: Modern Primitives

The eruption of fashionable body piercing and tattooing is closely connected to the emergence of primitivism. 'Modern primitives' have broadly influenced the body modification scene even for people who would not call themselves 'primitivists'. The movement was born in the 1960s and 1970s in California, coming out of various underground lesbian, gay, hard-core and S&M groups. It developed alongside the 'tattoo renaissance' and the repertoire of styles expanded to include Japanese, tribal and so-called fine-line styles. There was a growth in piercing associated with various journals, such as *Piercing Fans International Quarterly*. The growth in piercing often interacted with modern social anthropology in providing positive or sympathetic information about native or indigenous customs and practices.

The key figure in this development is Fakir Musafar, who in 1979 coined the phrase 'Modern Primitive' and who established publications such as *Body Play* and *Modern Primitives Quarterly* in 1991. Known as the 'father of the Modern Primitive movement', he created an ideology for the movement which associated body piercing with the political struggles and plight of indigenous people, and as a result some primitives revived the Sun Dance rituals of American Plains Indians. Musafar rejected modern civilisation and its technologies, celebrating the primitive as a critique of progress. Primitivism borrowed heavily from science fiction writing such as William Gibson's *Neuromancer* (1984) and even attempted to incorporate feminist academic writings such as Donna Haraway's 'A Cyborg Manifesto: Science, Technology and Socialism' ([1985] 1991). It promoted the idea of pain as defining the self, creating a definite boundary between the inside and outside world, providing sensations of ecstasy and spiritual insight and claimed that pain was a method of self development and enhancement.

Musafar advanced the idea of the 'primal urge', describing it as the instinct to change or modify the body in a ritualistic fashion, and described it as manifested spontaneously in response to a lack of ritual and spirituality in American culture. He claimed that the term 'Modern Primitive' was used to describe a non-tribal person who, in responding to primal urges, does something to transform their body. As a result, he observed that there was an increasing trend among young people to get pierced or tattooed. This development is often claimed to be the consequence of a 'real' response to primal urges and not simply a passing fashion. Hence the authenticity of a person's motives for becoming tattooed or pierced is commonly of great concern to Modern Primitives. Musafar argued that Modern Primitives are born, not made and the idea that there is a 'primal urge' to mark and manipulate the body assumes a link between all people of all cultures across all time periods.

From the perspective of Douglas's cultural anthropology, one would want to argue that Modern Primitives are a reaction to the erosion of rituals and social coherence, and that the transgressive direction of Modern Primitives is the outcome of a society based on weak grid and weak group. However, in modern societies these forms of primitive resistance are easily co-opted by consumerism and the fashion industry. Rather like the consumer co-option of subcultures in Britain – punks, mods and rockers, hoodies, heavy-metal groups and so forth – primitive styles were partially incorporated into a global popular culture in the forms of a piercing fad and the incorporation of tribal designs in tattooing culture. Genuine primitives rejected these 'trendies', whose motives were seen to be impure from their perspective, but the trend in consumer society has been to blur the boundary between transgression and fashion. In contemporary culture, scarification, implants, piercing and branding were combined with the restoration of aboriginal 'rites of passage' to bring the body back into the centre of experience and to celebrate pain as a traumatic but ultimately therapeutic method of (re)defining the self. As primitivism was rapidly absorbed by MTV and youth fashion, Modern Primitives became more radical in offering followers horns inserted in the head, tails attached to the body, bone-sculpting and finger removal. In some American cities it is now possible to hire spaces to practise ritual hanging from hooks and less traditional forms of S&M play. In response to fashionable body modification, radical primitives adopted more extreme practices. Modern versions of the Sun Dance of the Lakota Sioux Indians of North Dakota were adopted by white American primitives as a rituals practice that would offer genuine spiritual insight. These modern urban simulations of the ceremony were eventually rejected by a council of Native American spiritual leaders who objected to the infiltration of New Age beliefs into traditional customs, the sale of sacred pipes and the consumption of drugs at tribal gatherings.

From Douglas's conservative cultural position, these developments demonstrate in fact the failure of rituals and classification and the emergence of societies where stable meanings have disappeared along with strong grid and group structures. Clifton Sanders (1987: 395) argued that 'The tattoo is both an indication of disaffiliation from conventional society and a symbolic affirmation of personal identity'. In this sense, tattoos are used to carve out a new communal affiliation for the individual, but the communities that are produced by customised rituals tend to be ever-changing and dissolving niches for the recreation of the social.

The fragmentation of the social

Whereas Durkheim had presented an image of mechanical solidarity in *The Elementary Forms* ([1912] 2001) as a society based on commonalities, collective rituals and shared emotions, the contemporary social world has given rise to very different images and theories. With the growth of world-wide urbanisation and the rise of global mega-cities, social life was thought to be increasingly fragmented, giving rise to urban ghettoes, parallel communities and subcultures. The idea of the 'lonely crowd' painted a picture of passive and isolated urban dwellers glued to their TVs. In the sociological literature from the 1950s onwards, it was claimed that there were new youth subcultures associated with a growing consumerism. Ethan Watters (2003) in *Urban Tribes* argued that these new social groups were composed of 'never-marrieds' between the ages of 25 and 45 years who formed common but ephemeral interest groups. Their new lifestyles were always shifting forms of identification with these fragmented groups. Dick Hebdige (1981) wrote a classic account of these developments in his *Subculture: The Meaning of Style* to describe the oppositional movements that followed 'rock 'n' roll' namely punk, Goths and other rave cultures.

These studies had in fact been preceded by Michel Maffesoli's *The Time of the Tribes* in 1996. The subtitle of this work in the English translation was *The Decline of Individualism in Mass Society*. Maffesoli argued that various micro-groups were emerging in modern society who share a common, but shallow and informal, culture. These 'tribes' are fleeting, but their members share a common emotional bond, which is very different from the cold bureaucratic and formal ties of modern organisations. Punks were probably the classical illustration of such youth interest groups. The growth of consumer society, youth cultures and fashion rendered much of the Marxist emphasis on production obsolete, and in 1967 Guy Debord published his *The Society of the Spectacle* in which he developed Marx's theories of alienation to argue that modern society was further alienated by the impact of the mass media. Everyday life had been colonised by commodities, producing what Marx had called the fetish of commodities. We can only experience our world through this mediation – being had become merely appearing and the relations between people had become a spectacular world of artificial appearances and events. Debord's work on a spectacular society was the ideological foundation of the movement (mainly among students) of the *Situationist International*. Debord, who encouraged events and demonstrations as a protest against the alienation of a media-dominated world, had a profound effect on the student protests of 1968.

Ideas about the media and alienation became part of post-modern theory. Jean Baudrillard was influenced by both Marshall McLuhan and Karl Marx, but criticised Marxism as a theory of production for neglecting consumption. In any case, Marx could not have anticipated the growth of modern media of communication. Baudrillard emphasised the ways in which reality and fiction, substance and appearance, had merged, in his *The System of Objects* (1968), *The Mirror of Production* (1973) and *Simulation and Simulcra* (1981). Baudrillard gained world-wide notoriety through his argument that the Gulf War was a TV spectacular in *The Gulf War Did Not Take Place* (1991). These ideas about social fragmentation, corrupted social systems and simulated representation began to influence science fiction and cultural theory around the themes of cyberspace and cyberbodies. The works of William Gibson(1984) were said to give expression to a new community of hackers and the technologically literate who were socially disaffected and searching for social forms that could express the new connectivity made possible by computerisation. These new possibilities might overcome the 'electronic industrial ghettoes' (Stone, 1991: 95) that characterised modern society. Some social theorists began to speculate about 'cybersociety' as a more attractive alternative to the information city. These theories also celebrated the merging of fiction and social science writing, arguing that traditional social sciences had no chance of capturing even the basic features of the information age. One example is Davis's *Beyond Blade Runner. Urban Control – the Ecology of Fear* (1992).

Modern tattooing and piercing provide an interesting insight into the mobile, ephemeral social world of modern primitivism in which gangs flourish in cities in which social order is often tenuous. Some modern writers suggest that in fact social control is breaking down in the global mega-city giving rise to a disorganised world, in which there is an underworld of grinding poverty and squalor lurking below the surface of organised consumerism. The alternative to societies that are highly regulated might be the emergence of a dystopian future in the shape of the 'feral society'. If modern governments cannot find adequate solutions to issues arising from unemployment, youth alienation, urban crime and social dislocation, one can anticipate that mega-cities will become increasingly ungovernable. With the erosion of welfare safety nets, there is the growing prospect of urban unrest in which migrant ghettoes become no-go areas beyond the reach of modern policing. In this emerging scenario of sporadic violence, 'the feral city is an area in which state power is nonexistent, the architecture consists entirely of slums, and power is a complex process negotiated through violence by different factions ... The feral city is an extreme endpoint of failed communities' (Sullivan and Elkus, 2009). Delinquent gangs are a function of such urban decay and the decline of communal control in which tattoos define social membership for young men whose familial and kinship networks are breaking down.

Members of the new lumpen-proletariat or underclass who inhabit the unskilled or deskilled sector of the casual labour market are neither culturally nor physically mobile in the world economy. Because they are stuck in a sector of the market which is underdeveloped, they are more likely to adopt neo-tribal mentalities that address their wish for urban sociality. Gangland, football clubs, the 'local community' and the rock bands of English pubs simulate both their alienation and their desire for membership. When neo-tribalism spills over into genuine fascism, this version of belonging and membership can become overtly hostile to the cosmopolitanism of workers in global communication markets. Tattoos survive in these groups as a primary mark of social loyalties, while for the fashion model they are reversible adornments. For young men, these urban gangs provide some temporary respite from the instability of the urban landscape by giving them, at least in the short run, an experience of strong group and strong grid.

While modernisation brought about both individuation and separation, affective groups survived in everyday society as sites of collective solidarity. These 'little masses' are distinguished by their special clothing, sports and adornments, and body art. These emotional communities have resisted the processes of rationalisation and bureaucratisation which are typical of the public sphere based on the new 'contractarian' forms of citizenship (Somers, 2008). As the framework of citizenship erodes, the vacuum is filled at the level of civil society by dysfunctional social groups. Maffesoli identifies these neo-tribal groupings – football clubs, working-class gangs, social movements and primary groups in the everyday world – as sites where Dionysian affective and orgiastic experiences are still possible, but these assumptions may be misplaced forms of romanticism. The gangs of the feral city are the recruiting ground for terrorist groups and the spread of urban violence rather than warm and cosy sites of a new sociability, and they are, of course, also far removed from Douglas's vision of modern purity and danger.

Conclusion: the loss of ritual

Within Douglas's theory of ritual, all societies must be guided by ritual activities, and in this sense we cannot draw a line between 'primitive society' and 'modern society'. Nevertheless her perspective suggests that modern ritual life will be thinner and weaker than the societies described in her work on Africa or the Aboriginal societies described originally in *The Northern Tribes of Central Australia* (Spencer and Gillén, [1904] 1997). Her fourth rule on purity suggests that, with respect to the body, modern existence is no longer defined by these embodied rituals. The fact that ritual observance is now seen to be archaic was illustrated by the post-Vatican II attempt to define Friday observance as an obstacle to modern spirituality. Douglas claimed that the decline of ritual practices has robbed modern individuals of a sense of belonging and purpose and it has the function of disconnecting the natural and the social body.

However, apart from her spontaneous comments on the racial categorisation of the Irish migrant in London, Douglas undertook no serious ethnography of urban society. Her later work on economics in, for example, *The World of Goods* (Douglas and Isherwood, 1978) was clearly an analysis of the contemporary world, but it was not an anthropological investigation of urban culture as such. One consequence of her focus on the anthropology of pollution was a lack of attention to some of the fundamental characteristics of modernity. There are at least three dimensions of modernity that receive no treatment in her work. The first is that multiculturalism has contributed profoundly to modern cultural complexity; the second is the partial collapse of the hierarchical organisation of gender and the rise of gender pluralism; and the third is that the creation of symbolic worlds in modernity often depends heavily on the typically ironic and playful adoption of 'primitive' rituals and symbols. These social changes have created complexity and confusion about cultural identities and a corresponding erosion of hierarchical authority. These social changes clearly have their maximum impact in youth cultures. Within urban spaces, gangs can function to recreate Douglas's notion of strong group and strong grid, because in a multicultural society gang membership typically expresses and preserves both social solidarity and ethnic differentiation. Tattoos play a crucial role in these groups by marking the body in relation to social membership (group), and within these gangs discipline is hierarchical and where necessary violent (grid).

Douglas's work had a political dimension which was that hierarchical authority is important for sustaining social solidarity. My comments on the issue of rituals in popular culture do not ultimately contradict her position, because gang solidarity does not necessarily produce any increase in trust or social capital across social groups. Gangs give rise to ample intra-group solidarity, but little or no inter-communal sociality. On the contrary, the general social order remains as divided and fissiparous as ever. More importantly, attempts to create or recreate rituals in the service of popular culture are necessarily ineffective, because the surrounding cultural system in which those rituals originally resided cannot be recreated as a whole. This outcome follows from her argument that we can never understand a cultural item – such as the prohibition on pork – without taking into account the whole edifice of culture that distinguishes between the clean and unclean. The authority and efficacy of a ritual – such as Friday abstinence – cannot be preserved without the total framework of piety in which abstaining from meat was originally located. At least within religious systems of belief, this principle raises serious difficulties. For instance, the notion of Christ as the Lamb of God can only have any genuine meaning in an agrarian civilisation in which sacrifice had significance in relation to the idea of the disinterested exchange of a gift. In societies that are based on the industrialisation of agricultural production, the significance of the lamb as a symbol of love has been denuded of any concrete significant meaning.

We might push Douglas's conservative argument further by claiming that in the contemporary world we no longer possess the rituals which anthropologists have described in their research on aboriginal communities. Instead we have a secular system of rules to regulate behaviour, and our collective rituals have become infrequent, contested and ineffectual. At the same time our religious rituals are submerged into rules and our bodily codes expressed in hygienic formulae. What remains of our ritual world has been submerged in morality that is into assumptions about correct behaviour and any attempt to restore tradition or primitive practices will be merely imitations of a passing world.

6 | *Pierre Bourdieu and religious practice*

Introduction: public religions

Whereas in recent years many sociologists and philosophers have come to the conclusion that religion has to be taken seriously in debates about the nature of modern politics and the public sphere, such was not the case with many post-war social theorists. What has changed? The obvious answer is that there are various transformations of social and political life that have placed religion as an institution at the centre of modern society. Religion now appears to be closely related to identity politics, ethnicity and gender, medical technology and security issues. It has been the ideological driving force behind many social and nationalist movements such as Solidarity, 'engaged Buddhism' and Hindu nationalism. The earlier post-war generation of social scientists accepted the secularisation thesis that, with modernisation, religion would decline and hence there was little point investing research effort into an institution that would inevitably disappear. In Europe, there was the additional factor of Marxist social and political theory, which was in France and elsewhere an influential if not a dominant tradition in the post-war period. For critical theorists, there was no assumption that religion could continue to exercise significant ideological influence over secular modernity. Religion was simply a set of false beliefs that comforted the disinherited and legitimised the rich and powerful. Religious ideologies would disappear with the spread of secular science, urbanisation, literacy, working-class struggles, the decline of the family and the emancipation of women.

However, the dramatic collapse of organised communism in the early 1990s and the erosion of Marxist–Leninist ideology allowed religion to flourish once more in East European societies, especially in Poland, the Ukraine and the former Yugoslavia. In Russia, the Orthodox Church has become closely associated with nationalism and, while the Communist Party has not disappeared in Vietnam, the modern Renovation Period has allowed the return of religion to public life. In Vietnamese towns Roman Catholicism is returning and the Protestant sects are flourishing among ethnic minorities. Spirit possession cults are also attracting members of an emerging middle class from the expanding capitalist sector. Globalisation and the Internet have created new opportunities for evangelism even in societies where the Party still attempts to regulate or suppress the flow of information and interaction. In China, Charter 08 calls for, among other things, freedom of religious assembly and practice. While these dissident movements are unlikely to shake the control of the Party or its authoritarian responses to religious revivalism, these developments are likely to see a significant growth in religious activity across both the existing communist and the post-communist world. As a result of such social transformations, there is a need to rethink many aspects of modern secularity.

One obvious feature of globalisation has been the growth of flexible labour markets, mass migration and permanent settlement, producing the world-wide emergence of diasporic communities in societies with expanding economies. These diasporic communities are typically held together by their religious beliefs and practices in such a way that in modern societies the distinction between ethnicity and religion begins to become irrelevant. Indeed the 'Turks' in Germany have become 'Muslims' and around the world Chinese minorities, for example in Indonesia and Malaysia, are almost automatically called 'Buddhists'. The result is that religion has become a major plank of public culture and the politics of identity.

Religion has often emerged as the principal site of ethnic and cultural contestation, and states have become involved in the management of religions, thereby inevitably departing from the traditional separation of state and religion in the liberal framework. Paradoxically, by intervening to regulate religion in the public domain, the state automatically makes religion more important and prominent. In societies as different as the United States and Singapore, the state intervenes to manage Islam in the name of supporting 'moderate Muslims' and bringing them into mainstream society (Kamaludeen, Pereira and Turner, 2009). Throughout the modern world, there is a complex interaction between religion and national identity – from Hinduism in India to Catholicism in Poland to Shinto in Japan – whereby religion becomes part of the fabric of public discourse.

Perhaps the critical event in bringing religion back into the global public arena was the Iranian Revolution in 1978–9. The fall of the secular state, which had promoted a nationalist vision of society as a Persian civilisation over a traditional Islamic framework, provided a global example of a spiritual revolution. It offered a singular example of the mobilisation of the masses in the name of religious renewal. In 1978, Michel Foucault wrote articles for the Italian newspaper *Corriere della sera* describing the revolution under Ayatollah Rubollah Khomeini as a new 'political spirituality' (Arfary and Anderson, 2005). The message of the Iranian intellectual Ali Shariati against what he called 'Westoxification' was embraced by a wide variety of religious movements outside the specific Iranian context (Akbarzadeh and Mansouri, 2007). Islam became at least one conduit of the political idea that modernisation could take many forms and that the domination of American capitalist society could be opposed (Halliday, 2003). Reformed Islam came to encapsulate the notion that secularism was not the inevitable shell of modernity. The other defining moment was the 9/11 attack on the Twin Towers – the very symbol of the financial dominance of the West over the developing world. This attack has come to be interpreted as a symbolic as much as a terrorist event (Göle, 1996). In a similar fashion, the cultural and social ambiguities of veiling stand for the problematical status of the veil and women in modern secular cultures (Lazreg, 2009).

The rekindling of academic interest in religion and modernity has been sparked off by the (unexpected) attention shown by Jürgen Habermas in his *Religion and Rationality* (2002). For sociologists working in the sub-discipline, Habermas's reflections on religion do not provide any new insights or conclusions that are not already familiar to social scientists. He has claimed that the secularisation thesis rested on the assumption that the disenchanted world (as described by Max Weber) rests on a scientific outlook in which all phenomena can be explained scientifically. Secondly, there has been (in terms of Niklas Luhmann's systems theory) a differentiation of society into specialised functions in which religion becomes increasingly a private matter. Finally, the transformation of society from an agrarian basis has improved living standards and reduced risk, removing the dependence of individuals on supernatural forces and reducing their need for religious meaning and psychological support.

Habermas notes correctly that the secularisation debate is based on a narrow European viewpoint. America, by contrast, appears to be vibrantly religious in a society where religion, prosperity and modernisation have sat comfortably together. In more global terms, Habermas draws attention to the spread of fundamentalism, the growth of radical Islamic groups and the presence of religious issues in the public sphere. The privatisation of religion – the cornerstone of the liberal view of tolerance in the legacy of John Locke – is thought by many observers to be no longer a viable political strategy in the separation of state and religion (Spinner-Halevy, 2005). Habermas's solution to the problems surrounding radical fundamentalism and radical secularism is to propose a dialogue involving the inclusion of foreign minority cultures into civil society on the one hand and the opening up of subcultures to the state in order to encourage their members to participate actively in political life. Religious groups have to state their views and beliefs within the public sphere, where there can be a genuine communication between different religious traditions.

In some respects Habermas's debate about the pre-political foundations of the liberal state with Joseph Ratzinger (subsequently Pope Benedict XVI), at the Catholic Academy of Bavaria on 19 January 2008, was perhaps more interesting, or at least more revealing. Both men were in a reconciliatory or conciliatory mood (Habermas and Ratzinger, 2006). Habermas recognised that religion had preserved intact values and ideas that had been lost elsewhere and that the notion of the fundamental equality of all humans was an important legacy of the Christian faith. Habermas has also shown himself to be aware of, and possibly sympathetic to, much of the Jewish quest for otherness in the first generation of critical thinkers in the Frankfurt School. In retrospect, it is very clear that, for example, Walter Benjamin's interpretations of modern secular culture were deeply coloured by Jewish Messianism (Wolin, 1994). This issue raises an important question about the continuities and discontinuities between the early and late members of the critical tradition. Indeed it poses a problem about the continuity of Habermas's own philosophical work.

Habermas's debate with Ratzinger can be understood against the German background of *Kulturprotestantismus*, in which there is a general respect for religion and where religion is far more prominent in public life than is the case in the United Kingdom. Habermas's response may have been generous, but it does rest upon the idea that political institutions and in particular the state cannot really function without a robust civil society or without a set of shared values. The role of religion, contrary to much critical theory and contrary to the secularisation thesis, may be important to provide a necessary support of social life as such.

One of the most important sociological interventions in this debate was José Casanova's *Public Religions in the Modern World* (1994), which provided a robust framework for understanding key developments that had put religion at the centre of political life in many societies. At the same time, there is discontent with the conventional emphasis in mainstream sociology of religion on the decline in belief and church membership in the conventional approach to secularisation. There is no necessary or simple connection, for example, between Christian belief and religious practice. In Britain, Grace Davie (1994; 2006) pioneered the phrase 'believing without belonging' to capture these discontinuities between belief, church membership and worship. Although there is a strong temptation to abandon the secularisation thesis in its entirety, Casanova does not support any wholesale and premature abandonment of the entire argument about secularity but instead proposes that we can think of secularisation as simply a sub-theme of the more general notion of modernisation and that modernity involved the differentiation of the religious and the secular sphere. He has been critical of the idea that secularisation means simply the decline of religious belief and practice. He therefore identified three components of secularisation: (i) differentiation of various spheres of the social system (such as religion, state and market); (ii) secularisation as the decline of religious belief and practice; and finally (iii) the marginalisation of religion to the private sphere. Through a number of comparative studies, he demonstrated that secularisation as differentiation is indeed a key component of modern secularisation.

However, his critical contribution was to identify important developments in what he called the 'deprivatisation' of religion. His examples of public religions included the Iranian Revolution, the liberation theologies of Latin America, the Solidarity movement in Poland, and the rise of the Moral Majority and the Christian Right in America. Taking the Christian Right as an example of the 'deprivatisation' of religion, he argued that by the 1950s 'the American way of life' was characterised by the plurality of ways of life, by what could be called 'moral denominationalism' (Casanova, 1994: 145). Consequently, an adequate sociology of religion has to evaluate these three components separately and independently.

There is much discontent among contemporary sociologists of religion with traditional approaches to religion in the secular world and hence Casanova's work was welcomed, because it created a new interest in public religions. Nevertheless, there is still much turmoil in the sub-field and some degree of uncertainty about what might come after the secularisation debate. As a result, sociologists of religion have started to look towards the work of Pierre Bourdieu to give them a more adequate framework for understanding religious practice, ritual and habitus (Furseth, 2009). Although Bourdieu's actual production of essays in the sociology of religion was slight, his influence can be seen in recent work such as Terry Rey's *Bourdieu on Religion* (2007). Other writers have also begun to draw on Bourdieu's notion of symbolic capital and field to study religion (Bell, 1990; Braun and McCutcheon, 2000; Engler, 2003; Swartz, 1996; Verter, 2003). There has also been interest in his early work on Algeria, in which there was some discussion of religion (Loyal, 2009).

Bourdieu's sociological work in relation to religion has also received a sympathetic reading from Kieran Flanagan (2008), who suggests that Bourdieu was more interested in theology than religion. He also claims that Bourdieu's vision of sociology was deeply influenced by the Church, that Bourdieu was 'uniquely proximate to Catholicism' and that his sociology was infused with 'metaphors derived from its theology' (p. 251). The notion of sacramental powers with the ecclesiastical institutions provides Bourdieu, or so Flanagan claims, with an insight into how power is exercised within the cultural field in terms of its symbolic violence. Recognising that Bourdieu absorbed the concept of habitus from Aristotle and Aquinas, the real influence on this concept came form the art historian Erwin Panofsky. What are we to make of these extraordinary claims? Bourdieu was no doubt influenced by the surrounding culture of French Catholicism, but only in the weak sense that in Catholic Europe culture and religion have become constituent parts of national frameworks. Similarly, the notion of habitus is present in Catholic theology for the simple reason that Aristotle's philosophy provided the framework for the elaboration of Christian theology. The main influence on Bourdieu in his approach to religion was certainly Max Weber, but his general sociology owes more to Marxism than to Catholicism.

In this chapter I want to consider whether Bourdieu's work holds out any significant interest or provides a new conceptual framework for the student of religion. My answer is somewhat paradoxical. What Bourdieu actually says about religion in his limited collection of essays on religion is not very interesting and most of it appears to depend on Max Weber explicitly and Louis Althusser implicitly. Having said that, his conceptual framework – social capital, symbolic violence, field, hexis and habitus – does provide a powerful perspective, avoiding in my view many of the pitfalls arising from the exaggerated attention to religious beliefs rather than embodied practices in the work of many contemporary sociologists and philosophers of religion. Although Bourdieu's contribution to the sociology of practice is considerable, insights into practice and embodiment are obviously present in alternative traditions such as pragmatism (Barbalet, 2000).

In this chapter I develop a critical view of Bourdieu's interpretation and use of Weber's sociology of religion. These critical remarks on this aspect of Bourdieu's work need to be set within the context of recognising that Bourdieu was deeply familiar with Weber's sociology. For example, he read *The Protestant Ethic* in the German original before any French translations were available (Schultheis and Pfeuffer, 2009) and he quarrelled with Raymond Aron about interpretations of Weber, in which Bourdieu rejected any artificial opposition between Marx and Weber. Bourdieu was an assiduous student of *Economy and Society*, and his emphasis on the struggle over religious legitimacy in Weber's comparative sociology of religion provided an important alternative to both Talcott Parsons and Raymond Aron who, while themselves occupying different positions in politics, sought to distance Weber from Marx. In short, Bourdieu was clearly enthusiastic in his response to Weber's sociology as a whole.

Bourdieu interpreted Weber as salvaging the symbolic in Marx's economic sociology and hence Weber became useful at various stages in Bourdieu's development. For example, Bourdieu started reading Weber's *The Protestant Ethic and the Spirit of Capitalism* (2002) during his time in Algeria and it was Weber's analysis of religious asceticism that gave him a genuine insight into the economic ethics of the Khajirites, who were a radical movement in Islam that from the seventh century claimed the right to revolt against any Muslim leader who deviated from the teachings of the Prophet. In this group, who now live primarily in the Mzab region of Algeria, Bourdieu saw the importance of inner-worldly asceticism as a powerful economic ethic. He later recognised the importance of Weber in the concept of 'the field', in which Bourdieu sought to capture the notion of struggles over symbolic capital. Finally, Bourdieu appreciated the value of Weber's work in capturing the idea of 'character studies'. With respect to this notion, I would prefer to use Weber's own expression of 'personality and life orders' and to extend this phrase to argue that Weber was constructing a sociology of piety, where we can see immediately the connections between piety, habitus, disposition and Aristotle's notion of virtue or excellence. From Bourdieu's interview with Franz Schultheis and Andreas Pfeuffer (2009), it is clear that, avoiding the futile debate about whether Weber was on the left or the right of European politics, Bourdieu made good use of Weber in his various works on distinction, symbolic violence, practice and so forth. Having recognised Bourdieu's appreciation of Weber, we need to turn to what Bourdieu actually has to say about religion.

Bourdieu on religion: a preliminary critique

There is no need here to present an account of Bourdieu's general sociology. I shall merely select certain aspects that are germane to a discussion of religion. According to Rey (2007), Bourdieu produced some ten essays on religion, which were mainly confined to Roman Catholicism in France and to Islam in Algeria. His early work on the Kabylia in Algeria became the basis of a critique of the anthropological structuralism of Claude Levi-Strauss. When Islam does appear in the work on Algeria, the main influence on Bourdieu appears to be from Weber's comparative sociology of religion, including Weber's commentaries on the sociology of law. Bourdieu's analysis of the differences between *Shari'a* and Kabyle customary law with respect to women and inheritance was probably influenced by Weber. Bourdieu did not pursue any subsequent empirical, specifically ethnographic, research that engaged with religion with the possible exception of the study of Catholic bishops with M. de Saint Martin in 1982. Bourdieu undertook an empirical study of his home town Denguin in France in 1959 and 1960, publishing the work in 2002 as a collection of essays. Although this work subsequently led Bourdieu to think more seriously about the emotional relations between biography and research, this study of marriage strategies did not involve any significant discussion of the role of religion in peasant life (Jenkins, 2006).

Rey (2007: 57) has summed up Bourdieu's legacy in the study of religion by saying that his contribution was based on two firm convictions: 'that religion in the modern world is in decline; and that the ultimate function is to help people make sense of their position in the social order'. These two notions could be said to be a crude combination of Marx's view of religion as an opium of the people and Weber's treatment of religion as an aspect of power struggles between social groups over legitimacy. In this respect, the dominant influence was Weber, not Marx, and unsurprisingly the attention of most commentators has been focused on 'Une interpretation de la theorie de la religion selon Max Weber' (Bourdieu, 1971), a revised version of which was translated as 'Legitimation and Structured Interests in Weber's Sociology of Religion' (Bourdieu, 1987a).

Bourdieu's sociological reflections on religion have to be seen within the larger context of French secularism, that is, within the tradition of *laicité* and French republicanism. After the Second World War, the legacy of occupation and resistance meant that Marxist and other critical theories were far more prominent in intellectual life in France than elsewhere. For the left, religion has meant in practice Roman Catholicism which, for obvious reasons, has been associated with French conservatism, both political and cultural. The fact that France has been more deeply divided politically between left and right is also reflected in the development in France of a specific tradition of 'religious sociology' rather than 'sociology of religion'. In this French tradition, religious sociology was primarily an arm of the pastoral outreach of the Catholic Church, providing useful sociological data on church attendance, recruitment, belief and so on. These data were then used to identify regions of low adherence to the Church and thereby to make missionary activity more effective. Among the left in France, there has been the justifiable suspicion that the sociological study of religion has not been – and possibly cannot be – a neutral or objective inquiry, because belief and investigation have become hopelessly entwined. This situation led Bourdieu to the conclusion that a science of religion was a contradiction in terms and that religion therefore was not a suitable topic for sociology. In a lecture to the French Association of Religious Sociology, which was subsequently published as 'Sociologues de la croyance et croyances de sociologues', Bourdieu (1987b) cast doubt on any sociological capacity to understand the institutions of religion without the intervention of the screen of belief. Those sociologists who were Catholic could by definition not study the Catholic Church, while those who had left the Church might be equally 'contaminated' by belief – or more so. Finally, those sociologists who had never had any connection with Roman Catholicism would either not be interested in the topic or would miss important aspects of the phenomena out of ignorance. It follows that religion cannot be studied by sociologists! As Danièle Hervieu-Léger (2000: 14) points out, however, this lecture was a clever professional intervention, but not a convincing account of the epistemological issues involved. The same arguments might apply, for example, to the study of sexuality. It would mean that gay sociologists could never study homosexuality or that prisons could never be studied by sociologists with a criminal record. And in any case Bourdieu himself went on to publish some thirteen articles on religion – just to disprove his own argument?

This also opens up the question, ironically, about Bourdieu's own political commitments. For example, in secular republican France, the Islamic veil is an inescapable problem, because it signifies the injection of religion, which is a private matter from a secular perspective, into the public domain. Bourdieu is reported to have regarded the debate about the veil as merely a smokescreen hiding a more sinister problem about race and ethnicity in French politics (Laurence and Vaisse, 2006: 163). However, this response has been criticised by Christian Joppke (2009: 28) as a 'knee-jerking charge of discrimination and exclusion' which 'obscures the fact that Muslim integration in France has been stunningly successful, at least in socio-cultural terms'. By comparison with Muslims in Britain and Germany, France's approach to schooling, the veil and broader questions of citizenship appears to be successful in the sense that, for example, the majority of Muslims place their French secular identity before their religious identity and believe that French democracy works relatively well. However, it is difficult for the left to accept such empirical findings. The decision to ban the *berqa* in public places in France in 2010 may of course damage relations between mainstream society and France's Muslim population.

One further issue with Bourdieu's approach is that it concentrated too much on formal positions, institutions and organised churches

(Dillon, 2001). Bradford Verter (2003: 151) made a similar criticism when he observed that 'Bourdieu perceives religion almost exclusively in organisational terms ... This leaves little room for imagining lay people as social actors capable, for example, of manipulating religious symbols on their own behalf.' In addition, Bourdieu had, unlike Weber, relatively little interest in the comparative study of religion and hence his work was to a large extent confined to Western Christianity. It might be more correct to say that his thinking about religion was confined to French Catholicism. Bourdieu's actual interests did not engage with the issues of explaining religious revivalism globally, the religions of the dispossessed, the restoration of spirit worship in Vietnam, liberation theology in Latin America, Solidarity in Poland and so forth. Bourdieu was obviously influenced by Marx throughout his sociological research (Lane, 2000). Marx's analysis of class and religion was compatible with Bourdieu's own approach to class, priesthood and the struggle to legitimise the symbolic power of the Church, but Bourdieu is probably less sympathetic to the Marxist notion that religion is the sigh of the oppressed creature and the heart of a heartless world. Religion is as much about protest against inequality and opposition to oppression as it is about the legitimacy of power. In arguing that a modern capitalist society is fundamentally secular, he borrowed from Weber in thinking about struggles over symbolic capital. In fact, he appropriated Weber's notions about the struggles between priest, prophets and sorcerers as a general model of the conflicts over status within the cultural field.

Religion, for Bourdieu, defines people and situates them in the social order. Both the secularisation argument and the idea about defining and inserting people in the social structure are similar to arguments put forward by Louis Althusser. Although there may be no direct or sustained intellectual connection between Althusser, structuralist Marxism and Bourdieu, there is an important analytical parallel between Althusser's theory of ideology and Bourdieu's interpretation of religion. In his development of Marx's theory of ideology, Althusser constructed the idea of the 'interpellation' of the subject. For Althusser, the functions of ideology are unchanging through human history or, as he said, 'ideology has no history' (1971: 150). The purpose of ideology is simply to constitute a subject and he explained this process in terms of the notion of hailing a subject or interpellation. For example, when a teacher shouts out to a pupil 'Pay attention!' and then the student turns towards the teacher, this simple fact of hailing the student creates a subject. But this very recognition as a subject is already a 'misrecognition' (*meconnaissance*) since the individual is always-already born as the subject of an ideology. Althusser illustrated this notion from Christianity by noticing that, in hearing the Voice of God, an individual receives instruction about his or her place in the world and what that person must do to become reconciled with Jesus Christ (Althusser, 1971: 166). By becoming subjected to themselves, individuals become subjects. Althusser in this respect conceived ideology in terms of an imaginary relationship representing the connections between individuals and their actual or real conditions of existence (p. 153). Finally, Althusser refused to see ideology as merely a collection of ideas, insisting instead that ideology is embodied in actions and behaviours that are governed by certain dispositions. In fact, ideas simply disappear, so to speak, in the material practices of persons in specific material settings. This idea of interpellation appears to be exactly Bourdieu's view of how religion functions in relation to the individual.

By interpreting ideology in terms of the dispositions that determine social actions, Althusser's theory of ideology appears to anticipate Bourdieu's notion of habitus fairly exactly. In short, to understand religion – for example, religious orthodoxy – we should not attend to the formal beliefs (or doctrines) which individuals may or may not hold, but consider the ensemble of practices by which individuals occupy a position within a religious field. I see no reason, therefore, to accept David Swartz's assertion that 'Bourdieu is not fundamentally Althusserian' (Swartz, 1996: 73). The problem with this relationship to Althusser is that it suggests that Bourdieu has not in fact resolved the traditional conceptual problems of sociology such as the agency/structure division. Similar concerns have been expressed about Bourdieu's interpretations of literature when it is claimed that he reduces literature to a power struggle. In relation to his commentary on Flaubert, Jonathan Eastwood (2007: 157) complains about Bourdieu's 'excessive reductionism' and claims reasonably enough that 'Literary activity is clearly more than a battleground for the control of power resources' (p. 166). Similar problems are raised about Bourdieu's theory of exchange, and especially with respect to the idea of the gift, where Bourdieu struggled unsuccessfully to deal with the possibility of the disinterested character of gift-giving.

While Bourdieu borrowed from the legacy of a structuralist Marxism, he also incorporated much from Weber, especially the analysis of charisma. The general notion of a religious field within which different social groups compete for control and domination is explicitly derived from Weber's general sociology. However, Bourdieu was critical of what he believed was Weber's psychological treatment of charisma. Allegedly, Weber interprets charisma as a property that belongs to an individual rather than undertaking an examination of the social relations within which charismatic power resides. Bourdieu (1987: 129) claimed that 'Max Weber never produces anything other than a psycho-sociological theory of charisma, a theory that regards it as the *lived* relation of a public to the charismatic personality'. Such a model is, for Bourdieu, defective because it ignores the interaction between prophet and laity. Social change can only take place when prophecy 'has its own generative and unifying principle a *habitus* objectively attuned to that of its addressees' (p. 131). While Bourdieu accepts the notion that charisma is a source of social transformation, it can only be so when the charismatic message is completely attuned to the dispositions or habitus of disciples and followers. However, such an argument appears in fact to rob charisma of precisely its transformative agency by making it look more like traditional authority that is a form of authority that is compatible with existing dispositions (customs, values and mores).

This interpretation of Weber is, in fact, completely misplaced and misleading. To take one crucial feature of the analysis of charisma in *The Sociology of Religion* (1966), Weber recognised that disciples or followers of a charismatic figure want demonstrable and tangible proof of charismatic powers. The authority of charisma tends to get confirmed by the capacity of the leader to provide health, wealth or political success for his (and rarely her) followers. Thus Weber observed that 'it was only under very unusual circumstances that a prophet succeeded in establishing his authority without charismatic authentication, which in practice meant magic. At least the bearers of a new doctrine practically always needed such validation' (p. 47). In other words, in a struggle within the religious field, prophets seek or require social vindication from followers typically through magical means. To understand charisma, we need to appreciate its manifestations in social relationships. Weber identified an interesting paradox here. While the charismatic leader desires a 'pure' commitment from his followers – 'Follow me because I come with the power and authority of God' – the followers ask for clear evidence of such powers that are beneficial to them. In Weber's view, therefore, there is a constant social pressure for 'pure' charisma to become 'mundane' or practical charisma as a consequence of the conflicting interests of leader and followers. This tension is intensified by the frequent competition between charismatic figures for domination. These issues are evident in the New Testament account of Jesus, whose pure charisma is illustrated by his claim – 'It is written but I say unto you' – signifying his overcoming of the Law. Nevertheless Jesus's pure charisma is demonstrated by such magical acts as the transformation of water into wine and the feeding of the five thousand. Although the New Testament shows John the Baptist as preparing the way for Jesus, and thereby subordinating himself to Jesus's ministry, we can interpret the relationship between them as an example of charismatic competition. Weber's analysis of charisma is parallel to his understanding of virtuosi and mass religion, in which the superior charismatic status of the virtuoso is parasitic on the material gifts of the followers, in return for which they can receive a charismatic blessing. Weber's analysis of Buddhist monks in relation to the laity is a very clear example of this interaction (Weber, 1958a).

Within the competitive field, some charismatic leaders will become sorcerers that are religious agents who provide services to an audience, such as healing by magical means. Over time other forms of charismatic activity will be subject to routinisation, being thereby converted into priestly roles. But some charismatic leaders, although subject to pressure from their followers to perform magical acts, will transcend the immediate habitus of their followers to issue a message that is transgressive and innovative. It is only when the message and the audience are not wholly 'attuned' that a charismatic breakthrough could occur at all. Interpretations of the actions of Jesus in the New Testament are obviously deeply divided, but one version would suggest that his followers expected him to take on the messianic role of a king in the line of David, who would drive out the occupying Roman forces. His crucifixion was totally incompatible with those expectations. It is only when a charismatic leader stands over and against the routine expectations of an audience that a radical message can emerge and only in such circumstances can one speak about the Other in history.

Bourdieu and the 'new paradigm' in the sociology of religion

In the last couple of decades, a 'new' paradigm has been heavily promoted in American sociology of religion, which has been commonly referred to as the 'new paradigm' or the economic interpretation of religion. These approaches, which have been influenced in many ways by rational choice theories, are associated with figures such as Rodney Stark, Roger Finke, Laurence Iannaccone and R. Stephen Warner. This 'new' approach is often contrasted disparagingly with 'old' European theories of religion. European sociology, it is alleged, has been too much focused on the symbolic dimensions which social actors require to make sense of life, and by contrast the new paradigm is concerned with the economic dimensions of religious behaviour, including both demand for and supply of religious beliefs, practices and objects. On the whole, the religious markets approach favours supply-side explanations, taking particular note of how state responses to religious pluralism may or may not encourage religious competition. This approach to religion and politics has often produced valuable insights into how states manage religious diversity (Gill, 2008). The economic approach to religion has also generated important insights into how the decline of communism has given rise to a flourishing religious market in post-communist China (Yang, 2007).

Although Bourdieu interprets religions and religious groups as existing within a competitive field, he nevertheless rejected the economic interpretation of religion in American sociology (Hamilton, 2009). Here again it is difficult to see how his criticisms of this approach and his attempt to distance himself from it can be easily sustained. I shall turn now to a more complete account of the development of what is variously known as the rational choice model of religion or the economic approach to religion.

What are the principal theoretical claims of this new paradigm? First, whereas traditional European social theory emphasised the centrality of secularisation to modernisation alongside urbanisation, increasing literacy and democratic politics, the new paradigm takes note of the resilience of religion, not only in the United States but globally. Bryan Wilson, in *Contemporary Transformations of Religion* (1976), argued that religion (that is, Christianity) had survived in America at the cost of its orthodox theological content. Wilson sought to explain the prominence of Christian belief and practice in America by saying that it had simply accommodated belief and practice to the predominant values and lifestyles of a consumer society. In short, the form of Christianity survived but only at the cost of its contents. Such a theory of religion implies that modern religious cultures are inauthentic and make few demands on their followers. One might say that religion, in this secularisation theory, has become merely religiosity. Another version of these arguments appeared in Robert Bellah's account of the growth of a civil religion in America in his 'Civil Religion in America' (1967), and through a subsequent series of influential publications (Bellah and Tipton, 2006) Bellah argued that alongside Christianity there was a vibrant national religion composed of American values, which treated American history as an unfolding of salvation. Christianity remained influential in public life when refracted through the lens of a civil religion. Bellah did not imply, however, that 'civil religion' was somehow less religious or less authentic than traditional Christianity. The new paradigm tends to bypass any discussion of the authenticity of religion, because it concentrates not on the meaning or importance of religion in the lives of individuals, but on the institutional framework within which religion is provided. It is therefore regarded in economic terms as a supply-side and not a demand-side theory of religious growth and decline.

Secondly, the new model directs research attention towards the function of religious or spiritual markets in which there is competition for 'brand loyalty' from consumers of religious meaning, practices and objects. The notion of spiritual markets has been explored empirically and systematically by Wade Roof in his *Spiritual Marketplace* (1999). In any historical understanding of religion and modern society, it is impossible to understand religious behaviour without taking into account the impact of the post-war generation (the 'baby boomers') in American culture, especially on religious practice and consciousness. Roof made an important contribution to the study of religion and generational change in his *A Generation of Seekers* (Roof, 1993), in which the post-war generations were defined as religious seekers, but also as eclectic in their religious 'tastes'. The 'culture wars' of the post-war period reorganised the map of mainstream religion in North America just as they challenged establishment culture generally. American denominational pluralism as a spiritual market-place in the absence of an established church continues to encourage organisational innovation and cultural entrepreneurship. The new paradigm emphasises the importance of the absence of an established church in American constitutional history and hence the importance of an open religious market in which competition is endemic.

The implication of the theory is that, paradoxically, the more a religion demands from its adherents, the more they will give to an organisation. In terms of a theory of the costs of commitment, the specific contents of a religious message are less important for success than the demands for commitment that it places on its members (Kelley, 1977). Ultimately, the costliness of commitment is measured by control over members' lifestyles, the development of a strong church and the seriousness of religious involvement. Although this thesis has been widely influential, Joseph Tamney's research in *The Resilience of Conservative Religion* (2002) provides only partial support for the strong church thesis. According to Tamney, conservative congregations support a traditional gender division of labour and conventional gender identities; in a society which is deeply divided over gender issues, such ideological reassurance can be psychologically attractive. Furthermore, given the general uncertainties of everyday life in modernity, the certainties of religious teaching on morality can also be psychologically supportive and comforting.

Thirdly, these sociological ideas about religious markets, demand for religious services and consumption of religious phenomena are primarily influenced by rational choice theory as an approach to modern spirituality. The paradigm has several interesting substantive claims, such as the notion that the religious demand for meaning is more or less constant across time – that is, the demand for meaning will remain more or less static (Finke and Stark, 1992; Stark and Finke, 2000). One cannot explain religious change by reference to the demand for meaning, which is seen to be constant. Hence variations in religious behaviour are influenced by supply rather than by demand. Religious pluralism in America, by offering innumerable outlets for religious taste, promotes greater involvement. The theory, in making a useful distinction between demand for and supply of religious products, effectively explains the proliferation of religious groups in the United States, switching between denominations by customers, the inflationary character of the market and the resulting hybridisation and experimentation that is characteristic of modern religiosity. Unlike popular forms of spirituality, fundamentalist churches succeed because of their strictness, that is, by the exacting demands they make on their members. Religions of high demand, such as Jehovah's Witnesses, aim to avoid the free-rider problem – joining without paying – by monopolising the commitment of their followers (Iannaccone, 1994).

In summary, the rational model of religious behaviour in competitive markets states that institutional pluralism, such as the American situation, strengthens and sustains the religious economy, and that monopoly, such as an established church, is inefficient. There are, in fact, no truly effective monopolies, only situations where religious markets are regulated. Historical variations in religious behaviour over time are best explained by institutional variations in the supply than by changes in individual religious needs for meaning and other religious services. Finally, secularisation is best described as 'desacralisation', but this development does not necessarily bring about any change in the behaviour of individuals.

The new model of religious behaviour in terms of rational choice assumptions has been subject to considerable theoretical and empirical criticisms and qualifications. These are too numerous to discuss here (Bruce, 1999; Bryant, 2000; Lechner, 2007). There are, however, probably two significant criticisms – one theoretical, relating to the inability of rational choice models to explain the institutional framework within which markets operate and consumer choices are made, and the other empirical, to do with the historical claims of the new model about European patterns of established religion. Rodney Stark's assumption that a society with a state church gives that church a monopoly position is questionable and the assumption that monopoly is an imposition on a society is dubious. If we look at the church in Poland, Russia and Serbia, we can see that in the religious field the monopolistic status of established churches is in fact variable and dependent on context. Steve Bruce's criticisms show that the empirical claims of rational choice theory, especially about the relationship between religious activity and competition or deregulation, are subject to many empirical qualifications.

The idea that competitive religious markets, like secular economic markets, automatically enhance choice of services, quality of products and efficiency of services is questionable. The majority of Pentecostal sects work in an unregulated institutional vacuum where other organised denominations and established churches are often absent. The religious field of charismatic movements, fundamentalist groups and Pentecostal sects is a market which is highly deregulated and in many respects free of competition. These evangelical or charismatic churches often flourish in economically depressed areas where other, more institutionalised, denominations are simply absent. Lack of competition in these inner-city areas with a clientele from the underclass may be the context in which these charismatic groups flourish. In brief, there is no obvious relationship between competition and religious dynamism.

We might, despite these criticisms, concede that the new paradigm has important, and testable, features (Beckford, 2003; Warner, 2004). It has produced some interesting insights intro the deregulated Chinese market in a period of post-communist regulation, but is it a new model? The idea of a religious supermarket was originally developed by Peter Berger in his analysis of the crisis of religious plausibility. The crisis of these 'plausibility structures' was produced by individuals 'shopping around' to satisfy their spiritual needs. Berger (1969: 137) wrote that 'the religious tradition which previously could be authoritatively imposed now has to be *marketed*. It must be "sold" to a clientele that is no longer constrained to "buy". The pluralistic situation is, above all, a *market*.' In other words, the transition from monopoly to competition seriously undermined authority. This approach provides creative ways of understanding the relationship between the state and religion, because the supply side of religion is often dependent on state policies towards religious competition in civil society. Although the new paradigm has produced interesting insights into many aspects of religious markets, the paradigm has also been criticised precisely because of its emphasis on free markets, individual choice and subjectivity (Bastian, 2006; Robertson, 1992b).

Because Bourdieu also concentrated on the competition over symbolic capital in the religious field, it might be argued that there is a strong parallel between his notion of a religious field and the rational model of a religious market. The counter-argument would hold that Bourdieu's theory is somewhat different because it does not assume the rational social actor of micro-economics who makes individual consumer choices in a free market. The distinctive characteristic of Bourdieu's theory is the idea of 'structuring structures' shaping the dispositions of the social actor. The contribution, therefore, of Bourdieu to the sociology of religion is the idea of religious interests and the role of institutions in organising the field. In my view, his essays on religion actually serve to pinpoint the real problem in Bourdieu's work, namely its failure to overcome the traditional dichotomies of sociological theory – action and structure, on the one hand, and materialism and idealism on the other. We might frame this comment by asking whether his sociology of religion was more shaped by the economic sociology of Marx and Weber or by the cultural sociology of Durkheim, Mauss and Maurice Merleau Ponty.

I have already suggested that there is little to distinguish Bourdieu's notion of religion as the consecration of economic inequality through the *illusio* of theological dogma and that for Bourdieu, as for Althusser, the individual is inserted into a place in the social field by the interpellations of religion. This legacy of Marx points to the deterministic undercurrent of Bourdieu's work. To quote again and at some length from the essay on Weber and religious interests, 'Competition for religious power owes its specificity ... to the fact that what is at stake is the monopoly of the legitimate exercise of the power to modify, in a deep and lasting fashion, the practice and world-view of lay people, by imposing on and inculcating in them a particular religious habitus' (Bourdieu, 1987: 126). This formulation of religion as ideology suffers from all the problems that have attended 'the dominant ideology thesis' in Marxist sociology (Abercrombie, Hill and Turner, 1980). It takes for granted the effective functioning of a dominant ideology; it assumes ideologies are primarily directed at the subordinate class; it assumes that the subordinate class cannot effectively understand their exploitation and subordination; and finally it cannot easily explain resistance and opposition except in a circular functionalist fashion, namely in terms of some failure of ideology. It neglects the alternative possibility, identified by Marx, that the dull compulsion of everyday life – such as the need of embodied agents for sleep and food – is sufficient to limit sustained resistance.

In rejecting the social actor of classical economics and developing his own analysis of hexis, habitus and practice, can we argue that there is an alternative component in Bourdieu's theory that is not just the legacy of mechanistic interpretations of religious ideology? Can we argue that in his notions of practice and habitus, Bourdieu drew on a tradition that included Wittgenstein, Durkheim, Mauss and Merleau Ponty and as a result formulated a more sophisticated view of religious practice? Can the concept of habitus lift Bourdieu's theory out of simple determinism? While Bourdieu gives us, through his emphasis on embodied action, a much richer and more satisfying description of the social actor than one can find in the world of economic theories of rational action, habitus does not as a concept escape the problem of determinism. Bourdieu allows for the fact that social actors are reflexive and that they engage in strategies that involve choice; the reflexivity of social actors does not allow them to escape from the logic of the situation – from the structural determination of the game within which strategies are played out. He provides no example of how and where social actors might change the structuring structures within a field of competition. No charismatic breakthrough can be explained by Bourdieu's sociology of religion and hence it is difficult to believe that in his development of the sub-discipline of religion the principle of reflexive sociology operates in any obvious or demonstrable fashion. Bourdieu's attempt to 'sociologise' charisma distorts Weber's typology of prophet, priest and sorcerer.

The basic issue is that Weber had to retain some notion of the difference between genuine and corrupted or fake charisma in order to recognise the difference between the radical transformation of history by charismatic intervention and the magical manipulation of charisma for mundane ends. In this sense, the sociology of religion is also stuck with the problem of 'false prophets'. We might reasonably compare Weber's notion of 'charismatic breakthrough' with Alain Badiou's notion of 'the event' as that moment that divides history through the 'eventual statement' that he explores, for example, in the life of Saint Paul. The 'Christ-event' changes the nature of the real and Paul, who is our contemporary, lays the foundations of the universal (Badiou, 2003). Although Badiou's language here is complex, he does recognise the significance of the 'eventual statement' in Saint Paul's letters as 'Christ is Risen!' (Badiou, 2005). Without some large notion of an eventful charismatic breakthrough, we are left with the rather uninteresting definition of a charisma as any person who is presumed by a collection of adherents to have some extraordinary qualities. In brief, Bourdieu transforms Weber's theory of charisma into a rather conventional theory of religious institutions and their struggle to monopolise the power of the symbolic.

Conclusion: making use of Bourdieu

Much of the debate about religion in modern society has been dominated by philosophers who typically neglect anthropological and sociological research on religion. Philosophical commentaries on religion, for example from Richard Rorty, Gianni Vattimo and Jürgen Habermas, have no empathy for the ethnographic study of religion in modern anthropology. In particular, they neglect religious practice in favour of the idea that the problem of religion is a question of belief. Whereas the analysis of religion in Durkheim and Wittgenstein pinpointed the importance of religious practices, the concentration on belief to the exclusion of religious practice is a major defect of these contemporary philosophical approaches. Belief can only survive if it is embedded in practice and practice can only survive if it is embodied in the everyday world (Turner, 2008a). This argument seems to me to be the central but unintended conclusion of twentieth-century anthropology, especially in the work of Mary Douglas. Religion in Western society is weak because it has become de-ritualised, cut off from a religious calendar and disconnected from the human life-cycle. Pierre Bourdieu did not make a major contribution to the sociology of religion. His notions of embodiment, habitus, practice and field offer a fruitful way of thinking about religion which avoids many of the pitfalls that one finds in recent philosophical approaches to religion. However, Bourdieu failed ultimately to transcend the problems that he so skilfully identified in classical sociological theory.

Religion, state and post-secularity

7 | *The secularisation thesis*

Introduction: the secular in historical and comparative perspective

There are many social and political reasons that may explain why the topic of secularisation has become a major issue in the humanities and social sciences and why it has also become such a critical problem of *— Is it?* modern political life. One obvious reason is that in the modern world many important social movements find their inspiration in religious ideas and they are often directed by religious leaders. It is, of course, often difficult to separate out the nationalist, ethnic and political dimensions of what we call 'religious movements' that are the carriers of social protest, and hence one has to be cautious about attributing religious causes to political phenomena or religious motives to their adherents. One example would be the plight of the Hui in Yunnan and Uighurs in Xinjiang in modern-day China (Berlie, 2004) or the enforced use of Islam in Chechnya to define a form of ethno-nationalism that is still acceptable to the state in Putin's Russia. In any discussion of secularisation, we have to keep in mind that much of the debate has been generated not just by the growth of radical forms of Islam, but more generally by the rise of fundamentalism (Marty and Appleby, 1991). What has been identified as a crisis of liberalism around the separation of the church and state is nevertheless closely connected with the Western response to the growing influence of Islam in Europe.

The debate about religion is connected to wider changes in Western societies as a whole. In this respect, Talal Asad's analysis of the *Formations of the Secular* (2003) has drawn our attention to the ways in which this debate about religion in general and Islam in particular masks issues that relate to how Europeans understand themselves, about the legacy of the Enlightenment and about the role of national-ism in the West. As a result, the current debate about secularisation goes to the heart of a range of unresolved and deeply problematic questions in modernity about how we understand others, how we respect (or do not respect) others and hence about the social and political conditions of tolerance. In short, the 'return of the sacred' raises questions about the liberal tradition of tolerance and the prospects of multiculturalism in modern societies. Although it could be said that all world religions now stand in a problematic relationship to the state in multicultural societies in which citizens and denizens often belong to minorities that are connected to dispersed global networks, the basic political issue has become defined as a Muslim problem – can Muslim minorities be integrated in a mutually satisfactory manner within a secular and liberal environment? There are no easy or simple answers to this question, but we should note that the issue of secularism, religion and politics is not simply a problem for Western intellectuals. Many Muslim intellectuals, such as Abdolkarim Soroush (2000), have also argued that Islam can best flourish in a secular polity rather than in an authoritarian theocracy.

Before one can enter into such detailed considerations, it is important to start with the equally intractable problem of definition, namely to establish the meaning of such basic terms as 'the secular', 'secularism' and 'secularisation' (Smith, 2008). Within the context of European religious history, the notion of the secular was originally applied to the religious who had taken vows to live either for a period or more permanently in the outside world (*saeculum*). These religious people lived outside the cloister while still maintaining the calling within the religious institution itself. This secularisation of priests could in fact assume many forms, including the dispensation of vows in which the priest was no longer under the full panoply of religious obligations. In this historical context, the suppression of religious houses could also be referred to as a process of secularisation. In such cases, the ecclesiastical property was handed over to a secular authority. These ecclesiastical terms help us to understand early notions of the separation between the religious and the world, but they are not entirely relevant to the tasks of the sociology of religion.

The concept of 'secularism' was first defined by George Holyoake in 1846, and the ideas of a 'secular' society grew out of the establishment of the British National Secular Society, which at its peak in the 1880s had a membership of some 6,000 people (Royle, 1974). Holyoake proposed that 'secularism' should simply refer to any social order that was separate from religion without engaging in any direct criticism of religious belief. In more detail, it involved the view that human life could be improved by purely secular means, that science can provide perfectly adequate guidance for this life and that in ethical terms the idea of doing good to others – Kant's moral imperative, for example – requires no religious foundations. Secularism, when under the inspiration of militant atheists such as Charles Bradlaugh, Member of Parliament for Northampton in Great Britain, assumed a more strident, uncompromising and critical relationship to religious belief.

In the nineteenth century, Christian belief came under attack from two very different quarters. The first was from Darwinism, in which the theory of evolution appeared to dispense with any notion of divine creation or the guiding hand of a divine Father. Nature, being subject to the law of the survival of the fittest, had no space for either a Creator God or benevolent Design. The second was the tradition of biblical criticism in which academic scrutiny of the New Testament raised questions about the coherence and authenticity of the biblical text, promoting the idea that biblical inerrancy was not a requirement of Christian faith. In the twentieth century, Christian theology was further challenged by theologians such as Rudolf Bultmann who sought to demythologise Christianity and by Dietrich Bonhoeffer who prepared the way for a God-less theology. In European philosophy, a more strident doctrine of atheism was launched by Friedrich Nietzsche who, through the prophetic figure of Zarathustra, announced the death of God, but Nietzsche's prophetic and poetic claims never had any widespread appeal, whereas his impact on modern intellectual trends has been profound.

In Britain, organised atheism can be said to have come into existence with the establishment of the Secular Society in 1866 by Bradlaugh, who was its first president. Secularism became a public and political issue when Bradlaugh, who had been elected to Parliament, refused to take the Oath of Allegiance which was required in order for him to take his seat in the House, and as a result his constituency was declared vacant. The Oath was eventually abandoned in 1886. However, it was Holyoake who built up the local groups that formed the backbone of the Society. These groups had emerged out of the Owenite and Chartist movements, and the secularism of the Chartists was always subordinate to their political and economic doctrines. In fact Chartism was ultimately a political failure and secularism, especially in Britain, never gained any serious foothold among the urban working class. It is for this reason that it is often suggested that the British working class owed more to John Wesley than to Karl Marx, that is to Methodism rather than to militant socialism. The British working class has consequently been characterised by the absence of any ideological commitment to scientific Marxism or secularism and British society as a whole has been noted for its pragmatism, gradualism and tolerance, unlike Italy, where class differences produced deeper ideological and social divisions (Anderson, 1976).

One might argue that the whole notion of tolerance was a precondition of a secular society in which neither religious nor political dogmatism offers a promising basis for civil peace. Anglicanism, one might argue, offered exactly the theological and social compromise that was suitable to a society otherwise pulled apart by class interest. In England, there has been a long tradition of doctrinal compromise that sought to create a broad national Church capable of absorbing internal differences in belief and practice. The architect of this tradition was Richard Hooker, who most clearly understood and articulated the conditions that underpinned the Elizabethan Settlement. Hooker played an important part in securing a pragmatic compromise with the Puritans to avoid further conflict in the Anglican community. He argued that treating the Bible as the only source of our knowledge of God would open up an endless debate about correct interpretation and would paradoxically drive the faithful towards an extreme individualism (Rasmussen, 2002). Hooker's commitment to a multiplicity of avenues for receiving God's goodness created a broad theological basis for social consensus.

Hooker's tolerant view of the sources of authority had an influence on the evolution of the American Constitution through the early settlement of the colony of Virginia by such figures as Edwin Sandys. Virginia, unlike Puritan New England, was not created by ministers fleeing religious persecution and hence it is not surprising that James Madison, the fourth President of the United States and a co-author of the *Federalist* essays, recommended to Thomas Jefferson that Hooker's *Laws of Ecclesiastical Polity* should be included in the library of the University of Virginia (Dackson, 1999). One can easily see why Hooker's tolerant position chimed well with the American Founding Fathers, because he had argued that laws are simply the products of reason, and as circumstances change so must the law change. When he applied this view not to the Church but to civil society he concluded that, where there is no general consent then there is no legitimate compulsion to follow a law that no longer has communal support. John Locke adopted Hooker's arguments to support the doctrine of resistance in the Glorious Revolution in the United Kingdom (Tanner, 1960). However, Hooker's doctrines about ecclesiastical organisation provided further ammunition against British colonial rule and Jefferson's separation of church and state can also be seen as a pragmatic solution to the ever-present prospect of religious conflict.

The English Civil War of the seventeenth century and the American War of Independence created a foundation for secularisation that was obviously unlike the experience of Roman Catholicism in relation to the French Revolution and the creation of a secular state. Both France and Germany were probably more exposed to the Enlightenment than Britain – the exception being the influence of David Hume. In Europe, the conflicts between Protestant and Catholic brought Rousseau in *The Social Contract* ([1762] 1973) to argue that the state should not be concerned with the truth of religion but only in its social functions. A state that was concerned not to breed division between its citizens should embrace a civil religion to promote domestic harmony. In the period leading up to the French Revolution, writers such as the Marquis de Condorcet developed the idea of human perfectability and the need for social reform, including the enfranchisement of women. For Enlightenment figures such as Voltaire and Diderot, Christianity was irrational and based on a false understanding of empirical reality, and hence Enlightenment rationalism sharpened the distinction between revelation and reason as the means of understanding natural and social reality. The Enlightenment associated political intolerance with monotheism in general and Catholicism in particular, and advocated the separation of church and state as a necessary condition of individual liberties. It was the Enlightenment that laid the foundation for the republican ideology of 'liberty, fraternity, equality' and contemporary French secularism. Because France had been based on a confessional state, conflicts around religion have been highly divisive and they partly explain the secular nature of republicanism.

The importance of the idea of laicity (*laicité*) in France also helps us to understand why in republican France the wearing of the veil by

Muslim girls in French schools has become, at least on the surface, a more controversial and problematic political issue than in either Britain or America. The difference between Britain and France can be summed up as a difference between John Locke (freedom from the state) and Rousseau (freedom through the state). This contrast was further elaborated in Isaiah Berlin's famous definition of the difference between negative and positive freedoms. For Berlin, 'Liberty means non-enchroachment; liberty means non-impingement by one person on another' (Hardy, 2002: 53). For Berlin, Rousseau's doctrine of the general will – in giving myself to all, I give myself to nobody – laid the foundation for European dictatorships in which a Leader, who understands my wants better than I do, can forcefully make me free. Thus Rousseau was the 'most sinister and most formidable enemy of liberty in the whole history of modern thought' (Hardy, 2002: 49). The liberal Lockean version of the liberty of negative freedom is quite unlike the republican tradition of positive freedom and in part this difference explains the contrast between Britain and France over veiling and other religious insignia. The British sense of compromise produced the ruling that religious attire was acceptable in schools provided they were consistent with school policy on dress codes, which in practice meant consistent with the school colours! The British experience with respect to multiculturalism therefore brings out the weakness of Berlin's position, since the notion of 'non-encroachment' tells us nothing about how a wider consensus might be created within which negative freedoms could be enjoyed. British liberalism has only served to illuminate the hollow character of multiculturalism in the absence of any overarching shared tradition. The republican tradition was by contrast sharply and clearly proclaimed in March 2004, when the French national assembly passed a law prohibiting the ostensive display of religious symbols or signs in French public schools. The struggle around legislation in France has been drawn-out and complex. The debate has been about whether the prohibition on overt religious symbols applies more appropriately to teachers or to students. However, one might reasonably assume that French Muslims would be deeply alienated from the French secular state and yet, as Christian Joppke (2009) decisively shows, 42 per cent of Muslims think of themselves as French first and Muslim second, 70 per cent of Muslims think that French democracy works well and 80 per cent of French Muslims are comfortable about dating and

Relating
to the church
of us clergy

marrying people of other religions. French republicanism appears to have been more successful than British liberalism in incorporating Muslims into a secular multicultural democracy.

Secularisation is a theory that describes the historical contraction of the power of ecclesiastical institutions and the authority of Christian belief in relation to secular institutions (especially the nation-state) and secular belief (especially natural science). It would appear, therefore, that secularism and secularisation are peculiarly Western 'problems' and therefore have little relevance to Asia – the position taken by Talal Assad, among others. The issue here is made more complicated by the fact that there is no stable agreement among academics about whether the notion of 'religion' applies easily and comfortably to the cultures of Asia. This issue has been endemic to sociology since at least the publication of *The Elementary Forms of Religious Life* in 1912 when Émile Durkheim ([1912] 2001) struggled with the problem of classical Buddhism. Belief in a High God is largely absent from Asian religious cultures and Confucianism is a state ideology relating to social order and respect for authority (Kapstein, 2005). Similarly, Buddhism may be thought of as 'the Righteous Way' or the *Dharma* that develops meditation practices to regulate desire. Daoism is typically a set of beliefs and practices promoting health and longevity through various exercises such as breathing techniques (*gigon*). Japanese Shintoism might also be defined as a state ideology rather than as a 'religion' in this Western sense.

However, these arguments in favour of anthropological relativism ignore the impact of globalisation over the last two centuries. Firstly, British, French and Dutch colonialism left behind a legacy of European law and administration based on the separation of church and state throughout their Asian colonies. Secondly, the early development of the idea of citizenship in China and Japan was based on the German experiment with social security policies and on the liberal ideas of Herbert Spencer. Thirdly, Marxism–Leninism clearly had an impact on the revolutionary traditions of China and Vietnam and contributed to the suppression of religion in the communist period. Finally, missionary work has throughout the period of European colonialism carried Western ideas about church and state, reason and revelation, and sacred and profane to Asian shores. The notion, therefore, that one can draw a neat and convenient distinction between East and West is naive and misleading.

Furthermore, it is important to preserve some distinction between religion and the sacred. If religion is the ensemble of beliefs and practices that bind people together into a moral community – to quote Durkheim's famous definition – then the sacred refers to those experiences of the holy that periodically transform the lives of individuals and social groups by disclosing some aspect of divinity. This idea was classically described by Rudolf Otto in his *The Idea of the Holy* ([1923] 2003). The experience of this world fills the individual with a sense of awe and wonderment, but the 'message' of this sacred world is ultimately ineffable (Turner, 2009c). From a sociological point of view, while it is possible to measure religious decline quantitatively in terms of religious membership and church attendance, it is clearly difficult to describe and more difficult still to measure whether the sacred has also atrophied with the spread of urban, industrial and secular society.

The sociology of secularisation

As I have demonstrated in the opening chapters of this volume, the sociological study of religion and modernisation lies at the very root of the sociological imagination being an important topic in the work of Marx, Weber, Durkheim and Simmel. With the collapse of European feudalism, the development of an industrial society, the decline in the authority of the Catholic Church and the revolutionary overthrow of the 'old regime' in France, sociologists such as Auguste Comte and Claude H. Saint-Simon asked themselves what new consensus might sustain society. Their answer involved a complex and ambitious mixture of science, positivism and the 'religion of humanity' (Wernick, 2001). The crisis of industrialism was taking place at all levels – intellectual, institutional and emotional – and sociology was seen to have a unique position in understanding the laws of social change by which France could be guided out of the abyss of political turmoil. Two novels – Honoré de Balzac's *The Centenarian* in 1822 and Mary Shelley's *Frankenstein* in 1818 – signalled the decay of the old order, dissected the social and moral problems thrown up by new technology and anticipated the birth of science fiction as the genre of modernity. Balzac's work, published under the pseudonym of Horace de Saint-Aubin in four volumes, transforms the traditional religious paradigm of the search for immortality into a purely scientific quest within specific

Cartesian limits and at the same time recognised the inward turn of science to deal with the problematic status of mind (Chatelain and Slusser, 2005). It would not be preposterous to date the modern age of secularism from France in the 1820s, which was simultaneously the birthplace of positivism, sociology and socialism.

A cult formed around Saint-Simon and carried the ideas of the religion of humanity and the theory of social evolution as a spiral alternating between critical and organic periods to a new generation of French intellectuals. Saint-Simon had sought a scientific basis for morality and promoted the idea that, just as the natural world was governed by Newtonian gravity, the social world was governed by a force of universal attraction. This secular principle was to replace the Pauline conception of love in Christianity. We can see, therefore, that Comtean sociology combined a theory of secularisation as a social process and a commitment to secularism as a moral system in which secular principles would ultimately replace the idea of revelation in Christianity. His secularism was summarised in his final work on the *Nouveau christianisme* of 1825, in which traditional Catholicism was to be replaced by a communitarianism of love.

These early doctrines of French socialism were influential in the intellectual development and political outlook of Karl Marx (1818–83). However, a more dominant figure in the philosophical background to the Marxist understanding of the sociology of capitalist society and the historical role of Christianity was G. W. F. Hegel. The philosophical study of religion was, for Hegel, an important stage in the historical development of human understanding. While different cultures gave religion a different content, Christianity was a world religion. In Hegel's dialectical scheme, the increasing self-awareness of the Spirit was an outcome of the historical development of Christianity. For Hegel, Christianity was the highest and most comprehensive historical stage in the emergence of human reflexivity. Marx took over Hegel's historical account of consciousness but turned it on its head to give a materialistic interpretation in which the socialist consciousness of the working class would replace Christian spirituality.

Marx's view of Christianity was mediated by Ludwig Feuerbach. In *The Essence of Christianity* (1957), Feuerbach developed the idea that Christian theology was a spiritual inversion of the material world in which man's powers had been attributed to God. From Feuerbach, he also acquired a view of humanity in terms of material practice; to survive, humans must constantly labour to reproduce themselves and their society (Wartofsky, 1977). Marx, in volume one of *Capital* ([1867] 1974), went on to elaborate these ideas to construct a theory of reification to describe this upside-down world and to grasp the notion that in capitalism there was the development of a fetish of commodities. He claimed that the 'religious world is but the reflex of the real world. For a society based upon the production of commodities ... Christianity with its *cultus* of abstract man, more especially in its bourgeois developments, Protestantism, Deism, etc, is the most fitting form of religion' (p. 83). From Marx's 'critical criticism' has flowed a long heritage of Marxist analysis in which religion has been interpreted as an alienation of human capacities which are re-ascribed to the gods, creating a society in which religion functions to obscure the real relations of economic exploitation. In Marxism, overcoming religion is thus the first step to human liberation.

Although there have been many crude imitations of Marx's ideas among socialist intellectuals, including Karl Kautsky and Joseph Stalin, there have also been brilliant applications of Marx's embryonic ideas about religion in relation to social class. In *The Hidden God* ([1956] 1964), Lucien Goldmann explored the relationship between Racine and Pascal in terms of the rising and falling fractions of the dominant social class in France. These Marxist ideas, including Goldmann's analysis of the pessimism of Pascal's view of the world, played an important part in Alasdair MacIntyre's studies of *Marxism and Christianity* (1995) and *Secularization and Moral Change* (1967). MacIntyre's early analysis of religious change suggested that the urbanisation of Britain with the Industrial Revolution had led to the destruction of the forms of communal life 'to which religion had given symbolic expression', and that the general function of religion 'is always at least an expression of a society's moral unity, and it lends to that unity a cosmic and universal significance and justification' (1967: 12). MacIntyre, through his engagement with both Catholicism and Marxism, came to elaborate a coherent theory of secularisation as the separation of the sacred and the secular, arguing that 'if our religion is fundamentally irrelevant to our politics, then we are recognising the political as a realm outside the reign of God ... A religion which recognises such a division, as does our own, is one on the point of dying'. In his later work, MacIntyre went on to demonstrate, in *After*

Virtue (1984), that a secular society was one in which there was no authoritative language within which to settle moral disputes and that in contemporary society the dominance of emotivism in philosophy – all moral judgements are nothing other than expressions of preference or feeling – is the consequence of secularisation.

Although these developments provided a powerful set of ideas within which to think about Western secularism, the creation of a full-blown sociology of secularisation first appeared in the theory of the rationalisation and demystification of the world of Max Weber. In simple terms, this development meant that more and more aspects of everyday life came under the influence of science and that explanations of the world relied less and less on religious presuppositions. In more complex terms, he argued that in such a society there was a progressive differentiation of the spheres of life into separate sectors of aesthetics, religion, the economy, politics and so forth. Over these 'value spheres', religion had relatively little authority and control. The result of these structural developments in the differentiation of society is the emergence of the disenchantment of the world in which humans are increasingly confronted by the meaninglessness of the world. It is this pessimistic or fateful view of the world that has attracted more interest than his more descriptive sociology of secularisation. It has been argued that Weber embraced a fatalistic analysis of modernity in implying that the unintended consequences of action have negative consequences for human life (Turner, 1996). The best example is the Protestant ethic thesis, in which the unintended consequence of piety was the emergence of rational capitalism in which human life is eventually converted into a standardised existence and society appears in the form of an iron cage. In the transition from community (*gemeinschaft*) to association (*gesellschaft*), we have in Western capitalism lost our roots in a communal world of emotional social attachments. Secularisation in this framework is the erosion of those strong communal bonds that wrapped individuals into meaningful social groups. Placing this argument in its biographical context, Weber in his youth enthusiastically embraced the world of all male society – military service, the university brotherhoods, student drinking clubs and the society of male university colleagues. For Weber, early warrior societies produced closely knit social groups in which there was a strong and enduring relationship between the cultivation of the soil, the family and the affective life of communal living.

The problem was that the modern rational world was eroding these close relationships between humans and nature, and hence the disenchantment of the world became a corrosive dimension of modernity (Radkau, 2009). We can in this framework better understand Weber's theory of charisma as also a theory of secularisation, since charismatic power was a basic feature of leadership in these pre-modern communities. In modern political life, bureaucratic authority and rational–legal norms determine political action.

Weber's sociology of routinised charisma was significantly influenced by the God-less philosophy of Nietzsche (Eden, 1983; Hennis, 1988). There is a striking parallel between Nietzsche and Weber in terms of both life and philosophy. Both men retired from their professorial positions at an early age as a result of ongoing health problems that were both physical and mental, and they sought recovery from mental strain through convalescence in the Alps. Both men had unfulfilled ambitions to significantly influence the public sphere – Nietzsche as a prophet and Weber as a charismatic politician. As critics of German, or more precisely Prussian, society, there is an important convergence in their ideas. While Nietzsche developed a battery of ideas around the will to power, nihilism, the overman, the soul and fate to form a critical theory of an emerging industrial society, his principal concern was the disappearance of the heroic individual who had achieved self-mastery through struggle against conventional morality and modern society (Stauth and Turner, 1986). At times Nietzsche argued, in a manner wholly parallel to Weber, that the heroic individual was cultivated in the ancient world, in warrior societies and in the military. This view was Nietzsche's version of Weber's notion of 'personality and life orders'. Against the view that the ancient world was one of tranquillity, Nietzsche showed that Greek society was characterised by an endless struggle between eroticism and passion (Dionysus) and rationality and formalism (Apollo), and that any healthy life for the individual would require some reconciliation of these two dimensions of human nature. The problem with modern society was that the emergence of an industrial civilisation and the growth of a mass society had eclipsed the opportunities for heroic individualism. This was Nietzsche's version of the theory of charisma.

In his approach to the history of Christianity, Weber was, however, directly influenced by the work of his colleague Ernst Troeltsch, who had argued in *The Social Teachings of the Christian Churches* (1931) that the institutional development of the Christian West could be seen in terms of the dynamic between the church and the sect. Against the atrophied religion of the ecclesiastical organisation, sects periodically arose to renew the genuine foundations of religion, thereby demanding greater commitment and loyalty from their followers. Over time, these sects begin to acquire the formal characteristics of a church and hence the dynamic oscillation between church and sect is once more re-enacted. Troeltsch went on to argue that with the decline of the Universal Church, this dynamic was replaced by religious individualism in the form of modern mysticism.

We can see that this view of sectarianism is in fact a theory of secularisation, since the charismatic enthusiasm of sect development is constantly being diluted by the institutional emergence of the church form. This theme was eventually taken up in the sociology of denominationalism in which the denomination was regarded as an important addition to Troeltsch's model and provided a more appropriate model of religious development in the United States. The sociology of denominations subsequently became a major feature of the sociology of religion in America, where H. R. Niebuhr's *The Social Sources of Denominationalism* (1957) and Liston Pope's *Millhands and Preachers* (1942) were regarded as classic contributions. Denominations do not enjoy the same general authority over society as the church and hence they can be regarded as further evidence of secularisation. A further development in American sociology was the attention to cults (Dawson, 2009). The fragmentation of religion in modern societies into a myriad of cults also attests to the erosion of institutionalised religion and its place in the public sphere.

Perhaps the most influential work on the church-sect typology and secularisation generally was undertaken by Bryan Wilson in a series of publications. Adopting Robert K. Merton's model of social action and adaptation to social values, Wilson published one of the most prominent approaches to sect formation in his 'An Analysis of Sect Development' (1959). He examined sects that, for example, retreated from the world, challenged the world or accommodated to it. He argued that the conversionist sects, which attempt to transform the world by converting people to Christianity, for example early Methodism, were also the most exposed to the process of institutionalisation and that their eventual transformation into denominations was consequently more rapid than sects which withdrew from society. Wilson combined this analysis of sectarianism with a more general theory of secularisation, in which he argued that the decline of church membership and the erosion of the authority of the church could only be allayed temporarily by sectarian enthusiasm and that in modern society denominationalisation in fact meant the decline of the overarching embrace of a Universal Church. By contrast, the survival of Christian commitment in America and the impact of Protestantism on American politics were only possible by surrendering the orthodox core of the faith to the exigencies of secular consumerism (Wilson, 1966). Success in terms of denominational growth meant accommodating to, not triumphing over, secular society.

In the ensuing debate about secularisation, Wilson has often been unfairly accused of promoting a restrictive, partial and perhaps jaundiced view of the decline of the Christian Church. One valid criticism of Wilson's approach, however, was that it concentrated too much on formal institutions, thereby defining secularisation in terms of the erosion of official religion. Subsequently, sociologists sought to demonstrate the importance of what was called 'implicit religion', namely an unofficial religion of everyday life (Bailey, 1983). Similar issues were raised by Thomas Luckmann in *The Invisible Religion* (1967). Another approach was to suggest that, especially in Britain, religious behaviour in a secular society could be summed up under the heading 'believing without belonging' (Davie, 1994).

In the United States, the principal exponents of secularisation were Peter Berger and Thomas Luckmann. Their argument was originally founded on the exploration of the sociology of knowledge, in which they emphasised the notion of the social construction of reality. By combining various aspects of classical sociology with the philosophical anthropology of Arnold Gehlen, they examined the fact that everyday life is precarious and that its constructed characteristics are normally hidden from view (Berger and Luckmann, 1967). These ideas were developed by Berger (1967) in his sociology of religion to describe the social world as a 'sacred canopy'. In modern societies, the traditional canopy is under considerable stress, because the 'plausibility structures' that support that overarching canopy are fragile. Secularisation involves the gradual erosion of the religious framework of modern society and the religious legitimacy of modern institutions is subject to constant questioning. In his *A Rumor of Angels* (1969), he left open the possibility of the intimation of the divine in the everyday world, especially around issues of fundamental human concern, such as death and suffering.

In 'From Secularity to World Religions' (1980), Berger revised his interpretation of secularisation, recognising the continuing import- ance of religion world-wide and the force of religion in the Third World. His acceptance of this global view also forced him to think more deeply about religion outside the Judaeo-Christian framework of his earlier work. As with many Western scholars, Berger's views about secularisation were shaken by the eruption of the Iranian Revolution in 1979. The consequence for Berger is the necessity of rejecting a unilinear model of modernisation and rethinking secularisation theory to recognise the possibility of counter-modernisation and counter- secularisation. Some aspects of this rethinking were published in *The Desecularization of the World*, which he edited in 1999.

American exceptionalism

The idea of 'American exceptionalism' has typically referred to the absence of a socialist movement in the United States – a thesis associated with Seymour Martin Lipset in *The First New Nation* (1963). In this chapter, 'exceptional' refers to the exceptional histor- ical differences between America and Europe in terms of the role of religion in politics and society. Against the background of the decline of mainstream Christianity in Europe, sociological discussion has focused on the question of America's historical, cultural and insti- tutional differences from the European experience. Although church and state were separated, for example by the Virginia Statute on Religious Freedom, religion and politics have been significantly inter- connected in American history. In the absence of any established church, freedom of conscience subsequently became a cornerstone of American democracy. Starting with Alexis de Tocqueville and his journey to America in 1831, European observers have been fascin- ated by the prominence of religion in American public life (Offe, 2005). Tocqueville and his companion Gustave de Beaumont arrived in New York on the pretext of an official visit to study the American penitentiary system. His observations on American society in *Democracy in America* in 1835 and 1840 are widely regarded as the most influential interpretation of democracy in the nineteenth century (Tocqueville, [1835/1840] 2003).

Tocqueville argued that, given the constitutional checks on a powerful state, religion, once separated from politics, played a major part in America's emerging civil society and that the individualism of the Protestant sects was highly compatible with secular democracy and the spirit of equality on the frontier. Protestant churches operated as a buffer against the levelling onslaught of mass egalitarianism. The American Protestant sects offered a sharp contrast to the conservative role of the Catholic Church in resisting the French Revolution. In *The Old Regime and the French Revolution* ([1856] 1955), Tocqueville sought to understand the French Revolution and its descent into Terror by a comparison with the successful revolution in the American War of Independence. The separation of church and state has subsequently figured prominently in the sociological analysis of secularisation, on the one hand, and American exceptionalism, on the other.

In studying American religious history, it is common to refer to various 'Great Awakenings' that in diverse ways achieved a 'revitalisation' of American culture. The first was Puritanism itself and the creation of the American settler experience in which the new colony was to be based on the Covenant. America was the Israel of the New World with a mission to install the Kingdom of God on the new land. This conception of society as ruled by divine law and yet the recognition that membership of the community was nonetheless voluntary provided a religious impetus towards the growth of democracy (Lechner, 1985). While Puritanism is one basis for religious fundamentalism, the First Great Awakening in the eighteenth century was an evangelical movement in that it sought to promote personal piety rather than a reform of society and government. Although the emphasis was on faith rather than belief and practice, this evangelical revival may have contributed to the Revolution in providing a basic national consciousness.

After independence, Protestantism had to find a place in the new republic and the Second Great Awakening was clearly more fundamentalist in seeking to shape the public values of the new society through the conversion of the nation. The First New Nation was to be a 'Righteous Empire' (Marty, 1970) but, given the separation of church and state, religion would work through education and conversion to secure a Christian foundation to society. Despite the constitutional separation of church and state, religion has been deeply entangled in American politics. In his study *The American Civilizing*

Process, Stephen Mennell (2007: 267) observed that 'even at the highest levels in the USA, rhetoric is deployed about a personal God who actively gives direction through prayer. Presidential prayer meetings are publicised, especially at times of international crisis' and that by contrast 'religious belief is regarded in Europe as largely a private matter'. Religion has played an important role in many presidential elections in recent American political history, most notably in the election of Ronald Reagan in 1980 through the influence of the Moral Majority. But religious issues were also significant in the election of President John F. Kennedy in 1960, when questions were raised about the personal independence of a Roman Catholic President. The question of the separation of the church and state also emerged during the 2008 presidential campaign around Mitt Romney, a Republican candidate who was also a member of the Church of Latter-Day Saints. In all of these presidential races for the White House, the candidates have universally supported secularisation (the separation of church and state) and at the same time warmly affirmed their deep religious commitments (Daniel and Holladay, 2008). How might we explain the vitality of religion in American life?

Bryan Wilson (1966) argued that religion had survived in America but at the cost of its orthodox content, that is, Christianity could only persist in America by embracing the secular culture of consumer society. In order to explain this development Wilson appealed to an argument put forward by Will Herberg (1955), for whom the vitality of religion in America was connected with the history of migration. In *Protestant–Catholic–Jew*, Herberg argued that a religious label became inseparable from a secular American identity as wave after wave of migrants arrived in America. In Europe, religion had often provided the basis of national identity, but in America the acquisition of American nationality had received its affirmation through a religious identity. A good and upright American citizen has a religious faith – albeit one severely constrained by secular practice. American denominations provide an associational life that is the social glue connecting every new generation with the nation through denominational affiliation. This attitude towards the positive benefits of religion in American life was frequently asserted by President Eisenhower, who was famously quoted in *The New York Times* in 1952 as saying 'Our government makes no sense unless it is founded on a deeply held religious faith – and I don't care what it is' (Herberg, 1955: 97).

Another version of this argument can be seen in Robert Bellah's analysis of civil religion in America. Developing the notion of civil religion from J.-J. Rousseau's *The Social Contract* ([1762] 1973), Bellah argued that from its inception America had developed a system of beliefs and practices that, while not opposed to Christianity, was neither sectarian nor specifically Christian. Certain key events have defined the content of this civil religion. The Declaration of Independence and George Washington's leadership established the idea of America as a new Israel that had called people out of political bondage. The Founding Fathers have become saints in a political hagiography that celebrates the fundamental values of American history and society. Of Washington the 'Father of his Country', an American writing in 1777 observed: 'Had he lived in the days of idolatry, he would have been worshipped as a god' (Longmore, 1989: 204). The Civil War created the ideas of sacrifice and rebirth as critical components of the civil religion, and the notion of a sacrificial historical burden was reinforced by the loss of American lives in the two World Wars and later in Korea and Vietnam. Subsequently, the Gettysburg National Cemetery and the Arlington National Cemetery have become sacred ground in the national mythology of suffering and sacrifice (Bellah and Tipton, 2006).

Many minorities in America necessarily or at least frequently fall outside this sacred narrative. Although Native Americans went to fight in America's foreign wars in the twentieth century, they have not found a comfortable place in this history of suffering and redemption, and their spirituality is not commonly regarded as an aspect of mainstream religion in America. In fact, most sociological textbooks on American religion rarely include any discussion of these aboriginal traditions. In the modern period, it is also the case that Islam does not sit easily in the American national landscape and it does not fit into the national narrative of redemption.

Any account of the growth of this civil religion should not, however, overshadow the growth of religious fundamentalism in the United States. In the twentieth century, the conservative churches grew rapidly in response to the liberal secularisation of American society, and against these trends fundamentalists held to the literal truth of the Bible, rejected evolutionary thought in science, condemned the decline of the family and the rise of sexual promiscuity, and feared that cultural relativism would contribute to the decline of America as the leading nation (Marsden, 1980). The modern influence of the Christian Right on American politics contrasts sharply with earlier periods. In the decades between the Civil War and the First World War, there was 'the secularisation of American higher education and the loss of Protestant cultural hegemony over the public sphere of American society' (Casanova, 1994: 137). With the urbanisation of America, religious influence declined and the individualistic message of evangelical Christianity did not lend itself to the public discussion of major political and economic issues such as the Great Depression, war and foreign policy.

It was not until later in the century that the arrival of television presented a great evangelical opportunity to Protestantism, which rapidly embraced televangelism and quickly developed expert marketing techniques to reach large audiences. By 1979 there were three significant groups on the New Christian Right – the Moral Majority, Christian Voice and Religious Roundtable. Under the leadership of Jerry Falwell, the Moral Majority raised huge funds. Falwell abandoned his old position in which Christianity had nothing to do with politics and began to articulate a conservative political agenda. Falwell claimed that Christians should do something about the crisis surrounding the family, gender and homosexuality. The result was the eventual transformation of the privatised religion of evangelical Protestantism into the Moral Majority as a public religion. While the secular character of consumer society has not been reversed, certain branches of the Protestant Church (re)entered the public domain over moral issues, especially over homosexuality, alcoholism and general social anomie.

Why did religion come to be influential in American politics from the Reagan election onwards? There is in more recent sociological approaches the so-called market or economic explanation of religious activity that argue that, precisely because America did not have an established church, competition between denominations created a more robust and 'efficient' set of circumstances in American religious life (Finke and Stark, 1992; Stark and Finke 2000; Warner, 2004). Ultimately, the costliness of commitment is measured by the degree of control exercised over members' everyday lives by the church. At the same time, conservative congregations provide ideological support for conventional gender identities and, in a society which is deeply divided over gender issues, such psychological reassurance can be attractive.

Furthermore, given the general uncertainties of modern life, the certainties of religious teaching on morality can also be psychologically supportive and comforting. For some critical theorists, religious fundamentalism, following the military failures of the Vietnam War, provides a vehicle for the expression of resentment against a range of social targets – gay men, black Americans, central government, intellectuals and strident feminists. These resentments were crystallised around right-wing populist politicians such as George Wallace, Patrick Buchanan and Oliver North, and the frustrations were concentrated in male workers in the blue-collar sector of the labour force that suffered most from the decline of the manufacturing industries (Connolly, 1995: 123). Although there is evidence that fundamentalism is more common in low-income strata that have been marginalised by the growth of the service sector, there is also agreement that fundamentalism cannot be seen only as a working-class movement of protest.

Despite the growth of the Moral Majority, other sociologists have argued that we should not exaggerate the continuing influence of the Moral Majority on American politics. The social and political impact of fundamentalism is somewhat limited in social class, generational and geographical terms. In contemporary America, the South has been slowly urbanised and industrialised and this has reduced the social base of evangelical Protestantism. The growing importance of individual spirituality among younger generations may also indicate that the religious landscape of America is changing rapidly (Roof, 1993; 1999). In addition, American religions are becoming more diverse with the spread, for example, of Islam and Buddhism, which do not easily fit into notions of civil religion or spirituality. With these reservations, American exceptionalism will remain an important issue in the comparative study of modern religion.

Post-secular society

The idea of 'post-secular society' has emerged in recent philosophical debate about the changing relationship between the religious and the secular in late modernity. Major works on secular society have recently caught the attention of a wide range of intellectuals concerned with the character of the public sphere. The dominant commentaries have included Charles Taylor's *Varieties of Religion Today* (2002) and his *A Secular Age* (2007). Jürgen Habermas (Habermas, 2002;

Habermas and Mendieta, 2002) has explored the legacy of critical theory in relation to modern religion, thereby opening up the traditional debate about reason and revelation in human societies. This philosophical debate has also played an important role in how sociologists think about their subject matter. While it is the philosophers who have raised the major issues concerning the place of religion in apparently secular societies, their characterisation of religion has been almost exclusively focused on Christianity and Islam, and there has been little engagement with the comparative empirical data that are generated by anthropologists and sociologists. In short, while secular philosophers have set out the broad terms of the debate, their work often lacks empirical substance and the quality of their discussion now hangs on the injection of anthropological and sociological fieldwork, especially from outside the European and American context, into the public debate. What is at issue here is the very character of secular society, and as a result we are now obliged to give an answer to, or at least attend seriously to, the question raised forcefully by Habermas: Are we living in a post-secular society?

Most Western sociologists and philosophers have unsurprisingly had little to say about religion outside northern Europe and the United States. The recent debate about post-secularism has in part been to recognise the peculiarities of the European experience of secularisation, to question the notion of American exceptionalism and to create a dialogue on the public sphere with religion, especially with Islam. It is increasingly obvious that it is difficult to generalise from the European experience, in which the separation of the state and church in the Westphalian settlement of religious wars presupposed a particular history of confessional politics. By contrast, contemporary anthropological and comparative sociological research clearly illustrate both the complexity of secularisation as a process and the vitality of religion in the rest of the world, especially as a result of modern pilgrimage, religious revivalism in Southeast Asia, and Pentecostal and charismatic movements in South America and Africa (Martin, 2002). However, when serious attention is given to religious movements outside the West, both sociologists and philosophers have given far too much attention to fundamentalism in general and to radical Islam in particular. There are many contemporary forms of religious revivalism and growth other than radical or political religion. While secularisation and post-secular society are clearly issues in Western

Europe, religion in its various and complex manifestations is obviously thriving in many parts of Asia, Africa and Latin America. Religious reformism in Indonesia and Malaysia, the restoration of Confucianism and Daoism in China, the reinstatement of spirit possession cults in Vietnam with the Renovation Period, shamanistic religions in South Korea, the spread of Buddhism from Taiwan to the USA, the mobilisation of Tibetan Buddhism as a global model of meditation, the transformation of Hinduism outside India and so on – these are well-known developments outside the Western world that bring into question the narrow focus of much sociological and philosophical debate.

It is now widely held that the conventional secularisation thesis of sociologists was too narrow in its focus on the United States and Great Britain, and consequently in contemporary research sociological attention has shifted to consider religious phenomena that flourish outside the institutional framework of official religions. One example is the growth of 'spirituality' – a form of religion which does not necessarily depend on ecclesiastical institutions, and where individuals pick and choose between different religious traditions. The result is a hybrid mixture of religious beliefs and practices.

Another development in the sociology of religion has involved research on religion and nationalism. While there are major tensions between religion and politics that characterise modern Israel and India on the one hand and Vietnam and China on the other, religion and politics are not inevitably in a contradictory relationship. Politics often embraces religious motives and narratives to give expression to a nationalist agenda, especially a nationalist revival which appears to be essential, for example, to contemporary Russian politics, where there has been a dramatic recovery of Russian Orthodoxy. In the opposite direction, religion often appears to produce the vitality and substance of successful political movements. Perhaps the most telling illustration of the strange marriage of religion and politics would be the Polish Solidarity movement, in which Polish trade unionists and political activists used religious sites and symbols to pursue distinctive political objectives. Crosses were regularly carried by protesting workers leaving the Gdansk shipyards in the 1980s and pictures of Pope John Paul II were also part of the paraphernalia of protest. In this religio-nationalist discourse, Poland is presented as the suffering and broken nation, caught between powerful and aggressive neighbours.

This sense of being the victim of military ambition from both fascism and communism has been captured in the icon of the Black Madonna, Our Lady of Czestochowa, whose scarred face epitomises this national grief. Roman Catholicism became the iconic carrier of such nationalist sentiments in which to be Polish is to be Catholic (Zubrzycki, 2006). However, the majority of ethno-nationalist movements that are driven by religious identity and membership have occurred outside Europe, especially in South Asia (Van der Veer, 1994).

The criticism of traditional approaches to the sociology of secularisation also includes an exploration of the idea of 'political theology', in which both philosophers and theologians have sought to expand our limited concentration on the (juridical) separation of church and state. There are broadly two main approaches here. The first is from political philosophers who work within the legacy of Carl Schmitt and Ernst Kantorowicz (Vries and Sullivan, 2006). Schmitt had argued in his *Political Theology* ([1934] 1985), which was first published in 1934 and which in turn owes a lot to Max Weber's notion of the state, that political philosophy came into existence with the transfer of theological notions of sovereignty and omnipotence to the state. The second approach to these issues includes a group of theologians around the theme of 'Radical Orthodoxy', most notably John Milbank (1990), who argues that (secular) sociology has failed to provide a universal, rational language of the social and that theology is a social science. The task of modern Christian theology is to recognise the challenge of elaborating a genuinely universal discourse of the social.

Although there has been a general criticism of secularisation and growing interest in post-secularism, there is also the danger of demolishing the secularisation thesis too profoundly. If we treat secularisation as the absorption of secular culture, especially a commercial culture, into modern religion, then secularisation is manifest through the growth of mega-churches, drive-in confessionals, buy-a-prayer, popular religious films, religious shopping outlets and the sale of amulets and other paraphernalia. I have elsewhere called this commodification of religious belief and practice an example of 'low intensity religion' (Turner, 2009d), by which I mean that many forms of religiosity are low on commitment, individualistic, highly subjective and post-institutional. Because these religious styles are distinctly post-institutional, it is doubtful that they will have a lasting impact on social structure or culture. Religion has joined the process of modernisation insofar as religious lifestyles are crafted onto secular lifestyles that are promoted through a vast array of advertising strategies and financial inducements. These lifestyles circulate in religious markets that sell general therapeutic rather than specifically religious services. Of course, historians are likely to argue that the circulation of religious goods on a market is not a commercialisation of religion that is peculiar to modern societies. The commercialisation of religion in modernity involves a global commodification of religion, the creation of religious sites as places of tourism, the emergence of religious salesmanship and the construction of mega-churches in societies where there is no longer a dominant Universal Church or a global Islamic community (*ummah*) with the power to enforce orthodoxy. While this argument that religion has been commodified can recognise pre-modern forms of commercial religions, in the contemporary period of cultural globalisation the phenomenon of commercialised hybrid religiosity is widespread, embracing Buddhism in Thailand through the sale of amulets, popular Islamic preaching in Indonesia and Egypt, charismatic movements in Africa and Pentecostalism in Latin America.

Conclusion

Despite the growth of fundamentalism, national religions and public religion, the concept of secularisation, provided we remain imaginatively responsive to the diversity of modern religions, can still be safely applied to the contemporary world. Secularisation involves, as Niklas Luhmann (1984) has persuasively argued, the differentiation of spheres of activity in modern societies between religion, the economy and the polity. It means that religious institutions have to compete with a wide range of agencies (such as welfare providers) in the delivery of welfare services. Religion has to compete, normally unsuccessfully, with secular scientific interpretations of reality. It means that the overarching authority of religious traditions has been eroded. It means that, in a secular commercial culture, religious belief and practice is infused with commercial ideas and practices about selling religion and marketing religious institutions. Finally, it means that a religious cosmology explaining the place of human beings in the universe has little purchase on the modern world, where evolutionary theories of human development, despite fundamentalist objections, are dominant.

8 | *Legal pluralism, religion and multiculturalism*

Introduction: in principle and in practice

Islamic holy law (the *Shari'a*), along with the veil, has become one of the most contested issues in Western liberal societies. The possible introduction of the *Shari'a* raises significant problems for multicultural policies as a specific example of legal pluralism. In this chapter I briefly outline four positions one might take towards the recognition of *Shari'a* law in any secular state with a diverse multicultural society. The first option would be to take up some normative in-principle position either to accept or to reject the *Shari'a*. This would involve public debate about religious law in a secular state along the lines suggested in Jürgen Habermas's recent comments on a post-secular society (Habermas, 2002; Habermas and Ratzinger, 2006). The second option would be to follow a pragmatist strategy either for or against. This approach might equally accept or reject *Shari'a*, but in this case the reasons are practical and not normative. A government might decide to accept or reject the introduction of religious courts depending on the possibility of their integrative or disruptive social consequences. The pragmatist approach suggests that a government might just see what happens (partly from historical experience and partly from contemporary observation) when there is some piecemeal recognition or introduction of legal pluralism. If this piecemeal departure from legal uniformity does not cause too much public uproar, a government might feel comfortable with some slow evolutionary departure from state sovereignty, legal uniformity and secularism. Alternatively, a government might pragmatically ignore or cautiously reject any attempt to introduce some version of legal pluralism through recognition of the *Shari'a*. In many societies we already have the existence of religious courts – both Jewish and Islamic – that offer legal decisions especially for minorities in secular societies in which they act as third-party arbitration. These courts rarely appear in discussions about multiculturalism, religious tolerance and legal pluralism. One reason may be that the debate about the veil has overwhelmed all other issues.

Different legal traditions stand in a different relationship to the possibility of legal pluralism. In a common law tradition such as the legal system of England and Wales and many commonwealth societies such as Australia, in contrast to the Roman tradition of continental law that is characteristic of France and Germany, some degree of fuzziness is not incompatible with an evolution towards pluralism. The sociology of law following the criticisms of Max Weber might adopt the critical view that the common law tradition lacks logical coherence anyway. Common law is an inductive system in which case law dominates. Weber famously compared what he regarded as the instability of a *fatwa* given by a religious teacher in Islam with the decision of a judge in English case law. There is a provision in the English common law tradition in which lay people can devise a process to settle a dispute in front of a third party provided both sides agree to the process. One might say that legal pluralism has been around a long time and is an almost inevitable outcome of post-colonialism, in which secular European law, Islamic *Shari'a* and tribal or customary provisions have existed side by side (Snyder, 2004).

Max Weber on *Shari'a*

Sociological assumptions about law in Islam have undoubtedly been influenced by Weber's account of the irrational characteristics of *Shari'a*. Weber (1978) argued that both English common law and '*kadi*-justice' are remarkably similar in drawing on precedent and legal decisions by judges (Turner, [1974] 1998). From Weber's point of view, both systems are irrational; they do not have the same logical consistency as Roman continental law, which is a deductive system from general principles. In addition, he argued that decision-making in both common law and *kadi*-justice is exposed to political interest. Furthermore, he regarded English common law as expensive and open to manipulation by class interests. Judge-made decisions were too easily influenced by the economic and political interests of the dominant class. However, in the case of Islam, there was the additional difficulty that, because it is holy law, it had become in principle closed to further interpretation. The gap between the frozen normative content of the *Shari'a* and the inevitable evolution of empirical social reality is resolved by (arbitrary) decision-making or the issue of a *fatwa*.

This characterisation of Islamic law is not entirely accurate – at least for the contemporary period. Modern legal decision-making in Islam has been subject to continuous debate and assessment in which individual decisions are constrained by and open to public debate (Peletz, 2002). In this respect, *kadi*-justice is a product of communal consensus. Throughout the twentieth century, there were consistent and largely successful efforts to rationalise, systematise and modernise Islamic law to make it relevant to modern conditions. *Shari'a* is not a timeless and frozen religious law, but a set of diverse traditions that are open to criticism and evaluation.

In feminist criticisms of Islam, it is often claimed that holy law silences women's voices, but in reality there is equally an internal debate in Muslim societies about the inconsistency of legal decision-making in Muslim courts with respect to gender issues. We should therefore not refer to Islamic law as an unchanging and coherent body of laws, but rather as a system of prescriptions that are open to continuous debate and internal judicial scrutiny. The unresolved debate in Islam about so-called temporary marriage (*mut'a* or *sigheh*) is a good illustration of this internal diversity, uncertainty and debate (Haeri, 1989). There is nothing fundamentally different between the reform of Islamic law and the reform of Western secular laws. For example, criticisms have been raised about the role of legal judgments in English common law with respect to rape cases. Traditionally the law courts have not favoured female victims of such crimes and sentencing practices appear to have been highly inconsistent. There is a case to be made that both Islamic law and common law rest on a social consensus and both tend to be conservative in dragging behind more advanced public opinion. The common law is common, in the sense that it reflects, through the legal decisions of judges, the common view of socially appropriate behaviour. Islamic law reform in a society like Indonesia also illustrates the ways in which law can be regarded as a summary of common practice (Bowen, 2003).

This comparison between common law and *Shari'a* law as practice brings us up against a philosophical problem that makes the debate about legal pluralism particularly complex (Williams, 1956).

Weber, in regarding law as command, necessarily tied law-making to state sovereignty. Law is simply a collection of rules that are enforceable by states that have sovereignty over a territory. Weber's definition of law as the command of a sovereign state would appear to preclude any evolution of legal pluralism which implies some degree of political devolution and the relaxation of state sovereignty. This conceptual restriction also recognises implicitly that Weber's political theory is not conducive to the development of liberal democratic systems; his political views had more to do with authoritative leadership than with inclusive politics. Whatever the demerits of either common law or *Shari'a*, their very messiness is seen to have the virtue of allowing for the emergence of a consensus around social issues. The jury system that in part recognises the importance of lay opinion has been a significant component of Anglo-Saxon notions of democracy.

Any in-principle position (normative acceptance or principled rejection) about religious courts runs into obvious problems around the question of sovereignty. The pragmatist position can be defined as a de facto alternative to holding any normative view of *Shari'a* and secular common law. Pragmatism might be more attentive to the negative or positive social outcomes of pluralism even if the result was some partial erosion of sovereignty, and in the case of England and Wales the more specific issue of the long-held insistence on parliamentary sovereignty. From the perspective of the sociology of religion, we have seen that *Shari'a* is basically a traditional method of expressing a social consensus within any Muslim community. The problem for modern Muslims living as diasporic communities (and typically therefore as minority communities) as a result of worldwide migration is that achieving a consensus about how to live as a good Muslim in modern societies has become problematic. It is problematic for at least two reasons. Firstly, new situations emerge. Can a female Muslim living in Germany join a secular football team and if so what should she wear? Secondly, much of this debate occurs on-line with new sources of authority and therefore outside the traditional framework of communal consensus. Hence it is unclear who has authority to speak on such matters. From the perspective of the sociology of law, I want to propose that the total collection of Internet activity (blogs, Facebook, Twitter and so forth) within the diaspora constitutes a new type of Muslim consensus, but it is an emergent consensus outside the normal or traditional framework. In one sense, because Islam lacks a centralised authority system, the global Internet is the Muslim *ummah*.

An informal, creeping, populist version of Islamic law may in fact challenge the authority of traditional forms of religious authority. In attempting to understand the current situation of Muslim minorities, it is important to focus on actual practice rather than on formal systems of belief. What constitutes Muslim belief cannot be found in sociological terms by reading the official texts; it can only be found by observing actual Muslim practice. For example, what constitutes piety for contemporary Muslims cannot be grasped simply through a study of the Qur'an. We might take the issue as to whether a good Muslim could have a tattoo or some other body modification. Sources from the Qur'an and *hadith* tell us little about piercing, tattooing and other aspects of popular youth culture. According to the *hadith* (customary teaching), God has made human beings perfect and therefore it is a blasphemy to change the human form. If one examines on-line discussions about tattoos among young Muslims, there are interesting problems thrown up about the issue. For example, is the use of henna also prohibited? If one already has tattoos before conversion to Islam, is it important to undergo surgery to have them removed? It appears that some young Muslims are already experimenting with tattoos and jewellery that have what one might call Islamic themes. There is an equally lively and dense debate about appropriate sexual behaviour – homosexuality, polygamy and gender roles – among young Muslims on-line (Marcotte, 2010). In diasporic communities, this question is typically resolved through on-line discussion. Where there is an emerging modern consensus in popular discourse about body modifications, then the on-line discussion functions as something approaching a third-party arbitration of these puzzles.

This development represents a de facto Islamisation of everyday behaviour, but it is a development that does not necessarily have the oversight of traditional sources of authority. The situation is very fluid, but it has the characteristic of modern Muslim piety in producing an inflation of pious norms to cope with new situations in a diasporic context. It gives rise to what I have elsewhere called 'halal consciousness' as the outcome of pietisation or *halalisation* (Kamaludeen, Pereira and Turner, 2009; Tong and Turner, 2008).

These on-line legal discussions contribute to the pietisation of everyday life but often in ways which do not satisfy the more conventional or traditional sensibilities of Islam.

A pragmatic acceptance of this communal development would simply recognise the fact that in modern secular societies there is already *Shari'a* in operation in guiding Muslims towards pious behaviour. It cannot be avoided and therefore governments might as well accept it. The final pragmatic position, however, would be a weak strategy of attempting to ignore this creeping evolution of a form of legal pluralism. A secular government could not control the emergence of such a communal consensus and as Islamic practice became more entrenched and institutionalised over time, a pragmatic group of politicians might, as it were, simply sweep these local developments under the carpet, pretending that nothing was occurring that could compromise the secular framework of a liberal society. We might invent a concept to describe this evolutionary development of law through localised, communal decision-making that, so to speak, takes place behind the back of the official secular framework, namely the process of de facto '*sharia*-isation'. Thus, creeping '*sharia*-isation' cannot be prevented since it emerges spontaneously through communal practice and it becomes necessary in order to answer questions about new situations. However, practical politicians might try, at least for the time being, to ignore it. If diasporic communities begin to practise their own form of *Shari'a*, a secular state might ignore such a development provided it is confined to local areas where migrants happened to be dominant. The only problem from a pragmatist position of ignorance or implicit rejection would occur when a local problem – for example a Muslim woman objects publicly to the use of *Shari'a* in a domestic dispute – becomes a national issue through the intervention of the media.

Religious courts

Looking at these options in more detail, there are then two possible normative positions or ideal type constructs that can be identified with respect to the state's response to the proposal that *Shari'a* operate as a domestic legal option for Muslim communities living as in a diaspora. The first in-principle argument is that, if one takes multiculturalism very seriously, then one ought to take *Shari'a* law

seriously. If one believes that cultural traditions should not be culturally swamped in a secular, tolerant multicultural environment – in
other words that multiculturalism is not a smokescreen for de facto
assimilation – then it is difficult to reject the legal pluralism position.
Any coherent and convinced multicultural position has to embrace
legal pluralism. However, legal pluralism creates problems. To mention the most obvious questions: Does it compromise the sovereignty
of the state? Does it lead to a system of parallel societies? Can
Muslim women opt out of a conservative interpretation of *Shari'a*?
Is modern multicultural society becoming an 'enclave society'?
(Turner, 2007a). Should we oppose the minimalist recognition of
Shari'a, because it might be the first stepping-stone towards the
growth of more authoritarian forms of Islamic law? As a result, we
have open to us the normative argument that *Shari'a* law is not
compatible with a secular multicultural tradition which accepts the
right of citizens to enjoy access to courts that recognise their individual rights. In this normative position, *Shari'a* law is seen to be
divisive in a culturally diverse society and actually corrosive of
multiculturalism.

The objections to accepting *Shari'a* have already emerged, for
example, in legal debate in Ontario, Canada where from 1991
onwards the secular courts authorised the use of *Shari'a* in civil
arbitrations over divorce, child custody and inheritance cases. The
Arbitration Act allowed individuals to access religiously based tribunals within the province (partly to relieve the overburdened existing
tribunals). The Act was in part a response to an overburdened legal
system for which the creation of these arrangements would address
these administrative problems. These provisions included not only
recognition of Islamic legal traditions but also the legal legacy of
rabbinical, Catholic and aboriginal faiths. These developments gave
rise to concerns not only among secular Canadians but among Muslim
migrants to Canada. There are some 600,000 Muslims living in
Canada, and many who came from Iran as refugees strongly objected
to these developments. The arguments against such arrangements,
which were reported in the *Globe and Mail*, included the fact that
many Muslim women are poorly educated and do not easily understand their rights under Canadian law. The *imams* can make judgments where there is no oversight and consequently how would one
know whether they contravened the secular law? Because the women

are often living in social enclaves where there is little understanding of women's rights, they are vulnerable and may not be able to access third-party oversight. These debates were aggravated by sensational reporting of a murder case in which a young girl aged sixteen years from a Toronto suburb was strangled to death by her father following her refusal to wear a headscarf. In response to the debate and the problems it threw up, Premier Dalton McGuinty determined to repeal the Act without prior discussion with his Cabinet. The issue has been explosive within the public domain. In August 2005, Ayaan Hirsi Ali, whose apostasy and public criticisms of Islam had by now become internationally famous, attended a conference in Toronto in support of Homa Arjomand, the co-ordinator of the International Campaign Against *Shari'a* Court in Canada. Similar conflicts emerged from the Archbishop of Canterbury's lecture 'Civil and Religious Law in England: A Religious Perspective' on 7 February 2008. In the light of these public conflicts, the normative position might say either that, despite the practical problems, we should accept *Shari'a* because we have to accept legal pluralism as a consequence of being committed multiculturalists, and we should also accept the public confrontations that go with it, or we should reject these developments because we believe there is a higher principle involved, namely the integrity and coherence of secular liberalism and the idea of a uniform citizenship for all as a basis for the empowerment of individuals regardless of their religious identities.

   In practice, however, it is probable that these in-principle solutions will break down into some pragmatic compromise where either group rights, as adumbrated by Will Kymlicka, will be regarded as a short-term solution, thereby allowing some partial recognition of *Shari'a*, or implicitly as a stepping-stone to some more ample acceptance of *Shari'a* that would operate with the condition that it was ultimately subordinated to the secular law. Some compromise position might be more likely as an outcome and the implication of compromise might be the recognition that we do not entirely take multiculturalism seriously, because we do not want this issue to emerge as a divisive problem in the public arena. We might think that Habermas's notion of a post-secular society in which religious issues should be taken seriously is in practice too problematic, because dialogue might provide a platform for the expression of extremist views.

Customary law and post-colonialism

These pragmatic positions therefore start out in the opposite direction from any normative argument. If some level of legal pluralism (and therefore the recognition of religious tribunals) causes no serious public issue, then let us either quietly accept it or quietly ignore it. In the first pragmatic response then, at the very least a community could hang on to multiculturalism. In the second position (pragmatism), a community would finally let go of multiculturalism by gently ignoring it. Both pragmatist positions would probably want to argue from political experience. In modern Britain and in many post-colonial societies – such as Malaysia and Singapore – there is a hybrid system where religious courts operate with limited jurisdiction and generally under the umbrella of English common law. The experience of Dutch law and legal pluralism in the colonial context of Indonesia provides an instructive case of legal confusion and ambiguity (Burns, 2004). In Indonesia, outside the *Shari'a*, *adat* and *adatrecht* or 'custom' and 'customary law' were the legal framework for local communities. Customary law became the site of an ongoing legal struggle between the law of the Dutch colonial state, *Shari'a* and traditional practice. In 1901, Cornelis van Vollenhoven, who accepted an academic appointment to the chair of colonial law and administration at Leiden University, in his inaugural lecture redefined *Mohammedaansch recht* as *adatrecht*. The change of name indicated a new field of inquiry – the customary laws of Indonesia that were not merely a pale reflection of Islamic law. This perspective on the law was a product of the German *Historische Rechtsschule* as expounded most notably by Friedrich Karl von Savigny (1779–1861). Its core doctrine was that the law is always the evolutionary expression of the development of a nation. This school was a nationalist–romantic reaction against the abstract legal rationalism of the Enlightenment. Because the law is necessarily deeply embedded in a national culture and language, it is impossible to graft external, alien laws onto such a body of 'living law'. Therefore the Leiden School came to see customary law as the natural expression of Indonesian culture.

Van Vollenhoven published his *Miskenningen van het adatrecht* in 1909. It was an open juridical challenge to the conventional view that the Dutch state was the supreme master over the lands of the Netherlands East Indies. The *Miskenningen* exposed the bureaucratic muddle of decrees, statutes, ordinances and regulations. Of course this problem in fact went back to the very foundation of the Dutch East India Company, which had become a self-perpetuating, self-justifying administrative system. The attempt to defend the idea of universal abstract law against local customary law came then to be associated with the so-called Utrecht School. The doctrines of the Leiden School did not fit easily with the economic and administrative needs of empire or capitalist enterprise and the romantic view of law was an implicit threat to Dutch authority in, for example, giving legitimacy to the indigenous process of adjustment. The Leiden School argued that in Indonesian law there was no equivalent to 'customary penal law' and the idea of '*adat* tort law' was nonsensical. Indonesian penal processes were closer to the idea of 'remedy', in which the judge seeks to avoid potential danger to the community rather than exacting a punishment on the individual. The Utrecht School claimed that customary adjustment as a restoration of communal harmony was clearly inferior to a rational legal system that demanded recognition of evil intention and which balanced punishment with the scale of an offence. An imperial power that recognised such irrational customary practices had simply forfeited its right to rule. For Nolst Trenité, a senior government adviser on agricultural policy, and his colleagues who opposed van Vollenhoven, there was just too much scholarly attention given to *adat* practices. In the ideological confrontation between these two positions, the technical debates about land rights, legal process, tort and punishment were basically controversies over the issue of sovereignty. Whereas the function of the Leiden School was to invent Indonesian nationhood, the Utrecht School sought to nurture the Dutch polity. In the long run the ideals and methodology of Leiden were vindicated in Indonesia's political independence, but paradoxically the Basic Agrarian Legislation of 1960 was a triumph of Utrecht legal realism. While the Legislation affirms *adatrecht* (*hokum adat*) as a national tradition, in reality it appropriated the right to allocate land to the state. Under the notion of 'in the interests of the state', New Order governments did not concede any priority of local rights. The Legislation in reality recognised the arguments of the Utrecht School that the right of land allocation belongs to the state. Customary law or *adat* became an anomaly in an independent Indonesia and, as with most post-colonial states, the government was confronted by legal pluralism involving the *Shari'a*, customary law, the remains of Dutch colonial law and various components of international law.

The theoretical conundrum of legal pluralism is solved by 'forum shopping' (seeking out an appropriate legal framework that will satisfy partisan interests), but the results tend to produce a juridical mess.

Modern European states are not confronted by this post-colonial situation, but they do confront problems about different legal systems. In Great Britain in any case, Scots law survived the Union of the Crowns and has retained its separate (more Roman) tradition. In many white-settler societies, in the United States, New Zealand and to some degree in Australia, indigenous peoples have been able to enjoy the right to use customary tribal law on aboriginal land. One might add that laws made in European courts, in human-rights decisions and so forth, now impinge on national sovereignty. But turning once more to Islam, in British towns with large Muslim populations, something like *Shari'a* law operates in domestic issues where local people obtain a *fatwa* or religious judgment about some domestic dispute. As a result the Archbishop of Canterbury's 2008 public lecture on *Shari'a* law caused, from a pragmatic perspective, a lot of fuss when it was not necessary. But is the implication here that legal pluralism is acceptable provided we do not advertise it too widely? Provided the Archbishop does not make another speech, we can get on with creeping legal pluralism. Certainly getting the *Shari'a* option out in the public domain often produces an unfortunate backlash. In the provisions for *Shari'a* in Toronto, it certainly galvanised right-wing groups who clearly did not want the liberal principle – religion is essentially a private matter and should not be brought out into the public domain – to be compromised, but it also brought Muslim feminists (especially Iranian feminists) out against the idea.

The pragmatist solution supporting an evolutionary response runs into problems partly because the headscarf has become such a public symbol of deeper issues about women's rights, racism and recognition. The feminist literature on the topic is deeply polarised. On the one hand there is the deeply moving account of misogyny and suppression of women's rights in the Iranian Revolution from writers such as Azar Nafisi in her *Reading Lolita in Tehran* (2008), and on the other the persuasive but more cerebral account of Egyptian female empowerment from Saba Mahmood in her *The Politics of Piety* (2005). Hence the issue of *Shari'a* law raises questions about recognition, difference and equality. While sociologists have typically examined the problems of cultural recognition in terms of identity, difference and cultural rights, they have all too often neglected the legal framework within which recognition might take place.

In the following discussion, I take a fairly pessimistic view that the preservation of cultural, religious or legal differences can only be sustained if there is an overarching framework of citizenship that binds people together into a shared community. Without that commonality and a common or shared project, there is a real danger that societies will break down into isolated enclaves or parallel societies in which communities with separate schools, with little spatial propinquity and retaining separate cultural traditions – and in this case their own legal traditions – will fragment. The wider society becomes simply a collection of gated communities. The problem of parallel communities is real and in the worst case scenario one can image the growth of modern societies dominated by global mega-cities in which there is relatively little shared civil society. John Rawls (2001) in *The Law of Peoples* has spoken of the importance of an 'overlapping consensus' of fundamental doctrines if a liberal society is to survive, but such a liberal consensus cannot function without a system of overlapping social groups. Taking multiculturalism seriously may force us to take social solidarity seriously, namely to take a critical look at the celebration of difference at the cost of the things that hold us together. From a sociological point of view, multiculturalism without some powerful framework of shared interests and shared institutions cannot provide an adequate cultural framework for any complex society. More problematically, there are powerful processes in modern societies that are undermining public life – neo-liberal policies of the privatisation of pensions, health care and education, the powerful imprint of subjective individualism in consumer culture, the loss of social capital with modern forms of communication and the decline of active citizenship through the outsourcing of state functions. Legal pluralism is simply one component of what I want to call 'the erosion of citizenship' (Turner, 2001b).

Group rights and trust

Cultural recognition of differences represents a weak theory of social integration. Recognition ethics can only work if we can give full recognition to the cultural claims of others, especially minority groups. The modern theory of recognition ethics is in large measure a product of Hegel's master–slave analysis (Williams, 1997) and this perspective has been criticised on the grounds that one needs redistribution as well as, or prior to, recognition. The point is to develop a critical recognition theory that goes beyond the soft option of merely recognising cultural diversity. A well-developed multicultural policy giving full recognition to minorities as the basis of citizenship must examine the legal framework within which such recognition could take place. As I have argued, a thorough multicultural policy must address the question of legal pluralism: Does cultural recognition of the Other require us to take other legal systems or rights claims seriously? We might consequently call this legal dimension the hard question of multiculturalism. Any solution to this problem must simultaneously defend the notion of the rule of law as a basic condition of cultural dialogue and establish the conditions under which legal pluralism can give expression to different legal traditions. Cultural dialogue between social groups about cultural differences can only take place where a framework of debate has been accepted. Legal pluralism clearly illustrates the limitations of cultural relativism, but also holds out the promise of recognising the importance of separate and distinct legal traditions.

Kymlicka's contribution to liberal theory implies that societies can survive as effective democracies provided they are able to accommodate divergent cultures and identities. In a recent publication, Kymlicka (2009) has criticised the assumption that increasing ethnic and religious diversity reduces trust and social solidarity, and as a result public commitment to welfare declines. Kymlicka claims that recent empirical research does not support this view, but concedes that previously homogenous societies that experience very rapid incoming migration may be less willing to support such collective approaches to welfare. Other writers have taken a far more pessimistic interpretation of the issues confronting social order in the face of social diversity. For example, Jack Knight (2001) notes that cultural consensus in modern societies is unusual and that increasing social diversity undermines the cultural homogeneity of more traditional stable societies. Following Knight's argument, it is useful to make a distinction between two forms of consensus – sharing a common set of beliefs that are positively valued, and knowing about a set of beliefs that provide common expectations. In the cognitive sense of sharing, 'cooperative predictable behaviour is guaranteed by the existence of mechanisms that converge expectations toward actions that satisfy the requirements of mutual benefit' (Knight, 2001: 358). Agreements over social norms affect attitudes towards how other people will co-operate, and in turn this expectation shapes assumptions about future behaviour. Knight develops this argument to make sense of Robert Putnam's counter-intuitive observation that social capital is a moral resource that increases with use (Putnam, 2000). The Putnam thesis is that the growth of generalised trust is a function of everyday compliance with norms, and the more individuals co-operate with each other, the more they trust one another. Past experiences of reliable co-operative inter-action tend to enhance our general sense of the trustworthiness of other people in a community. In short, trustworthiness routinely generates trust, and conversely lack of reciprocity tends to deflate trust (Hardin, 2001).

In the light of this analysis, what diminishes trust in modern soci-ety? Knight's argument, in following a similar position taken by Steven Lukes (1991), is that social diversity undermines community and the erosion of community undermines trust. Ethnic and multicul-tural diversity is now an obvious feature of most advanced societies and trust in culturally diverse societies is difficult to achieve because there are important differences of interest, of basic social ends, and of social beliefs and values. In culturally diverse societies, it is rational for social groups to employ strategies of social closure to secure advan-tages over scarce resources against outsiders who are seen to be competitors. One problem with the development of denominational schools and separate religious education is that children growing up in separate educational institutions are unlikely to share norms or even know about the beliefs and practices of other religious traditions. It is unlikely in these circumstances, other things being equal, that school-children will acquire the trust that is necessary for a society to function adequately.

Informal conditions of social regulation and normative regulation do not work effectively in social environments where social equality and fairness are manifestly absent. The greater the distributional bias in resource allocation, the greater the propensity of disprivileged groups to become resentful and to disrupt existing social arrange-ments. The greater the social disadvantages, the greater the incentive of disprivileged groups to avoid interaction with dominant groups. The greater the disadvantage, the lower the probability that marginalised groups will respond positively to normative appeals to comply with existing social norms. The history of apartheid in South Africa would be an extreme instance of this system of social closure, but social conflict between groups on the basis of ethnic classification remains a common aspect of political division and social violence in many contemporary societies. In Great Britain, the conflicts between Catholics and Protestants in Northern Ireland would be another example of the existence of parallel communities with their own schools, neighbourhoods and clubs, where it took many decades to bring the 'Troubles' to an end.

In societies that are culturally diverse, generalised trust cannot be sustained by reliance on informal mechanisms, like customs, to ensure compliance and co-operation. Weber's treatment of formal rules in *Economy and Society* (1978) suggests that the consequence of formal legal institutions is to increase dependence on impersonal formal mechanisms to secure productive, co-operative social interactions. In this sense, the growth of a litigious society is paradoxically a measure of the decline of trust. Knight (2001: 365) argues that the task is 'to construct a conception of the rule of law in a socially diverse society that satisfies the requirements of social order and co-operation and, as a *possible* by-product, creates the conditions for the emergence and maintenance of informal mechanisms like trust'.

While Knight is pessimistic about achieving such a desirable outcome, he supports a pragmatist interpretation of the rule of law as a mechanism for satisfying the interests of different social groups in a differentiated social order. To accommodate the different interests of culturally distinct social groups, law must develop a range of mechanisms that avoid the adversarial character of legal dispute. Legal proceduralism as a juridical principle underlines the importance of overt and predictable legal processes in the resolution of conflict. In this respect, the work of Lon Fuller (1969) has been important in developing legal procedures (adjudication, mediation, managerial discretion, contract and legislation) that can contribute to social co-operation. Pragmatism suggests that legal decisions have to satisfy a condition of equal respect and treatment of members of different social groups.

While Knight provides a useful interpretation of how the rule of law might operate in a culturally diverse society, he remains pessimistic about the efficacy of such formal processes in generating

generalised trust. In my view, we need to see the rule of law within a broader social and political framework, namely social citizenship. The institutions of modern citizenship have been the principal mechanisms of social inclusion in contemporary society, and citizenship has played a major role in mitigating the negative consequences of the market. In particular, social citizenship is important in containing and reducing the negative consequences of social class differences in capitalism.

There are important connections between citizenship and social capital. Much of the discussion of social capital has assumed that trust will emerge informally from the everyday network of social relationships that are associated with church attendance, club membership or participation in neighbourhood groups. Run-down and under-privileged neighbourhoods are urban areas in which the informal wellsprings of trust have run dry. This analysis of trust is parallel to conventional views about how money functions. It is argued that money can only function where there is confidence (informal trust) in money. However, any 'extension of monetary relations across time and space requires *impersonal trust and legitimacy*. Historically, this has been the work of states' (Ingham, 2004: 187). In a large and complex social environment, informal trust requires the backing of the rule of law and state institutions. With globalisation, societies have become disorderly and difficult to govern. The management of transnational, diasporic communities whose relationship to the host society often remains distant, problematic and uncertain, requires a legal framework that is fair and transparent.

By bringing the question of law into our understanding of the issue of legal pluralism within the framework of post-national citizenship, I simply argue that any comprehensive recognition of cultural differences requires recognition of legal differences. The possibility of legal pluralism is an important test of the limits of multiculturalism, or at least public support for multicultural policies. To take one major example, Turkey is an important test of the limits of the European Union, because its inclusion would certainly raise questions of the relationship between European law and *Shari'a* norms. In order to grasp what is at stake here, we need to look more closely at the idea of recognition ethics as a basis for multicultural understanding and ultimately as a basis for legal pluralism.

Towards critical recognition theory

Any in-principle positions on multiculturalism and legal pluralism require some recognition of the value of *Shari'a* as a legal system. In short, the achievement of some degree of social order in complex societies requires recognition of the cultural differences of minority communities. In turn, this discussion will have to take a position on so-called recognition ethics. There has been a remarkable revival of Hegelian recognition ethics, mainly through the application of recognition ethics theory to multicultural society. However, there are also difficulties with this tradition. Much of the intellectual effort in this field has gone into the analysis of cultural rights. This inquiry is, so to speak, the 'soft' end of the debate; recognition ethics often neglects the problem of economic redistribution, and it often favours recognition of difference over the establishment of justice. More importantly, this debate has neglected the legal framework within which recognition might take place, and which can provide a stable framework for dialogue.

When we talk about recognition between two or more communities, we need to recognise that within communities there may be no consensus about correct practice or belief. In critical recognition theory, we must take into account the importance of these internal or 'indigenous' debates. We must avoid prejudicially assuming that something called 'Islam' does not accord women the same rights as something called 'the West'. These monolithic notions mask the fact that within Islam as well as in the West there are more or less endless debates about how women (men, children, the elderly, the sick and so forth) should be treated. Neither the common law nor the *Shari'a* are static, homogenous or consistent systems. Each is internally contested. These issues are clearly relevant to the framework developed by Jürgen Habermas around the idea of communicative rationality.

Let us imagine a debate between two communities (A and B) about the nature and function of marriage. In a democracy we might argue that there are two conditions of open, continuous debate. The first rule of Habermas-type communication discourses is that debate and disagreement should not be silenced. The role of a democracy is to permit dialogue about diversity. Democracy is also a framework for achieving compromise between apparently irreconcilable positions. In critical recognition theory, we notice that the debate between A and B should not be constrained, but equally the debates internally to A and B should not be inhibited. Furthermore, A should be free to join in the internal debate in B and vice versa. We might therefore object, for example, to the fact that neither Christian nor Islamic fundamentalists appear to recognise this openness. A critical dialogue can only take place where there is already some agreement about the rules of debate.

What we might call the 'exit-issue' has emerged in the scholarly debate between Chandran Kukathas and Will Kymlicka over cultural rights. The ultimate guarantee of female rights is probably the liberal right of an individual to leave his or her community. The right to leave one's own country or community is a fundamental right (Saharso, 2000). Thus in a debate over recognition between A and B, there must be a provision that, if an individual member of A decides that the cultural practices of B appear to be more congenial for her needs, that individual can migrate. In practice, this right is very difficult to enforce, because the survival of a group (especially a minority group) may depend on the ability of the group to exercise control over its women to ensure reproduction, including the repro-duction of language, culture and religion. Preserving the boundaries of a social group – and therefore having a clear notion of an inside and an outside – may be fundamental to the survival of a social group. In his famous *Ethnic Groups and Boundaries* (1998), Fredrik Barth argued that what defines an 'ethnic group' may have less to do with the presumption of a stable and shared culture as the mainten-ance of a boundary. The existence of an inside and an outside becomes fundamental to the idea of continuity. Whether members of a group have dissimilar behaviour or values may be ultimately unimportant. What matters is whether 'they say they are A, in contrast to another cognate category B, they are willing to be treated and let their own behaviour be interpreted and judged as A's and not B's; in other words, they declare their allegiance to the shared culture of A's' (p. 15). There may be serious disagreements within the Muslim community about what constitutes good behaviour or piety, but adherence to practices that are the products of *Shari'a* interpret-ation – the headscarf, *halal* food and restaurants, and abstinence from alcohol – defines the boundary of the group against other social groups. While Barth's work is very pertinent to this discussion of law, such a theory of social groups has also to allow for the possibilities of defection, migration and apostasy.

There are therefore serious sociological issues facing any normative theory of recognition. A critical recognition theory, based on communicative principles, provides tough criteria of mutual acceptance. We have to recognise the right to disagreement, but we must also recognise a right to persuasion. Accepting somebody else's argument would then be rather like migrating to another country. We might put this in Wittgensteinian terms. There has been an 'argument' between the English and the French for centuries, but there are also internal disagreements within English society about French culture. There are both Francophobes and Francophiles. Critical recognition ethics must allow Francophiles who love the French way of life to migrate. Accepting the truth of an argument might be like adopting a new way of life. This porosity between cultures is what is at stake, because Francophobes are inclined to regard Francophiles as disloyal. A critical recognition theory can only function when a society is willing to accept 'cosmopolitan virtue' as a necessary adjunct of globalisation (Turner, 2002). But cosmopolitanism appears to be shrinking rather than expanding. Survey data suggest that identification with nation and locality are far greater than what we might call world identification. What we might call 'pure cosmopolitans' are in a definite minority and they are overwhelmingly drawn from upper social groups with higher levels of education. Tolerance for others has declined significantly in many European countries, and even among people with cosmopolitan attitudes there is often little evidence in practice of cosmopolitanism (Holton, 2009: 136–9).

The possibilities for pluralism and tolerance have since 9/11 been severely tested and constrained by a discourse of terrorism and security. The development of an intelligent and cosmopolitan treatment of Islamic communities in Europe and elsewhere has been halted (hopefully temporarily) by legal and political responses to 'terrorism'. In particular, the clash of civilisations thesis has identified Islam as a civilisation that is fundamentally incompatible with Western values. While Muslim communities are been marginalised by the processes of securitisation, it is unlikely that Islamic traditions will receive any sympathetic understanding in the West. There is therefore considerable political pressure on Muslims in the diaspora to accept the Westphalian definition of religion as a matter of private practice and personal belief. In the United States, Islam could become acceptable as a denomination in the melting pot of multiculturalism, but only on the condition that it becomes a 'religion' in *our* terms.

We cannot just rely on improvements in attitudes without both government support and legal foundations for multiculturalism. In summary the legal conditions for a critical theory of recognition that goes beyond poly-ethnic rights would involve:

1. recognition of the validity of different legal systems;
2. acceptance of claims of minorities to exercise their own jurisdictions;
3. mutual recognition that laws are socially produced and subject to dispute and hence to evolution;
4. acceptance of legal norms that function across communities – essentially the acceptance of the rule of law which I have interpreted as meaning acceptance of rules of debate and evaluation;
5. recognition of rights of appeal against sentences; and
6. acceptance of some process whereby members can exit from their own communities without reprisals.

What are the implications of these norms? It suggests that Kymlicka's group-differentiated rights are at present underdeveloped by not recognising the importance of legal self-determination or 'poly-juridicality'. Legal pluralism would thus stretch the assumptions of liberalism to their limits. What are the implications for religious communities? These norms rule out the idea of religious law as immutable and fixed. This consequence may not necessarily be a significant problem in the sense that Islam in practice has accepted the idea of legal interpretation (*ijtihad*).

The notion that individuals can opt out of their own communities is perhaps the most problematic. In the case of minorities, the survival of their cultures and traditions requires continuity of socialisation and transmission – a process that has historically depended on women. Hence, women are typically subject to excessive (and at times brutal) subordination to group norms. But this fact offers no normative reason for supporting gender inequalities.

What is the law?

Whereas there was no shared term for 'law' in the Indo-European languages, there has been a common notion of 'order' underpinning the law-like orderliness of the natural world, the relations between God and men, and social relations within communities. This paradigm in which law is equivalent to social order was common to the Abrahamic religions, and in these cultures there was no distinction between secular laws, rituals and the sacred. In this interpretation, both law and religion refer to custom, to the individual's place in the world and to order. In sociological language, the social norms of a community are merely particular manifestations of a greater *Nomos* that shields people from disorder or chaos.

With the development of the secular state in the West, law came to be conceived as the command of the state, and hence laws were institutionally separate from both religion and morality. The decline of the Holy Roman Empire, the separation of church and state, the decline of the authority of ecclesiastical courts and the emergence of law issued by a secular state were important stages in the separation of law from morality in the Western tradition. The positivist tradition went further in seeking to convert jurisprudence into a science and to remove any (subjective) evaluation of law. Moral rules and legal rules can only be distinguished by the procedures by which they come into existence, and the scope of positive law has to be determined by an appropriate official such as a judge. In the sociology of the law, this command theory was developed by Weber in his definition of the state as that institution which has a monopoly of force in a given territory. This positivist tradition was hostile to the legacy of natural law in which just laws expressed a (religious) notion of the good society. In the natural law tradition, procedural correctness was never a guarantee of the existence of a just law. In the West, 'legality' and 'legitimacy' came to have separate and distinctive meanings and significance.

Before the rise of the modern state and the development of secular legal systems, it was not possible to make such clear distinctions between law, religion and morality. In the Abrahamic religions, for example, religious laws determining the relationship between people and God, and people and community were produced by revelation and their authority depended on charismatic powers. The ultimate authority of the law was divine. In Judaism, the texts dealing with law and ritual were known as the *halakhah*, the root of which means a way or path. In this sense it describes the customary ways of the people. More specifically, it describes religious customs. Moses was the central prophetic figure behind halakhic laws, because it was through Moses that God revealed the law. Islam shares with Judaism this centrality of law to ritual and religious practice. The Prophet was the divinely appointed lawgiver of the community and subsequently the caliphs were deputies responsible for the good order of the Household of Faith. The Prophet created a polity at Medina that was held together by a constitution that spelt out the legal obligations of newly converted tribes to Islam, and on his death, when some tribes attempted to terminate their contract the Apostasy War broke out. The *Shari'a* is governed by *fiqh* or understanding, and in Sunni Islam there emerged four major schools of law (Hanafis, Hanbalis, Malikis and Shafi'is). Shi'ite Islam had its own systems. The term *Shari'a* literally means the way to the watering place, namely the source or fountain of life and good order. Islam has no church or priesthood, and in this sense its legal structure is the core of its religious consciousness and the expression of its social solidarity.

Because Islamic legal systems were often dislodged or reorganised by Western positive law during colonisation in the nineteenth and twentieth centuries, in the post-colonial period there has been a significant revival of Islamic legal thinking in order to modernise legal practice and to make the impact of Islamic law more widespread in the community. This modernisation of law often results in legal pluralism, as in, for example, Malaysia, where *Shari'a* competes with English common law, tribal codes and human-rights legislation (Peletz, 2002). In the Malay case we might say that Islamic legal practice has been modernised by lawyers who implicitly shared Weber's critique of the 'irrationalities' of traditional Islamic legal practice. And so *Shari'a* has been made more central by lawyers who were as often as not trained in English legal practice, and who wear pin-striped suits rather than customary garb, and whose mental attitudes and professional *habitus* are distinctively Western. This development is not to say, however, that *Shari'a* has achieved a dominant or monopolistic position. Rather it is modernised, and shares the legal stage with international law, human-rights conventions, global corporate law and an English common law tradition. In this context, how is the authority of religious law discovered and how is it implemented?

Legal pluralism must lead to new questions, and possibly new answers, about the status of religio-legal norms. The debate about authority in Islam is underpinned by the realisation that the debate over the opening of the gate of interpretation (*ijtihad*) in modern Islam has produced, not a restoration of tradition, but a modernisation of Islamic legal thinking and practice. In short, the attempt to impose or implement *Shari'a* in post-colonial and multicultural contexts has brought about a wholesale debate about the relevance and nature of Islamic legal custom in new contexts. Modern communications technology has greatly facilitated this global legal discussion. Because of the weak institutionalisation of religious hierarchies in most Islamic settings, the legal debate over authority becomes localised, devolved and fissiparous. It is difficult to impose any transnational authority over this debate where local *mullahs* pass legal judgments on websites for an audience that has no clear cultural or spatial boundary. The fundamentalist or maximal view that *Shari'a* has to have some sort of monopoly or definite authority becomes very problematic in a multi-faith context and especially in diasporic communities where innovation is an inevitable outcome of migration and cultural adaptation.

Conclusion: public reason

In conclusion, there is a danger that the formal recognition of religious laws in general and *Shari'a* in particular would contribute to a further fragmentation of modern societies – societies that are already deeply divided and low on trust. If we were to extend multiculturalism to recognise *Shari'a* courts, then we would need to invest in many more processes to sustain some form of common citizenship. Acceptance of a public role for the *Shari'a* provides an acid test for the criteria of post-secularism that have been outlined in Habermas's recent work. In a democratic society, secular citizens have to offer public reasons for their political statements and attitudes, because 'only in this way can political power shed its repressive character' (Habermas, 2008: 122). At the same time, religious citizens must be able to reflect objectively on their religious convictions and connect them with life in a secular society. In this discussion of 'public reason', Habermas has developed John Rawls's *Political Liberalism* (1993) by introducing his own version of deliberation as the cornerstone of democracy. A similar view is embraced by Amartya Sen in *The Idea of Justice* (2009), in which he considers the empirical limitations on deliberative democracy such as the failures of the media and the press to provide critical views and objective knowledge about modern conditions. Although Rawls, Habermas and Sen have made major contributions to the theory of democracy, their understanding of the *sociological* conditions of critical debate is often underdeveloped. The key problem is how, in Rawls's terms, we can achieve a consensus in modern political systems. The argument running through this book is that divisions between religions in a globalising context have increased rather than diminished and there is a danger that multicultural societies will become enclave societies. A philosophical consensus about constitutional principles or post-secular values is very different from a social consensus. An overlapping consensus requires overlapping social groups – the product of high levels of inter-marriage, common experiences, a shared welfare system and a common school system. The growth of parallel communities undermines the prospect of overlapping social groups. Without social solidarity an overlapping consensus is unlikely and there is a danger of increasing social fragmentation. In the meantime, the sociological fact is that *Shari'a* is already operating in modern secular societies wherever third-party adjudication of disputes takes place according to religious norms. In addition, there are major changes taking place within Muslim communities about the norms that are appropriate to living in a secular society. These Internet debates already transcend local or national jurisdictions, but they also transcend all traditional forms of religious controversy. These small changes may be an indication of an emerging vernacular cosmopolitanism that may, in the long run, be a basis for engaging in debates, namely participating in public reasoning.

9 | *Managing religions: liberal and authoritarian states*

Introduction

When sociologists refer to 'the management of religion' or the crisis of multiculturalism or the problems of secularism, they are essentially talking about how modern liberal states respond to the radicalisation of modern religions, that is, to the alleged 'depersonalisation' of religion (Casanova, 1994) or, more crudely, to 'fundamentalism'. In this context, the particular issues surrounding Muslim minorities in non-Muslim secular states can be seen as simply one instance of the more general problem of state and religion in modern multicultural societies. There is some agreement that virtually all modern societies are multicultural. Because in practice it is difficult to separate 'religion' from 'culture', all multicultural societies are by definition multi-faith societies. Therefore any policy relating to multiculturalism is automatically a policy about religion. Despite the separation of church and state in liberal constitutions, modern governments find themselves dragged into forming religious policies, however implicit or covert, in order to manage the resulting tensions between competing religious traditions. This development is one reason for the growth of political interest in religion, not necessarily because of 're-sacralisation' but simply because 'identity politics' means 'religion and politics'. Much of the literature has been concentrated on religion in Western liberal societies, where Islam, as a result of large-scale migration and settlement, has been seen as a threat to democratic cultures. In addition, there is the argument that societies that have experienced very rapid waves of migration, and as a result have become diverse ethnic societies, have experienced a decline in public commitment to taxation to support welfare states (Freeman, 1986). Against a background of the threat of terrorism and growing political pessimism about finding a security solution that does not automatically undermine liberal rights, religious diversity is seen as a social as well as a political problem.

There is consequently an awareness of the limitations of the West-phalian solution to religious wars and Lockean liberalism as political strategies to manage such conflicting interests (Spinner-Halevy, 2005). This issue of church and state is not simply an issue in the West for liberal democratic societies. In this chapter, I want to show that the issue also confronts authoritarian regimes which have to find strat-egies to respond to religious minorities without endless civil war. These issues are endemic to modernity as a consequence of migration and the multiplication of diasporic communities. To take one more initial example, Singapore has developed a strategy of 'upgrading' Islam through educational strategies primarily through the agency of MUIS (*Majlis Ugama Islam Singapura* or the Islamic Religious Council of Singapore) and it provides a model, albeit an authoritarian model, of religious management (Kamaludeen, Pereira and Turner, 2009). Singapore might, in the language of John Rawls (2001), be considered as a 'well-ordered hierarchical society' in which the various religions are not only managed but upgraded through various educa-tional strategies.

In the West, societies such as France, Germany, Britain and the United States have different policies to manage religion, but their approach will in general terms remain primarily liberal. In liberal post-secular consumer societies, their constitutions and histories may well prevent them from adopting explicit and systematic policies of religious management and they are more likely to continue to treat, or attempt to treat, religion as a private lifestyle option. In short, they will probably attempt to resist the 'deprivatisation' of religion. These policies towards the veil, religious schools and the law suggest that we must always examine policies towards religion against the back-ground of different forms of citizenship. French republicanism on the one hand, and British liberalism on the other, produce very differ-ent responses to religion in public life and very different outcomes. The fact that French Muslims are more content with French secular-ism than British Muslims are with British pragmatic multiculturalism may at first appear counter-intuitive (Joppke, 2009). One aspect of the explanation may well be that British pragmatism sends an unclear, ambiguous and shifting message to both host community and to Muslim minorities. However, even liberal societies may be forced, perhaps reluctantly, to take an interest in religious goods and services. If we adopt the so-called economic or market approach to religion, then states will be interested in the 'quality' of religious products on the market. Just as states intervene in issues to do with secular consumerism – for example testing the quality of food and the cleanliness of restaurants through various agencies charged with the oversight of public health and hygiene – so we can expect secular states to manage religions through testing the quality of their products, especially their relations with minors. The recent example of Scientology in contemporary France is a case in point. In a consumer society, there may well be an ironic convergence between the emergence of passive citizenship in which there is a general withdrawal from active involvement in the society and polity as manifest, for example, in a low turn-out at election time and the growth of spiritual markets on which individuals may 'mix 'n' match' religious products as religious consumers. The growth of post-institutional, post-Christian spirituality appears to be the perfect counterpart to the erosion of citizenship and the emergence of the passive subject.

In liberal democracies the active citizen is increasingly becoming a passive consumer in which work, public service and reproduction are no longer the fundamental bases of effective citizenship entitlement. This erosion of citizenship was dramatically illustrated by the recent credit crunch in which citizens in Britain, Australia and the United States were admonished by their governments to shop in order to save both the economy and the society. The new duty of the citizen is to consume and, paradoxically, at the same time to save. States increasingly treat citizens as an audience that must be managed by sales techniques (focus groups, opinion polls, marketing strategies and national identity as branding) and the quality of political leadership is tested by ratings in opinion polls. The new spirituality in the West and commodified religions in Asia may also fit into a pattern of citizenship as consumerism. Modern spirituality is post-institutional, subjective and privatised. A similar argument had been put forward more generally for the consumer lifestyles that can sit comfortably alongside Pentecostalism (Martin, 2002).

These developments perhaps cast a different light on traditional political questions about tolerance and liberty. Employing once more the idea of competition in religious markets, the analysis of religion in the public sphere will be a function of the relationship between majorities and minorities. Anthony Gill in *The Political Origins of Religious Liberty* (2008: 47) claims that 'religious liberty is a matter of government regulation'. Dominant religious groups, in order to establish their legitimacy and authority, will seek state regulation of minority religions. In other words, majority religions are unlikely to welcome religious liberty and will attempt to define marginal religious groups as mere sects or, worse still, as cults. By contrast, religious liberty will be the political objective of religious minorities who can prosper in a more open market situation. In terms of political life, this approach leads to the perhaps unsurprising but important observation that 'politicians seek to minimize the cost of ruling' (p. 47). Governance is clearly more problematic in pluralistic environments where there is plenty of scope for religious competition and conflict. Such societies are probably also characterised by low trust, and hence the costs of political transactions are higher. Because virtually all modern societies are multicultural and multiracial, the 'management of religion' is an inevitable component of political secularisation (Turner, 2007b; 2008c). In other words, precisely because religion is important in modern life as the carrier of identity, it has to be controlled by the state to minimise the costs of government, even in constitutional settings that overtly espouse the separation of church and state.

The capacity of the state to exercise control over religions is, of course, highly variable. The disciplinary management of religions in well-ordered hierarchical regimes such as Singapore and South Korea may remain unavailable to liberal democratic regimes such as the United States and Britain, which must aspire to define religion as simply one aspect of the lifestyle of post-secular consumerism. In short, they will hang on to the myth of the private nature of religion and at the same time treat religion as a matter of public concern. There is obviously a pessimistic aspect to this argument, insofar as liberal societies may slide inevitably towards authoritarian systems with the global development of political securitisation and the cultivation of passive consumer citizenship. The modern citizen is both regulated by the state and entertained by a powerful mixture of secular culture, consumerism and popular religion. This is simply the modern version of 'bread and circuses' that served the Roman state in its quest for security and sovereignty. The management styles of modern states will also vary according to the churches, denominations and cults to which they have to respond, such as the Moonies and Scientologists in the West, the 'cults' of post-communist states such as Falun Gong in China, the Protestant evangelicals in Vietnam or the Muslims of Chechnya in Russia.

One might assume that the obvious response of authoritarian states would be simply to suppress, violently if necessary, such minority religions. Indeed, various religious movements are suppressed in China because they are seen as a threat to the authority of the Party. However, I propose a less obvious interpretation, which is that one strategy for managing religions in authoritarian regimes is to commercialise them as objects or sites of religious tourism. There is evidence from China that Buddhism and Daoism, for example, are being allowed to enjoy a partial revival, but only as forms of modern tourism. Religious sites are useful means of attracting overseas Chinese visitors who contribute financially through gifts and remittances. Similar strategies are employed in the rebuilding of temples in eastern Tibet. While there has been a significant decline in the number of Buddhist monks, some 1,550 out of 1,886 monasteries have been rebuilt in eastern Tibetan areas (Kolas and Thowsen, 2005). However, as I have suggested, the Chinese promotion of Buddhist sites and institutions generally is connected with the expansion of global religious tourism. Shrines can grow and flourish only if they can be contained within religious theme parks – perhaps the counterparts of the science parks that are so popular in modern universities. Religion and science would therefore no longer need to compete with each other, as both contribute to the growth of the economy.

Managing religions

As the modern economy becomes increasingly global, especially in terms of the flow of finance and commodities, states and their bureaucratic agencies have to defend the principle of state sovereignty in a context of growing cultural diversity and complexity. There is as a result a profound contradiction between the economic requirements of flexibility and fluidity in the capitalist labour market and the state's objective of defending its territorial sovereignty. In particular, with the growth of a global war on terror after 9/11, states, rather than becoming more porous and open, have redefined and sharpened their legal and political borders with increasing determination. Singapore is no exception. It is a society that regards its neighbours with some degree of suspicion and anxiety. The threat of Islamic radicalism for a society that is overwhelmingly Chinese provides ample official reasons for vigilance and for controlling its own citizens.

The modern state therefore has a contradictory relationship to multiculturalism and migration on the one hand, and to security and sovereignty on the other. To satisfy the needs of business elites and to protect its economic position in global capitalism, the modern state must encourage labour migration, porous economic boundaries and minimal constraints on labour fluidity and flexibility. The state is under political pressure from economic elites to reduce the resistance of labour to the logic of capital accumulation by limiting the scope of strike action and controlling any prospect of wage inflation. In the name of fiscal prudence and good economic governance, the resistance of organised labour to structural change has been addressed by a determination to undermine trade unions, make strikes illegal and import foreign labour to reduce the unit costs of production. States also need to attract overseas 'talent' to sustain its professional classes and to ensure a steady flow of skilled labour. However, the state also has an interest in sustaining its own sovereignty, and hence wants to create and impose a cultural and moral unity on society. Sociologists occasionally refer to this nation-building activity of the state in terms of creating the cultural fabric – the great arch – of the society as the real foundation of political power (Corrigan and Sayer, 1985). The paradox is that its economic interests inevitably produce social and cultural diversity through high levels of migration, but its commitment to its sovereign power requires the state to sustain an overarching moral unity, to contain cultural complexity and to assimilate the migrant, at least culturally. In terms of the theory of modern governance (Foucault, 1991), the modern state is an administrative order that seeks to maximise the social potential of its population (and hence it has an interest in supporting migration) and at the same time has an interest in the enforcement of a particular type of territorial sovereignty.

This contradiction means that state policies towards citizenship and migration tend to be unstable, vacillating between treating migration and multiculturalism as aspects of economic policy and constructing multiculturalism within a framework of national sovereignty and cultural coherence. While many sociologists have noted that 'we are all multicultural now' (Glazer, 1997; Kymlicka, 1995), much of the recent evidence from Western societies is that multiculturalism is in retreat, because these policies have failed for various reasons – for example to deliver an equal share in social resources. More importantly, they often appear to have divided rather than united societies (Barry, 2001; Joppke, 2004; 2009; Levy, 2000). Political and social problems in recent years in Britain (the Bradford riots of 1995), France (the Foulard Affair), Germany (the case of Mrs Ludin), Denmark (the Cartoon Crisis) and Australia (the Cronulla Riots of 2005) have served only to refurbish doubts about existing multicultural policies. Singapore is somewhat different. As an international port, it has always been a migrant society and its Chinese majority, although a political elite, is also a migrant rather than a strictly indigenous community. Singapore has been largely successful in embracing multiculturalism – or multiracialism to use its own terms – without jeopardising the social supremacy of the Chinese, but it has achieved this end through careful management of religion, urban housing policies that reward compliance and strict controls on inward migration.

Theories of multiculturalism have attempted to make a distinction between the social and the cultural dimensions, thereby identifying four types, namely cosmopolitanism, fragmented pluralism, interactive pluralism and assimilation (Hartmann and Gerteis, 2005). The typology suggests that multiculturalism can involve various forms of association, including a situation (of parallel communities and fragmented pluralism) where social groups retain their internal solidarity, but where the society as a whole is fragmented. In this typology, social groups within a multicultural environment can clearly be in conflict-ridden competitive relationships with each other. Within this paradigm, assimilation is not strictly speaking an example of multiculturalism, since it is based on the assumption that difference is harmful and should be abandoned in the process of absorbing foreigners into a host society. Assimilation is the opposite of cosmopolitanism, which recognises the value of cultural integrity rather than the suppression of cultural differences. Finally, both cosmopolitanism and interactive multiculturalism praise difference, recognise group rights and accept principles of recognition and reciprocity. Cosmopolitanism involves a normative vision of this cultural diversity in which individual civil liberties are preserved (Appiah, 2006), but such policies can only work, I have argued, if there is an overarching legal and cultural framework to offset the diversity.

Typologies of state responses to religion can obviously be misleading if they are not treated with some scepticism and caution as modest methodological and heuristic devices. In the following typology, I shall attempt to categorise the logical range of possible government policies extending from inclusion to exclusion. Obviously any one government may have several policy strategies in place at any one time, and these policies may not necessarily be compatible or coherent. Governments are likely to follow contradictory strategies, because they are trying to balance economic openness with state security and political closure. There will be an oscillation between authoritarianism and liberalism, depending on the shifting nature of public opinion towards outsiders. The more extreme state policies of what I have called 'enclavement' involve the creation of ghettoes or social quarantine such as Guantá-namo Bay or the apartheid system of colonial South Africa (Turner, 2007a). These extreme forms of separation and exclusion might also include repatriation and expulsion on the one hand and extermination and ethnic cleansing on the other.

One can also imagine that the most extreme policies would include the repatriation of peoples and ethnic cleansing. In situations where territorial boundaries are ambiguous and there is much ethnic diversity within a society, then failing states may also redefine citizenship in order to transform unwanted resident populations into stateless peoples. This process of exclusion by changing the very nature of citizenship status has regrettably been a common occurrence in post-colonial Africa (Manby, 2009). In this discussion, however, I do not intend to examine such extreme measures as repatriation, genocide or expulsion, but rather to consider more routine measures of government control. For the majority of liberal governments, such extreme policies are unlikely instruments of government. While some politicians – for example Enoch Powell in the British post-war debate about migration – may recommend repatriation as a policy, such methods are rare and repatriation would be a difficult strategy for a liberal democracy to justify, let alone implement. In short, draconian policies of repatriation, expulsion and genocide are problematic even for authoritarian states, because they may well come under pressure from international law, the United Nations and human-rights activists. In liberal states, it would be difficult to implement such policies because their very enactment is likely to contradict the rules of procedural justice in a functioning democracy. The laws that were enacted in Germany to declare that Jews were not citizens were in some sense extraordinary laws (Agamben, 1998). For similar reasons, the use of 'extraordinary rendition' by the United States security agencies appears to contradict the principles of rule of law upon which democracies are based.

Inclusive policies, although in some respects benign, can nevertheless be criticised as patronising. By an inclusive policy of 'adaptive upgrading', I borrow a term from Talcott Parsons's sociological theory of social systems to suggest that some governments may adopt strategies to improve the education and social status of migrants with the view that such policies may help to integrate and domesticate minorities by re-educating and retraining its leadership with the long-term objective of bringing them into the middle classes through social mobility. Parsons (1999: 76) defined 'adaptive upgrading' as 'the re-evaluation of the older, previously downgraded components to constitute assets from the point of view of the broader system'. The opposite strategy would be to downgrade or even to degrade a population by transforming it into a minority whose main function in society would be to provide menial services. Degrading prevents a group achieving even minimum standards of civility. All under-classes could be said to experience degrading and, taking a phrase from Weber ([1921] 1952: 3), such policies would transform a minority into what he called a 'pariah group'.

Policies to achieve the integration of a social minority is probably the most common multicultural strategy which aims simply to bring a subordinate or minority group into the mainstream, but with the implication that over time they will lose their cultural distinctiveness. These strategies are in effect strategies of domestication. The opposite strategy is to force minorities into various types of enclaves, including the use of physical impediments such as walls to stop the flow of people. Cosmopolitanism is ambiguous. It has been criticised by some as an elite strategy that recognises differences but from a position of privilege. In order to avoid this criticism, cosmopolitanism needs to be taken to a higher stage of mutuality that I have called 'critical recognition ethics' (Turner, 2006). Although recognition appears to be an essential step in the development of cosmopolitanism as a moral attitude and a culture necessary for complex multicultural societies, there are, by that very fact, ample opportunities for misrecognition and resentment.

States and management strategies: authoritarian strategies

I have attempted to show that all modern states are now involved in some form of the management of religions. Given the growing problem of urban security and political insurgency, one can predict a slide towards more interventionist and authoritarian responses towards minorities and their religious traditions. In the majority of liberal democracies before 9/11, there was an inclusive laissez-faire policy in which the state guaranteed freedom of conscience on the principle that religion remained a private affair. The main exception has been with the treatment of so-called 'cults', and hence states in liberal democracies have been forced to intervene in what they have seen as problematic behaviour. States tend to intervene in the religious field when there is a perceived threat to minors, namely when children or other vulnerable groups are seen to be at risk from the evangelical activities of cults. Such behaviour tends to be regarded as brainwashing and hence a foundation for legal intervention. I shall not, however, concern myself with liberal and republican strategies in the West. These have already been widely discussed elsewhere (Asad, 1991; 2003; Joppke, 2009; Laurence and Vaisse, 2006). I shall instead concentrate on various authoritarian responses to religious pluralism and the rise of religious radicalism. Pessimistically, authoritarian solutions are likely to become the dominant mode of the modern management of religions.

The Singapore model

As a British colony Singapore became a multiracial society when migration in the nineteenth century created a small but diverse and complex society. However, today the state must manage even more diversity in its role as a cultural hub in Southeast Asia. Like many other modern societies, Singapore has a declining fertility rate despite all government attempts to reverse that trend. It must consequently seek to import labour, especially talented professionals. With a population of just over four million (plus some two million migration workers) and with little opportunity to recover more land, the Singapore state has nevertheless decided to increase its population to just over six million. With greater economic openness, there is also the prospect of greater ethnic diversity unless there are direct controls on the ethnic composition of immigrants. The Singapore state, in order to sustain its sovereignty over society, has to create the myth of a morally coherent and integrated community. In building an 'imagined community' (Anderson, 1991), it has to invent a nationalist ideology. It must find ways of projecting a common purpose around the state and some sense of a unified national community. It must foster a vivid and meaningful feeling of what it is to be a 'Singaporean' rather than simply a Chinese person living in an island in Southeast Asia. A delicate balance is required between nationalism, internal harmony and openness to foreign talent, and at the same time it must continue to give the impression that it does not favour one community over another.

Singapore has in the past experienced racial and religious tensions. There were riots in 1951 over the religious identity of Maria Hertog – a European girl who had been raised by a Malay family (Aljunied, 2009), and again in 1965. The government has responded to religious diversity by preventing religious labels playing any overt public role. The Maintenance of Religious Harmony Act of 1990 prevents the use of religion for political ends. The state has also been willing to respond forcefully to eliminate any signs of religious opposition, for example in its response to what it saw as a Marxist conspiracy among Catholic intellectuals in 1987. Twenty-two members of Catholic Church organisations who had promoted awareness of the plight of foreign workers were arrested on the grounds that they were plotting a Marxist revolt against the state. These arrests were carried out under the Internal Security Act but this blunt instrument was inappropriate in such cases. The Maintenance of Religious Harmony Act was designed to separate faith from social activism (Case, 2002: 91). However, the paradox is that, in order to keep religion and politics apart, the state must actively intervene in the 'religious market' to guarantee that religious services – preaching, teaching, healing, praying and so forth – are compatible with public security and nationalist goals.

In the Singapore case, this 'management of religion' has two dimensions, each of which is characterised by further ambiguities. The first dimension is the unintended consequence of creating religious enclaves. This outcome is a product of the classification of the population in which the state categorically divides the population primarily into four distinct communities: Chinese, Malay, Indian and Other. This means that these ethnic identities must play an important role in public life because the cultural identity of citizens is defined in these terms. Furthermore, since these ethnic categories are also in practice religious categories, it means that religion is significant in defining public identities. To illustrate, Malays are typically Muslim, Indians are typically Hindus and the Chinese are typically Buddhist, although there are a sizable number of Chinese who are Christians. Thus, there is an official ethnic 'enclavement' of groups despite the government's attempts to break these down through creating a national identity of being 'Singaporean'.

The second dimension is the specific management of Islam in Singapore; this is seen as necessary, in part because of the long-standing 'Malay problem', but also in part because the Singapore government prides itself on its technological rationality, ranging from urban planning to its family policies. Thus, the state feels it has a role to play in what we call 'upgrading' its own population. These upgrading strategies include everything from health (mosquito control and encouraging weight control for obesity) to automobile restrictions to education (including policies on 'Religious Knowledge'). Singaporean authorities have regarded individualism and 'shapeless multiculturalism' as aspects of Western decadence, contrasted with the moral superiority of Confucian Asia (Harvey, 2006: 61). The upgrading therefore manifests itself through the self-assumed responsibility of the state to intervene directly in the arena of religion, morals, reproduction and family life (ostensibly to make life better). Singapore's strategies towards its Muslim population have been conducted primarily through MUIS and its related policies of improving Muslim education, and modernising the *Shari'a* and its courts, in seeking to regulate and improve Muslim family life. In this case, despite religion technically being situated in the private or personal sphere, it is heavily regulated by the state.

Singapore is a small and insignificant island city-state in Southeast Asia and it is surrounded by societies that have much larger populations and resources. However, it is a society that is sociologically instructive. It illustrates in stark and clear terms the paradoxes of a market-driven society that claims to follow the principles of liberal capitalism. While the dominant form of global capitalism has been neo-liberal, few Asian societies have fully embraced deregulation in economics and liberalism in social life. The idea of a harmonious society based on a strong state and a Confucian value system has been far more attractive as a state ideology. Asian societies have sought to regulate family and religion in the interests of social stability. The Singaporean experience shows that any society that wants to separate religion and politics (in order to guarantee freedom of religious belief and practice) must interfere systematically in society to manage religions. The success or failure of these policies will have profound implications for the wealth and wellbeing of its citizens, and in the regions that surrounds the island.

Post-communist authoritarianism: China and Russia

The situation of religion under communism comes in my typology under downgrading or degrading. Religion in general was regarded as a superstition and as a threat to the monopolistic role of the Party. In China, in the period of the Cultural Revolution, Mao attempted to liquidate Confucianism as feudal and directly attacked the traditional customs of filial piety. It is said that both Stalin and Mao came implicitly to support some aspects of religion if they were useful in supporting or legitimating the Party. In Vietnam, Roman Catholicism was seen by the Party as a bastion of French colonialism and under American influence the Diem regime came to support Catholicism as a state religion against Buddhism. Despite these conflicts, it is possible to argue that Confucianism remained an official ideology and its commitment to an orderly society often served Party objectives.

The traditional legal arrangements of imperial China were based on Confucian values and can be described as a system of moral 'familialism'. This system involved unconditional filial piety, the welfare of the dominant status group over the individual and reverence for seniority. This 'Confucianisation of the law' meant that both judge and ruler drew directly from morality, especially where strictly juridical guidelines were absent or ambiguous. This traditional system promoted the idea of rules of law and virtue. The criminal law was the cornerstone of this system, because it was the basis of social control. This system broke down during the Cultural Revolution and one can interpret the post-Cultural Revolution period of institution building and law reform as an attempt to prevent any relapse into the excesses of class struggle and generational conflict. The 1999 national plan for managing public order sought to contain the growth of criminal gangs, the production of fake agricultural goods, the proliferation of cults and the emergence of juvenile delinquency, and to manage China's floating, dislocated populations. With these reforms, there has been a political emphasis on the need to combine rule of law with the rule of virtue. As an antidote to 'blind Westernisation', Chinese citizens are called upon to embrace Confucian virtue in the form of the 'four beautiful virtues' or *si mei* of beautiful thought, language, behaviour and environment and the 'four haves' (*si you*) of consciousness, morality, culture and discipline (Bell and Chaibong, 2003).

China's legal reforms and modernisation are in many respects a reassertion of traditional Confucian norms of respect, duty and stability. This feature of traditional rule and the failures of China's criminal law institutions is perhaps nowhere better illustrated than in the Party's response to the 'Falun Gong problem'. Between 1949 and 1997 cults were regarded as secret societies and hence constructed by the political elite as counter-revolutionary movements. The current treatment of Falun Gong continues a tradition of such criticism and displays the worst aspects of legal flexibility in which policy needs replace legal procedure. The ethos of 'state instrumentalism' and the use of the notion of 'social harm' give rise to considerable human-rights abuses. The worst features of state instrumentalism include detention without trial, extra-legal detention and custody for investigation. These procedures are enforced on the basis of the extra-judicial authority of public agencies.

Falun Gong ('Wheel of Law'), which combines Buddhist–Daoist beliefs and traditional exercises, claimed the right to assemble to practice their healing exercises in public spaces. Its founder Li Hongzhi was born in 1952 and embraced the teachings of *qigong* (on breathing exercises) at an early age. He established his own school of traditional healing in 1992 and initially gained political approval for these practices. Falun Gong appealed to the powerless and the dispossessed. When they were banned by the Ministry of Civil Affairs in 1999, Falun Gong responded with acts of civil disobedience. In response, the authorities adopted a mixture of extra-judicial measures that amount to administrative discipline: hard labour for re-education, 'custody for repatriation', detention for 'further investigation', loss of jobs and so forth. The Chinese Communist Party has defined religious heresy as crime and employed state institutions to reinforce 'socialist spiritual civilisation' against 'feudal superstition' (such as the beliefs and practices of Falun Gong). On 12 July 2006 it was reported in *Embassy*, the Canadian foreign policy newsletter, that the Canadian government had announced its intention to investigate allegations that Falun Gong prisoners in Chinese jails were being murdered and their organs sold to transplant patients. One piece of evidence is that prior to 1999, when Falun Gong were banned, the state was harvesting organs from 1,600 prisoners executed each year. Since 1999 there has been a rapid increase in organ transplants and it is estimated that some 41,500 organ donors in that period are unaccounted for. If these allegations prove to be true, the removal of prisoners' organs without consent will give 'extra-judicial procedures' a new and sinister meaning.

The case of the Uighurs and Chinese Muslims (Hui) has also recently become a matter of international concern. The Uighurs have a complicated history. With the collapse of the Second Eastern Turk Qughanante in 742 CE, the Uighurs created a steppe empire in 744. In 755 they helped the Tang to suppress the An Lushan uprising and extracted important resources from the Tang, including silk and royal brides. However, with internal political struggles and inclement weather, which destroyed their herds, famine contributed to the collapse of this empire in 840. Some Uighurs then sought sanctuary with the Tang and over time some sections of the Uighur community became sedentarised merchants, even joining the cosmopolitan aristocracy of the Tang administration. Other Uighur groups were dispersed and those that resisted Tang dominance were killed. In his *Tang China and the Collapse of the Uighar Empire*, Michael Drompp (2005; 156) concludes that the majority of Uighurs who sought support from the Chinese perished, while the Uighurs who lived in China were finally acculturated and dispersed. The pacification of the Uighurs along the northern frontier zone was brought about in large measure by the administrative skills of Li Deyu, whom Emperor Wuzong had put in charge of the political and military crisis. The seeds of Uighur nationalism were sown in the late nineteenth century and cultivated through the modernisation of the Uighur education system. Through the 1930s there were nationalist rebellions on the part of both Uighurs and Hui. The creation of the East Turkistan Republic in 1933–34 was a turning point in Uighur political consciousness. The contemporary political history of the Uighurs starts in 1949 when the Chinese Communist military leader General Wan

Jen occupied Xinjiang and, despite sporadic resistance, the Party was successful in bringing the Muslim establishment under control. The traditional social structure of Uighur society was undermined by land reform, which dispossessed the Uighur landholding class and redistributed land under the control of mosques. With the demobilisation of one million soldiers in 1952 there was increasing population pressure on the province. As a result, the proportion of Han people has steadily increased. In 1949 the Uighurs represented 76% of the population, in 1967 it was 50% and in 1984 the Uighurs were down to 40%. The Chinese government also started nuclear tests in Lob in East Turkistan, which it is claimed has caused significant damage to the fertility of the local Uighur population. In summary, it has been argued that the modernisation of the Uighurs is taking place through the filter of sinicisation, but the main question is whether the Chinese version of modernity will spell the end of Uighur culture (Berlie, 2004).

At present the prospects for respect for human rights in China are not promising. The partial erosion of the achievements of the new liberalism of 1997 to 1998 is depressing and where religions survive they do so because they can be useful to the state. In reviewing China's development, it is helpful to make a comparison with the recent history of Russia. Like China, Russia is faced with serious problems resulting from the confrontation with its Muslim population. With the collapse of the Soviet empire in 1992, there was, of course, considerable optimism about the prospects of human-rights improvements, but the main beneficiary so far has been the Orthodox Church, which can offer some veneer of legitimacy to the state.

Perhaps the most striking cultural development, therefore, in modern Russia has be the recovery of the Russian Orthodox Church in relation to both society and state. Although the Orthodox Church was severely repressed in the early years of the Russian revolution, the close relationship between Orthodoxy and nationalism meant that Christianity could also play a useful role in Russian politics. Since the fall of the Soviet system, the Orthodox Church has made an important comeback under the skilful political leadership of Patriarch Alexy II, who has forged a powerful alliance with both Vladimir Putin and Dmitry Medvedev (Garrad and Garrad, 2009). In 1983, Alexy was successful in securing the return of the Don Monastery in central Moscow to ecclesiastical use. In 1991, he managed to restore the veneration of St Seraphim of Sarov who, dying in 1833, was revered as a patriot by Tsar Nicholas II. The saint's relics were restored to the Cathedral of Sarov. In 1997, a law on the freedom of religious conscience gave a privileged status to Orthodoxy while Roman Catholicism has been politically marginalised. In Putin's Russia, Orthodoxy has continued to prosper as an official religion offering some degree of spiritual and national legitimacy to the Party and the state. There is also a close relationship between the military and the Church in that religious icons are used to bless warships and the Patriarch offered a thanksgiving service on the anniversary of the creation of the Soviet nuclear arsenal. Although the public role of Orthodoxy has been largely restored, the Church's influence is largely based on cultural nationalism rather than on its spiritual authority. Thus, while some 80 per cent of Russians describe themselves as 'Orthodox', just over 40 per cent call themselves 'believers'. This relationship between the political and the social allows us to say that, while Orthodoxy is a powerful public religion and that public space has been partially re-sacralised, Russian society remains secular. The legacy of atheism and secularism from the past still has a hold over the everyday social world, even when religion now plays a considerable part in a nationalist revival. Therefore, in any assessment of the notion of a 'post-secular society' we need to be careful about whether secularisation refers to formal institutions at the political level or whether it refers to lived religion at the social level.

The most extreme test of Russia's policies towards minorities and various autonomous regions has been the problem of managing Islam, especially in Chechnya. In November 1994, President Yeltsin decided to attack the Chechen capital Grozny to crush the separatist movement of Jokhar Dudayev. Human-rights critics of the war, such as Sergei Kovalev, having been denounced as enemies of Russia, predicted that the war would result in intolerance, revenge and civil violence (Gilligan, 2005). These criticisms came horribly true at the school massacre in Beslan. While Kovalev was highly critical of the Chechen leadership, he argued that the second war in Chechnya allowed Vladimir Putin to consolidate his power. Putin, who has done much to curtail human rights, undermine foreign non-governmental organisations, silence opposition and restore centralised power, has enforced the ideology of the Great Power and the doctrine of *derzhavnost* – the view that the state is a superior mystical being that every citizen must serve without question. The good citizen is a *derzhavnik* who is indifferent to the fate of other citizens and who accepts state crimes as necessary and justified.

After two wars in Chechnya (in 1996 and 1999), the Russian solution has been to create a powerful Chechnyan government that is ultimately subordinate to Moscow. This pacification of Chechnya is fragile and depends currently on the capacity of its leader, President Ramzan Kadyrov, to implement the policy of economic development and urban reconstruction of Grozny, the surrender of the former separatist rebels and the promotion of 'traditional' Islam to counteract its more radical variations. Under a new religious leadership, Kadyrov is promoting the idea that Chechnyan Sufism is in fact the national culture. The principal sign of Islamisation in Chechnyan society is the compulsory veiling of women, at least in public buildings and at the university. The other elements are the banning of alcohol, which nevertheless remains freely available to the political elite. Finally, President Kadyrov promotes polygamy as necessary to replace a population destroyed by warfare and as a means of making women behave. Islam has become politicised by the Chechnyan state as a policy of state building and social control (Littell, 2009).

Conclusion: states, sovereignty and space

Religious diversity has, with the collapse of communism and the rise of fundamentalism, become a major political issue in democratic societies, because we do not, in general terms, possess effective social policies and institutions to manage the social tensions that flow from increasing cultural complexity, and the conventional liberal solutions, especially the legacy of the Treaty of Westphalia, are problematic. The quest for political security has raised increasingly difficult issues for existing multiculturalism and religious diversity in relation to the state and the law. There is no shortage of evidence of terrorism. Although Singapore has not as yet been the target of a successful terrorist attack, there is considerable anxiety in the city-state that such an attack would have devastating social and economic consequences. It is also obvious that, as a secular capitalist state, Singapore must be a potential target of some significance. Economically advanced societies can no longer rely on the conventional division between politics and religion, and have entered a new phase that will have to involve the direct management of religions. In the current context of global anxieties over security, liberal states have evolved from policies of benign neglect to the active management of religious institutions. In practice, these new strategies are primarily concerned with 'managing Muslims' under the banner of social pluralism and multiculturalism. Managing religions is important if the state is to reassert its authority over civil society, especially over those religious institutions that seek to articulate an alternative vision of power and truth, and if it is to command the loyalty of its citizens over and above other claims of membership. While in the West governments struggle to reorganise liberalism to cope with the new reality of public religions, in other regimes, where the pressure for security and sovereignty is more prominent, more direct and authoritarian strategies are in place to either promote traditional religion in the service of the state or to create religious leisure parks and religious tourism as lucrative state activities. In short, just as there are multiple forms of modernisation, so there are multiple forms of secularisation.

10 | *Religious speech: on ineffable communication*

Introduction

Sociology broadly defined consists of the study of social interaction involving the exchange of meaning, symbols, values, objects and occasionally persons. At the core of this notion of exchange is language, and hence there has always been a close proximity between the philosophy of language and social theory. Recent critical theorists such as Jürgen Habermas (1984) have sought to construct the whole edifice of normative social theory on the idea of communicative acts. This definition of sociology is, of course, hardly controversial, but the very ordinariness of this definition points to some interesting gaps in sociological theory. The first is that it takes the social actor for granted, but what is a social actor? More specifically, can what we might call 'immaterial agents' (ghosts, spirits or angels) communicate? The second question is how do communicative systems manage the ineffable nature of religious speech? Religion is interesting from the point of view of a (secular) sociology of social action, because the communication of religious truths is typically ineffable, and hence religious systems tend to require a stratum of intermediaries (such as theologians and other intellectuals) to interpret and translate the ineffable meaning of sacred realms.

In societies where the great majority of people in the past could not read and write, the sacred written word had a special authority and power. There is always a tension between religious messages that are received by prophets and holy people as revelations and the process by which these messages are converted into texts. Over time these divine messages tend to get encoded into languages that we now regard as dead and hence the whole panoply of interpreters (saints, prophets and priests) became the intermediaries who make the ineffable effable. Literacy becomes a key issue in matters of religious authority. Historically, a literate religious elite has confronted an illiterate laity. As a result, translations of the divine word are often unavailable to the masses, who depend either on a literary elite that seeks to exert a hegemonic control over divine speech or on popular teachers or agents (such as spirit mediums) to render the invisible visible. In an illiterate world, the unreadable nature of the sacred word creates an important gulf between the priests who know the word and the laity who cannot read it or understand it. Often it was illiterate women who presented a significant challenge to the literate male priestly hierarchy. Joan of Arc was a challenge to the authority of the Church because she claimed to have a direct contact to the sacred world through the mediation of angels.

The ineffable nature of the sacred in a traditional society becomes the intellectual property of elites that can read and interpret Hebrew or Latin, or Arabic or Sanskrit. The sacred texts of Judaism, especially the written Torah or Hebrew Bible and the Talmud became a key source of social distinction in which the educated elite of male scholars were able to 'talk in Talmud', and thereby were separated from the inferior world of women and the uneducated. These literate religious elites stand in opposition to popular movements such as Sufism, in which the ineffable is rendered intelligible through ecstatic experiences, dance, trance or divination. In the modern period, where there is perhaps greater literacy, a democratisation of knowledge and access to knowledge through the Internet, the sharp distinction between the elite and the mass becomes blurred. In a democratic environment, the very idea that some truths are ineffable contradicts the ethos of modern society in which everybody claims a right to understand. Democracy tends to promote plain speech. The elite's control of ineffable knowledge is compromised and the whole idea of hierarchically organised wisdom evaporates. We are moving from the age of revelation to the age of information where everything is effable. The resulting crisis of authority is perhaps the real meaning of secularisation and, despite all the talk of re-sacralisation, the world of deep ineffability appears to be remote from everyday experience. Where is prophecy today? Where are the ineffable messages of yesteryear?

A theoretical paradigm: the media of exchange

One of the few attempts in sociology to understand religion in terms of the media of exchange is to be found in the late systems theory of Talcott Parsons. The notion of the 'media of exchange' grew out of Parsons's voluntaristic theory of action in which people exchange meaning through the medium of language. The notion in *The Structure of Social Action* (1937) that sociology is the study of action and inter-action rather than behaviour carries with it the idea that human interaction is always an exchange of meaning in which actors have to interpret the symbolic media of exchange in order to make sense of any communication. The difficulties in Parsons's original formulation of social action theory laid the grounds for subsequent attempts in sociology to better understand the actual dynamics of communication, such as symbolic interactionism and ethnomethodology.

However, Parsons went on to develop his original action theory in *The Social System* (1951), to argue that we can understand the four subsystems of the social system (culture, personality, economy and polity) as connected to each other through various media of exchange. Politics involves power as a medium of exchange; culture, an exchange of meaning; the economy involves money as a symbolic medium for the exchange of value; and personality satisfies wants and needs through the communication of affect. Parsons developed these notions further in his later work when he began to consider how these exchanges might relate to religion and ethical systems, and here he came up with the idea that what defines and determines the 'human condition' is the idea that life itself involves a gift relationship in which each individual is ultimately faced with the burden of life as simply something that is on loan to us and for which we have responsibility. These ideas were worked out in a series of interesting papers such as 'The "Gift of Life" and its Reciprocation' (Parsons, Fox and Lidz, 1972). Many of these papers reflecting on death and religion and exchange appeared in *Action Theory and the Human Condition* (Parsons, 1978). Perhaps one of the last attempts to spell out how the symbolism of gift and exchange enters the modern world appeared in 'Religious and Economic Symbolism in the Western World' (Parsons, 1979).

Parsons's views on the nature of money have continued to influence modern sociological theory relating to the economy, for example in Geoffrey Ingham's *The Nature of Money* (2004). However, Parsons's contributions to the sociology of religion through the idea of media of exchange have perhaps been less influential, apart from the work of Roland Robertson (1978) and Niklas Luhmann. Rejecting the restrictions of the four subsystem paradigm in Parsons's *The Social*

System that examined exchange in terms of economy, polity, value integration (culture) and personality, Luhmann has also rejected the idea that sociological theory refers to human beings, but instead conceives the social system as consisting of communicative acts.

Luhmann extended much of Parsons's framework to examine such media as truth, love, money and political power. One of Luhmann's most provocative contributions was to analyse love as a system of communication, especially a communication of the ineffable. In *Love as Passion* (1986), Luhmann showed how individuals need to share a code or interpretation to make sense of something that cannot be communicated when somebody says 'I love you'. He also showed how the code of love has changed over time by becoming a self-referential code, thereby increasing its autopoiesis with respect to the social system as a whole. The problem with modern love is whether more or less life-long commitments can survive the need for individual fulfilment on the part of the individuals (Arnoldi, 2001).

Luhmann developed similar arguments with respect to religion in *Religious Dogmatics and the Evolution of Societies* (1984). The medium of communication in religious systems is faith. Like love, religion deals with things that cannot be communicated, and religion in primitive societies is carried through the medium of ritual as a repository of the ineffable. In what Luhmann calls the 'religions of revelation', the role of the Church and the creeds is to translate revealed wisdom into creeds that can be memorised and recited and to organise a hierarchical system of interpretation through the training of religious functionaries such as priests. More could be said here, for example, about the nature of angels as carriers of otherwise incomprehensible meanings whose appearance can be interpreted by humans as conveying a message that is ultimately capable of human comprehension. The most powerful images of such events in Christianity were the message of the Angel Gabriel to the Virgin Mary and the Visitation of Mary to her cousin Elizabeth, whose offspring became John the Baptist according to the Gospel of Luke. As Jean-Luc Nancy (2005) points out, *visitation* in ecclesiastical Latin is more than a mere visit; it is the procedure for becoming aware of something. The Visitation became an occasion to recognise Mary as a significant religious figure in her own right, and so Elizabeth says 'Blessed art thou among women and blessed is the fruit of thy womb' (Luke 1:42–3). As these words indicate, the earliest Latin manuscripts of Luke attribute the Magnificat to her.

We could say that in religions of revelation angels are inserted into human interaction when two incommensurable systems – the sacred and the profane – collide in this-worldly time and space. In the Annunciation scenes from the life of Mary, the raised finger of the Angel Gabriel indicates a communication crisis, pointing to the arrival of a new code that will translate the incomprehensible into a gospel. The visitation of angels transforms the unreadable into the readable; the ineffable, effable.

The central paradox in Luhmann's theory of communication is that communication is necessary only when misunderstanding or lack of shared information is present. If there was no lack of understanding, then communication would not be necessary. If the conception of Mary had been intelligible, there would have been no Gabriel. The word 'effable' from *effabilis* comes from *effari* or 'to speak out'. Thus the ineffable is that which cannot be uttered. The *Shorter Oxford English Dictionary* notes that the ineffable is the unspeakable, unutterable and inexpressible. It also carries the meaning from 1597 that some things must not be uttered. In religious systems of communication, therefore, faith is an essential component of religious life, since the actions of the gods are ultimately unknowable. In monotheistic systems such as Judaism and Islam, even his Name is a secret; hence the use of the Tetragrammaton or YHVH or Yahweh. In Judaism, the worship of Yahweh was 'aniconic', that is without images or icons and His personal Name could never be known.

Luhmann's analysis of such media of exchange as love and faith is always set within his theory of the evolution of society, and in the case of religion he developed a theory of the secularisation of religion that is parallel to the study of love. In his evolutionary scheme, there are segmented, stratified and differentiated systems. In the first two, the religious sphere operates across the various components of the social system, giving an overall coherence to society. In this respect, Luhmann follows Émile Durkheim's account of social change in *The Division of Labor in Society* (1960). In a differentiated society, however, religion can no longer provide the general rationale for society as a whole, and it becomes increasingly functionally specific to the provision of what we might broadly call 'human services'. These therapeutic or welfare services are provided to people who are to some extent the victims of the social problems that arise in modern societies. Luhmann's theory of secularisation therefore recognises that religion becomes increasingly specialised as a quasi-welfare agency in modern societies (Beyer, 1984).

In summary, we can argue that in the age of revelation, religious communication had certain key elements that defined what constituted 'religion'. Firstly, the structure of the system of communication was essentially hierarchical in the literal sense that meaning came down to earth from above. However, the social structure of these religious codes was also hierarchical, and there was little differentiation between religious and political authority. We might borrow a term from Max Weber in volume one of *Economy and Society* (1978: 54) to describe this structure, namely a hierocracy.

Secondly, because religious communicative acts were necessarily tied to general structures of power, the metaphors of religious language reflected the structures of power in a society. The metaphors of divinity tend to be couched in the language of an absolute monarchy. In ancient Judaism, the words for God reflect the idea of lordship. In Moses Maimonides's *The Guide to the Perplexed* (1956), we find a discussion of the names of God in which *Adonay* or Lord is commonly used to describe a being that is gracious, merciful and just.

Thirdly, in the Abrahamic religions of revelation, the messages of God require intermediaries who are the vessels of these commandments, moral codes and ritual guidelines. As we have seen, prophets and angels mediate between these incommensurable communication systems, but there are as it were strains in this system. Given the absence of God, there is a tendency for the system to require persons who can intercede on behalf of people on earth. Figures such as the Virgin Mary have become crucial in communicating between the wretched of this earth (especially the persecuted, the powerless and the despised) and a merciful God, as we find in countries such as Mexico and the Philippines in the Virgin of Guadalupe (Warner, 1983). In Poland, the Black Madonna, Our Lady of Czestochowa, represented the suffering of the whole nation (Zubrzycki, 2006). On the other hand, monotheistic religious traditions tend to condemn any appeal to intermediary figures who might compromise the singular authority of God. It is as if any system based on a monotheistic or singular source of all messages condemns any shortcuts in communication. Through such notions as idolatry of false gods, these monotheistic religions gave us the modern idea of ideology as a system of false communication or misrepresentation.

Finally, in the age of revelation a system of hierarchic communication has always given priority to intellectual elites who are charged with the responsibility of guarding and reproducing a sacred language as the earthly means of divine communication. These are represented by the army of rabbis, mullahs and bishops who have defended the orthodoxy of the original message. Perhaps the logical conclusion of such institutional processes was the doctrine of papal infallibility and the early closure of interpretation in Islam. The transition from Latin to the vernacular in the West during the Reformation is an indication of a major shift of power from religious to secular authorities.

Towards a critique of Parsons–Luhmann

In attempting to create a theoretical framework for understanding religion in an age of ubiquitous media, I offer two basic criticisms of the Parsons–Luhmann schema. Firstly, their arguments are primarily couched within an interpretation of the Abrahamic faiths (Judaism, Christianity and Islam), namely religions which are monotheistic, revelatory and prophetic. We would need to make some important modifications to these arguments if we were to consider the so-called 'religions of Asia'. For example, Buddhism as a philosophical system rejects the idea of a monotheistic Creator-God, and encourages human beings to achieve personal enlightenment without the trappings of a theistic theology. We might say that Theravada Buddhism sought to reduce the amount of noise in systems of religious and ethical communication. Similarly, neither Confucianism nor Daoism had any notion of a singular source of revelatory knowledge. Confucius might achieve the status of an immortal in popular Chinese culture, but his wisdom was not regarded as a matter of revelation. Hence Confucianism and Daoism have no need for angels.

Secondly, neither Parsons nor Luhmann gave any consideration to the role of popular religion. By concentrating on the issues of faith and meaning in religious communication systems, they were in fact primarily concerned with the elite and its world of sacred texts, theological systems and scholarly debates about the meaning and significance of revelation. In popular religion, by contrast, we might argue that meaning is relatively unimportant, and what the laity demand from religion is succour to cope with the basic tribulations of bare life. Popular religion is typically based on an exchange system in which the laity communicates with a great variety of divine figures, objects or spaces through offerings that are designed to win the favour and attention of a pantheon of gods and goddesses. In exchange for such offerings, humans expect protection from disasters, the promise of wealth and the prospects of health. The basic goal of Daoist practice was longevity.

Precisely because the official communication system is ineffable, the laity depends on more concrete methods of manipulating divine figures and of making their wishes known. For example, many aspects of religion in Asia are concerned to communicate with ancestors, to help ancestors and to receive the protection of these ancestors. The whole role of filial piety in Confucianism expresses this need for an exchange system with the dead ancestors and with the need to avoid 'hungry ghosts'. Communicating with ghosts occupies much of the mundane world of popular Chinese religions; here is a religious communication system that is popular, local and diverse, with no sacred language and no system of priestly control (Ikels, 2004). Modern Vietnam is a country which is, so to speak, over-populated with these displaced ghosts (Leshkowich, 2008).

In modern Asia, Daoist temples still function rather like banks or market-places, and it makes sense to talk about both 'grey' and 'black markets' in terms of the provision of services and goods (Yang, 2006). Throughout the Chinese community, there is a large market for the production and circulation of votive money as offerings, especially in the Chinese New Year. There is also in modern Thailand an important local industry in terms of the manufacture and distribution of amulets. In short, the media of exchange in the religious market includes both actual and votive money, as well as other goods and services. The economy of religious merit as an exchange system between laity and religious personnel is deeply embedded in the economy of secular goods and services.

The religious sphere, whether in the Christian West, in folk religions or in the religious traditions of Asia, is therefore stratified in terms of what Weber in *The Sociology of Religion* (1966) called virtuoso and mass religion. Whereas the virtuosi are concerned with the meaningfulness of religious communication, the mass are concerned with health and prosperity. The orientation of the masses to religious communication is pragmatic, this-worldly and utilitarian. In the age of revelation, the elite could contain and occasionally liquidate popular religions, because the power of the elite gave them control over the temples, the sacred language and rituals.

The main change that has taken place with the growth of new information systems in the age of ubiquitous media is that the power relationship between popular and virtuoso religion has been levelled out, if not reversed. The struggle between popular and elite religion in the field of symbolic capital has given an important if unintended advantage to popular religious communication, which can now bypass the hierarchal organisation of orthodox information. The principal thesis of this chapter is therefore that the new media have brought about a democratisation of the systems of religious communication in terms of both codes and contents. We can briefly consider these changes in authority and the partial democratisation of religion that are associated with the new media.

Religion in the age of ubiquitous media

The major changes that have taken place in religion can be simply described in the following list. Firstly, whereas the religious system of communication in an age of revelation was hierarchical, unitary and authoritative, the system of communicative acts in a new media environment are horizontal rather than vertical, diverse and fragmented rather than unitary, the sources of authority are devolved rather than centralised, and the authority of any message is negotiable and negotiated. The growth of these diverse centres of interpretation in a global communication system has produced a crisis of authority in the formal system of religious belief and practice. In Islam, for example, there has been an inflation of sources of authority since, through some local and specific consensus, almost any local teacher or *mullah* can issue a *fatwa* to guide a local community (Volpi and Turner, 2007).

Secondly, because new media provide multiple channels of access and encourage discursive interaction on blogs and other sites, they bring about a partial democratisation of information. Although there is clearly a digital divide, more and more people have access to religious sites of communication. There is a corresponding democratisation of religion. Many young Muslims bypass their *ulama* and *imams* in order to learn about Islam in English from pamphlets and sources such as *The Muslim News* and *Q-News*. The majority of Muslim users of the Internet are resident in Europe and North America. These diasporic Internet users are typically students in Western universities undertaking technical degrees in engineering, chemistry and accountancy. There is an important affinity between their scientific backgrounds and their neo-fundamentalist interpretations of Islam. Because Internet access is often too expensive to be available in many communities in the Middle East, Asia and Africa, it is again the student population of Western universities who are accessing the Internet for religious and political purposes. There is evidence that the Internet is used by radical activists to promote terrorism against the West, but the Internet can also promote reasoned argument and discussion in a context where everybody can in principle check the sources of communication for themselves. In the absence of firm criteria by which information can be guaranteed by recognised institutions, young Muslims are inclined to generate their own standards. Much of this Internet discussion is about the proper conduct and piety required by a 'good Muslim' in new contexts and circumstances. The majority of sites are not developed by official Muslim organisations such as the Muslim World League, and it is for this reason that the Internet is a means of bypassing the traditional gatekeepers of Muslim orthodoxy.

The Internet has only served to reinforce an existing problem of authority. Within the Muslim diaspora, where young Muslims face new problems relating to personal conduct, the new intellectuals create personal websites, providing religious or ethical rulings on various questions relating to religious conduct. These email *fatwas* are not recognised by *Shari'a* courts as admissible evidence and they cannot be readily enforced, but they clearly have an influence within the diaspora. They become authoritative as users can compare these rulings against other sites and e-*fatwas*. In summary, the Internet is an important technology for creating an imagined community for individuals and groups that are separated from their homeland and exist in alien secular cultures that are often hostile to Islam. These Internet sites also serve to reinforce the individualism which many observers have associated with neo-fundamentalism, because the global virtual *ummah* is the perfect site for individuals to express themselves while still claiming to be members of a community on whose behalf they are speaking (Mandaville, 2001). We can conclude, therefore, that the modern form of religious communication is characterised by a principle of subsidiarity where authority rests in the local and specific act of communication rather than from a principle of hierocracy.

Thirdly, therefore, the ubiquitous media contribute to a growing individualism that is very different from the rugged ascetic individualism of nearly Protestantism. The religious subjectivity of the media is a facet of the 'expressive revolution' that had its roots in the student revolts of the 1960s. In the new individualism, people invent their own religious ideas, giving rise to a DIY religiosity and, with the prevalence of the Internet, to 'online-religion' where the individual is free to navigate their own personal pathways through religious messages.

The result has been a social revolution flowing from both consumerism and individualism, and as a result there has been a slow erosion of the more traditional class identities of early capitalism. Consumerism and a new emphasis on status, consumption and lifestyle have blurred the old cultural divisions between social classes. Although income inequality has increased in the decades of neo-liberal economics, class identities are weaker and government strategies to reduce union power and to control strike behaviour have been generally successful (Mazower, 1998). Religious identities, at least in youth cultures, are as a result more fluid. Religious lifestyles get modelled on consumer lifestyles in which people can try out religions rather like they try out a new fashion in handbags or shoes. In a consumer society, people want goods not gods, and to a large extent their desires can be satisfied by consumer credit. A new industry has emerged concerned with spiritual advice about how to cope with the modern world while remaining pious and pure. Pious lifestyles are marketed by religious entrepreneurs who need to brand their products in the spiritual market-place.

The consequence of these developments is a growing division between 'religion' and 'spirituality' (Hunt, 2005). Globalisation thus involves the spread of personal spirituality and these spiritualities typically provide not so much authoritative guidance in the everyday world as a subjective, personalised meaning. Such religious phenomena are often combined with therapeutic or healing services, or the promise of personal enhancement through meditation. While fundamentalist norms of personal discipline appeal most to social groups that are upwardly socially mobile, such as the lower middle class and newly educated couples, spirituality is more closely associated with middle-class singles who have been thoroughly influenced by Western consumer values.

Whereas the traditionally religious find meaning in existing mainstream denominational Christianity, spiritual people create their own religious space in the general spiritual market-place, deliberately avoiding any overt connection or commitment to traditional religious organisations and their legacy of orthodox theology. The new religions are closely associated with the themes of therapy, peace and self-help. Of course, the idea that religion, especially in the West, has become privatised is hardly new (Luckmann, 1967). However, these new forms of subjectivity and private spirituality are no longer confined to Protestantism or the American middle classes; they now have global implications.

These religious developments are no longer local popular cults, but burgeoning global popular religions carried by the Internet, movies, rock music, popular TV shows and 'pulp fiction'. These can also be referred to as 'pick 'n' mix religions' because their adherents borrow promiscuously from a great range of religious beliefs and practices. These forms of spirituality can be transmitted by films such as *Hidden Tiger, Crouching Dragon* and *House of Flying Daggers*. This development is one aspect of 'a new techno-mysticism most spectacularly presented to us in the use of special effects in blockbuster films' (Ward, 2006: 18). These phenomena have been regarded as aspects of 'new religious movements' (Beckford, 2003) that are, as we have seen, manifestations of the new spiritual market-places. Such forms of religion tend to be highly individualistic: they are unorthodox in the sense that they follow no official creed, they are characterised by their syncretism and they have little or no connection with institutions such as churches, mosques or temples. They are post-institutional and in this sense they can be legitimately called 'post-modern religions'. If global fundamentalism involves modernisation, the global post-institutional religions are typical of 'post-modernisation'.

Fourthly, because authority has been devolved by the principle of subsidiarity, the result is the hybridisation of religious traditions. This hybridity is reinforced through globalisation and through the processes of borrowing from different religious traditions in a global religious market. To quote from Courtney Bender's *Heaven's Kitchen* (2003: 72) in his description of 'Anita', an informant from the kitchen (known as God's Love We Deliver), Anita 'attended the Sunday morning services at the Episcopalian and Catholic churches on her block. She spirit channelled, took astrology courses, read Deepak Chopra, and dabbled in Catholic mysticism. She grew up in a Jewish family, but since childhood she had been attracted to the "mysterious" black habits that Catholic nuns wore. She recently learned that she had been "a nun in a past life". Anita emphatically told me that her inner spirit guided her to ideas that would be "helpful".'

Fifthly, we live increasingly in a communication environment where images and symbols rather than the written word play an increasingly important role in interaction. In a visual world that is iconic, new skills for reading images no longer duplicate the literary skills of the written word. It is a new experimental context in which the iconic can also be the iconoclastic as Madonna in her Catholic period switched to Rachel and for a while explored the Kabbalah (Hulsether, 2000).

Finally, I call this combination of self-help systems, subjectivity, devolved authority structures, iconic discourses and experimental syncretism an example of 'low-intensity religion'. It is a mobile religiosity that can be transported globally by mobile people to new sites where they can mix and match their religious or self-help needs without too much constraint from hierarchical authorities. It is typically a passive religiosity with controlled emotions, because modern conversions tend to be more like a change in consumer brands than a traumatic transformation of the self. If the new religious lifestyles give rise to emotions, these are packaged in ways that can be easily consumed. Brand loyalty on the part of consumers in low-intensity religions is also fluid and unstable.

One can argue that these developments were in fact anticipated by emotional forms of evangelical Protestantism starting with John Wesley and somewhat later with Friedrich Schleiermacher. Traditional evangelical Christianity does, of course, play a large role in the spiritual market-place where Christian groups have made successful use of more conventional media. One illustration of the process of selective modernisation is the use of television and radio by fundamentalist Christian groups in the United States. Religion has for a long time been a prominent feature of American broadcasting and the 'radio preacher' became a familiar figure of popular culture. The development of satellite broadcasting and the distribution of programmes through the cable television industry greatly expanded their influence. For example, Pat Robertson's *700 Club* was particularly successful and CBN is now the third largest cable network in America, and funds the CBN University, offering courses on media production techniques. Another example is James Dobson's radio programme *Focus on the Family*, that offers psychological advice and counselling services. This programme has evolved into the equivalent of a Christian call centre that receives 1,200 daily calls on a toll-free number. However, the new global media have given these more conventional developments in the use of media a new pace and intensity, creating an avalanche of religious signs and services that threaten to drown more traditional forms of practice. They begin to replace the traditional book culture of the world of preachers in the old evangelical religions.

Conclusion: religion and nostalgia

I turn finally to the problem of intellectual nostalgia (Turner, 1987). Cultural nostalgia has played an important role in cultural and critical theory, and was an important component of the critical theorists. For example, Adorno's work on the 'culture industry' is essentially a backward-looking criticism of capitalism and art. We might say that many Jewish intellectuals in the twentieth century embraced a nostalgic critique of modern post-Holocaust society, especially in the work of Walter Benjamin and Gershom Scholem (Scholem, 1997), whose study of the mystical Godhead in Kabbalah mysticism is exemplary. In the sociology of religion, critics might argue that the work of Bryan Wilson (1966) had a nostalgic element insofar as he developed a significant criticism of popular religious forms – the use of guitars in churches, the interaction between religious themes and popular culture, and in general the impact of youth cultures on the representation of the sacred. However, the principal example of nostalgic cultural criticism in recent years was developed by Philip Rieff (2006) in his notion of three cultures – first, second and third – and the idea of 'death-works'. By the concept of death-works, Rieff points to artworks and other phenomena that stand at the juncture of two cultures where one of them is collapsing. A death-work is a destructive and deconstructive work that signals and contributes to the collapse of a culture. Rieff believes that we are standing at the collapse of the second culture and the arrival of a third. The third culture is post-sacred, post-literate and post-communal. The death-works are represented by Pablo Picasso, Marcel Duchamp, Piero Manzoni, Robert Mapplethorpe and Andres Serrano. The first and second worlds were sacred spaces, characterised by a high literature and a priestly class. For Rieff, the modern world still has a priestly class – sociologists, welfare workers, psychoanalysts and so forth – but it no longer has a sacred space or a literature.

Rieff recognised that the democratisation of culture in the third world involves a celebration of illiteracy – 'The democratisation of death-works is seen in the rise of armies of principled illiterates' (Rieff, 2006: 92). However, the implication of Rieff's nostalgic critique is that no social order can survive without some notion of the sacred as a foundation for a shared sense of what constitutes authority. His condemnation of Andres Serrano is possibly the clearest statement in his work of this issue. Serrano's *Piss Christ* in 1987 is seen as a direct and pathetic assault on the sacred that seeks to rob identity of its underpinnings in the sacred. In this sense, Serrano is the archetypical artist of the historical moment of the death-work.

Rieff's critique of modern culture in many respects parallels my analysis of religion in the age of information. We might say in a Rieffian framework that Madonna's 'Like a Prayer' in 1989 is a death-work in which Catholicism as an authoritative and meaningful system is collapsing under the weight of the democratising feminist message of the video as a means of communication. In the information age, religion has become part of the leisure industry that offers entertainment rather than salvation and therefore the rise of low-intensity religion can be regarded as a death-work signalling the end of authentic and viable forms of personal piety. Although this might be regarded as merely a nostalgic criticism, the defence of this position is the claim that modern spirituality does not have the socially transformative potentialities of organised religions that sustained a division between the sacred and the profane – between the world and its alternative.

11 | *Spiritualities: the media, feminism and consumerism*

Introduction: urban mythologies

In the contemporary world, there are obviously porous boundaries between religious fiction and religious fact. Hollywood films and popular fiction compete spiritually and culturally for the modern 'religious imaginary' in ways that ecclesiastical institutions and their intellectual spokespeople find hard to comprehend, even less to control. In this discussion, I compare two recent but very different examples of popular culture, namely Dan Brown's *The da Vinci Code*, which came out in 2003, and Mel Gibson's *The Passion of the Christ*, which was launched on 25 February 2004. The former severely annoyed the authorities within the Catholic Church, because it appeared that many lay people were attempting to follow the trail for the Holy Grail in France and Britain in imitation of the novel's main storyline as a modern pilgrimage. Brown's book became the target of several academic criticisms, such as Darrell Bock's *Breaking the da Vinci Code* (2004). Both the book and the subsequent film globally enjoyed large sales. Although the film was judged by many to be a box-office failure, the book sold some four and a half million copies within the first nine months. Brown's other novels have also been enjoying high sales. There is now a Dan Brown industry in which *The Lost Symbol* (Brown, 2009) competes to overtake previous sales figures.

Gibson's *The Passion* was also a major commercial success. It had within two months of its release already generated box-office receipts of around $387 million. The film was skilfully managed and directly promoted at the grass roots by ministers of Evangelical churches, conservative Roman Catholics and charismatic groups. The film's mass marketing strategy had the support of local church leaders who also encouraged their congregations to attend, often through block-booking tickets (Maresco, 2004). The film was simultaneously promoted through various ancillary markets. For example, more than one million 'witness cards' were printed and circulated in support of the evangelical aspect of the film. The soundtrack was promoted by Sony Music and Integrity Music. Four million copies of the film were sold on the first day of release, and *The Passion. Photography from the Movie* has gone into eight reprints and sold over 650,000 copies.

Brown's book, by contrast, is controversial as a doctrinal challenge to Christian orthodoxy, but especially to Catholic traditions. For example, many of the claims within *The da Vinci Code* have some affinity with scholarly arguments from within feminism and feminist theology about the subordination of women within traditional Christian institutions and teaching. Feminist criticisms of the patriarchal assumptions of Christian theology have had a long history in the works of Simone de Beauvoir, Carol Christ, Mary Daly and Julia Kristeva (O'Connor, 1989). Whereas in *The da Vinci Code* these feminist themes became one aspect of Brown's successful novel, *The Passion* was staunchly compatible with orthodox Catholicism, but it too caused public controversy, mainly around accusations of latent anti-Semitism.

These two popular works as examples of contemporary popular culture are in many respects a mirror image of each other: heretical versus orthodox theology; traditional Catholicism versus anti-Catholicism; patriarchal versus matriarchal narratives. What they have in common is the representation of religion as a powerful dimension of the popular imagination and post-institutional spirituality. Both are also popular representations of religious themes that circulate as commodities outside the official religious institutions, and therefore outside the control of ecclesiastical authorities. These are simply two examples of how popular culture constantly appropriates religious symbols and themes. Such commercial developments are paradoxical, because they keep religious themes in the public domain, but at the same time they challenge traditional, hierarchical and literate forms of religious authority. There are many other examples from popular culture. Madonna plays with Catholic images on the one hand and with Jewish Kabbalah on the other. Whereas Dan Brown's book and Madonna's records directly challenge religious orthodoxy, Gibson sought the approval of religious leaders before shooting and releasing his film, but he could not control the unintended consequences of the film once it was in circulation. *The Passion*, unlike

The da Vinci Code belongs to a well-established genre of popular representations of Christ in postcards, domestic paintings and films. In one sense, there is nothing particularly new about popular religion, but what is important is the global scale and the social impact of such religious commodities. Popular religion corrodes the formal authority structure of official religious institutions by simply bypassing them, and therefore it is an example of what I have described in this volume as social or everyday secularisation.

The da Vinci Code and the feminist critique of religious studies

The da Vinci Code is overtly a traditional detective story in which the hero Robert Langdon and heroine Sophie Neveu uncover the real secret behind the apparently senseless murder of the renowned curator Jacques Sauniere. The plot that unfolds uncovers the historical attempt to disguise the true meaning of the quest for the Holy Grail, the subordination of a feminine cult in Christianity, the true identity of Mary Magdalene and the sinister involvement of the Catholic order of Opus Dei in a series of brutal murders. This historical account of suppression starts with Leonardo da Vinci, who was allegedly a prominent member of a secret society whose purpose was to protect the true history of the Christian faith until the world is ready to receive that message. The book traces the role of cryptology in hiding the secret message of Christianity, and in order to transmit that message da Vinci employed his technological genius to invent a portable container for these secret documents. The novel explores how Langdon and Neveu, more or less by accident, luck and perseverance, hit upon the hidden meaning of Christianity and the importance of the da Vinci code.

The book is an account of the uncovering of the cult around Mary Magdalene. The hidden secret of orthodox Christianity is that Jesus was married to Mary and that his divinity was not accepted until the Council of Nicaea in AD 325. This marriage, according to the novel, is part of the hidden theme of Leonardo's *Last Supper*, in which Mary sits at the right hand of Jesus. In uncovering this deep secret, the novel involves a series of confrontations between the hero, the French police and Opus Dei, all of whom are either attempting to find the truth behind the murders or attempting to cover up the truth about Jesus and the origins of Christianity.

At another level the novel is an intellectual romp through European religious and intellectual culture. Langdon is a Harvard Professor of Religious Symbology and much in demand from the organisers of lecture tours and controversial presentations, as we discover at the beginning of the plot. However, the story takes place in Europe and the novel is in this sense a form of intellectual tourism. The reader is transported to high-culture travel locations – the Louvre, Hotel Ritz Paris and Westminster Abbey – and at the same time the novel invites us to join a pseudo-world of intellectual puzzles about the Church, Western history, ecclesiastical history, cryptology, theology and 'symbology'.

One pivotal scene occurs in Chapter 56, where Robert Langdon explains the real meaning of the common symbols for male and female. The ancient symbol for male is a 'rudimentary phallus' or 'blade', and this icon 'represents aggression and manhood' (Brown, 2003: 237). By contrast, the true icon of the female is V or 'chalice', because 'it resembles a cup or vessel, and more important it resembles the shape of a woman's womb. This symbol communicates femininity, womanhood, and fertility ... legend tells us that the Holy Grail is a chalice' (p. 238). Professor Langdon goes on to explain that the power of the female was always a threat to the predominantly male Church and therefore the female was demonised and cast out as unclean. The biblical story of Adam and Eve was the creation of a patriarchal religion in which woman has to be categorised as the weaker, inferior and dangerous vessel. Christianity thus appropriated many of the myths of ancient religions and the mother goddess theme of pagan cults became the hidden goddess of the Christian period. The conclusion of Langdon's analysis is that the Holy Grail is in fact the symbol of the lost goddess of the pre-Christian traditions.

Despite the enthusiastic applause of *The Washington Post*, *The Boston Globe* and the *Chicago Tribune*, Brown's thriller will not be regarded as a contribution to any serious study of religion, but it does ironically incorporate many themes from academic religious studies, specifically from the feminist critique of the mainstream sciences of religion. It is not a contribution to literature and feminists may criticise the book as a typical male-dominated action thriller. It is, after all, the male hero Langdon who has to explain to Sophie that Christianity has suppressed the female principle in Western religions. Nevertheless, *The da Vinci Code* contains a feminist account of Christianity that is more successful in reaching a mass audience than the work of academic feminists. It also appears to be more effective in reaching a mass audience than the literature of mainstream Christianity.

The feminist critique of the science of religion has taken three directions. Firstly, there is the criticism of religious studies as such that the absence of women is not just academic absentmindedness but an actual exclusion (Warne, 2001). Male scholars – Durkheim, Mauss, Robertson Smith, Evans-Pritchard, Müller and so forth – dominated the development of the sciences of religion, thereby excluding and suppressing the feminine on the religious. Secondly, the scientific study of religion was essentially a by-product of the rational Enlightenment, which sought to make religion intelligible by simply collecting an exhaustive assemblage of facts about religious phenomena. Thirdly, this rational quest of classification was in many respects parasitic upon colonialism, because the data for the new science were often collected by colonial officials, or it was made available as a result of colonialism. Perhaps the most prominent example was indeed Émile Durkheim's *The Elementary Forms* ([1912] 2001), which was made possible by British colonial administrators conducting their work among the Aboriginal communities of central Australia. The academic study of religion in France did not, however, begin to generate its own colonial anthropology and its own fieldwork until Michel Leiris and others joined the great field expedition from Dakar to Djibouti between 1931 and 1933, thereby laying the foundations for what became the *College de Sociologie* (Richman, 2002). Fourthly, with the association between European colonialism and the science of religion, the Judaeo-Christian notion of religion – as an institutionalised system of belief and practice with reference to a single creator-God – was eventually exported to Africa and Asia. The consequence has been that 'the comparative study of religion remains founded on a conceptual framework that is unmistakably theological and Christian in orientation' (King, 1999: 40). Finally, in conjunction with these academic traditions, women remain substantively excluded from the institutions of religion. This exclusion is clearly manifest in the doctrine of the masculine character of the sacerdotal nature of priesthood in Western Christianity – an exclusion that was all too clear in the controversial conflict over the nature of the priesthood between Anglicanism and the Catholic Church in late 2009.

The feminist response has been twofold. Firstly, it has challenged the science of religion in order to recognise women's experience as a legitimate category of analysis and has promoted new theories and methodologies to challenge the allegedly existing masculine nature of conventional science. Secondly, in political terms women have, through cross-cultural research, demonstrated how women have not only resisted religious oppression, but have been creative and innovative agents within the religious field. As a result of these critical endeavours feminist academics have 'assessed the ambiguity of gendered symbolism within many religious systems' (Hawthorne, 2009: 143).

The idea of the feminine sacred has been a concern of feminist scholarship from the beginning (Atkinson, Buchanan and Miles, 1985), but it is perhaps ironic that the Max Weber household was a distinctive example of the patriarchal household and yet Marianne Weber was a leading feminist of her generation, arguing in her *Ehefrau und Mutter in der Rechtsentwicklung* (1907) that women should have complete legal control over their own disposable income. Both Max Weber and Marianne Weber were deeply influenced by Albrecht Dieterich's *Mutter Erde. Ein Versuch uber Volksreligion* (1905), in which he argued that the origin of all religions lay in a 'mother cult' out of which sprang the monotheistic–patriarchal religions that had subsequently suppressed the feminine. When Weber made his famous visit to North America and his journey to Oklahoma, one aspect of this research was to examine traces of the mother goddess cult in Native American spirituality (Scaff, 2005). There is, in short, an established tradition of scholarship researching the historical decline of the matriarchal foundations of religion and the evolution of feminine spirituality.

My argument is not, however, that *The da Vinci Code* is a contribution to feminist literature, but rather that popular religious culture plays a major role in circulating such beliefs. Moreover, such popular literature by definition more effectively addresses a mass audience than academic literature. Paradoxically, popular religion is typically corrosive of the erstwhile dominant and hierarchical culture of the official institutions. What is less clear is exactly how this popular genre is absorbed into the everyday beliefs of the lay audience for such works. Perhaps what is more obvious is that the media – TV, film and the Internet – are no longer marginal to religion but instead occupy a central place. Modern examples might be the commemorations of the assassination of Present Kennedy and the death of Princess Diana as major aspects of a civil religion that is global rather than simply national (Zelizer, 1993).

The Passion as pornography

The Passion is part of a genre of 'the Christ film', such as Cecil B. DeMille's *The King of Kings*, Pasolini's *The Gospel according to St Matthew* and Zeffirelli's *Jesus of Nazareth*. The film is therefore a modern representative of so-called 'biblical epics' (Babbington and Evans, 1993). While Brown's novel has caused some embarrassment to the Catholic authorities, Gibson's film is unquestioning in its representation of an official version of the Passion. As we have seen, Gibson made strenuous efforts to make sure the film would be well received by Christian audiences. Tickets for *The Passion* were sold in large numbers to congregations. While the film is a violent and graphic description of the death of Jesus, the New Testament has relatively little to say about the final crucifixion of Christ. In Paul's letters there are few descriptive references to the agony of Christ, because the message of Pauline Christianity is simply 'The Lord is risen!' Gibson has relied on an old Catholic tradition such as 'The Dolorous Passion of Our Lord Jesus Christ', which was published in 1833 by the German Romantic poet Clemens Brentano ([1833] 1970), who provided a detailed account of the violent death of Christ. This account was in turn based on the visions of a nineteenth-century Catholic nun, Anne Catherine Emmerich. Gibson's film was shot in Italy, the characters speak in Aramaic and Latin, with English subtitles, and the principal actor James Caviezel is unquestionably beautiful rather than just handsome. The film is mainly concerned with the flogging, beating, scourging, torture and final death of Jesus. There is little or no relief from the violence and the scenes and photography appear to be modelled on the dramatic painterly techniques of Caravaggio, such as his painting of Christ at Emaus from the late sixteenth century.

The film can, in fact, be regarded as a medieval passion play that is transcribed through modern cinema technology. Its unrelenting pornographic representation of violence comes eventually to challenge the overt attempt to remain true to the physical reality of the crucifixion. Gibson's film was in addition regarded as implicitly anti-Semitic, and thereby remained true to its medieval counterparts. Within its

Orientalist paradigm, Gibson's Jewish priests are presented as small, dark and unattractive creatures in stark contrast to Jesus. The film manages to avoid the fact that Jesus and his disciples were also Jewish, and had more in common in cultural and religious terms with the High Priests than they did with the Roman colonialists. In this sense the film was also problematic for the Church's public relations.

The realism of *The Passion* is in part reminiscent of Pier Pasolini's Marxist version of *The Gospel According to St Matthew* (1964), Franco Zeffirelli's *Jesus of Nazareth* (1977) and Martin Scorsese's *The Last Temptation of Christ* (1988). However, the blood-splattered figure of Christ in Gibson's film is also similar to the image contained in the famous Isenheim Altarpiece of Matthias Grünewald from the early sixteenth century. In this modern passion play, the tortured figure of Jesus is pure south German Baroque. By contrast, the Jewish religious leaders are opulent and corrupt, while Pilate is a subtle politician who would help Christ but cannot. The guards who harass and abuse Christ are represented as British thugs, thereby continuing Gibson's post-colonial anti-British theme from such films as *The Patriot*. Satan is a chillingly alien figure of ambiguous gender, and Caiaphas is sinister and corrupt. The overwhelming effect of *The Passion* is that of pure emotionality. We are only expected to *feel* the events of Christ's death and not to hold any intellectual views about what is occurring in the film. We are invited to feel the pain, not to understand it.

Again like a medieval play, the film assumes that the audience understands the plot and the characters, and therefore Gibson does not fill in any background details. Without the background understanding it is, in fact, not clear why Jesus receives so much punishment from the guards, or why the ordeal lasts so long. A Christian audience knows that Christ died to save us from our sins and that crucifixion expresses the doctrine of the immanence of divinity and the resurrection of the body, and therefore Christ has to experience the pain and suffering of mankind in order to dwell among us. Nevertheless, the extent and duration of the flogging is still puzzling. The violence is in this sense pornographic and this theme of physical brutality runs throughout Gibson's previous blockbusters such as *Braveheart* and the early films such as *Mad Max*. Unlike the feminist undercurrent of *The da Vinci Code*, Gibson's film obviously makes few concessions to a feminist consciousness, being completely infused with violence and masculinity. Mary the Mother of Jesus is without any specific characteristics and is a passive agent in relation to the central activity of the crucifixion, which is dominated by men, and in the film she appears at the edge of the crowd rather than central to the story.

Although there is an important difference between a traditional print society and the modern world of media technology and consumerism, popular images of Christ have clearly been around a long time. Precisely because we have no description of Jesus the man, artists through the centuries have been more or less free to speculate. Whereas the Byzantine world depicted Christ as the divine King with the emblems of majesty and power, in the conservative Catholic tradition Jesus often appears as an anorexic ascetic. In later periods, a romantic picture card image of Christ was favoured by the puritanical Victorians. William Holman Hunt's depiction of Christ – *The Light of the World* in 1852 – is reassuring and familiar, whereas Vincent van Gogh's *Pieta* is disturbing and mentally tortured. Clearly, images of Jesus follow historical fashion and embody contextualised assumptions (Kitzinger and Senior, 1940). Gibson's image of Jesus resembles the posters of Jesus as a film star complete with Harley Davidson motorbike that are popular in the Philippines, except that in *The Passion* Christ as a beautiful young man is brutally murdered by an invading imperial force for reasons that remain obscure.

Why then does Gibson dwell so heavily on the physical punishment of Jesus – a man whom we do not get to know or understand in the film? The New Testament account of the death of Jesus is striking in its brevity, whereas the film is a long and laborious account of physical destruction in which the mutilated body occupies the screen, not the divine Jesus as the saviour of mankind. The Gospel according to St Mark in some eight verses of Chapter 15 tells us with a remarkable economy that 'they gave him to drink wine mingled with myrrh, but he received it not. And when they had crucified him, they parted his garments, casting lots upon them, what every man should take' (15: 23–24). There is little concern here for the violence that fills Gibson's baroque imagination. *The Passion* is successful because, while looking backwards to a medieval miracle play and a baroque crucifixion, it also speaks to modern times.

Firstly, we live in a world where our TV screens are filled with images of people being blown up in Iraq, shot in Palestine, tortured by corrupt regimes in Africa or kidnapped and raped in Latin

America. The human body, in a 'somatic society' where our political problems are manifest in corporeal images, has become the vehicle of our conception of political instability (Turner, 1992; 2008a). Modern society has, to borrow an idea from the anthropological imagination of Arjun Appadurai, become a 'death-scape' and so the violent images of *The Passion* look like today's media pictures from Baghdad and Mumbai rather than scenes from the Jerusalem of the New Testament. Secondly, we can read the film as a story of ethnic conflict between Jews and Romans, in which the conflicting groups speak a language that is unintelligible to the other side. This ethnic conflict is overlaid with religious differences between different interpretations of the truth. This is in part why the film is seen to contain an anti-Semitic theme and why it has a contemporary message of distrust and misunderstanding. Thirdly, it involves a clash of nationalisms and a struggle with colonial rulers. Gibson's film itself has a critical political edge in associating the origins of colonialism with the Roman occupation of the Holy Land. It is in this sense a film with a conventional Christian message – the inhumanity of man against man – but it is also decidedly modern – a film about identity politics, ethnic cleansing and the clash of nationalisms, albeit coated in the vicarious violence of the modern pornographic imagination and overlaid with Baroque sensuality.

New media technologies

New media technologies have contradictory effects. Early theories of the media and religion had an instrumentalist framework in which it was assumed that audiences would be easily influenced by the new programmes. Notions about 'brainwashing' were common and because the viewer was conceptualised as a *tabula rasa*, it was further assumed that the dominant evangelical Protestant message of TV evangelism would exclude other perspectives and traditions. Later, more sophisticated, sociological research on audiences showed that the media in fact reinforce existing values and attitudes rather than creating new ones (Abercrombie and Longhurst, 1998). Rather than being a threat, the media were seen to build up religious identities and create new forms of solidarity. More recently, the emphasis has shifted to the idea of 'mediation', in which the media are no longer cast in an instrumental light but are seen to be constitutive of modern societies as such. In particular, the religious media are well placed to assume a commanding position in the rise of post-institutional spirituality in which the new individualism can absorb religious images in producing a new cultural hybridity. We can also argue that the modern world is a post-print world in which visual culture, especially among younger generations, is particularly influential. One additional reason, therefore, for the success of *The Passion* is its striking and powerful use of images, which one might compare to the techniques of Caravaggio.

The transition of modern societies from print to digital image is a major civilisational shift with significant, if contradictory, consequences for modern religions. Print was important in the Judaeo-Christian traditions because the word of God was manifest in a written tradition. At the same time, these religions were specifically hostile to images and convinced of their potential for idolatry. The God of the Abrahamic religions disclosed Himself, not through rational discussion, but through revelation, the carriers of which were charismatic figures: Moses, Paul, Muhammad. However, in a post-prophetic time, revelation can be approached routinely by human beings through the written word encased in holy scriptures – the Hebrew Bible, the New Testament and the Qur'an – and increasingly through religious websites that offer advice and free-flowing interpretation. With what Weber called the routinisation of charisma, these religious cultures of the Book required scribes and scholars who interpreted the Word and passed on knowledge through repetitive forms of learning. Before the invention of printing, memorising these revelations was an essential requirement of the survival of a religious community, and recitation was proof of piety. Traditional Islamic and Quranic learning are classical illustrations of a print-based religious culture that has promoted oral transmission through a discipleship relation with elders and religious teachers. Their traditional elites required specialised hermeneutics as the basis for their authority of interpretation. The Qur'an, which according to tradition was originally written down on the shoulder blades of camels, is now available in a multimedia environment. The Mosaic code, which according to tradition was originally written on tablets of stone, is now available in the storyline of innumerable Hollywood films. In the contemporary world, children grow up in a learning environment in which multimedia techniques are taken for granted. For example, educational programmes for Muslim children regularly use animation to present Islam in a modern context.

Consequently, we live in a communication environment where images and symbols rather than the written word play a dominant role in interaction. This visual world is constructed around icons rather than around a written language. It is important not to exaggerate these changes with the arrival of a digital age, because religious books are still a major component of the commercial culture that surrounds modern religious activity. There is, as we have seen, the stunning commercial success of Dan Brown's novel, but there are other examples in popular religion, such as the best-selling *Left Behind* series in America, which combines science fiction, end-of-the world fantasy and evangelical emphasis on rebirth and renewal (Frykholm, 2004). However, there are also important examples from Jewish fundamentalism or Haredism, where the globalisation of orthodox Jewish texts such as those published by Art Scroll has contributed to the growth of Jewish piety (Stolow, 2010). In particular, the publication of the seventy-three volumes of the *Talmud Bavli* (*The Schottenstein Edition*) by Art Scroll, which was launched in February 2005 at the Mesorah Heritage Foundation, is simply one indication of the contemporary success of Jewish ultra-Orthodoxy within the Jewish Diaspora. In the print-orthodoxy of modern Judaism, the globalisation of these texts points to the expanding importance of Haredi intellectuals within the public sphere and the continuing importance of the written word as a measure of authenticity. In the Judaeo-Christian and Muslim traditions, the physical book maintains a material authority despite the revolution of digitalised information. However, when the sacred texts are translated in order to reach an English-speaking diaspora in all three religions, there is the suspicion that some element of truth and authenticity has been compromised.

My discussion of the media, religion and authority has concentrated, therefore, on the contradictory effects of information technology at the local level, where the circulation of cassettes and video clips was initially an efficient method for religious revivalism and evangelism. At the same time, the flexibility and volume of this religious traffic in information threatens to swamp traditional voices. This contradiction is nicely expressed by Ronald Niezen in his superb ethnographic study of religious fundamentalists in the Songhay village of Dar al-Salam in the Republic of Mali: 'In the Muslim world in particular the billboard now competes with the Book as the purveyor of truths to live by (or, according to some, of dangerous falsehoods to resist by every means possible), not to mention the cultural influence of television and the Internet' (2005: 168). Much of the sociological research on spirituality that is post-institutional, subjective and hybrid religiosity has been confined to the West, but it also has a remarkable similarity to the reinvention of Sufism in Southeast Asia. Whereas both Ernest Gellner and Clifford Geertz associated Sufism with the disappearing peasant cultures of Asia and North Africa, more recent research by Julia Howell (2001) shows how the Sufi tradition has been revived in Indonesia, where its rich ritual life and less authoritarian culture appears to appeal to those disaffected with fundamentalist piety. What we might call 'neo-Sufism' appeals to younger generations, university students and to the educated middle class. These developments in personal spirituality have received some endorsement from intellectuals such as Nurcholish Madjid, leader of a modernist student group, and from Abdurrahman Wahid, leader of the Nahdlatul Ulama and subsequently President of Indonesia. For young Indonesians, the Internet is increasingly a major vehicle for the transmission of neo-Sufi spirituality.

In many respects the Internet rather than film may be more consequential for religious life. While 'religion on-line' may be compatible with more traditional forms of evangelism, the emergence of 'on-line religion' opens up channels of experimentation and development that are outside the control or even sight of ecclesiastical institutions. It has been claimed by sociologists that the modern world is characterised by a new form of individualism that is fluid, creative and mobile. Individuals in a risk society, according to Beck and Gernsheim-Beck (2002), are disconnected from deeper social structures such as status and class and in some sense have to create their own world. This notion of the individual as a seeker appears to fit well with the unfolding digital world in which religious actors have become seekers in a spiritual market-place.

While the Internet has major, often negative implications for religious authority, modern religions have also benefited considerably from modern media, including Hollywood epics. DeMille claimed with some justification that more people understood the story of Jesus of Nazareth as a result of seeing his film than through any other medium apart from the Bible itself. *The Passion of the Christ* probably did more for the restoration of Christian commitment in America than any number of Sunday sermons, but it also did much to revive anti-Semitism. A new brand of Christianity also emerged in post-war America that made considerable use of the opportunities created by expanding TV channels and it was Protestantism rather than Catholicism that creatively exploited these new means of evangelism. However, Catholicism eventually caught up with the new technology and the death of Pope John Paul reminded us that he was the first media Pope, who fully recognised the power of the media in shaping attitudes and beliefs. Interestingly the Pope employed much of the media paraphernalia of a TV celebrity, including the famous 'Popemobile'. Although modern fundamentalism benefits considerably from the global communication media, there are important differences, as Marshall McLuhan warned us, between a world constructed on print-based knowledge and learning and a modern world based on multimedia communication. In contemporary youth cultures texting is probably the most important means of communication for young people. While globalisation theory tends to emphasise the triumph of modern fundamentalism (as a critique of traditional and popular religiosity), perhaps the real effect of globalisation is the triumph of heterodox, commercial, hybrid popular religion over orthodox, authoritative professional versions of the spiritual life. Their ideological effects cannot be controlled by religious authorities, and they have a greater impact than official messages.

Spirituality, emotion and the confessional culture

The Passion and *The da Vinci Code* are therefore typical examples of popular religious culture. Although their values may be very different, they are both representative of a post-institutional and commercial religiosity. They are both indicative of changes to religion in late modernity. I will attempt here to provide a summary of some of the major changes that one can observe in religion in modern societies by taking a comparative perspective on the commodification of religion. Religious lifestyles are constructed on consumer lifestyles in which people can experiment with religions rather like they can experience different lifestyles that have been designed by the fashion industry. Perhaps the most important example of this contemporary development of spirituality is provided by the spectacular career of Oprah Winfrey.

Born in 1954 in Kosciusko in the state of Mississippi to unmarried parents, she experienced a childhood of poverty and sexual abuse but, mainly through the supportive influence of her grandmother, she eventually in the 1980s enjoyed success on a Chicago TV talk-show. In 1986 *The Oprah Winfrey Show* was expanded to a full hour and broadcast nationally. In the mid-1990s the show departed from its tabloid format and began to explore significant public issues about race, women's health, meditation and spirituality. Her skills as an interviewer produced famous encounters when celebrities would explore profoundly personal issues relating to sexuality, drug abuse and marital breakdown. Her interview with Michael Jackson was watched by an audience of one million people and over time her media influence expanded to include *The Oprah Magazine, The Oprah Winfrey Network, O at Home* and *Oprah.com*. Her shows are characterised by a high level of personal disclosure and raw emotion, including her propensity to cry on air. She has been praised for the success with which her show has brought gay, bisexual, transsexual and transgender people into the American mainstream and at the same time she has been criticised for creating a therapeutic hosting style that pandered to the American obsession with self-help. Indeed, her shows are said to have created an American confessional culture, and it was *The Wall Street Journal* that coined the notion of 'Oprahfication' to describe this emerging culture of therapy, confession and emotion.

The significance of Oprahfication has been brilliantly captured by Eva Illouz in her *Oprah Winfrey and the Glamour of Misery* (2003) in which she demonstrates how the Oprah show has contributed to the culture that reflects obsessively on pain and suffering. The talk-show interviews allow the victims of suffering to affirm their right to be heard and they satisfy the audience by showing how the recognition of suffering, a public confession and the display of deep emotions of guilt and remorse can produce holistic healing. These themes of suffering, trauma and healing represent a tradition that is rooted in Western Christianity, but they are also profoundly American. The triumph of the individual over adversity sits well with the tradition of self-reliance and individualism. Perhaps the special feature of the TV programme is the centrality of Oprah Winfrey's own biography of suffering and personal recovery to the therapeutic trope of the show itself. Sherryl Wilson, in her *Oprah, Celebrity and Formations of Self* (2003: 93), draws a parallel between the talk-show and the black church 'with its call and response patterning, its dependence on participants – the congregation – under the steerage of the host/minister' (2003: 93). Oprah, however, was able to address the general problems of women – black and white. Even more remarkable then, according to Eva Illouz, is the fact that the show, which was dominated by the charismatic personality of a black American, found a large audience among white women searching for a message of reassurance and self-renewal. This interpretation of the Oprah Winfrey interviews also supports the argument that it is spirituality, rather than organised religion, that finds an obvious resonance with this world of the emotive confessional. But what is the source of this emotional dynamic in American culture? One answer is provided in Eva Illouz's *Cold Intimacies* (2007), in which she argues that in the first half of the twentieth century American corporations started to employ psychologists to advise them on how emotions could be used to sell commodities and as a result emotion now plays an important part in advertising and promoting commodities. To this argument, we might add that the long-term consequence of pietism, which also promoted the importance of an emotional response to the message of a loving God, has been to emphasise the emotional life in mainstream Protestantism and consequently in American civil religion.

Conclusion: globalisation, religion and subjectivity

In a period of rapid globalisation, religion can be said to have assumed three forms (Cox, 2003). There are various global movements that are broadly involved in religious revivalism, often retaining some notion of and commitment to institutionalised religion (whether it be a church, a mosque, a temple or a monastery) with an emphasis on orthodox belief and practice that are imposed authoritatively. Within this revivalist tradition, there are conventional forms of fundamentalism, but there are also new strains of Pentecostalism and charismatic religion. Secondly, many aspects of traditional folk religion continue, especially in rural communities which are less exposed to globalisation. These folk traditions are embraced predominantly by the poorly educated and the oppressed, for whom religious activity promises to bring healing, comfort and riches. Of course, even these traditions of folk religion are never completely immune from global changes and they can often provide a basis for the spread of modern witchcraft

(Comaroff and Comaroff, 1999; 2000). Spirit possession in Vietnam is a revival of traditional practice with roots in northern hemisphere shamanism, but it is also combined with the networks of businessmen and with the payment of remittances from overseas Vietnamese communities. Thirdly, there is the emergence of new spiritualities that are heterodox, urban, commercialised forms of religiosity typically existing outside the conventional churches, and often appealing to the new middle classes in the service sectors of the global economy. In particular, the development of spirituality – such as on-line religion – caters to the individual need for meaning, but these post-institutional forms of religion do not necessarily put high demands on the individual. Privatised forms of religious activity do not contribute significantly to the vitality of civil society, but simply provide psychological maintenance to the individual. The growth of consumer society has had a significant impact on religion in terms of providing models for the commodification of religious lifestyles, and much global religiosity involves a complex chemistry of spirituality, individualism and consumerism. There is no doubt, therefore, that the locus of authority has shifted, in the West at least, from ecclesiastical elites to secular intellectuals, but these intellectuals themselves are increasingly marginalised by the elites that control the media, the financial markets and consumer culture. Television celebrities such as Oprah Winfrey are the intellectuals of the modern information age with an influence that is now global rather than local and specific.

The principal characteristics of religion in modern society, especially Western society, are its individualism, the decline in the authority of traditional institutions (church and priesthood) and awareness that religious symbols are constructs (Bellah, 1964). Modernity appears to be wholly compatible with the growth of popular, de-institutionalised, commercialised and largely post-Christian religion in the West. In a differentiated global religious market, these segments compete with each other and at the same time overlap in providing comparable services. While the new spirituality is genuinely a consumerist religion, fundamentalism appears to challenge consumer (Western) values. However, even the most pious religious movements can become saturated with the consumer values and practices against which they overtly protest, as, for example, when the veil becomes a fashion object or when Christians promote supermarkets that behave according to Christian standards. Piety often involves selling a lifestyle based on special diets, alternative education, health regimes and religious tourism.

Gender issues are a prominent feature of these new patterns of spirituality, where women increasingly dominate in the public religious sphere rather than simply in the domestic consumption of religion. Women will be and to some extent already are intellectual leaders in the emergent global spirituality. Once more it is female TV stars such as Oprah Winfrey who give expression to the anger of women against social arrangements that are associated with domestic violence and sexual abuse, and against ecclesiastical institutions that often abuse women and children.

Throughout this chapter I have assumed a parallel between the emotive individualism of the market and consumer sovereignty on the one hand, and the powerful emotions that are expressed in films such as *The Passion* on the other. But there is also a parallel development in the growth of 'emotivism' in moral philosophy and the rise of modern spirituality. In this discussion, 'parallel' has the same meaning as the chemistry metaphor in Weber's notion of 'elective affinity'. There is a chemistry between popular religion as represented in *The Passion* and *The da Vinci Code* and the market-place that is between spiritual and commercial markets. The chemistry of public emotion, confession and spirituality is, as I have argued following the research of Eva Illouz, especially pronounced in *The Oprah Winfrey Show* in which intimacy and the authentic self are made into public spectacles. What feels good is true and authentic.

As a conclusion of this discussion, I can perhaps switch from the notion of a social chemistry to the stronger notion of a causal narrative. The rise of literacy in the nineteenth century gave Western populations access to popular science and some understanding of the significance of secularism and Darwinism. These changes were described in Alasdair MacIntyre's *Secularization and Moral Change* (1967). As the laity gained access to literacy and a basic education, from the 1870s until the aftermath of the First World War, there was a gradual decline in the authority of ecclesiastical institutions and their spokespersons. In the second half of the twentieth century, the rise of consumer society made the traditional theodicy of the Church – suffering, redemption and resurrection – increasingly irrelevant and this change was reflected in the sharp decline in recruitment to the priesthood. Religion has survived in the West in the form of spirituality, which is a post-institutional, hybrid and individualistic religiosity. Spirituality is the religious parallel of the sovereign consumer. Both the secular and the religious markets promote the idea of the individual as the sovereign agent in charge of their own actions and emotions. The idea of the holy as a transcendent reality that takes hold of the individual, often against their will, is now an alien conception to a world in which democratic notions of personal agency are predominant. The paradox of a post-secular society is that religion is booming, while the sacred is in terminal decay (Luckmann, 1990). Of course, for many sectors of society, the promise of consumerism and a happy life are rarely or never attained. Within an affluent consumer society, there are necessarily many social groups who fall outside the American dream or the message of affluence in neo-liberalism. For the disprivileged who form an underclass in this society, the Christian theme of suffering, healing and redemption continues to have a powerful appeal, but this message, once shorn of its more religious content, is now promoted more successfully and prominently on secular chat-shows rather than from the pulpit.

12 | *Religion, globalisation and cosmopolitanism*

Introduction: paradoxes of religion and modernity

In the modern world, religion and nationalism have often functioned as modes of individual and collective identity in a global political context. Both religious and nationalist modes of self-reference are products of a common process of modernisation, of which globalisation can be regarded as the current phase. Just as nationalism can assume either liberal or reactionary forms (Kohn, 1944), so religion can adopt either an ecumenical/cosmopolitan or an exclusive/fundamentalist orientation. From the late nineteenth century, citizenship became increasingly the dominant juridical framework of civil society as the mode of national membership and individual identity. In Europe and North America, national citizenship emerged as a secular form of solidarity that either competed or combined with the Church to provide a potent channel of nationalist identity and fervour. With growing national assertion and competition, citizenship became primarily an institution of 'national manhood' (Nelson, 1998), in which entitlements to citizenship benefits were based on work and warfare. As state sovereignty was territorial, citizenship became an exclusionary principle of identity and membership within a given terrain. With the collapse of communism in the Soviet Union and the transformation of China towards authoritarian capitalism, religion can once again blend with nationalism to provide the cultural glue that national citizenship requires to develop common rituals and communal organisation. However, the precise relationship between religion, nation and state is clearly variable. There is, nevertheless, a tension in many Islamic societies between nationalism and Islamic faith, insofar as reformed Islam offers a post-secular identity – Iran being perhaps the most obvious example.

Let us consider some of the paradoxical consequences of globalisation that have disrupted the traditional relationships between religion, national identity and gender. Taking both nationalism and fundamentalism as responses to the 'de-traditionalisation' of identity and membership, I attempt to defend the notion of cosmopolitan virtue as a normative commitment towards more tolerant patterns of intercultural contact. This discussion is normative in its intentions, partly because the caring virtue of cosmopolitanism is treated here as an important complement to the general idea of human rights in a world that is subject simultaneously to powerful forces of global integration and to political fragmentation. The background problem that surfaces periodically in this argument is that if national citizenship has in the past attempted to define a civic culture, then we need to identify, if we are to talk about global citizenship at all (Held, McGrew, Goldblatt and Perraton, 1999), a corresponding set of cosmopolitan virtues. In fact, cosmopolitan virtue can be treated as the obligations side of human rights, where cosmopolitan rights and obligations are mutually dependent and combine to form a normative framework for political action and responsibility. In this argument, cosmopolitanism is a normative standard of public conduct, and its development is politically urgent given the fact that empirically the global order is breaking down into antagonistic ethnic, regional and national identities (Delanty, 2009).

We can regard sociology as a discipline that has had a close engagement with the intellectual exploration of social and cultural paradoxes. This argument about religion, globalisation and cosmopolitanism is based on four controversial claims that turn out to be paradoxical. The first is that, contrary to much of the received wisdom, fundamentalism is a modernisation movement rather than a defence of traditionalism. Fundamentalist modernism is an attempt to impose certain conditions of uniformity and coherence on societies in order to reduce the uncertainties that result from the hybridity and complexity of the globalisation process, and at the same time to instil personal discipline in adherents and believers. Fundamentalism often paradoxically prepares individuals to enter successfully into a modern, urban environment. It may be true that the growth of global fundamentalism is a reaction to modernisation (including commercialism, sexual liberation and secularisation), but it is not a traditional reaction. We might call this situation the 'Nietzsche paradox', in which a religious attempt to control the world results in the unintended consequence of modernisation. Such a development might illustrate the maxim that a people is always destroyed by its strongest values.

The second paradox is from the sociology of Talcott Parsons. Modernisation and then globalisation begin to constitute 'religion' as a separate, differentiated and specialised sector of modern society, a sector that is often thought to refer to, and assumed to manage, the private world of values and activities. Religion in the modern world is about what troubles individuals, namely what they think is of ultimate concern. Secularisation makes 'religion', in this sense, a 'problem of modernity', and thereby makes the religious question more prominent in public discourse. Of course, this specialisation of 'religion' is not entirely unfamiliar to theological thinking about *religio* in the sense that it has been common to distinguish between 'religion' as a social system and 'faith' as an authentic response to God. One could argue that globalisation has involved the export of this model of private and individualistic religion and the idea of religious institutions as functionally specialised. Fundamentalism attempts to ensure the dominance of religion in the public spheres of law, economy and government through a process of 'de-personalisation' (Casanova, 1994). This process of exporting an individualistic version of Latin Christianity, and global reactions to it, has been described (not very elegantly) by Jacques Derrida as 'globalatinisation', which he defines as 'this strange alliance of Christianity, as the experience of the death of God and tele-technoscientific capitalism' (1998: 13). However, the attempt to impose religion in civil society as an integrating principle in the name of fundamentalism often has the unintended consequence of raising questions that may turn out to be corrosive about the value and meaning of traditional institutions. Fundamentalisation has the unintended and unanticipated consequence of exposing the traditional world to religious inspection with the result that its taken-for-grantedness and authenticity become critical issues. This unintended 'de-traditionalisation' of values and practices is particularly evident in the Islamic debate about the status of women in Muslim society. The unveiling of women by secular authorities – or at least a prohibition on the veil in public spaces – and the re-veiling of women by religious authorities has ironically exposed 'woman' to an endless public debate. In fact 'woman' becomes an object of public gaze precisely as she puts on the veil.

The third paradox, which I shall call the Marshall McLuhan paradox after the founding father of media studies, concerns the compression of time and space, and arises from the current globalisation of the world as such. Religion becomes intricately and inevitably bound up with the conflicts that arise from this new phase of globality. It is clear that the religions with which I am concerned in this discussion are primarily the Abrahamic religions; these religions in turn have been traditionally regarded as 'world religions'. In the case of Islam and Christianity in particular, we are considering religions that are literate in their emphasis on the written word, monotheistic in their adherence to a High God and evangelical in their strategies towards 'the world'. From their inception, the prohibition on idolatry forced them to develop notions about an outside world of unbelief, of difference and of 'other religions'. They had also to deal with the presence of secular powers and authorities which were of 'this world'. In this sense, because the world religions had to construct a notion of 'alterity', the Abrahamic religions were early or primitive versions of globalisation, and they had to respond to difference and otherness through various discourses and strategies of ecumenicalism, apostasy and evangelism. In this sense the problem of Orientalism is generic to world religions (Hart, 2000; Said, 1978; Turner, 1978). An Orientalist world-view comes almost inevitably into existence with the very commitment to an evangelical orientation to the world. There is therefore an indigenous discourse of difference/otherness that emerged out of the problem of understanding and explaining the presence of cultures that lay outside the Chosen People or the Household of Faith or the Universal Church.

For much of world history, these different but related religions existed side by side on a continuum of tolerance, indifference and ignorance. Crusades, *jihad* and Holy War were exceptions rather than the norm. The paradox of globalisation is that, because it compresses time and space by creating the world as a single place, it intensifies the problem of otherness. Competition between religions is no longer local or national but global. Precisely because the world becomes a global village – or better still a global city – the incommensurability of human values and cultures becomes an issue that cannot be easily ignored or trivialised, or from which we cannot easily escape. It is no accident that human-rights legislation such as the Universal Declaration of Human Rights by the United Nations (1948), the International Human Rights Covenants (1966), Bangkok Declaration (1993) and so forth are a key development in the rise of a global society. The concept of human rights (that is, the rights of humans as humans) is distinctively modern and derives from a series of revolutions that took place in the late eighteenth century and that give rise initially to the idea of the 'rights of Man'. We can find philosophical foundations for these developments in John Locke's defence of tolerance and in Leibniz's attempt to forge a notion of respect for other cultures, but the real work on formulating a notion of individual rights emerged out of the American War of Independence and specifically from the pen of John Adams.

Despite criticisms of the Western character of human rights and despite attempts to find notions of rights in other traditions such as Confucianism (De Barry 1998), no alternative, viable framework to the rights that developed as a radical legal category from revolutionary conflicts against monarchy in France and America has emerged. Notions of individual entitlement, elaborated through a series of twentieth-century conventions, came to be the dominant legal framework of modern rights conventions. Modern theories of so-called neo-Confucianism have not delivered any effective guarantee of individual rights for the simple reason that Confucianism was and remains a secular ideology of social order that favours state power over individual rights.

The final paradox is taken from the legacy of Montaigne and is concerned with the inevitability of Otherness as a requirement for self-understanding. It is the paradox that to understand ourselves we need another world of strangers about whom and through whom we can become self-reflexive. In Hegel's account of the master–slave relationship neither party can come to self-awareness. The master does not recognise the slave and in turn the slave is a mere object. Recognition of others and self-understanding are dialectically necessary components of reflexive consciousness (Williams, 1997). However, our empathetic understanding of other cultures and their specificity leads in the first instance to cultural relativism and hence to the realisation that our own cultures are contingent social constructs with no necessary and automatic authority. Understanding ourselves means facing up to, and where possible overcoming, our own sense of contingency. Globalisation therefore simply deepens the conventional problem of relativism.

Notions about the peculiarities and specificities of different cultures have been basic to the social sciences since the historicism debate of the 1890s, but it has been to some extent endemic to Western thought since the historical writings of Herodotus. This legacy of relativism was in the late twentieth century reinforced by cultural anthropology and its critique of 'culture' and by post-modernism, which further elaborated the idea that 'there are no facts only interpretations'. Few social scientists have, however, commented on the oddity of relativism in a global age. If we are moving into a global world, and indeed into a world social system, then relativism is itself challenged by the possibility of a global culture. Relativism is itself historically specific and contingent. One additional feature of this chapter is that, from a defence of cosmopolitanism, we can challenge relativism through the argument that human rights, for example, requires a corresponding set of obligations and virtues that I call cosmopolitan virtue. A comprehensive defence of this position requires a more extensive justification than is possible here, in which I present merely a sketch of the more substantial argument (Turner, 2002; 2006). Cosmopolitanism and human rights raise other issues with respect to nation states and citizenship.

Nation-state citizenship has been in the modern world a powerful agency for creating individual identities. Modern citizenship is a political and juridical category relating to liberal individualism. This juridical identity of citizens has evolved according to the larger political context, because citizenship has been necessarily housed within a definite political community, namely the nation-state. Of course, citizenship was originally a product of the Greek city-state, and later Renaissance humanism, in which the ascending order of the state and the horizontal ordering of citizenship contrasted with the descending theme of the Church and its hierarchical order of institutionalised charisma (Ullmann, 1977). This tradition of citizenship became linked to the norms of civility, civil society and citizenship. The rise of nation-state citizenship in the late nineteenth century somewhat replaced the traditions of humanism and urban cosmopolitanism with an exclusionary national ethic. Now the problem for the development of contemporary forms of citizenship is twofold: global society is not (as yet) a definite political community with an effective system of governance to which cosmopolitanism could be attached, and the continuity of national citizenship necessarily constrains the possibilities of global membership.

In the traditional terminology of sociology, citizenship-building is also and necessarily nation-building. The creation of the institutions of citizenship in legal, political and social terms was also the construction of a national framework of membership within the state – the historical process that dominated domestic politics in Europe and North America through much of the late eighteenth and nineteenth centuries. The production of an institutional framework of national citizenship created new national identities. Whereas citizenship identities during the rise of the European cities had been local and urban, with the rise of nationalism they became increasingly connected with strong nationalistic cultures that sought greater domestic coherence and at the same time struggled to acquire colonial territories in the international competition for power. Modern politics became a politics of friend or foe along the lines indicated in political theology by Carl Schmitt (1976). Nationalism does not automatically assume an illiberal and intolerant form, but in the eighteenth and nineteenth centuries nationalism, when mixed with a potent brew of imperialism and militarism, became closely infused with notions of racist superiority. This development was not exclusively Western. Japanese modernisation and state-building followed along an almost identical pathway, and Japan evolved through the idea of the greater prosperity zone into a modern colonial power.

Now the dominant narratives of nationalism are typically masculine. They record and celebrate the heroic rise of the nation against a variety of internal and external enemies through a pattern of civil conflict, warfare and liberation. The blood bond between rulers and community in a feudal structure has over time been converted into a national myth of civil loyalty based on the principle of the formal equality of citizens. The national mythologies of a society cement individual biographies with the collective biographies of generations, and generations are the cultural building blocks of a nation-state and its people. Although the nation-state typically adopts a patriarchal value system, women are not excluded from nation-building. On the contrary, they are crucial for family formation and biological reproduction, that in turn reproduce society. However, women's voices in the grand narratives of nationalism tend to be muted and overshadowed by a warrior ethos. Epic poetry, tragic romances and national mythologies combine collective emotions and sentiments with stories of nation-building. The sacred narrative of the Founding Fathers with George Washington at its core is a classic example

(Brookhiser, 1996). Such nation-building ideologies almost always assume a religious character.

This religious framework of nationalist ideology can either take a very direct form, as in the case of Israel and Iran, or it can be understated, as in the case of England, or it can take the form of a civil religion, as in America. In Christianity, the resurrection story has proved to be a potent theme of national resurgence and revival, and in the history of Poland there was a direct appeal to Christianity to express national suffering, but this time in the female figure of the Virgin of Czestochowa (Rubin, 2009). In the history of secular nationalism, religious themes have therefore provided a fertile source of collective myth-making. It is difficult, however, to imagine how religion might come to play a central role in the creation of a shared global mythology or cosmology that might unite the great diversity of world cultures. Perhaps the only contemporary candidate would be an apocalyptic religion of the destruction of Nature.

The Nietzsche paradox: fundamentalism as modernity

Whether we like it or not, the primary models of modernisation have been Western models. The idea of 'multiple modernities' is politically attractive, but it has not entirely replaced more unified and standardised models of *the* process of modernisation (Eisenstadt, 2000). There is a legitimate sociological argument therefore for claiming that the sociology of Max Weber provides us with the classical model of the origins and contents of modernity; it also provides us with a basic insight into its paradoxes. In this respect, I follow Alasdair MacIntyre in that 'The contemporary vision of the world, so I have suggested, is predominantly, although not perhaps always in detail, Weberian' (1984: 109). In this respect, Weber closely followed Nietzsche in seeing modernisation as the product of resentment, and thereby involving many negative, nihilistic and destructive features (Stauth and Turner, 1988). Although *The Protestant Ethic and the Spirit of Capitalism* (Weber, 2002) may be fundamentally flawed as a historical argument in terms of detail, it nevertheless provides us with an unrivalled analysis of the general archaeology of modernity. In the Protestant ethic thesis, Weber argued that the irrational drive to find convincing evidence of personal salvation in a theological system, where ultimately God's purpose could not be fully known and understood, was resolved through a religious life order that emphasised asceticism, hard work, personal rectitude and seriousness of purpose. In more elaborate terms, this soteriology was displaced onto daily practices that encouraged control, discipline and hard work. In the long run, Protestant piety produced an ethic of world mastery that encouraged scientific rationalism and scepticism towards ritualism, liturgies and magical manipulation. From these sectarian origins, Protestantism emerged as a religious culture that emphasised hard work, this-worldly asceticism, a critical rejection of ecclesiastical authority that was not grounded in biblical sources and a hostility towards religious symbolism and idols. The traditional economic doctrines of the Church regarding the just price and the fair wage disappeared in favour of righteous economic accumulation. The medieval sins of greed and gluttony were slowly modernised. The tragic vision of Protestantism was that its quest for personal salvation had an elective affinity with secular values and rational capitalism.

The Protestant ethic is the cultural basis of modernity because in sociological terms it encouraged a teleological view of history; it embraced a uniform view of truth and authority; it promoted a quasi-democratic form of governance that was opposed to priestly powers; it encouraged a view of authority that gave priority to the Word in the vernacular language of the people; and finally it created a set of ideological resources that could be mobilised to attack absolutism and patriarchy in the form of bishops and princes. One must guard against exaggeration here. In 1520 Luther threw a copy of the canon law into a bonfire of books and he took the view that the Mosaic Law was for Jews, whereas Christians had to live by faith, but this trust in faith alone could easily lead to anarchy, given the depravity of the human heart. Luther's response to the Peasants' Rebellion of 1524–25 was brutal and he joined the princes in crushing the rebellion. While he rejected their violence, Luther came to depend on the authority of the sword to control society. In his *An Admonition on the Twelve Articles*, Luther argued that Christians must adapt to their local social and political conditions rather than oppose them (Tappert, 1967). Their role was one of obedience and suffering, but the consequence of the *Admonition* was to turn Lutheranism from a popular social movement into a conservative doctrine of godly rule that left the peasantry shorn of any common religious practices (Marius, 1999).

Although this account of Protestantism may be criticised on historical grounds, it is nevertheless useful in presenting the argument that Protestantism is par excellence a modern world-view. In this sense, it laid the foundations for the modern ideology of individualism. The Counter-Reformation against Protestant modernism was the Baroque cultures of the absolute monarchies, who employed opulent designs, imposing grandiose architecture and an appeal to the senses as an attempt to halt the growth of Protestantism individualism, scriptural religion and rationalism. Whereas Protestantism demanded minimalism in architectural design and plainness in cultural representation in order to discipline mind and body, Baroque culture celebrated decoration, sensuality and ornament. Lutheranism placed the sermon as the centrepiece of Christian worship in which the chapel became a lecture theatre. The exuberance and sensuality of Baroque culture in southern Germany corresponded to an attempt to revive and refurbish political absolutism, while the plain chapels of northern Europe welcomed in an aesthetic principle that concentrated on the spoken word rather the visual display of ecclesiastical authority.

Protestantism is the prologue to modernity in creating a culture of control, asceticism and discipline. The paradox of Protestantism, as of contemporary Christian, Jewish and Islamic fundamentalism, is that it attempts to find some legitimacy for its version of fundamental principles in sacred texts, but frequently these texts provide little actual support for such ideas. Indeed the quest for textual authority – that is, scripturalism (Geertz, 1983; Stolow, 2010) – exposes traditionalism to a discursive evaluation and eventual critique. If fundamentalists reject existing sources of authority – clergy, ecclesiastical traditions, legal codes, religious custom and so forth – they have to face the problem of an internal critique that can also question the fundamentals of authority. If the early Protestant Reformation faced the problem of antinomianism, then modern religious reformism ultimately confronts the problem of perspectivism or competing forms of fundamentalism.

We can take perspectivism to mean in practice that there can be no final assurance; there is no authoritative *nomos* by which social practices can be safely and unambiguously legitimated. It was through this hermeneutic questioning of the text that historicism emerged in the late nineteenth century from biblical criticism. Critical analysis of biblical texts demonstrated, for example, that there was no single source for biblical authority in the sacred texts, that there was disagreement between the sources and that the texts were themselves post-hoc interpretations. Jacob Taubes (2004) argues, for example, that late-nineteenth-century liberal theology in the works of Theodosius Harnack and Adolf von Harnack continued the critique of Marcion of Sinope in treating the Old Testament as irrelevant, in fact antithetical, to modern Christian belief and practice. In short, there was no pristine and definitive Text; there were only texts about which there can be unending dispute. In the words of Richard Rorty (Zabala, 2005: 17) hermeneutics announces the age of the end of any metaphysics because it affirms the dictum of Nietzschean philosophy that there are no facts but only interpretations.

These considerations provide a useful prologue to a discussion of Islam. There are three issues to be considered. In the first case, we must reject or at least question the view taken by sociologists of religion who have argued that 'fundamentalism itself has become a global category, part of the global repertoire of collective action available to discontented groups, but also a symbol in a global discourse about the shape of the world' and go on to claim that this perspective interprets 'fundamentalism as a form of anti-Modernism' (Lechner, 1993: 28). Clearly, fundamentalism has been a response of discontented and disconnected social groups caught up in the processes of secularisation, urbanisation and de-traditionalisation. The Iranian Revolution against the social change programme of Reza Shah is in contemporary history the classic case. However, it is misleading to regard Shi'ite fundamentalism as simply anti-modernist. The *ulama* opposed the Iranian nationalism of the Shah's regime and they regarded America as their principal enemy, but they employed modern means to implement their ideology, such as the media, mass mobilisations and modern technology. To quote from Masoud Kamali's study of civil society during two revolutions in Iran – the Constitutional Revolution and the Islamic Revolution:

The radical clergy's participation in modern political events in Iran provided them experience in playing modern politics, using modern political concepts and discourses, and negotiating and forming coalitions. Their prominent position in civil society of Iran, their capacity to mobilise people and perhaps most important of all the appearance of a large urban group, the marginal migrants, which provided them with their own army, put them into a leading position in the opposition to the Shah. Utilising modern political strategies and their own army, they led a major revolution of this century. (Kamali, 1998: 274)

There is also a parallel between puritan reform movements in Christianity and the modernist movements of Islam in the second half of the nineteenth century (Adams, 1999; Turner, [1974] 1998: 145–50). Reformers such as Muhammad Abduh (1849–1905), Rashid Rida (1865–1935), Rifa'a al-Tahtawi (1801–73) and Jamal al-Din al-Afghani (1839–97) had argued, in a context where Islamic civilisation was profoundly threatened by European imperialism, that the modernisation of Islam required a reform movement that would make it compatible with its origins. Islam had declined in power and significance because it had moved away from its charismatic foundations. Reform Islam required true Muslims to explore the Qur'an and the *hadith* for passages that encouraged hard work, frugality and diligence. A correct interpretation of the Qur'an should show that it was compatible with modern science and rational thought. This reform of Islam showed that fundamental Islamic concepts supported rational civilisation, modern capitalism and democracy. Islam had become corrupted by the social accretion of folk beliefs and by the survival of pre-Islamic practices in the popular movements of Sufism. In this sense, the fundamentalisation of Islam was a necessary step to its modernisation. Contemporary fundamentalism has accepted this model of modernisation, which often combines with anti-Americanism. In particular, religious fundamentalism is often hostile to the Western media, despite the widespread penetration of the modern media and commercialism into local Muslim communities. Islamic fundamentalism has thereby often created 'Occidentalism' as the unintended consequence of the criticisms of the West. These anti-Western ideas are often an ironic parallel to the 'Orientalism' of the West (Ahmed, 1992: 177).

Furthermore, fundamentalist commitment to textual origins has paradoxical consequences that parallel the problems of biblical criticism in nineteenth-century Christianity. The case of women's rights in Malaysia and Indonesia is interesting as an illustration of the debate over Quranic textual authority. The problem in Southeast Asia is that in addition to struggles over modernist and traditionalist readings of the Qur'an, women's lives have traditionally been regulated by local custom or *adat* that affirm women's public roles in a positive and non-hierarchical way. The rule of *hijab* (covering and seclusion) is not deeply embedded in the traditional Malay world. However, throughout the 1980s and 1990s local *ulama* in several of the Malay states have attempted to argue the case for polygamy, claiming that Malaysia in demographic terms has a surplus population of women. Women's groups in Malaysia and other Islamic societies have often been successful in challenging the argument that the right of polygamy is enshrined in the Qur'an. The traditionalist view of the Qur'an has been that women are a secondary creation (from the rib of Adam) and that they exist to satisfy men's needs (under the injunction that men have a right to tilth). Women's groups have challenged these arguments on three counter-claims: the anachronistic elements of the Qur'an are not essential or compatible with the theme of gender equality in the rest of the Qur'an; the anachronistic verses are products of local historical circumstances (a principle of Islamic historicism); and because the Qur'an expects that a husband will protect his wife and promote her welfare, polygamy is difficult to reconcile with these ideal aims and objectives of marriage. The most sophisticated defence of women's equality has involved an appeal to a common ontology. Norani Othman (1999: 173) has argued that Islamic law is not opposed to human rights because it supports the notion of a shared ontology. This awareness is by no means alien to Islam. It is grounded in the Quranic notion of a common ontology (*fitna*) and couched in an Islamic idiom of moral universalism that predates much of the Western discourses about human rights. It is thus doctrinally a part of the Muslim world-view itself.

The attempt to introduce polygamy to a community that has traditionally operated as much by local customary practices as by Islamic norms has produced a critical reaction: What is tradition? What is orthodoxy? The idea that 'regressive' norms are the product of the historical specificity of the Quranic teachings raises very difficult long-term issues about what teachings are in fact not historically specific. Similar struggles of interpretation are taking place in Indonesia over the issue of women in public office, especially judicial office. Conventional Quranic interpretation, particularly in the Middle East, accepts the view that only men can hold judicial office, but in Indonesia there are at least one hundred women judges in the *Shari'a* courts. The appointment of women is justified on a variety of grounds. The Qur'an itself (as distinct from *hadith*) does not directly prohibit women. The Hanafi legal school argues that women can sit on civil but not criminal cases and in Indonesia the Islamic courts cover only civil cases; hence women can be judges. However, when they are functioning in criminal cases, women are not within Islamic jurisdiction, and so they can be judges! Since the Qur'an enjoins men and women to prevent evil, it is permissible for women to be judges. The most interesting argument is about historical authority. For example, the fact that the Rightly Guided Caliphs did not appoint female successors is explained by historical circumstances that need not apply in modern times. Finally, these debates in modern Islam take place against a cultural and social background in which Southeast Asia was not a profoundly patriarchal culture and in which matrilocal norms were widespread (Reid, 1988).

These contemporary examples are features of the argument that a fundamentalist quest for foundations will expose any such religious investigation to the classical hermeneutic dilemma of interpretation. Fundamentalists are in this sense not traditionalists, because a traditionalist would argue that there is no need for interpretation – the gate of interpretation (*ijtihad*) is closed. By contrast, fundamentalists are in practice involved in reinterpretation by the very act of imposing their reformed perspective over customary practices that existed without reflection in the past.

The Parsonian paradox: the rise of religion and the status of women

Thomas Luckmann (1988) has argued that there are broadly three structural arrangements for sacred universes. Firstly, religion is diffused throughout the entire social structure – the situation characteristic of archaic societies. Secondly, there can be a differentiation of religion in close proximity to the political institutions in traditional society. Finally, differentiation and institutional specialisation of religion as a distinct field of activity has been characteristic of modern societies. This thesis of functional differentiation as religious modernisation is shared by a number of authors including Talcott Parsons, Peter Berger and Niklas Luhmann (Beyer, 1994). It follows, as Frank Lechner and others have argued, that fundamentalism represents a protest movement in favour of de-differentiation that is opposing the growth of the autonomy of other subsystems (the political, the aesthetic, the economic and so forth). This sociological interpretation of fundamentalism places it in the role of an anti-modern movement. For example, Peter Beyer argues that one strand of religious responses to the specialisation of religion as a system of belief and practice relevant to the private sphere will include 'conservative, anti-global, particularistic, and often politicized "fundamentalisms"' (1994: 104).

Although these observations about globalisation are insightful, it is not clear that Islamic fundamentalism falls under the classification of conservative, anti-global and particularistic movements. For one thing, Islam sees itself as a global religion and historically has not accepted the notion that it is locked into a particular territory or confined to some specialised subsystem of a given society. It is not anti-global in the sense that its global spread and appeal depends heavily on the existence of modern means of transport without which the modern mass pilgrimage to Mecca would not be possible. It is true that Islamic fundamentalism has rejected differentiation by attempting to enforce religious law over the operations of secular institutions such as banks, airlines, armed forces, educational systems and gender relations.

Again the legal regulations regarding the public role of women are interesting as a basis for exploring the public/private division, the role of law and the unintended consequences of fundamentalist values for modernisation. The problematic status of women in fundamentalism has opened up a human-rights debate about the legitimacy of the traditional norms of gender relationships. These debates offer a point of intersection between internal debates over authority, universal human-rights legislation and cosmopolitan virtue.

Throughout the Islamic world, the modernising debates between secularists and fundamentalists have centred on the status of women, the role and nature of marriage and the authority of family law. Again the comparison with debates in Christianity and Judaism suggests that there are common issues for religious institutions in the face of modernisation and globalisation. The theology of the Abrahamic religions is fundamentally patriarchal, in that God sends his Son, his Messenger or his Prophets to establish a relationship with men for the proper organisation of their souls and their communities. In this chain of authority, women are either marginal or disruptive. Their very natures are corrosive of divine purpose. Because spirituality is focused on the control of sexuality, it is not surprising that women were regarded with some degree of anxiety. In the case of Christianity, the hostility of Pauline theology to women is well known. Marriage was a necessary evil to control the passions of men and it was seen as a status below that of celibacy. Judaism did not wholly share this view of women. The Mishneh Torah, in Book Five on holiness, while warning against 'forbidden unions' and 'lewd discourse', recommends that a man should not 'live without a wife, since married estate is conducive to great purity' (Twersky, 1972: 124). Maimonides, in *Laws Concerning Character Traits*, warned against excessive sexual indulgence but mainly on medical grounds, because 'semen is the strength of the body and its life' (Weiss and Butterworth, 1975: 40). Obviously there was variation in traditional forms of patriarchy, but in general we can conclude that in traditional societies women were characteristically in subordinate roles. Given the powerful status of men in world religions, there has always been a countervailing presence of the female offering consolation to women and the downtrodden. The female alternative theology in Christianity has centred on the Virgin Mary, and in Buddhism on Kuan Yin (Paul, 1985).

The process of modernisation has done much to change the status of women by bringing them into the formal labour market and often providing them with access to some level of literacy and education. In some Muslim societies, these economic changes have provided them with some basic legal protection, permitted divorce on a 'no-contest basis' and facilitated their promotion to public office. These social developments are obviously uneven, but throughout Southeast Asia they have transformed the status of young women leaving rural communities to work in urban areas in transnational corporations (Brooks, 2006). There has also been some degree of social experimentation with gender identities in Asia (Peletz, 2007). These transformations of gender relations and identity have put both traditionalists and fundamentalists into defensive positions.

At the centre of these public contests, the veil in Islam has assumed considerable cultural significance. The marriage contract in Islamic belief is a so-called 'root paradigm' that provides people with a cultural map for everyday behaviour. In its legal form, marriage is a contract, namely a contract of sale (*'aqd*) involving a sale of goods and services. In exchange for a bride price and maintenance, a husband gains exclusive rights over a woman's sexual services and thus over her personality. As a contractual relationship, it has to be entered into voluntarily and thus assumes consent on the part of the woman. The tension in this traditional formula is that the woman is both legal person and property, but the consequence of marriage is to impose on women a duty of obedience. According to Islamic convention, the disobedience of women would be simultaneously an erosion of male privilege and an attack on the social order. Universities in the Middle East have become effective sites for fundamentalists to recruit rural women into protests against secularism and Westernisation. Although the veil has many meanings, it has a significance as a statement against Westernisation (Botman, 1999; Brenner, 1996).

Let us briefly take the case of Iran. At various stages in modern Iranian history, women had been encouraged to unveil (for example the Unveiling Act of 1936 and the Family Protection Law of 1967). During the secularisation of Iranian society under Reza Shah, Muslim women had unveiled as they entered new urban occupations and interacted with Western culture. With the growth of religious opposition, Ayatollah Khomeini had encouraged women to adopt the veil as a protest against the Shah and as a symbol of their religious commitment. Fundamentalists supported protests of veiled women against the Pahlavi regime and cultivated respect for and identification with Zainab, the granddaughter of the Prophet. In short, women were politically motivated to form a mass movement against a nationalist and secularist regime and were organised around a set of religious symbols that did not always and necessarily coincide with the official theology of the ayatollahs. In recent developments in Iran in the post-revolutionary context, the veil has, of course, become deeply contested as an image of the revolution, as a patriarchal symbol, as a protest against Westernisation, as a symbol of repression and as a sign of compliance. Possibly for this reason, there is no settled assessment of the current status of women in Iran and opinions vary between the feminist critique of Azar Nafisi's *Reading Lolita in Tehran* (2008) and the claim of Anouar Majid in *Unveiling Traditions* (2000: 130) that Iranian feminists can occupy spaces where it is possible to challenge the subordination of women from within the Islamic tradition.

This reflexivity in the public debate about the status of women is an unintended consequence of political mobilisation and duplicates the issues of marriage and the public role of women in Malaysia and Indonesia. As Shahla Haeri (1993) argues, the fundamentalists have to confront the unintended consequences of their success as revolutionaries. These consequences included a heightened political consciousness amongst women. The figure of Zainab, who represents woman in a public role, has served as a radical cultural force in women's lives. Having been exposed to radical Shi'ite discourse, urban women have engaged with the clerics over the interpretation of religious law and custom. Such critical women are often portrayed as weak, nagging or neurotic in the press. The situation of women was compounded by the consequences of the war with Iraq in which, with the decline in the number of young men available for marriage, men were encouraged to adopt polygamy. Iranian women have replied by arguing that only in a true Muslim society can men maintain justice between several wives and thus under present circumstances women can only suffer from neglect and brutality. In both Iran and Pakistan, the nervousness of the authorities is illustrated by edicts to regulate the nature of veiling and to insure that 'bad veiling' is avoided.

This example is important, partly because it illustrates the polyvalent nature of religious texts and their openness to divergent interpretations. Fundamentalists are not traditionalists in the sense that a traditionalist response would involve, in the case of Malaysia, an assertion of the value of local customary practice. The attempt to impose an Islamic orthodoxy necessarily raises problems where the Text is silent or divergent. This textual strategy thus makes it difficult to impose *Shari'a* norms as a response to the specialisation of religion as simply a matter of private practice. These difficulties in the application of sacred law to changing circumstances were recognised, it has to be said, only too clearly in Weber's sociology of law (Turner, [1974] 1998). The attempt to create a closed Text through the closing of the door of interpretation must of necessity create a gap between the normative world of the Qur'an and the brute exigencies of the everyday world. In modern Islam, the gap is closed by a world-wide debate about what constitutes appropriate Muslim practice in multicultural, especially secular, societies. The debate now takes place more often than not on the Internet rather than in customary settings.

The McLuhan paradox: globalism and cultural relativism

Claims about the universality of knowledge and in particular about the universality of rights have become distinctly unfashionable among social scientists, at least since the publication of J.-F. Lyotard's *Postmodern Condition* ([1979] 1984). The assumption that there might be Truth by which our beliefs about society could be measured has been criticised from a variety of positions. For philosophers such as Richard

Rorty, we should embrace pragmatism to ask, not whether a belief system is true, but whether it serves some useful purpose. Any notion that one could speak confidently about shared moral codes has also been increasingly regarded as open to question. In this debate Rorty has been particularly important as a figure in the revival of pragmatism as a specifically American version of relativism (Dickstein, 1998). Jürgen Habermas rejects relativism but he nevertheless believes that we live in a post-metaphysical world. For Habermas, 'the secular awareness that one is living in a post-secular society finds expression at the philosophical level in a post-metaphysical mode of thought' (2008: 119). This mode of thinking refrains from making 'ontological pronouncements on the constitution of being as such' (p. 140). Habermas is sceptical about the ultimate reach of rational science and its self-reflexivity prevents reason from making hasty judgements about religion, but at the same time he maintains a distinction between faith and knowledge.

Habermas, however, does not equate post-metaphysical thought with post-modernism, and has remained a critic of relativism. He has opposed the late-twentieth-century alliance between anthropological relativism and post-modern critiques of the universalistic assumptions of traditional moral discourse. Of course, anthropology, given its commitment to ethnographic detail, has probably been relativistic through most of the twentieth century, but it has in recent years found additional support from both post-modernism and the literature on decolonisation and subaltern studies. The erosion of the literary canon has also done much to reinforce this relativistic tendency. Intellectuals working in this stream of modern thought have therefore moved a long way from the Enlightenment, and especially from Kant's epistemology and his cosmopolitan ideal (Bohman and Lutz-Bachmann, 1997).

With some well-known exceptions, such as Ernest Gellner and Alasdair MacIntyre, cultural and moral relativism came to be a widely shared view in the humanities and social sciences. In the study of non-Western societies, Edward Said's criticisms of Orientalism added further fuel to the fire of 'the cultural turn'. The contemporary debate about globalisation and cosmopolitanism suggests, however, that the relativist position may itself be under attack. If the world is increasingly global, can it also be relativistic? Does globalisation require us to rethink notions about cultural specificity and particularity? Of course, an assumption that the modern world is subject to global pressures in economics, politics and culture does not necessarily mean that there is any corresponding set of assumptions that the social world is becoming more uniform. A global age does not automatically result in McDonaldisation, because there can be equally powerful pressures towards localism and hybridity. The idea of 'glocalisation' was invented to describe these mixtures of global culture with local customs and practices (Robertson, 1992a), and globalisation should not be conceived merely as Westernisation; it is important to recognise the growing impact of Asian cultures on globalisation processes (Turner and Khondker, 2010). While remaining aware of powerful resistance to cultural standardisation, there is a widespread view in sociology that there are powerful pressures towards the experience of a global village. The rise of global tourism, world sport, global communication networks, global agencies like WHO and UNESCO, the spread of human rights both as law and consciousness, and the global experience of common health crises in the AIDS/HIV epidemic and more recently SARS and swine flu are features of globalisation. Optimistic globalisation theory may, however, lull us into a false vision of the world as culturally integrated, or at least capable of such integration. We might ask nevertheless whether Kantian cosmopolitanism can ever be revived?

Obviously, cultural relativism has a much longer history than nineteenth-century historicism or twentieth-century cultural anthropology. In this commentary, I want to approach the question of cosmopolitanism and cultural relativism from the point of view of sixteenth-century thought, when Europe was divided by religious wars, and Islam (in the shape of the Ottoman Empire) was a powerful and real threat to European political autonomy. In order to give this discussion some shape, I examine the cosmopolitan scepticism of Michel de Montaigne (1533–92), whose moral views had been determined by religious conflicts between Huegenots and Catholics. Montaigne's predicament with respect to his own period is a useful point with which to open a discussion of Orientalism, religious tolerance and relativism. His attempt to come to terms with religious conflict and moral diversity through a theory of scepticism is a valuable corrective to our contemporary amnesia in which relativism and notions of Otherness and difference are somehow exclusively modern dilemmas. Although Montaigne appears to be a relativist, it turns out that his cultural relativism was simply a rhetorical smokescreen. In terms of relativism, Montaigne ironically asserted that 'what we call barbarism is simply what others do'. However, his *Essays* ([1580] 2003) actually challenge that aphorism because he recognised that questions of justice cannot be easily discussed if relativism is accepted naively.

Cultural relativism precludes any serious debate about justice and suffers paradoxically from the same dilemma as liberalism. What does a liberal do in a world which is inhabited by people who don't accept liberalism? For example, a liberal must have problems with reactionary conservatism, when authoritarian arguments do not accept liberal norms about such basic rights as freedom of speech. Cultural relativists have, however, similar problems when fundamentalists regard relativism as an aspect of the disease of secularism. My argument attempts to tackle these questions of relativism through an opening commentary on Montaigne in order to defend cosmopolitan virtue as a necessary adjunct to the possibilities of global citizenship. McLuhan's ideas about a global village create a puzzle, because we need to know whether there are many global villages each with its own local customs or whether there is one global village with a growing cosmopolitanism. It may be that it is only when the global village becomes the global city that the world citizen begins to share something like a common culture. The prospects of any coherent world consciousness such as cosmopolitanism continue to look remote.

The Montaigne paradox: the question of Orientalism

Living in the context of the French religious wars, Montaigne wanted to achieve a moral reform of the French nobility, whose warlike behaviour prevented any possibility of political compromise and compassion. Montaigne, who in this respect could be seen an early theorist of civilisation in the mode of Nobert Elias, argued that the violent ethos of noble life had resulted in the destruction of French society. His question was simply: What is appropriate behaviour for a noble class if we are ever to restore peace and civilisation? How can French society be sustained when faced with such violence?

Through a close examination of the essays on revenge and clemency, we can see that Montaigne presents an argument which gives priority to 'humanity' as the basis for mercy and sympathy, because in his view only a commitment to a common humanity could begin to moderate an aristocratic social world of vengeance and resentment (Quint, 1998). Montaigne was deeply shocked by the cruelty and violence of his own times. Men had become like beasts; they took delight in the torture of others. How can this behaviour be regarded as truly noble? Hunting as the principal pastime of the nobility prepares them for a warrior calling in which they take up a lifetime of inflicting terrible violence on human beings. He drew a parallel between various types of extreme behaviour – refractory French noblemen, intransigent religious zealots, Roman gladiators and Brazilian cannibals. In many respects these different types all exhibited the virtues of Stoicism, but Montaigne argued that they had negative consequences. The unyielding, almost compulsive, behaviour of the warrior rules out any possibility of compromise and co-operation. Montaigne therefore embraced what he regarded as the softer (feminine) values of mercy, compassion and tenderness.

Montaigne's interest in the Brazilian cannibals was an ironic device for analysing the violence of his own society. His version of 'Orientalism' is used as a literary strategy to expose the difficulties confronting his own society. This attitude was in fact an important part of the humanistic goal of understanding one's own society through the study of other societies. Montaigne's ethics – yielding, forgiveness, clemency, talking it out rather than fighting it through, adopting feminine virtues rather than masculine Stoicism – were designed to make men behave more humanely to one another, and perhaps ultimately to lead his countrymen out of their civil war and restore conditions of peace and justice. Montaigne's ethical position contained an unresolved tension between sympathy and understanding towards the other on the one hand, and the quest for justice on the other. The search for justice does not in itself lead to sympathy and compromise.

This brief commentary on Montaigne draws attention to the fact that the so-called 'problem of other religions' (and thus the problem of other societies) is not an exclusively modern problem. The problem of the truth or falsity of other religions was intensified by the beginning of European colonisation of the Americas and by the subsequent colonisation of Asia in the nineteenth century. However, while modern discussions about Western views of the Orient are a product of twentieth-century global conflicts, the controversy about 'other cultures' can be traced back historically to the ancient encounter between the Abrahamic religions. The fundamental issue is that Islam, Christianity and Judaism are variations of a generic Abrahamic religion, but they have been differentiated from each other with the passage of time, in which missionary competition has brought them into conflict and the imperial struggle for power between Christendom and Islam sharply distinguished their claims to authority and authenticity. In historical and cultural terms, the Abrahamic faiths cannot be neatly and definitely assigned to specific geographical locations and destinations, but for political reasons such a designation has to take place. These religions share the tradition of a High God, a sacred book, a religious teleology and a lineage of charismatic prophets. While the modern equation of Christendom and the West may be unproblematic, Christianity is a religion whose theological roots are situated in the prophetic tradition of Jewish radical monotheism and whose geographical origins are Near Eastern. In this respect, Orientalism is a family feud, and hence the otherness of the other religions is both inevitable and curious. The East appears in Western imagination as the forbidden Other, which is simultaneously repulsive, seductive and attractive. Like the veil, the East is both secluded and inviting. From the eighteenth century, the Orient has existed within a literary and visual tradition which is both romantic and fantastic.

These contemporary tensions have a long history, beginning with the foundation of Islam as a 'household of faith' in the seventh century, and these inter-faith relationships are complex and diverse rather than simple and narrow, in which the religious connections between Islam and Christianity have been overshadowed by inter-regional conflicts over economic and political resources. Despite these conflicts, I am also concerned in my conclusion to this discussion to consider the nature of religious ecumenicalism as a model of secular cosmopolitanism and to explore the opportunities for inter-civilisational co-operation and understanding (Watt, 1991). I am less interested in the political economy of inter-religious conflict and co-operation, and more concerned to understand the assumptions which have shaped Orientalist discourse itself. The aim here is to grasp the principal components of Orientalism as a special type of ideology through an exploration of the writings of a number of influential authors. The textual qualities of this Oriental exchange have a special prominence in this overview.

It is this geographical Otherness which at the same time defines our subjective inwardness; our identities are articulated in a terrain of negativities which are oppositional and, according to Said, permanent and ineluctable. In *Culture and Imperialism* (1993), Said claims that the modern identity of the West has been defined by its colonies, but these colonies are not merely physical places in a political geography; they also organise the boundaries and borders of our consciousness by defining our attitudes towards, for example, sexuality and race. Within the paradigm of the Western modernity, the aboriginal is defined as somebody who is not only poor and traditional, but licentious and lazy. In the evolution of Orientalism, we can draw from an extensive range of Western sources. For example, the plays of Shakespeare present a valuable insight into the character of such Oriental figures. *The Tempest*, written in 1611, was based on naval records describing shipwrecks from the period. Caliban, who is probably modelled on early encounters with the indigenous peoples of the West Indies and North America, is treacherous and dangerous, contrasting as a negative mirror image of Miranda, who is perfect, naive and beautiful. Caliban's sexual desire for 'admir'd Miranda' is one aspect of the moral struggle of the play that unfolds between Prospero's island kingdom and the arrival of the survivors of the storm and the shipwreck. Shakespeare's Moor in *Othello*, who may have been based on Abd el-Ouahed, an ambassador to Queen Elizabeth I, has remained an ambiguous and much-disputed figure in Orientalist debate, being either of noble character or obsessively egotistical or simply foolish.

However, the study of Orientalism must also include an analysis of anti-Semitism. The negative view of Islam is part of a larger hostility towards Semitic cultures in the West. If Caliban represents one formative figure in the evolution of European notions of Otherness, Shylock presents another. *The Merchant of Venice*, which was written in 1596, has some parallel with Marlowe's *Jew of Malta* and expresses the anti-Semitism of Elizabethan England (Brown, 1955). Elizabethan hostility to Judaism was part of a general anti-Semitism in Europe, in which antagonism to Jews has often been parallel to hostility to Muslims. Generally speaking, the critique of Orientalism has not addressed the ironic connection between two forms of racism, namely against Arabs and against Jews. In his Introduction to *Orientalism*, Said wrote that in 'addition, and by an almost inescapable logic, I have found myself writing the history of a strange, secret sharer of Western anti-Semitism. That anti-Semitism and, as I have discussed it in its Islamic branch, Orientalism resemble each other very closely is a historical, cultural and political truth that needs only be mentioned to an Arab Palestinian for its irony to be perfectly understood' (1978: 27–8). In a reply to his critics, Said also noted the parallels between what he called 'Islamophobia' and anti-Semitism. There are, in fact, two discourses of Orientalism for Semites, one relating to Islam and the other to Judaism. These two discourses for Semites are constituted by 'the Islamic discourse of gaps and the Judaic discourse of contradictions' (Turner, 1991: 29). While Islam had been defined by its absences (of rationality, cities, asceticism and so forth), Judaism had been defined by the contradictory nature of its religious injunctions where, for example, its dietary laws transferred the quest for personal salvation into a set of ritualistic prescriptions which inhibited the full expression of its monotheistic rationalism, according to Weber's analysis in *Ancient Judaism* (Weber, [1921] 1952). For Weber, the rationality of Jewish monotheistic prophecy was undermined by a ritualistic dietary scheme.

The experience of Diaspora and ethnic hatred meant that displaced Jews were seen to be cosmopolitan and strange; the notion of the 'wandering Jew' pinpoints the idea that their commitment to the national polity could not be taken for granted. In the twentieth century, Hitler's hatred of Viennese Jews arose from the encounter in Austria with what he took to be a seething mass of unfriendly and strange faces. While Jews were strange, they were also guilty, according to New Testament theology, of religious treachery. These anti-Semitic stereotypes have been culturally crucial, because Christianity as the foundation of Western values has traditionally attempted to maintain its difference from other Abrahamic faiths. Precisely because Judaism and Islam shared so much in common (monotheism, prophetic and charismatic revelation, the religion of the Book and a radical eschatology), they had to be separated culturally by a discourse of ethnic and moral difference from the Christian tradition. Jewish separate identity raised significant questions about the character of civilisation processes in Europe (Russell, 1996: 83).

Finally, while there was religious conflict, there were also periods of religious co-operation and experiments with institutions that made possible tolerance of religious differences. In the discussion of Orientalism and decolonisation in the 1980s, there was a tendency to draw a wholly bleak and conflict-ridden picture of inter-religious relationships in the development of the modern world. Although Western political theory has often seen liberal patterns of power-sharing as the only basis for consensus, we should not forget the Islamic millet system as a limited but relatively successful pattern of managing religious and cultural differences. The millet system existed in the Ottoman Empire from around 1456 to its collapse in the First World War. Although it was certainly not based on a Lockean view of liberty, towards the end of the nineteenth century, reformers within the Ottoman system introduced changes that pushed the system towards a more secular democratic system. Will Kymlicka describes the millet system as 'a federation of theocracies' that offered 'perhaps the most developed model of non-liberal religious tolerance' (1995: 157–8). The system allowed non-Muslims such as Jews, Armenians and the Greek Orthodox collective rights to practise their religion within their own community boundaries. While they were not allowed to propagate their religion outside their community, the millet system compares favourably with the pattern of religious intolerance, for example in the Iberian Peninsular following the *Reconquista*.

Conclusion: cosmopolitan irony

In conclusion, one can suggest that the components of cosmopolitan virtue are as follows: irony both as a method and as a mentality in order to achieve some emotional distance from our own culture; reflexivity with respect to other cultural values; scepticism towards the grand narratives of modern ideologies; care for other cultures, especially aboriginal cultures arising from an awareness of their precarious condition and hence acceptance of cultural hybridisation; and an ecumenical commitment to dialogue with other cultures, especially religious cultures. Cosmopolitan irony is generally incompatible with nostalgia and is specifically a product of globalisation and modernity. It follows directly from Edward Said's vision of Orientalism as laid out in *The World, the Text and the Critic* (1984). His approach to the subject of Oriental knowledge in fact owed little to Michel Foucault and was based on his reading of Raymond Schwab's *La renaissance Oriental* ([1950] 1984) and Erich Auerbach's *Mimesis* (1968). Schwab's study was grounded in the assumption, in the analysis of the *Domaine Orientale*, that Western culture is but a particular version of the transcendental generality of human culture as a totality. Auerbach's study of the problem of representation in Western culture was also based on the view that the study of world literature and philology pointed to a common humanity. For Said, homelessness, nostalgia and Orientalism have been dominant aspects of his literary studies. It is not surprising that in *The World, the Text and the Critic* he quotes with approval Auerbach's moral observation – 'our philological home is the earth; it can no longer be the nation'.

At the beginning of the twenty-first century, there is increasing interest in the prospects of cosmopolitanism as a doctrine and consciousness that can give expression to Auerbach's normative philology in which we inhabit one home rather than many nations (Holton, 2009). The similarities between Greek, Latin and Sanskrit are sufficient to give us some plausible commitment, not to relativism, but to a belief in a common humanity. Yet we cannot feel too comfortable with the prospect of a new understanding. Auerbach also came to the conclusion that for all his talk about the political insecurity of the world, Montaigne remained too comfortable and too at ease with himself. Montaigne's *Essays*, despite their focus on the human condition, lack a sense of tragedy. For Auerbach, 'the tragic is not yet to be found in Montaigne's work; he shuns it. He is too dispassionate, too unrhetorical, too ironic, and indeed too easy-going, if this term can be used in a dignified sense' (1968: 311). In our over-crowded, militarised and unforgiving world, we cannot avoid a tragic sense so easily. The quest for cosmopolitan virtues appears to be thwarted at every turn. Examples are almost too numerous to discuss, but one incident may deserve closer attention. In November 2009, Swiss voters, possibly influenced by the right-wing People's Party, approved a ban on the building of minarets on Muslim mosques. Encouraged by these results, Walter Wobman, leader of the People's Party, claimed that they would now press for a ban on the *burqa* and bring in a law against forced marriages. This vote was seen to be yet further confirmation of Europe's slide away from a strong programme of multicultural tolerance and inclusion. The Swiss vote against minarets – which are in any case not used as a call to prayer under restrictions on noise and public inconvenience – is perhaps surprising in a country with a high proportion of immigrants, but it confirms the assumption that cosmopolitan tolerance, even in Europe, is still a distant prospect. Globalisation may paradoxically make integration more rather than less difficult to achieve.

13 | *Civil religion, citizenship and the business cycle*

Introduction: religious asceticism and consumerism

In this chapter I return to a familiar issue in classical sociology, namely the relationship between religion and economics. This relationship was famously explored in the Weber thesis on the 'elective affinity' between asceticism and rational economic activity (Weber, 2002). In this chapter I want to look at a more specific contemporary issue, namely the relationship between religion and the business cycle in the United States. In an examination of the Great Depression and the New Deal, I explore how America survived the economic crisis of the early 1930s and the public debates that surrounded that defining event in American political and economic history. I conclude the analysis with a brief overview of some of the issues that have emerged from the credit crunch of 2008–9. Franklin D. Roosevelt's economic measures clearly had some success in managing the Depression but the steep downturn in economic activity was solved eventually by America's entry into the Second World War, which created full employment by other means. This period was followed by the creation of a consumer society as yet another response to the business cycle and to the creation of modern citizenship, not by a welfare state, but by what Lizabeth Cohen (2003) called a 'Consumers' Republic'. With the election of Ronald Reagan in 1980, there was an intensification of strategies to liberate the market from state regulations and there was consequently a 'financialisation of America', which has seen, in sociological terms, an increasing dominance of financial elites alongside the long-term decline of American manufacturing industry. The general view of these changes was perhaps best summarised in two publications by Daniel Bell, namely *The Coming of Post-Industrial Society* (1974) and *The Cultural Contradictions of Capitalism* (1976). Bell captured both the cultural changes in attitudes that had accompanied these developments and the underlying structural changes in American capitalism.

Although American society has changed fundamentally between the two crises of 1929–34 and 2007–9, the moral and religious language surrounding the crises is remarkably similar. There are, for example, striking similarities between the language used by President Roosevelt and the language employed by President Obama. In March 1933, Roosevelt gave his first Inaugural Address as President (Rosenman, 1938). The same 'greed talk' is evident in response to both crises by presidents with very different social backgrounds. FDR complained about the fact that the practices of what he referred to as 'the unscrupulous money changers' were obnoxious to the law-abiding and honest American public. He went on in biblical language to criticise the bankers and financiers, saying that the 'money changers' had fled from their seats in the temple of modern society. His inaugural address also encapsulated the see-saw movement that we can observe in modern capitalism between acquisitiveness as a virtue in times of economic growth and asceticism in times of adversity. He told his audience that happiness has to be more than merely the accumulation of material wealth.

In any historical discussion of traditional religious responses to greed, it is evident that the Protestant Reformation had the effect of 'making money clean', that is, the Protestant sects abandoned the critique of the economic system by departing from traditional Catholic theological concerns with the just price or the fair wage. This observation is really the heart of Max Weber's *The Protestant Ethic and the Spirit of Capitalism* (2002). We may also note that in response to the Great Depression there was relatively little criticism of capitalism as an economic system and much concentration on the motivation of individual 'captains of industry' such as J. P. Morgan. The contemporary equivalent is the outrage against Bernie Madoff and his Ponzi scheme.

The constitutional separation between church and state implies that there cannot be an official church response to the business cycle. In addition, there is little evidence that fundamentalist denominations were critical of the Consumer Republic and that any attempt by the state to regulate the market or to interfere with such basic issues as profits and property rights is defined as a form of 'creeping socialism'. While the Christian denominations do not criticise capitalism since there is, as Weber showed, an elective affinity between the Protestant ethic and capitalism, the idea of greed provides what we might call a 'discursive space' by which the churches can enter the public sphere and engage with the issues of the day in a language that is compatible with a fundamentalist understanding of human behaviour. Greed talk provides a language that the layman can comprehend and which makes immediate sense of the crisis that envelops them. Furthermore, 'greed talk' is perfectly adjusted to the expression of resentment of the social strata who are most exposed to the risks of a post-industrial society.

Before entering into a closer analysis of the relationships between resentment, greed talk and the vulnerability of various social groups to the economic crises of modern capitalism, let us consider how sociologists have characterised American society in the twentieth century. Talcott Parsons was the most prominent sociologist in America in the 1960s and 1970s, during the period when the creation of a post-war consumer society was well under way. Parsons, who died in the year before Reagan's election, is also interesting because his critics – such as C. Wright Mills – regarded him as the ideological spokesman of triumphal post-war America.

Understanding America

Throughout much of his career Parsons worked on the sociology of America that was never completed in his lifetime. However, with the recent posthumous publication of his *American Society. A Theory of the Societal Community* (2007), we can get a better understanding of his intellectual endeavour. The phrase 'societal community' in the title of the book can be interpreted as Parsons's attempt to merge the notions of *gemeinschaft* (community) and *gesellschaft* (association). In this theoretical framework, the social solidarity of the community is seen to be constituted in modern societies especially through the institutions of citizenship. The other important components of solidarity for Parsons are the law, religion and general values. The aim of the book is to understand why the American societal community has been largely successful in coping with social and cultural pluralism despite a number of major strains – for example during the McCarthy period. In this volume, the main example of successful integration, or what he also called the adaptive upgrading of the system, was the transition from early slavery through emancipation to the emergence of the Afro-American community as one component of an ethnically diverse social order. The discussion of citizenship and race reflects his earlier work on the social rights of the black community (Clark and Parsons, 1966).

Few sociologists have the stamina to write about societies as a whole. It is worth noting, however, that Parsons made no reference to Robin Williams, whose *American Society* (1965) made ample use of Parsons's concept of the social system to describe America as a whole. With regard to the history of the United States as a revolutionary society, Parsons should be seen as part of the legacy of Tocqueville in concluding that the failure of European modernisation provides an interesting backdrop to the success of America. Similar views were taken by Harold Laski (1949) and Seymour Martin Lipset (1963), who praised the vitality of American civilisation. Of course, one important difference between Lipset and Parsons is that the latter paid little or no attention to Marxist social theory in *The Structure of Social Action* (1937) and no attention to socialism in his account of American politics or values, whereas for Lipset the absence of a strong socialist tradition in America, or more precisely that Progressivism in the United States was not labour-oriented, as was the case in Europe, was crucial. In *American Society* (2007), Parsons has set out not to describe America as an empirical society, but to select a complex of institutions and values which in his view characterise American modernity.

In trying to find an adequate point of comparison with Parsons, one must turn to the work of Robert Bellah on civil religion, America as a civilisation and the American empire. Bellah had been Parsons's student at Harvard but came nevertheless to present an alternative vision of the changing nature of religion and politics in such works as *The Broken Covenant* (1975). For Bellah, it was not the case that Protestant Christianity had evolved through American history, but rather that a new religion sui generis had emerged to give expression to such events as the Civil War and other 'times of trial'. Bellah's attitude towards American society remained far more critical than Parsons's liberal perspective. Bellah had at the beginning of his academic career been a communist sympathiser, believing that the message of equality at the core of socialism was also the main component of the Sermon on the Mount in Christianity. By contrast, Parsons has almost entirely ignored the work of Marx. Furthermore, Bellah takes the view in 'The New American Empire' that Americans 'have become an empire almost by default, leaving us in no way prepared for imperial responsibilities' (Bellah and Tipton, 2006: 351). In many respects, Bellah's analysis of America remains more satisfactory than Parsons's notion of the societal community because Bellah has a much better grasp of the relationships between religion and politics – historically, politically and sociologically. One important difference between the two sociologists is that Bellah, as a well-recognised scholar of modern Japan, had achieved a much greater sense of the centrality of civil religion to the construction of the nation in relation to the nation-state.

In his analysis of American society, religion of course plays a crucial role in Parsons's work – as it does in Bellah's sociology. In Chapter 3 of *American Society* (2007), Parsons examines a variety of historical factors that laid the foundations for this successful transition. These included its successful adaptation of the Christian legacy and the Enlightenment, the absence of any deep clerical–anti-clerical split and the relative devolution of political power to local units. Parsons refers to these historical factors in terms of the 'neutralisation of religion' (such as the separation of church and state), the 'decentralisation of politics' (such as the separation of powers and federalism) and finally the neutralisation of ethnicity since the founders were from a relatively homogenous cultural background. These factors contributed an evolutionary advantage to the new colony, the very isolation of which permitted important institutional developments that were denied to the mother country. The American experiment was unique in modern history and hence Parsons applauded the title of Lipset's famous study of *The First New Nation* (1963). Parsons extended this theme to argue that modern America was also a successful modern democracy by comparison with many of the failed attempts at modernity such as in Germany and Italy. His 1942 article on the resilience of the German aristocracy and military in the transition to modernity can be seen in this broader comparative context.

Parsons published *The Social System* (1951) at the beginning of post-war reconstruction and optimism. The democratic powers had triumphed over German, Japanese and Italian fascism. The end of the War had admittedly left the Soviet Union in control of large swaths of eastern Europe and in 1947, with the emergence of *Pax Sovietica*, Stalin began to adopt a much more aggressive policy in foreign relations. However, Vietnam and Watergate lay in the future and American dominance was not seriously questioned. Parsons's work stands out because it presents us with an unambiguous celebration of modernity (Holton and Turner, 1986). In contrast, Theodor Adorno's reaction to America in *The Culture Industry* (1991) and in *The Authoritarian Personality* (Adorno, Frankel-Brunswick, Levinson and Sanford, 1950) was profoundly negative. Parsons's sociology exhibits none of this ambivalence towards modernity. There is no sense of nostalgia in Parsons's sociology for tradition, community or certainty. Parsons's commitment to liberal democracy, capitalism and the values of achievement and universalism remained undiluted and largely unquestioned. It is interesting to compare Tocqueville's enthusiasm for American democracy (at least in the first volume of *Democracy in America* ([1835/1840] 2003)) with Weber's admiration of the vitality of Christian sects in early twentieth-century America. Following his brief visit to St Louis in 1904, Weber became convinced that America might avoid the routinisation of culture so prevalent in Europe. Adorno's response to America remained predominantly critical, especially towards American jazz, consumerism and popular culture (Offe, 2005). Parsons's *American Society* should be seen as a contribution to a long tradition of sociological speculation about the character of America from Tocqueville to Lipset.

Parsons defended modern society, but he was specifically the champion of the American version of liberal capitalism. Radical critics from C. Wright Mills to Alvin Gouldner had criticised American society as an aggressive capitalist system, which was imperialist in its foreign relations and exploitative internally through the class system and the caste-like hierarchy of racial groups. Whereas Mills in *The Power Elite* (1959) had portrayed the elite as an integrated system of power, Parsons (1968a) saw the American elite as diverse and fragmented, arguing that the senior figures in the legal system were outside the inner core of business interests. For Parsons, despite its obvious patterns of inequality and exploitation, American society and its values were the summation of a process of secular progress, starting in the seventeenth century with the Puritan sects and culminating in American denominationalism. Parsons's vision of secular social reality has none of the overwhelming sense of melancholy which saturates much of Weber's world view (Goldman, 1992), but Parsons's secular liberalism was clearly unfashionable in post-war social theory.

Given American economic dynamism after the War and the decline of British imperial power, the post-war outward thrust of America 'came as no surprise to those familiar with the history of international politics. With the traditional Great Powers fading away, it steadily moved into the vacuum which their going created; having become number one, it could no longer contain itself within its own shores, or even its own hemisphere' (Kennedy, 1990: 359). Americans have, of course, consistently denied that their ambitions were imperialist or predatory. The Marxist theory of imperialism condemned the expansion of Western capitalism, and regarded 'liberal democracy' as merely an ideological cover for underlying economic forces. In an influential argument in his *Reflections on the Causes of Human Misery* (1970), Barrington Moore attempted to show that there was no hard evidence to support the view that the economic success of American democracy depended on military expenditure and an imperialist agenda. In his defence of American politics, Moore coined the expression 'predatory democracy' and argued that it could not apply to the American experience. By contrast, the problem with many contemporary defences of American democracy is that they optimistically neglect the current possibility of an American Empire and the emergence of the predatory democracy. Despite America's global military presence, there is a popular American denial of imperialism (Ferguson, 2004). In *The System of Modern Societies* (1971: 137), Parsons described the 'imperialist phase' of Western society's relations with the rest of the world as 'transitional' and he argued that the majority of societies in the non-Western world had adopted crucial aspects of the values of modernity.

As I argued in Chapter 4, another important dimension of Parsons's theory of American society was that he rejected the secularisation thesis which described the inevitable decline of religious belief and practice with the process of modernisation. In the post-war period, sociologists typically embraced a naive and unidimensional theory of modernisation which stipulated an inevitable secularisation of religious institutions and values. The continuing importance of Protestantism in mainstream American life and the global impact of fundamentalism have obviously thrown doubt on the secularisation thesis and Islam in particular appears to have survived long periods of secular nationalism, communism and Western commercialism. However, Parsons's sociology of religion does not involve the proposition that religion can simply survive industrialisation. Because he followed in the footsteps of Durkheim's sociology of religion, Parsons had a subtle understanding of the contribution of religious values to cultural systems, and how religion as 'the serious life' in Durkheim's terms provided an underpinning of the human condition as such. Parsons does not share the pessimism of Alasdair MacIntyre's post-Catholic criticism of modernity (MacIntyre, 1984) or the optimism of those sociologists who treated religious resurgence as evidence of the universal human need for religion (Yinger, 1967). Parsons's argument was that with secularisation many aspects of Protestant culture are both transferred and transformed into pluralism, activism and individualism. Protestantism was incorporated into mainstream America as an aspect of the adaptive upgrading of the social system.

The entire purpose of Parsonian sociology, and especially *American Society*, was to develop a general theory of action (which would be common to all social sciences) as the foundation for theoretically informed social investigation. In his study of the American social system, we can see Parsons putting to good use the theoretical framework of *The Structure of Social Action* (1937). Parsons's sociology has often been criticised for its failure to deal with conflict and social change. In *American Society*, Parsons was clearly aware of the contradictions and conflicts in modern social systems, especially in terms of conflicts over equality and citizenship. These are issues which are reflected in his essays on the history of black Americans (Clark and Parsons, 1966). Parsons recognised that the establishment of procedural rules of democracy created a framework for the management of conflict rather than for the eradication of conflict. In this respect, Parsons was obviously influenced by the work of American philosophers of law such as Lon L. Fuller, whose analysis of the common law attempted to identify the procedural arrangements necessary for a sustainable social order. Parsons employed the idea of citizenship to deal with the tensions between solidarity and conflicts over interests. The concept of citizenship, which Parsons took primarily from the work of T. H. Marshall (1964), plays a major role in *American Society* in explaining the success of the progress of modernisation in America. The growth of social and political rights not only explains the success of ethnic minorities in integrating into American society but also explains the resilience of social solidarity against the strains of authoritarianism, racism and class conflict. Parsons shared a view with sociologists such as Reinhard Bendix (1964) that citizenship had been crucial in the process of nation-building in America.

Citizenship and civil religion

In the second half of the twentieth century there was considerable interest in social citizenship as an explanation of how societies, otherwise deeply divided by social class and racial tensions, could survive social conflict leading to political revolution. As we have seen, Parsons deployed Marshall's notion of citizenship to explain how, among other challenges, America began to overcome the deep divisions around race. Parsons's contribution to the theory of citizenship was not the real substance of his approach to America. Perhaps the most influential political philosopher on American citizenship was Judith Shklar, and in her *American Citizenship* (1991) she argued that most interpretations of citizenship in American political philosophy have overlooked the importance of employment and earning in the formulation of early colonial notions of citizenship. She noted that what the founding fathers feared most was slavery and aristocracy. Slavery obviously implied a loss of human status and dignity, while aristocracy was associated with idleness. In short, she argued, 'We are citizens only if we "earn"' (p. 67). We might say that earning was important if citizens were to undertake their proper obligations, such as paying their taxes and supporting their children, but Shklar wants to find a deeper moral meaning to earning which comes out when we think about aristocracy rather than slavery.

The founders of Jacksonian democracy feared that aristocracy would be re-established in America and that constant vigilance was required to prevent it. They feared in particular a 'new aristocracy of monopolists and especially the men who ran the Bank of the United States' (Shklar, 1991: 66), and furthermore, the rights of the industrious working class would be 'sapped by crafty and indolent bankers' (p. 74). The role of the President was to protect honest working men from such parasitic elites. In this context the education of the population was crucial to instil democratic values in young men and to protect them from any regressive aristocratic vices. She claims (p. 85) that these attitudes persist in modern America:

Resentment of the idle monopolist and aristocrat, and fear of being reduced to the condition of a black slave, or of a black second-class citizen, have not disappeared, because they are grounded in lasting political experiences.

Her analysis of American distinctiveness might be summarised by saying that voting was the synonym for active political citizenship and earning an income was the necessary condition for enjoying public respect, namely for coping with the difficulties of inherited inequality (Hoffman, 1993).

We might argue that the credit crunch has revived these notions about the evils of aristocratic leisure. The bankers and financiers of Wall Street are blamed for acting like aristocrats. They are the idle rich who have undermined America because of their personal greed and irresponsibility. Through their avarice, thousands of American workers are thrown out of work and, of course, they can no longer earn an income. By not earning, they have also stopped being citizens. These circumstances, in which the very citizenship of people has been undermined by the greed of a Wall Street aristocracy, may explain the storm of resentment that has been unleashed in American public life.

Let us compare Shklar on American citizenship with Ralf Dahrendorf writing about Britain and Germany. In *Class and Class Conflict in Industrial Society* (1959), he argued that Europe had escaped the class war predicted in Marx's sociology of revolution, because the development of citizenship had improved the lives of the working class in expanding their life chances, despite the continuity of overall class inequality. Capitalist society, he claimed, had changed radically with the 'equalisation of rights' and 'an extraordinary intensification of social mobility' (p. 105). A variety of institutions had emerged in European societies to manage and regulate the conflicts arising out of the class structure. In this regard, his work on social conflict combined Marx's economic sociology of capitalism with Max Weber's analysis of power. Rejecting Marx's definition of class in terms of property ownership as too narrow, Dahrendorf interpreted social class through the lens of Weber's analysis of authority. Classes can be conceptualised in terms of the distinction between those who give orders and those who take orders. Every institution contained this dynamic tension between those with and those without authority, and he went on to define social classes as 'conflict groups arising out of the authority structure of imperatively coordinated associations' (p. 206). Revolutionary conflicts are likely to emerge when these contradictions, existing in a wide range of separate institutional settings, converge and coalesce. Modern capitalism had to be analysed, therefore, in terms of the balance between these authority mechanisms, unequal wealth distribution and the enhancement of life chances made possible by the evolution of citizenship.

Capitalist societies had, however, been transformed by the political struggle for social rights and hence capitalist societies had to be understood in terms of an ongoing struggle between class and citizenship. In this respect, Dahrendorf, like Parsons, was deeply influenced by the work of T. H. Marshall (1950), who had developed a model of social rights in his famous Cambridge lecture on 'Citizenship and Social Class'. Dahrendorf extended Marshall's approach to citizenship by looking at the processes by which industrial conflict had become institutionalised in trade-union organisations, wage negotiations, industrial bargains and legislation relating to strikes and lock-outs. Out of these processes, a new social contract had emerged between the industrial capitalists and the working class. Although this new contract was unstable and open to constant contestation, it had converted open class struggle into industrial conflict through an industrial relations policy. The potential war between classes with opposed interests was avoided by the pragmatic evolution of trade unionism and wage bargaining, and as a result 'reformism' rather than revolution had characterised the history of twentieth-century Britain (Turner, 1986).

In what ways had capitalism evolved in the second half of the twentieth century? Dahrendorf's generation can be said to have assumed a model of capitalist society as one dominated by industrial production and large-scale factories in which, for relatively low wages, workers could expect to be forced to retire at 65 years on a minimal pension scheme. The factory system had become increasingly bureaucratic and authoritarian, and the modern worker was subject to continuous regulation and surveillance. In the meantime, their wives, after a relatively short period of employment, would spend much of the remainder of their lives in the domestic arena. In this respect, their lives were not much different from those of their parents and grandparents. However, the uncertainty of their world had been given a modicum of security thanks to the growth of the welfare state, that is, through the modest expansion of life chances.

Modern industrial society has been transformed by a consumer revolution that took hold in the late 1970s and, with the dominance of the Reagan–Thatcher economic strategy, trade unions were largely dismantled and Western capitalism was increasingly characterised by declining industries and an expanding service sector. In Marxist terms, consumerism can be said to have mitigated the harshness of 'wage slavery' and obscured the obvious exploitation of the worker, but a consumer society presupposes a passive citizen, or at least a citizen whose leisure time is spent in front of the TV or in the shopping mall.

The crisis of 2008–9 has confirmed the prevailing pessimism about the underlying sustainability of Western consumerism based on cheap money and deregulated mortgage markets (Krugman, 1994). The crisis has exposed the growing dominance of financial institutions in the United States and Britain. What does the 'financialisation' of America and Britain actually mean? Firstly, it involved the de-industrialisation of the economy as manufacturing declined and the service industry expanded. This involves a real change in the power of elites with the decline of the old industrial elites and the rise of financiers, bankers and investment CEOs. The crisis has been shaped by the emergence of a new system of elites (Savage and Williams, 2008). Secondly, it means that investment in manufacturing industries has been in foreign, not domestic, development. For some decades there has been a balance between Chinese production and American consumption. Following the economic reforms of Deng Xiaoping, China became heavily dependent on exports and on continuing consumption in the West. By concentrating on investment, China failed to create conditions for adequate domestic consumption and as a result China built up nearly two trillion dollars in hard currency reserves, which were primarily recycled back to the United States through the purchase of US treasury and dollar assets by China's central bank. American consumption was fuelled by cheap mortgages, credit-card consumption and easy credit. Almost a quarter of American economic activity is now made up of domestic consumption as opposed to other economic activities such as investment in manufacturing and personal saving. The sharp decline in the American housing market, the crisis in consumer confidence and the failure of key financial institutions on Wall Street produced a sharp fall in consumer demand, mounting job losses and mortgage foreclosures. Although the West in general and America in particular had been subject to the business cycle through much of the twentieth century, in terms of its depth and spread the current crisis may turn out to be worse than the Great Depression.

What is the implication of these developments? In general terms it involves the erosion of citizenship – at least in terms of Dahrendorf's sociological model of life chances and in terms of Shklar's emphasis on the importance of employment for autonomy and dignity. The casualisation of the labour market, the disappearance of employment contracts offering careers for life, the flexible nature of retirement and the de-unionisation of labour are changes that have produced a passive rather than active citizen. The rise of a consumer society has created a new type of individualism in which what we may call the 'consumer subject' is passive and private.

These developments pinpoint a surprising absence in Dahrendorf's general theory, namely the absence of any discussion of culture in general and of religion in particular. The problems of modern citizenship are closely connected to the intersection between ethnicity and religion in civil society and hence to the complicated nature of identity in post-secular societies. The evolution of weak or passive citizenship is parallel, in my interpretation of modern society, to the evolution of passive religiosity or spirituality, to employ the terminology of contemporary sociology of religion.

Conclusion: civil religion, greed talk and resentment

One major weakness in conventional interpretations of the post-war evolution of citizenship in America and elsewhere is the lack of attention to consumer society and the creation of what we might call the consumer citizen. In America, citizenship entitlement was not achieved by the creation of a welfare state (as in Britain) or through a state-run social security system for industrial workers (as in Bismarck's Germany) or through the creation of a developmentalist state, as in many Asian societies (such as South Korea and Singapore). America does not fit easily into the historical thesis of Michael Mann's (1987) typology of citizenship as a 'ruling class strategy' of incorporation of the urban proletariat. American citizenship grew through what we might call an 'affluence strategy'. State intervention was to be minimal and provision would be self-provision through employment, and full employment in the Consumers' Republic would be made possible by the universal right to consume. As we have seen, economic growth driven by mass consumption was made possible by high levels of productivity, but also by cheap money, easy credit, favourable mortgage conditions, a booming housing market and eventually through new financial devices such as the credit card.

The problems with American consumer-citizenship are firstly that it does not require or presuppose any political rights or political involvement. It is a form of passive citizenship that does not presuppose any social involvement. The activity of the consumer citizen is merely to consume – and thereby to make journeys to the mall or increasingly to the on-line shopping site. The second problem, as Cohen clearly demonstrated in the case of the American Consumers' Republic, is that the market as the conduit of this new form of citizenship results in a segmented citizenship. The third problem – and this may be an empirical observation and not a necessary consequence of this form of citizenship – is that the male blue-collar sector (along with the traditional agricultural working class) is marginalised by the growth of the service sector, by the emphasis on educational qualification in employment and by the entry of (educated) women in large numbers into the workforce. Other aspects of this transformation – most of which were described very adequately by Daniel Bell in the notion of post-industrialism – include the decline of the family, the slow erosion of patriarchy and, as a result, a more tolerant attitude towards gay and lesbian sexuality. Insofar as heavy industry is no longer the centre-stage of industrial production and wealth creation, the masculinity of the proletarian worker is no longer relevant as an identity relating to active citizenship. Finally, as we have seen, this type of society becomes highly vulnerable to the instability of the business cycle, namely to the history of boom, slump, crisis and recovery that has been the history of capitalism in the long twentieth century (Arrighi, 1994). The rights of citizens become closely tied to consumption and to creditworthiness, and the latter is largely dependent on regular employment and the absence of a history of defaults on mortgage and other loan repayments. This form of society tends to generate high levels of personal indebtedness and, because status depends on consumption, the modern consumer society demands that everybody should become greedy. Citizens acquire liabilities rather than assets and hence they are highly dependent for their status in society on the economic growth and recovery from periodic economic crises. Hence the paradox of modern society is the structural requirement of acquisitiveness and the moral discourse of greed talk and the ubiquity of the blame game, to use the language of Robert Skidelsky (2009).

Civil religion and fundamentalism fit this social system relatively well. The first offers an overarching system of values that makes sense of American history and society, providing the sense of solidarity and motivation that Durkheim saw as necessary to the maintenance of any society. The civil religion, as Bellah argued, combines a large measure of the Christian heritage, but it also absorbs and makes sense of much of America's traumatic history – slavery, civil war, world wars and eventual redemption. The American colonial period can be understood as an exile rather like the exile of Old Testament Israel and America can therefore be successful if it adheres to its redemptive history and its calling as the 'city on the hill'. To this legacy in the twentieth century, Americans have added greed talk – a moral language of condemnation for the periodic crises of the economic system – without directly attacking capitalism. The identification of the villains such as the AIG executives and finance managers of the large banks allows public criticism to fall on individuals rather than on the problems of the economy as a whole. Since the crises are unavoidable (at least according to economic theories of the business cycle), the greed talk is also necessary.

Another component of this civil religion, at least since the rise of the Moral Majority, has been the propensity for these structural crises to be experienced through a pervasive sense of resentment. In this regard, the greed talk maps perfectly onto the social structure of a declining industrial power, namely it provides a language for the male, blue-collar worker who experiences his economic redundancy as one of social decline. William E. Connolly (1995) has captured this general sense of resentment in his account of the creation of a fundamentalist ideology, the rise of the Republican Right, the social consequences of the Vietnam War and the transformation of manufacturing industry. He writes that '[t]he Southern Baptist Church was consolidated through a common feeling of betrayal and resentment. This combination of military defeat, deep resentment against the victorious forces, and aggressive moralisation to overturn those forces forms the recurrent basis of fundamentalism in America' (p. 110). The political fundamentalism of the South has combined with other dimensions of American life in the late 1960s. He invites us to '[c]onsider northern, male, white, blue-collar workers and white-collar workers of modest means' (p. 111). These sectors of American society found a common outlook with Southern white workers who were the backbone of fundamentalism. This constituency felt under siege from middle-class feminism, the welfare programme of the Great Society, the growth of the service sector, middle-class environmentalism and so forth. The result is that white working-class men aggressively assert their basic frustrations against feminists, gay men, east-coast intellectuals and

African-Americans. He also recognises that much of this resentment emerges in the academy, in the struggle against relativism, Post-modernism and so forth in the 'culture wars'.

The Republican Party was successful in tapping into these pools of resentment. The Republican agenda came to be orchestrated around George Wallace and Richard Nixon and consolidated by Ronald Reagan. Workers who had been traditional Democrats were attracted to the Republican Party by resentments conjured up by the Vietnam War, the cultural movements of the 1960s, affirmative action on race and gender, the decline of factory work, gay and lesbian marriage and so on. These sectors of society, who had already been victims of the rust belt and the Internet bubble have now been subjected to the housing market crisis, the liquidity crisis, the banking meltdown and the economic recessions, are relatively easily drawn into the public condemnation of bankers and fraudulent financiers. The greed talk and the blame game offer an explanation of their plight, a channel for their resentment and, in some cases, a spectacular show of revenge when the AIG executives refused to release the names of their managers, citing death threats against senior executives. The mass media compared current malefactors with Gordon Gekko, asking for the 'disgorgement' of such wrongdoers, and President Obama attacked banks for sitting on money designed to support recovery. There are historical precedents for such crises. For example, the Puritan Jeremiad had an important function in the New England colony in lamenting the current woes of the settlers and the bright future of a new Israel. Modern greed talk and the blame game are far more negative – they are about revenge and not about rebuilding; their content is moral rather than theological. It is about the allocation of blame on an individual basis for those whose behaviour exceeds what we might call normal greed. The public language around the modern crises of capitalism has a moral and occasionally religious framework, but the mainstream churches lack any effective language to analyse or comment on the contemporary structure and functions of a society that is going through a process of financialisation. The recent history of economic crisis brings into question the notion that in general there has been, according to José Casanova (1994), a profound 'deprivati-sation' of religion and the eruption of 'public religions'.

14 | *The globalisation of piety*

Introduction: the comparative sociology of religion

Any discussion of the possibility of 'the comparative sociology of religion' takes us immediately into the problem of a generic definition of religion and eventually into issues surrounding Orientalism, post-colonial theory, reflexive sociology and the nature of the social. These reasons alone – epistemology, ideology and ontology – are in themselves sufficient to compel us to take religion seriously (Turner, 2009a). It goes without saying that attempts to define religion have for a long time troubled the sociology of religion. To return once more to the question of defining religion, as we have seen in this volume, the definitional issue came out very clearly in Max Weber's comparative sociology of religion in which, for example, it is not clear that the 'Asian religions' such as Confucianism, Shinto or Daoism are religions at all (Turner, 2009b). Émile Durkheim, in the introduction of his study of Australian Aboriginal religion in *The Elementary Forms of Religious Life* ([1912] 2001), also wrestled with the problem of Theravada Buddhism, which in its orthodox form rejects any idea of God or gods. I return constantly to Durkheim and Weber because their legacy continues to shape debates about religion, secularisation and post-secularisation in the work of Charles Taylor, Robert Bellah, Pierre Bourdieu, Jürgen Habermas and (I would argue) Michel Foucault. Durkheim and Weber established why the sociology of religion continues to be important and created a set of categories with which we still think and, some would argue, that we still struggle with. In particular, their work raises in an acute form the problem of the differences on the one hand between official and popular religion and on the other hand between the sacred and the religious. In this volume I have referred frequently to the work of philosophers from whom we can derive enormous intellectual benefit. However, the philosophical discussion of religion by Richard Rorty, Jürgen Habermas, Jacques Derrida and Gianni

Vattimo are wholly about official religion and pay scant attention to the ethnographic work of anthropologists looking at religious practice in everyday life (Derrida and Vattimo, 1998; Zabala, 2005). Their discussion leaves open whether the decline of religion necessarily entails the erosion of the sacred. An article by Thomas Luckmann (1990) neatly summarised the issue – 'Shrinking Transcendence, Expanding Religion'.

We might argue that Durkheim's sociology was indeed about the sacred world as a phenomenon in some respects more important and enduring than mere religion. Let us for the sake of argument suggest that the sacred concerns the 'idea of the holy' (Otto, [1923] 2003) and, as I have argued, that it refers primarily to a world that is ineffable (Turner, 2009c). Although Weber might be said to raise the issue of the sacred in his theory of charisma, he in fact treats religion as primarily concerned with secular issues. The first page of Weber's *The Sociology of Religion* (1966) deserves close attention, since, starting with the declaration that a definition of religion can be achieved 'only at the conclusion of the study', he goes on to observe that the 'most elementary forms of behaviour motivated by religious or magical factors are oriented towards *this* world' and concludes by asserting that 'religious or magical behaviour or thinking must not be set apart from the range of everyday purposive conduct' (p. 1). I shall follow Weber in asking how can we, in a global economy, understand the various orientations of religions to the market and more generally to the commodification of reality? In other words, I want to reconstruct Weber's famous essay on 'Religious Rejections of the World and their Directions' (2009). If one prefers a more contemporary idiom, I want to understand how the *hexis*, dispositions and habitus of the world religions are positioned with respect to the globalisation of capitalist economic activity (Rey, 2007). In this respect, I am more concerned as a sociologist with the actual practices of everyday religion in the market than with the formal or orthodox perspectives of official religions.

What is religion? What is the sacred?

Various solutions have been put forward to solve some of these long-standing issues. One has been to distinguish between 'religion' as a generic phenomenon and 'religions', to recognise the huge diversity of cultural practices and beliefs that could in common-sense terms be regarded as manifestations of religion. A similar stance has been taken towards Islam by recognising that the term covers a bewildering diversity of phenomena and hence some scholars argue that one should refer in the plural to 'Islams'. Some anthropologists of religion go further in rejecting any notion of Islam and propose that we simply study what people who call themselves 'Muslims' do (Marranci, 2010). The debate can be further complicated by arguing that the categories of the religious and the secular are products of a Western Enlightenment imagination that was subsequently imposed on the Orient. The very category of 'religion' has been identified as a product of Orientalism (Hart, 2000), thereby indicating that the categories of religion and secular are deeply implicated in the whole project of Western cultural hegemony (Asad, 1991). The debate has in recent years become even more vexed as anthropologists begin to question the very notion of 'culture' under which one might have subsumed 'religion' (Turner, 2008b).

These problems lie at the core of the legacy of Weber's comparative sociology of religion – perhaps the most ambitious and the most complex project of comparative scholarship in classical sociology. The defence of the possibility of a comparative sociology of religion will inevitably involve some defence of the legacy of Weber's sociology as a whole. In contemporary sociology, there are surprisingly few examples of the comparative sociology of religion in modern scholarship. Perhaps the outstanding examples might be the work of Robert Bellah in his *Imagining Japan* (2003), Bryan Wilson's *Contemporary Transformations of Religion* (1976) and David Martin's *Tongues of Fire* (1990) and *Pentecostalism* (2002). The most self-conscious modern attempt to produce a comparative Weberian study can be found in Stephen Sharot's *A Comparative Sociology of World Religions* (2001). Other instances of such scholarship might include the work of Peter Beyer, Peter Clarke and Mark Juergensmeyer. But these are the exceptions, not the rule.

This brief overview brings us rather rapidly to an obvious conclusion. In contemporary sociology (and anthropology), there is relatively little that passes for the *comparative* sociology of religion and what we do have is heavily dependent on Weber's typology of 'Religious Rejections of the World and Their Directions' (Gerth and Mills, 2009). Furthermore, comparative macro-sociology in general does not have many contemporary exponents, with possibly such obvious exceptions as Michael Mann, Randall Collins and Theda Skocpol in the comparative sociology of the state. Also, with the exceptions of the late Shmuel Eisenstadt and Roland Robertson, few sociologists have attempted to examine religion at a macro-level in relation to modernity and globalisation.

One consequence of these definitional problems is the somewhat obvious methodological recommendation that we must remain sensitive to the actual meaning and origins of the words we use to describe religion and the sacred. In previous chapters I have drawn heavily upon Émile Benveniste regarding the two etymological roots (*relegere* and *religare*) of the word 'religion' (*religio*). Religion was originally about scruples and later about the social bond. Jacques Derrida, drawing on this Latin meaning of *religio*, follows Immanuel Kant's analysis of religion and morality in *Religion Within the Boundaries of Mere Reason* ([1763]1998). Kant distinguished between religion as cult and religion as moral behaviour. In Weber we have seen that the primary driving force of religion is the quest for practical secular benefits in terms of health and wealth. Only the virtuosi seek an ascetic or mystical orientation to a meaningful existence. I have further noted that Kant elaborated his understanding of religious action through an examination of 'reflecting faith' that compels humans to strive for salvation through faith, and that Weber cleverly developed these Kantian assumptions into a sociology of religion.

The basic issue in Weber's sociology of religion is the relationship between two distinctions: charismatic versus routinised religion or elite (virtuoso) religion versus mass religion. This distinction involves a value judgement that the religion of the charismatic leaders and the elite are always being eroded or corrupted by mass religiosity. It is the distinction between heroic and popular religion that lies at the core of the notion that world-rejecting religions have significant consequences for secular society. I have used the phrase 'low-intensity religions' to describe religious lifestyles that have been co-opted by consumer society (Turner, 2009c). One might coin an additional term to describe this position by suggesting that religions that are too thoroughly embedded in modern secular consumerism have become 'low-impact religions'.

My definition of secularisation is that in terms of social relations as a whole religion no longer has a major impact on the dominant structures of culture and society, because religion is increasingly part and parcel of the market. It does not, in Weber's terms, play a role in 'world mastery'. The modern world is secular, because religion is shaped by the dominant practices and values of a capitalist society which requires expanding consumerism to sustain the economy. Society determines religion and not, *pace* Durkheim, religion produces society. Paradoxically, the sacred is in retreat while commercialised religion expands. In this regard, my position is basically shaped by the work of Alasdair MacIntyre (MacIntyre, 1967; MacIntyre and Ricoeur, 1969). Consequently, this volume has argued against any general acceptance of such notions as the re-saclarisation and de-secularisation of modernity (Berger, 1999).

The issue here is not simply a methodological one about how an adequate definition of religion might guide research. It is not a matter of defending classical sociology against attempts to deconstruct in some wholesale fashion the very notion of 'religion'. It is even less a question of defending the legacy of Weber in the sociology of religion, whose work has been – we hardly need reminding – subject to intense criticism. We might suggest that there are two issues at stake and they are interrelated. The first issue is the viability of a comparative sociology as such. Are we forced to accept the notion that, ultimately, to study 'religion' is a question of studying texts, in which case religion only makes sense in a particular conceptual field or fields? The comparative sociology of religion could then only in the last analysis be a study of how the term 'religion' has emerged in a particular discursive framework. Secondly, and more importantly, what is at stake is the social as such. The point of my excursus into theories of modern tribalism in Chapter 5 was to suggest that the elementary forms of the social world, which Durkheim attempted to describe initially through the lens of Aboriginal tribal life, is fast disappearing, and new but fragmented and ephemeral forms of association such as the Internet or Network Society are emerging. The new forms of religion that we have broadly referred to as 'spirituality' on the one hand and 'commodified religion' on the other hand are the social expressions of this underlying fragmentation and commercialisation of the everyday world. If the division between the sacred and the profane was the cultural expression of the underlying patterns of what we might call 'thick solidarity', the new subjective and emotional individualism of modern religion is the cultural expression of the emergence of what we might correspondingly call 'thin solidarity'. What is at stake, therefore, in the revival of interest in religion is the possibility of discovering viable forms of social being in a global world of commercial and commodified sociality. The prospects of sustaining the vitality of the social world appear, however, to be decidedly unpromising. The comparative study of religion brings us face to face with whether 'the social' can survive at all in modernity.

Having skirted around the issue, let me attempt to lay out my approach to the definition of religion and the sacred as a preliminary step towards a sociology of comparative global religion and religions in terms of three unashamedly bold claims. I take the view that most of the so-called 'Asian religions' were not originally religions at all. Confucius and Mencius developed state ideologies connecting personal behaviour, family organisation and social order that were designed to minimise internal warfare. Shintoism was similarly a state cult and Daoism was the basis of much popular practice around healing and the practical management of life's exigencies. Buddhism is a secular technology of the self, to use Foucault out of context, that carved out a fundamental distinction between the *sangha* and the laity around a doctrine of suffering and its psychic extinction. Buddhism did, however, quickly evolve into a theory of society and in the long run became part of a critical component of a galactic polity. Throughout Central and East Asia, shamanism can be regarded, following Marcea Eliade, as a foundational set of practices around ancestor worship and spirit possession that survives today in Korea and Vietnam (Taylor, 2004). These spirit cults in Vietnam were often associated with struggles against China and came eventually to be included in historical interpretations of the heroic Trung sisters (Dror, 2007).

In terms of the notion of an axial age and axial cultures, as developed by Shmuel Eisenstadt (1982), the core meaning of the Abrahamic religions was established by the Old Testament prophets and by the early Christian community to signify a body of people drawn together by belief in a monotheistic God and held together by rituals, especially dietary practices and sacrifice, giving rise to a linear vision of history punctuated by catastrophic events. Islam is an authentic version of this axial foundation, but obviously much later than either Old Testament Judaism or Pauline Christianity. Islam came into the modern world, to quote the interpretation of William Montgomery Watt (1953) in *Muhammad at Mecca*, where there already existed models of institutionalised religions, namely Judaism,

Christianity and Zoroastrianism. From these religions, we also begin to get the distinction between 'faith' – a personal relationship to the divine – and 'religion' – the institutionalised beliefs and practices relating to human beings and the sacred realm (Smith, 1962).

These notions of faith and religion from the Abrahamic religions were eventually transferred to the rest of the world through trade, missions and colonial conquest, and were eventually imposed on subject societies, especially through the educational dominance of the Christian churches and their schools. What counts as 'religion' emerged out of this contact or confrontation between West and East, and eventually a competition emerged whereby in order to have a voice in the field of global religion – or in the language of Pierre Bourdieu, in order to establish their cultural capital in the field of 'real religions' – they had to create theologies, ecclesiastical institutions and something approaching a priesthood. This construction of a competitive field was signified originally by the meeting of the World's Parliament of Religions in Chicago in 1893 (Beckford, 2003). Over time, Hinduism, having been constructed by the British colonial administration, began to emerge as a religion with a universalistic orientation, and similarly Buddhism has been refashioning itself through the reform of the *sangha* and the slow emergence of a social movement called 'Engaged Buddhism'. In recent years, there have been attempts to modernise and revive Daoism, or more generally 'Chinese religions', by retraining men into the traditional practices in order to allow Daoism to enter this field.

In the modern period there are two interrelated changes that are important. Firstly, as religion has been constructed globally as a unified and recognisable institution, it is also increasingly managed by the state as a set of services that can contribute to welfare provisions in society. This management of religions typically involves an upgrading of religion to make it technically efficient and rational (Turner, 2008b; Kamaludeen, Pereira and Turner, 2009). Secondly, globalised religions are constantly and inevitably drawn into the global circuits of capital insofar as they are themselves converted into lifestyles and into agencies offering commodities and services that cater to the needs of their clients. While much of popular religion is shaped by consumerism, there are also powerful forms of opposition to capitalism that draw upon a more traditional language of asceticism and protest, most prominently, of course, 'political Islam'. While religion in this popular form has expanded globally, the sacred is shrinking because this Other world – what Otto called 'the Numinous' or the *Mysterium Tremendum* – shrinks before the secular world of modern science and industrialisation. My conclusion therefore supports a particular interpretation of secularisation, namely the merger between religion and consumerism and the destruction of the sacred by science, urbanisation and industrialisation. As religion expands, the sacred – the actual foundation of the religious world – contracts.

The traditional comparative sociology of religion has to be re-established within the framework of the sociology of globalisation. The reasons for this framework are relatively obvious: (1) the global migration of people in world labour markets, especially from South Asia and China; (2) the emergence of global diasporic communities connected by global networks; (3) the development of competition between world religions, often involving the adaptation of modern missionary techniques; (4) the development of world travel, making possible the more widespread practice of pilgrimage and religious tourism; and (5) the growth of religious revivalism, including religious nationalism, radical religions and fundamentalism.

Instead of the traditional research strategies of comparative religion, we should be looking for social trends and movements that are genuinely global and common to a variety of religious traditions. A number of trends are important in the reshaping of modern religions: (1) the growth of piety movements in diverse religious settings producing a general pietisation of everyday practice; (2) the commercial development of religions as they engage with modern markets and themselves become part of a widespread commodification of social activities (Turner, 2009d); (3) as a result of these movements deeply affecting the lay audience for religious goods and services, an erosion of religious authority through the decline of the status of the educated religious intelligentsia; and (4) the eruption of religion as a powerful mark of identity that cuts across national boundaries and national forms of political membership in secular citizenship. Hence there is a need for state management of religion.

Although I am here talking about 'global trends', I am not thereby implying some uniform set of outcomes and I recognise, for example, that pressures towards 'religious commodification' have local manifestations which are captured in the notion of 'glocalisation' (Robertson, 1992a). Religion maintains its place in the everyday world primarily in the shape of low-intensity popular religion – that is, in religious lifestyles that are part and parcel of modern commercialism. At the same time, and under very different circumstances, religion can play a significant role in the public sphere, where the national framework of citizenship often fails to capture the cross-national loyalties of diasporic religious communities. Religion can play an important political role where there is some intersection of nationalism, social crisis and religious identity – as was the case in such different circumstances in Iran and Poland. In short, any discussion of secularisation needs to distinguish carefully between secularisation in the public sphere (the church and state debate) and in the everyday world (the disenchantment thesis).

Religious rejections of the world and their directions

My principal thesis is simple: namely that, with the globalisation of religions, modern religious formations are profoundly influenced by the globalisation of economic life, specifically by the commodification of everyday life. Religion becomes part of the global economic system in terms of the circulation of religious commodities (amulets, prayer books, pilgrimages and so forth), by the creation and promotion of religious lifestyles (often associated with body management, veiling, diet and dining), by the adoption of modern communication technologies (the Internet, videos, cassettes, TV stations, computerisation and so forth), by the creation of religious youth cultures that among other things blend secular music with religious themes and probably, in the long run, by the commercial cultivation of the religious body.

In order to think about this profound global commercialisation of religion I shall self-consciously draw from Weber's celebrated essay on asceticism and mysticism in the *Zwischenbetrachtung*. In thinking about religious orientations to the world, Weber produced the basic distinction between 'the active asceticism that is God-willed *action* of the devout' and 'the contemplative *possession* of the holy as found in mysticism' (2009: 325). In relation to the transformation of human societies by religious dispositions, Weber argued that 'rationally active asceticism' is important in 'mastering the world'.

In traditional anthropology and sociology of religion, it was a commonplace to assume that religious cosmologies were often influential in social protest and hence there is a long line of outstanding research on the religions of the dispossessed, cargo cults, millenarian movements, radical sects, messianic movements and so forth. This legacy of research might be simply summed up in the title of Lanternari's classic work – *The Religions of the Oppressed* (1965). The modern version of this tradition involves research on radical or political Islam, which might be simply summarised as 'terror in the mind of god' (Juergensmeyer, 2000). By contrast, I suggest that the focus on religion and violence, specifically on Islamic radicalism in the popular media, is one-sided and misleading. The majority of Muslims are middle class and moderate, the overwhelming majority do not attend the mosque and they put their Muslim identity behind their citizenship identity (Joppke, 2009; Pew Centre, 2007). My focus has therefore been, by contrast, on piety and personal discipline as predominant forms of modern Islam, and I see relatively little evidence of religious radicalism but rather a subtle merger of secular, commercial and pious practices. Whereas Weber concentrated on world-rejecting religious orientations, I am struck by the world-accepting orientations of religion to global capitalism and the ineluctable subversion of the religious to the commodity. In this regard, I am obviously appealing to Karl Marx's discussion of the concept of the fetish and the 'fetishisation' of the world as the modern form of alienation.

Weber's model has been subject to endless criticism but it remains a basic assumption of much sociological work on religion – at least of Western sociology. However, I propose a new criticism or interpretation of this legacy by questioning whether it is appropriate to contemporary economic conditions. These religious orientations that Weber conceptualised emerged in a human world characterised by a material scarcity that was occasionally punctuated by periods of short-term abundance. The Judaeo-Christian tradition is complete with stories of seven fat and seven lean years, while medieval literature abounds with accounts of plagues and famines to be followed by the excesses of Cockayne. We need to understand the profound religious urge either to flee from the world (mysticism) or to control the world (asceticism) as shaped by the enduring and inescapable reality of scarcity. In such a world, paradise is always a land of abundance. In Islam, the world beyond scarcity presents an image of flowing water and palm trees. I have argued elsewhere, in 'Goods not Gods' (Turner, 2009d), that in traditional societies religion offers what I call a 'theology of unhappiness' that makes sense of a world of frequent famine, scarcity, short and brutal lives, high infant mortality and disease. A theology, or in more exact terms, a theodicy of unhappiness explains the scarcities of this world and the riches of the next world. Following Nietzsche, we might suggest that in such a world the resentment of the poor and the disprivileged is often directed against the rich and the privileged in theodicies of moral compensation.

But what happens to these theodicies of unhappiness, which were prominent in the Old Testament prophets, in Christian asceticism and the *karma-dharma-samsara* system of Buddhism and the Asian religions that were influenced by that form of asceticism, in a world where life expectancy is greatly increased, where deaths from childhood diseases have been largely eliminated or controlled, where famines are no longer regular occurrences and where modern consumerism holds out the promise of earthly pleasures and the immediate satisfaction of our senses? What happens to theologies of unhappiness in a modern world where the life expectancy of women in the West is around 78 years and where, in Japan, life expectancy for women in 2008 was 85 years and predicted to rise to 97 years by 2050? What happens to the Confucian doctrines of filial piety, duty and service across generations? One social change is that the notion of an afterlife or paradise as a garden or heaven as consolation disappears from modern theologies and there is little talk about heaven and an afterlife in a post-scarcity condition. Of course, traditional views of heaven were diverse, ranging from a beautiful garden to a heavenly city. Paradise could also be seen in both allegorical and literal terms. In the Gospel according to Saint Luke (14: 15–24), heaven or the kingdom of God is described by Jesus as like a marriage feast (McGrath, 2003). The idea of a feast only makes sense in biblical terms against a background of hardship and periodic hunger. It is difficult for us to treat a feast as a significant event, given the problems of obesity and diabetes in our affluent world.

My expectation is that modern religions will have to produce a theology of happiness to cope with a world of material wealth, longevity, mass consumption and the transition from scarcity to abundance. How will world religions manage and respond to the globalisation of consumerism, the financialisation of the major economies and the implementation of the project of human longevity? One obvious change, which I discuss in my *Can we Live Forever?* (Turner, 2009f), will have to be the creation of what I call an 'aesthetics of ageing' to justify the prolongation of human life and the rising inequality between generations. Christian teaching will in all likelihood move from the dialectic of asceticism and mysticism to a new dialectic of acquisitiveness and greed on the one hand, and thrift and restraint on the other. In the modern world, there has been an explosion of religious movements that treat secular prosperity in this world as a major reward for religious involvement and commitment, thereby replacing the dystopic visions of ancient societies in which life was merely a brief interlude before the next world. The modern world, where, for example, Americans spend a quarter of their day on texting and twitter, is now what I want to call an 'entertainment society', and modern religions will have to change accordingly if they are to retain an audience.

This development is especially characteristic of 'neo-Pentecostalism' which has embraced a Prosperity Gospel in which health and wealth are regarded as the gifts of the spirit (Chesnut, 2003; Coleman, 2000). These religious orientations place few ethical demands on their followers and their membership was drawn from the poor but increasingly neo-Pentecostalism appeals to the upwardly mobile lower-middle class, but I want to argue that the ethic of consumption is fairly widespread in the contemporary religious field. The Catholic hierarchy in Latin America has been both critical and suspicious of these trends, but charismatic movements inside Catholicism – such as the El Shaddai movement in the Philippines – also preach a gospel of prosperity. The Baptist congregations in the Philippines have also been suspicious of Pentecostalism (especially its form of worship), but they have nevertheless adopted many evangelical strategies from both Pentecostalism and charismatic Christianity (Howell, 2008).

I can foresee two immediate objections to the picture of global religions that I am seeking to describe. The first is from the historian who would probably point out that the commodification of religious objects in medieval Christianity was well established in the cult of relics. For the medieval laity, relics, especially of the saints, gave them a spiritual anchor to both place and person, concretely uniting the spiritual and the physical world (MacCulloch, 2003: 17). The second objection is simply that not all manifestations of religion are commercialised and there are clearly radical forms of religion that are public and associated with protest and political action. Regarding the historical issue, in Arjun Appadurai's *The Social Life of Things*, Patrick

Geary (1986) shows how in his essay on 'Sacred Commodities' there was a widespread and international trade in religious relics. I want to maintain that the modern world is different because: (1) the contemporary trade in religious objects, such as Buddhist amulets, is truly global; (2) the hierarchical organisation of power between the elite and the mass has been reversed in modern societies; and (3) it is the commercial values of the secular world that shape religion rather than religious values that shape markets. I can respond to the second objection by noting that for many human communities the world is profoundly precarious and human lives are vulnerable. The response to suffering and deprivation is rarely one of collective anger and political protest. Religion does not automatically galvanise deprived communities into action. Many commentators on political Islam and on religious fundamentalism have, of course, argued that religious radicalism is motivated by rage about and opposition to Western consumerism and that much of the Iranian Revolution was driven by the economic and social consequences of modernisation. In these circumstances, religion may offer the promise of future happiness and theodicies of resentment may still flourish, but these revolutionary movements can never be a permanent condition of society. There is within contemporary Iran much dissatisfaction with the outcome of the revolution as new generations emerge for whom Khomeini is a historical memory and not a living presence. In Poland, Solidarity is now also a part of history and many Catholics want their religion to become part of normal Polish life rather than a foundation of Polish resistance (Zubrzycki, 2010). The routinisation of charisma is an inevitable outcome of historical change and these religious manifestations of revolutionary fervour are gradually 'domesticated'.

In this discussion of globalisation and religion, therefore, I propose to develop an alternative to Weber's 'Religious Rejections' of the world to produce, not so much a typology as an empirical account of 'Religious Accommodations to the World and their Directions', concentrating on piety and pietisation, spirituality and mysticism, spirit possession and occult markets, and civil religion in modern America. In this summary statement, it is clearly impossible to go into any detail with respect to these various and diverse illustrations of the relationship between markets and modern religions, and I shall therefore concentrate on three aspects that provide the gist of this discussion, namely the sociology of piety, the role of the state in relation to religious markets and the consequences of these changes for politics, religion and authority.

The sociology of piety

Conventional interpretations of Weber in terms of Protestant asceticism and economic rationality, claiming that in some sense Protestantism produced capitalism, is the conventional view of Weber's historical sociology. It is accurate at one level, but it is simplistic and not always the most interesting. I want to suggest that we should rethink Weber's comparative studies of religion as a contribution to the sociology of different patterns of piety in the world religions and how those forms of piety shaped the cultural values of the life-world of various societies. If we interpret Weber through the framework of Wilhelm Hennis's 'Essays in Reconstruction' (1988), then Weber's sociology can be regarded as the comparative study of 'personality and life orders'. From this perspective, Protestantism inculcated a set of virtues (or pieties) that shaped the personality and the life orders of Puritans through training in religious excellence. I employ the idea of 'religious excellence' here in order to anticipate a subsequent reference to Aristotle, for whom virtue refers to a condition in which excellence has been achieved in a particular sphere such as morality, warfare or the gymnasium. If manly heroism is the excellence of the warrior, then we can for the time being regard piety as excellence in religious activities.

We can interpret Weber's *The Protestant Ethic and the Spirit of Capitalism* (2002) as a tragic narrative about religious piety in which the measurement of religious excellence is essentially hidden from view. In Weber's terms, the tragic fate of pious Puritans was that they, contrary to their known intentions, laid the foundations for capitalist rationality, or at least that they unwittingly laid the cultural foundations of capitalism by establishing new patterns of discipline and self-control (Turner, 1996). The problem of the pious is how to know that they possess it. The success of piety can never be displayed for fear of pride, and hence its measurement can only be indirect. Protestant anxiety about the perfection of piety eventually drove them to find substitute measures and activities. In the case of the most radical forms of Calvinist doctrines of predestination, the faithful could never know whether their piety was enough to guarantee salvation, and hence they came to depend on worldly success as a proxy measure of their inner worth and their ultimate Election into the Kingdom of Heaven. The rational life-world of the Protestant sects had, according to Weber, the unintended consequence of creating wealth, because the successful Protestant abstained from immediate consumption and instead invested his (or occasionally her) wealth in future-oriented projects. We can, with some freedom of interpretation, also read Weber as saying that the Protestant system of piety was a mechanism of personal control that brought about a modernisation of norms and practices by providing new standards of rational behaviour that challenged traditional ways of behaving in the everyday world.

Protestantism is, or more generally piety movements are, culturally creative. They typically involve the destruction or overcoming of many traditional or taken-for-granted ways of practising religion. They involve either a new emphasis on religious practices or the invention of practices that are then claimed to be orthodox, or more exactly orthoprax. Piety tends to have a radical impact on the everyday world of believers by encouraging devotees to change their habits or, in the language of modern sociology, to transform their habitus or their dispositions and tastes towards the material world. Piety is about the construction of definite and distinctive lifestyles involving new religious tastes and preferences. In short, piety or the pietisation of the everyday world, has these Schumpeter-like characteristics of combining new elements to create a religious habitus that stands in competition with other possible combinations in a competitive religious context. These new combinations are then defined as the orthodox standards by which the worth of a good Christian or a good Muslim or a good Jew could be measured.

This way of interpreting Weber allows us to begin to bring the emerging sociology of the body more decisively into the mainstream concerns of sociology as a whole. Of course, there is a tradition in the anthropology of religion of understanding the body as an important aspect of religious ritual and classification. As we have seen in Chapter 5, the most significant example would be the work of Mary Douglas (1966) on pollution. Connecting the sociology of the body to an analysis of piety provides an important theoretical linkage also to the work of Pierre Bourdieu and to the historical analyses of Michel Foucault. I have in mind here Foucault's lectures at the College de France in 1974–5 on penitence, confession, concupiscence and the body (Foucault, 2003). The paradoxical absence of the body in mainstream sociology of religion may be in part explained by the dominance of the Kantian–Protestant view of authentic religion as a denial of ritual and the body (Turner, 1991).

Penitence and confession in Foucault's interpretation required an inquiry into the organisation of parts of the body – what has the eye seen, what have the hands touched, what has the stomach consumed? Confession involved an investigation of the five senses and the result was an infusion of the penitential code with medical notions and medical cures. There was a regime of opposites in which, for example, greed is cured by charity (Foucault, 2003: 182). Greed sat at the centre of this medieval language of virtue and self-mastery, being fundamental to the doctrine of the seven deadly sins. Modern culture has lost this understanding of the relationship between sin and the body, between greed and the undisciplined soul. Our notion of 'culture' has become disembodied and the body in secular society is simply a blank screen on to which we inscribe various ideas and practices, typically connected to consumption (Robertson, 2001). In this volume, I have examined the embodiment of piety against the background of the historical evolution of a consumer society. A late capitalist culture or consumer society is in fact driven by greed, but we only engage in the critique of greed when the business cycle produces a crisis. However, our 'greed talk' is largely disembodied and consequently empty of substance. In *The Cultural Contradictions of Capitalism* (1976), Daniel Bell argued that the old language of asceticism has run its course and that modern societies are basically hedonistic. A consumer society swings between an ethic of acquisitiveness (excessive personal consumption is good for capitalism) and asceticism (excessive greed is bad for capitalism, leading to periodic crises). However the language of this critique – greed talk – is parasitic on an ethical system that has long since disappeared. Voluptuous greed may be morally offensive in a society of scarcity and occasional starvation, but can it have much purchase in Western affluent societies?

This Weberian narrative regarding Puritanism was therefore deeply paradoxical, since a movement to abstain from this-worldly activity (through abstinence and self-control) produced a rational, modern world that in Weber's view was also deeply secular. These processes brought about, as he claimed, the disenchantment of the world

(*Entzauberung der Welt*). We can in this respect easily recast Weber's sociology of piety into a modern idiom by arguing that piety is par excellence a technology of the self designed to produce religious excellence or virtues by the discipline of the body (Foucault, 1997). Being virtuous or pious can be effectively measured by contrast to those who are impious or lacking in virtue. There is therefore a competition over virtue – who, in a given community, is the most virtuous and how can that be measured and known? The central paradox of piety is, however, that to display it openly – we might say to provocatively flaunt it – is to demonstrate its very lack of authenticity. To show piety publicly is to destroy it, and hence piety must be subtly insinuated and suggested by indirect comparisons with those lacking in religious virtue. In Weber's scheme, however, piety necessarily creates hierarchies of religious virtue in the form of pious status groups that are defined by their successful combination of orthodox practices.

Within this competitive struggle over virtue, there is a hierarchy of virtuous values and practices which Weber expressed in terms of the distinction between virtuoso and mass religion in *The Sociology of Religion* (1966). Whereas the virtuosi adhere to the full range of orthodox demands, especially the moral demands of religion, the mass are always oriented towards this-worldly needs, primarily health and wealth. This essentially secular demand for security and sustenance from religious practice, rather than a meaningful life or spiritual perfection, is, for Weber, a corruption of the religious drive. However, the needs of the masses for mere survival are too pressing and too urgent to allow individuals time or motivation to engage with the demands of religious virtuosity. They want magical solutions to hunger and disease rather than an abstract theodicy of suffering. Religion for Weber is therefore a site of cultural struggles in which religious institutions are constantly purified by charismatic prophets and constantly compromised by the mundane needs of the masses (Bourdieu, 1987). This struggle is perhaps most clearly illustrated in his *The Religion of India* (1958a), in the contrast between the ascetic standards of Theravada Buddhism for mendicant monks and the secular needs for success which are captured in popular Buddhism. In terms of this dialectic between high and low religion, the true piety of the elite is measured by its apparent separation from the magical practices that characterise popular religion.

This basic distinction also becomes the occasion for another, more precise, contrast between the 'contemplative-orgiastic' virtuosity of Buddhism and Jainism on the one hand and the 'activist-ascetic' virtues of Protestantism on the other (Silber, 1995). In the former, activity in the mundane world is inferior to the life of contemplation and hence there opens up a chasm between the lifestyle of the monk and the everyday life of the laity. Given this separation, how does interaction between monk and layperson take place? Let me quote this lengthy statement from 'The Social Psychology of the World Religions': 'With such religions, a deep abyss separates the way of life of the layman from that of the community of virtuosos. The rule of the status groups of religious virtuosos over the religious community readily shifts into a magical anthropolatry; the virtuoso is directly worshipped as a saint, or at least laymen buy his blessing and his magical powers as a means of promoting mundane success or religious salvation' (Weber, 2009).

Charisma is, according to Weber, necessarily in short supply and hence it has a price that is driven by the economics of scarcity. Because religious goods (services and objects) are limited, there is a spiritual market for religious goods as there is for any 'good' that is in demand but of limited supply. Because these charismatic blessings are demanded by laypeople, there is a religious market in which charismatic values circulate. As with other goods, there are in principle problems of inflation, overvaluation and excess production. For example, in many Muslim societies that have been influenced by revivalism (*da'wa*), there is a tendency for more and more goods and services to come under the classification of acceptable and proscribed (between *halal* and *haram*). As the demand for pious goods and services increases with changes in behaviour, there is a corresponding inflation of religion that we can call the *halalisation* of everyday life (Kamaludeen, Pereira and Turner, 2009). One might – although the terminology is ugly – think of similar movements in Judaism taking the form of a *kosherisation* of everyday life.

One perennial problem which I want to address is how piety can be measured – what is the price of piety? In trying to provide an answer to this question, I argue the religious revival which we witness in Islam world-wide is a movement of piety that has important similarities to Weber's account of ascetic piety in several respects. Firstly, it is a movement to rationalise the everyday world through adherence to pious norms. Secondly, these movements are closely connected with a small, urban middle class in countries such as Bangladesh, Malaysia and Indonesia. In these predominantly Muslim societies, there is an interaction between the deregulated capitalist economy, the new elites and the growth of piety. There is distinctive merger of personal wealth and piety in the new middle class, especially among educated women.

Weber's Protestant ethic thesis can be interpreted as the sociology of piety that can be generalised to modern practices. The modernisation of the everyday world (or habitus) is articulated through acts of piety that create post-traditional lifestyles, but in competition with the semi-religious laity, and hence there is what one might call a tendency towards the inflation of pious acts. In creating virtue, piety tends to multiply the activities that can count as religious or pious. In the competition for virtue, there is an inevitable tendency towards inflation to cope with the demand for religious goods and services.

Recent interest in Muslim piety has been influenced by Saba Mahmood's *The Politics of Piety* (2005), which is important for several reasons. It challenges the general assumption about secularity in Western writing about religion, in which modernisation was an inevitable process of secularisation. Piety and revivalism are compatible with modern, urban lifestyles. Mahmood challenges the typical opposition, characteristic of Western feminism, between submission (wearing the veil) and resistance (discarding the veil). *The Politics of Piety* has to be understood within the wider context of American foreign policy and Western feminism. Research on Turkey, Indonesia, Bangladesh and Malaysia – specifically that addresses the issue of women, the veil and the new piety – comes to conclusions that are not dissimilar to those of Mahmood's study, namely that veiling can be empowering by allowing women to enter public spaces and compete with men in the religious field. The pious practices cultivated by women in Indonesia's Prosperous Justice Party are part of the creation of a certain middle-class habitus. It is a habitus that is oriented towards modernity and accords with essentialised notions of gender. It is one of several competing Islamic frameworks in contemporary Indonesia, and it remains unclear to what extent this pious habitus may be more culturally authorised than others (Rinaldo, 2010). There is an alternative view that gender is an important axis around which class distinctions are drawn and maintained, and that the habitus, as a form of socialised subjectivity, is in fact the means through which such large-scale inequalities are made real. Pious dispositions can also be part of the ways in which gendered class distinctions are embodied. One intriguing issue that emerged from research on Malaysia is the fact that pious women, who see child-bearing as an honorific *jihad*, have high fertility levels, thereby departing sharply from the general trend in Asian societies towards low total fertility rates (Tong and Turner, 2008).

The veil – as the principal sign of female piety – has, of course, become a contentious issue in liberal Western societies. There have been many moving and successful critiques of Islamic patriarchalism from within Islam by feminist critics such as Fatima Mernissi's (2003) *Beyond the Veil* and famously by literary critics such as Azar Nafisi in *Reading Lolita in Tehran* (2008). My own argument is that the meaning of the veil will vary significantly according obviously to the status of women in any given society. The subordination of women is clearly profound in the Middle East and North Africa, and therefore the Algerian experience is influential in Marnia Lazreg's critique in *Questioning the Veil* (2009). Bedouin society with its strong sense of male privilege, hierarchy and blood relationships does not allow much space for female empowerment – as Lila Abu-Lughod shows in *Veiled Sentiments* (1986). Perhaps the most repressive example of compulsory veiling comes from war-torn Chechnya under the contemporary process of reconstruction under the dictatorial presidency of Ramzan Kadyrov. In Chechnya, the obligatory veiling of women is equated with the necessary restoration not only of the society but of masculinity. An appeal to traditional Islam is used by the state to promote multiple marriages for men who are charged with responsibility to ensure that women are well behaved (Littell, 2009). In Europe itself, as Christian Joppke demonstrates in *Veil* (2009), the status of the veil and women as citizens depends to some extent on state policies towards public attire and secular education.

On the other side of the world there is a well-established argument from historians and anthropologists that women have enjoyed relatively high status in Southeast Asia. In pluralistic Indonesia, Islamic fundamentalism has not robbed women of their status in society (van Wichelen, 2010), and in secular Singapore, while veiling has become very popular among young pious women, the status of women remains high, being underpinned by state legislation. In Malaysia, much of the acceptance of veiling appears to be initiated by women rather than by men. In societies where Islam is a minority religion, women will be faced with the dilemma that, if they criticise the practice of veiling, they may appear to undermine their own communities. It is also important to realise that the veil can be an item of high fashion in many societies. Ethnographic research in Turkey suggests that the largest Muslim fashion departments employ an Islamic discourse about female modesty and fully embrace the secular commercial attitudes of Western capitalism. In popular Turkish culture, the veil is both a mark of Islamic identity and a commodity of capitalist circulation (Navaro-Yashin, 2002). Another issue raised by the debate about the veil is to what extent it is a product of the domination of men over women or the hegemony of religious culture over both. In Southeast Asia, where patriarchy has been historically much weaker than in the Middle East, women are more likely to be regulated by local custom than by overt male domination and aggression.

One further aspect of the sociology of piety concerns the ways in which the pious become distinguished from others (traditionalists and secularists) and hence how society may become divided ever more rigidly between the virtuous and the rest. Debates about the apostasy rule in Malaysia, for example, suggest that pietisation may encourage increasing social divisions between the household of faith and the household of war. It is here that the idea of 'rituals of intimacy' (Kamaludeen, Pereira and Turner, 2009) may be useful. These interaction rituals and strategies – such as 'defensive dining' – allow the pious to negotiate everyday life and to minimise the possibility of conflict over objects and activities that are *haram*. Such rituals permit a constant negotiation over issues that might pollute and hence cause communal friction.

What does the pietisation of Muslim practice among women in Malaysia and other Muslim societies tell us about the globalisation of religion? In fact, their piety is in part a product of their encounter with the secular West. Many Muslim women have now been educated in the West, and their encounter with secularism in Western universities has encouraged them, and possibly forced them, to reflect upon and reconsider their religious identities. Western secular students will often ask such Muslim women why they did not wear a veil, why they smoked and in some cases why they consumed alcohol. It was the clash between their Muslim background and secular education that led them eventually to adopt what they see as a more pious lifestyle in which they veil and force their husbands and children to conform to pious lifestyles. Of course, Malaysia is also in some sense a multicultural society in which the attempt at the Islamisation of the state is forcing citizens to make choices about their religious identities. Malay piety is also a product of the increasing importance of the *hajj* (the Pilgrimage) in defining personal identity, and hence fulfilment of this religious obligation further intensifies the sense of pious identity. The *halalisation* of everyday life is thus paradoxically an aspect of the pious transformation of everyday life and global consumerism.

The global commodification of religion

One can take interesting examples of these developments – the intersection of religion and market – from the limited and partial opening up of religion in China and Vietnam. The creation of a religious market in China has been described in a variety of influential articles by Yang Fenggang (2006; 2007; 2010). The disciplinary management of religions in well-ordered hierarchical regimes such as Singapore and South Korea may remain unavailable to liberal democratic regimes such as Australia and Britain, which must aspire to contain religious movements as the lifestyle of post-secular consumerism and passive consumerist citizenship. There is obviously a dystopian aspect to this argument. Insofar as liberal societies may slide inevitably towards authoritarian systems with the global development of both securitisation and consumer capitalism, passive citizens are policed and regulated by the state and at the same time entertained by a powerful mixture of secular popular culture, consumerism and popular religion.

As we saw in Chapter 13, post-communist states have unsurprisingly adopted rather different strategies in their attempts to come to terms with a more liberal environment. As in China and Russia, a similar pattern of communist suppression followed by a period of liberalisation of both society and economy has been characteristic of Vietnam. Under French colonialism, Buddhism was regarded as politically oppositional and the Catholic missions were obviously favoured. Diem's regime came to depend heavily on Catholic support, while the National Liberation Front supported various marginalised religious groups such as the Cao Dai. From 1975 onwards, there was a massive exodus from Catholic Vietnamese from the south and

Vietnam was caught up eventually in the Cultural Revolution that suppressed religion as mere superstition and a foreign import. Since 1986, Vietnam has become more open to religious resurgence in the so-called Renovation Period. Spirit possession and the problem of ghosts have been widely studied by anthropologists in the last two decades of research on Vietnam (Salemink, 2008). The consensus is that these are not simply a restoration of tradition but that spirit possession has a function in the capitalist development of modern Vietnam. Spirit possession networks are important in bringing business-men together and they serve as an important conduit of remittances from overseas, contributing to the circulation of cash among these networks. The votive burning of money to placate the grievances of ghosts also plays an important role in the everyday economy of ordinary Vietnamese citizens (Kwon, 2009). In more general terms, it is argued that the massive social disruption of Vietnam by decades of war has produced a generalised uncertainty that is partly ameliorated by the management of spirits, especially 'hungry ghosts'. These devel-opments in Vietnam may find a parallel in many societies in which a traditional world has been severely compromised and disrupted by war and capitalist agricultural development leading to what Comaroff and Comaroff (1999) have called 'the occult economy'. The social disruptions of modern Vietnamese society are replicated in the con-flict-ridden and competitive world of ghosts and spirits, and the post-war cultural landscape is overpopulated by the 'wandering ghosts of late capitalism' (Leshkowich, 2008).

Conclusion: resentment, religion and social mobility

In arguing that the tradition of the comparative sociology of religion has to become the sociology of religion and globalisation, I have con-sidered a variety of examples of how religion and the global consumer market interact. The various forms of religious commodification – in Islam, popular religion, spirituality, Vietnamese spirit possession, Protestant mega-churches, global religious publishing houses, health and prosperity cults and so forth – are not, of course, identical or even related responses. They form different, that is 'glocal', religious accommodations to the world and they are accommodations to the world, rather than in Weber's terms 'religious rejections of the world'. We can now provide a summary of these arguments.

(1) With urbanisation and economic development, huge numbers of peasants moved into mega-cities, especially in Asia. As they acquired new lifestyles, they also began to adopt a more sophisticated understanding of religion, and as their educational standards improved they became more open to new patterns of piety. The new urban lower-middle classes became more literate and at the same time more pious. These piety movements are more intensive when a religious group finds itself in a minority status and its intelligentsia has to answer questions about how to behave as a good Muslim or a good Christian in a diasporic community. Local leaders and new intellectuals have to compete for a clientele through the new media. Islamic communities in particular, in migrating to the West or into multi-faith societies in Asia, have found themselves confronted by diversity. The growth of global Islam often results in a challenge to traditional forms of authority. The veiling of Muslim women has become a typical feature of Muslim pietisation as urbanised women take up the veil. This issue of veiling is probably the most controversial aspect of the modern debate about women and religion. Veiling has been seen as the most damaging illustration of patriarchy and religious conservatism and has also been defended as an example of female empowerment. My own research in Malaysia (Tong and Turner, 2008) and Singapore (Kamaludeen, Pereira and Turner, 2009) lends support to the view that modern veiling is not traditional. Although the consensus is that veiling reproduces patriarchal power, I think that it points to some different issues – the massive decline in female fertility throughout Asia and the growth of education and literacy among Muslim women. Educated Malay women who were members of PAS (the Malaysian Muslim party) and who lived in conservative Kelantan had higher than average fertility rates, but they are also demonstrably empowered by reformed Islam in running their own Quranic study groups and questioning many aspects of traditional Islam.

(2) As men become marginalised within the occupational structure and as women acquire higher levels of education, there is considerable resentment from the blue-collar male workers who see lesbianism, gay rights, racial equality and the decline of the family as a challenge to their social standing and masculinity. These patterns of resentment, following Robert Bellah's commentary on modern

America, fuel the conservative religious response to cultural liberalism and to multiculturalism. The blame game and the greed talk surrounding the credit crunch of 2007–9 may be an illustration of these structural and cultural changes.

(3) As religious identities become more important for defining one's public status, religion begins to impinge on the public domain in new ways and the Westphalian system of secularisation and the Lockean vision of tolerance become less relevant to multicultural and post-Christian societies. However, the state has to manage religions in order to guarantee public order, and a complex set of arrangements has emerged to deal with such potential conflicts. In my Singaporean research, I came to the conclusion that in modern societies the state has to intervene to manage religions in the quest for security, especially in societies with large waves of migration, significant ethnic diversity and various diasporic religious communities. These strategies can vary considerably, but the modern state cannot simply ignore religion.

(4) It is useful to distinguish between the political and the social dimension in any discussion of secularisation. Political secularisation involves a paradoxical separation of church and state in which the state intervenes to control and regulate religions. This intervention is especially manifest in the attempt to solve the issue of the Muslim veil but in addition state involvement can be seen in the desire to control so-called 'cults' such as Scientology or to regulate the practice of polygamy in various religious traditions that lie outside the mainstream. State management can also be repressive, as in the case of the Chinese management of Falun Gong. Because religion and ethnicity become mutually reinforcing, ethnic conflicts and religious conflicts cannot be separated. The Chinese attempts to manage Islam in the case of the Uigars and Buddhism in the case of Tibet are clear illustrations. But social secularisation is something very different, involving the commodification and commercialisation of religions. This process is genuinely global and involves all the major religions – from Buddhist amulets to Protestant mega-churches.

(5) In this discussion, I have taken up a central issue of Weber's sociology – economics and religion. I have examined this issue through piety, the commercialisation of religion, greed and the credit crunch, the spread of female piety and the growth of

capitalism in Asia. In societies that are predominantly Christian, the new urban piety has spread through Pentecostalism and the charismatic churches. These piety movements appear, unsurprisingly, to be associated with social class and lifestyle. In the West, the post-institutional religions of youth or 'spirituality' do not involve inner-worldly asceticism or self-control. In Weber's terms, these forms of spirituality appear to be closer to mysticism, but they are not withdrawn from society as such. Spirituality in the West and neo-Sufism in the East both appear to be compatible with secular, mobile, urban lifestyles. They are typically low-impact or low-intensity lifestyles, but both spirituality and piety are heavily influenced by a consumer culture. Many of the religious movements I have discussed in this study can be regarded as aspects of global youth cultures that incorporate younger generations into the mainstream society. The paradox of much youth culture is that, while overtly deviating from society in terms of lifestyle, this often has the function of bringing youth into the mainstream.

(6) In the past, sociologists have been impressed by the connections between religion and political protest. The principal example of contemporary religious conflict with capitalism has been driven by political Islam (Kepel, 2002; 2004a; Roy, 1994). In the modern world, does resentment evolve into rage and revolutionary protest? While sociologists have given some attention to religious violence and suicidal protest, in many developing societies alienation and uncertainty produce an 'occult market' rather than revolutionary movements. Neo-Pentecostalism is one widespread example. In the case of modern America, the Protestant criticism of the credit crisis has mainly been directed at individuals rather than at the modern system of finance capitalism. It provides, in Durkheimian terms, an emotional discharge.

To conclude, throughout this volume my attention has been driven by the belief that the roots of the social are ultimately in the sacred. If we accept the direction of Durkheim's sociology of religion and Parsons's interpretation of it, the ultimate roots of community are sacred and thus that which binds people together into powerful, typically emotional groups, are religious forces. The sacred roots of collective culture are being eroded by globalisation in the shape of commercialisation and commodification, and in this sense we face the end of the social. We might further say that this formulation of the sociology of religion provides the linkage, therefore, with political theology. In a modern entertainment society, the citizen becomes merely a passive consumer of goods and services and with the commercialisation of religion the religious actor also becomes passive. There is, in short, an elective affinity between the passive citizen and modern spirituality. The 'chain of memory' that is constitutive of community has been broken by a long period of possessive individualism and by a more recent period of neo-liberal economic policies, and hence the roots of solidarity are very weak in modernity (Hervieu-Leger, 2000). This interpretation of our modern dilemma – the contraction of the sacred, the flourishing of religion as lifestyle, and the consequent erosion of the social – involves a metaphysics of nostalgia. This study of religion and the making of modernity has sought to provide a defence of nostalgia as a critical tool of analysis. In this respect the nostalgic imagination may be a defensible, and at least an intelligent, response to the end of the social.

References

Abduh, M. (1966) *The Theology of Unity*. London: Allen & Unwin.

Abercrombie, Nicolas, Hill, Stephen and Turner, Bryan S. (1980) *The Dominant Ideology Thesis*. London: Allen & Unwin.

Abercrombie, Nicholas and Longhurst, Brian (1998) *Audiences*. London: Sage.

Abu-Lughod, Lila (1986) *Veiled Sentiments. Honor and Poetry in a Bedouin Society*. Berkeley: University of California Press.

Adams, C. C. (1999) *Islam and Modernism in Egypt*. London and New York: Routledge.

Adogame, Afe (2010) 'Pentecostalism and Charismatic Movements in a Global Perspective' in Bryan S. Turner (ed.) *The New Blackwell Companion to the Sociology of Religion*. Oxford: Wiley-Blackwell, pp. 498–518.

Adorno, T. W. (1991) *The Culture Industry*. London and New York: Routledge.

Adorno, T. W., Frankel-Brunswik, E., Levinson, D. J. and Sanford, R. N. (1950) *The Authoritarian Personality*. New York: Harper.

Afary, Janet and Anderson, Kevin B. (2005) *Foucault and the Iranian Revolution. Gender and the Seductions of Islamism*. University of Chicago Press.

Agamben, G. (1998) *Homo Sacer. Sovereign Power and Bare Life*. Stanford University Press.

Ahmed, Akbar (1992) *Postmodernism and Islam. Predicament and Promise*. London: Routledge.

Ahmed, Leila (1992) *Women and Gender in Islam. Historical Roots of a Modern Debate*. New Haven and London: Yale University Press.

Akbarzadeh, Shahram and Mansouri, Fethi (eds.) (2007) *Islam and Political Violence. Muslim Diaspora and Radicalism in the West*. London: Tauris.

Alexander, Jeffrey C. (1988a) *Neofunctionalism and After*. Oxford: Basil Blackwell.

Alexander, Jeffrey C. (ed.) (1988b) *Durkheimian Sociology. Cultural Studies*. Cambridge University Press.

Alexander, Jeffrey C. and Smith, Philip (eds.) (2005) *Cambridge Companion to Durkheim*. Cambridge University Press.

Aljunied, S. M. K. (2009) *Colonialism, Violence and Muslim in Southeast Asia: The Maria Hertogh Controversy and Its Aftermath*. London: Routledge.

Alter, J. S. (2000) *Gandhi's Body. Sex, Diet and the Politics of Nationalism*. Philadelphia: University of Pennsylvania Press.

Althusser, Louis (1971) *Lenin and Philosophy and Other Essays*. London: New Left Books.

Anderson, Benedict (1991) *Imagined Communities: Reflections on the Origin and Spread of Nationalism*. London: Verso Books.

Anderson, P. S. and Clark, B. (eds.) (2004) *Feminist Philosophy of Religion. Critical Readings*. London: Routledge.

Anderson, Perry (1976) *Considerations on Western Marxism*. London: New Left Review.

Antoun, Richard T. (2001) *Understanding Fundamentalism. Christian, Islamic and Jewish Movements*. Walnut Creek: Altamira Press.

Appadurai, Arjun (ed.) (2001) *Globalization*. Durham: Duke University Press.

Appiah, K. A. (2006) *Cosmopolitanism. Ethics in a World of Strangers*. New York: W. W. Norton.

Arberry, A. J. (1950) *The Spiritual Physick of Rhazes*. London: John Murray.

Arjomand, Said A. (2004) 'Islam, Political Change and Globalization', *Thesis Eleven* **76**(1): 9–28.

Arkoun, Mohammed (1994) *Rethinking Islam. Common Questions and Uncommon Answers*. Boulder: Westview Press.

(2002) *The Unthought in Contemporary Islamic Thought*. London: Saqi Books.

Arnoldi, J. (2001) 'Niklas Luhmann' in Anthony Elliott and Bryan S. Turner (eds.) *Profiles in Contemporary Social Theory*. London: Sage, pp. 249–59.

Arppe, Tina and Borch, Christian (2009) *Distinktion. Scandinavian Journal of Social Theory* **19** (Special issue: 'The Sacred').

Arrighi, Giovanni (1994) *The Long Twentieth Century. Money, Power and the Origins of Our Times*. London: Verso.

Arrington, R. L. and Addis, M. (eds.) (2001) *Wittgenstein and Philosophy of Religion*. London: Routledge.

Asad, Talal (1991) *Genealogies of Religion. Discipline and Reasons of Power in Christianity and Islam*. Baltimore and London: Johns Hopkins University Press.

(2003) *Formations of the Secular. Christianity, Islam, Modernity*. Stanford University Press.

Ashiwa, Y. and Wank, D. L. (2006) 'The Politics of a Reviving Buddhist Temple: State, Association and Religion in Southeast China', *The Journal of Asian Studies* **65**(2): 337–59.

Atkinson, Clarissa W., Buchanan, Constance H. and Miles, Margaret R. (eds.) (1985) *Immaculate and Powerful. The Female Sacred Image and Social Reality.* Boston: Beacon Press.

Atkinson, Michael (2004) 'Tattooing and Civilizing Processes: Body Modification as Self-Control', *Canadian Review of Sociology and Anthropology* 41(2), 125–46.

Auerbach, Erich (1968) *Mimesis. The Representation of Reality in Western Literature.* Princeton University Press.

Babington, Bruce F. and Evans, Peter (1993) *Biblical Epics. Sacred Narratives in the Hollywood Cinema.* Manchester University Press.

Badiou, Alain (2003) *Saint Paul. The Foundation of Universalism.* Stanford University Press.

(2005) *Being and Event.* New York: Continuum.

Baert, Patrick and Turner, Bryan S. (eds.) (2007) *Pragmatism and European Social Theory.* Oxford: Bardwell Press.

Bailey, Edward (1983) 'The Implicit Religion of Contemporary Society: An Orientation and a Plea for its Study', *Religion: Journal of Religion and Religions* 8: 69–83.

(1990) 'The Implicit Religion of Contemporary Society: Some Studies and Reflections', *Social Compass* 37(4): 483–97.

Barbalet, Jack (1997) 'The Jamesian Theory of Action', *Sociological Review* 45(1): 102–21.

(2000) 'Pragmatism and Symbolic Interaction' in Bryan S. Turner (ed.) *The Blackwell Companion to Social Theory*, 2nd edn. Oxford: Blackwell, pp. 199–217.

(2008) *Weber, Protestantism and Profits. 'The Protestant Ethic and the Spirit of Capitalism' in Context.* Cambridge University Press.

(2009) 'Pragmatism and Symbolic Interaction' in Bryan S. Turner (ed.) *The New Blackwell Companion to Social Theory.* Oxford: Wiley–Blackwell, pp. 199–217.

Barber, Benjamin R. (2001) *Jihad v. McWorld.* New York: Free Press.

Barry, Brian (2001) *Culture and Equality. An Egalitarian Critique of Multiculturalism.* Oxford: Blackwell.

Barth, Fredrik (1998) *Ethnic Groups and Boundaries.* Long Grove: Waveland Press.

Bastian, Jean-Pierre (2006) 'La nouvelle economie religieuse de l'Amerique latine', *Social Compass* 53(1): 65–80.

Bataille, George (1992) *Theory of Religion.* New York: Zone Books.

Baudrillard, Jean (1968) *The System of Objects. For a Critique of the Political.* London: Verso.

(1973) *The Mirror of Production.* St Louis: Telos Press.

(1981) *Simulations and Simulcra.* New York: Semiotexte.

(1995) *The Gulf War Did Not Take Place*. Bloomington: Indiana University Press.

Bauman, Zygmunt (1987) *Legislators and Interpreters. On Modernity, Post-modernity and Intellectuals*. Cambridge: Polity Press.

(2000) *Liquid Modernity*. Cambridge: Polity Press.

Beck, Ulrich and Gernsheim-Beck, Elizabeth (1995) *The Normal Chaos of Love*. Cambridge: Polity.

(2002) *Individualization. Institutionalized Individualism and its Social and Political Consequences*. London: Sage.

Beckford, James A. (2003) *Social Theory and Religion*. Cambridge University Press.

Beckford, James A. and Demerath III, N. J. (2007) *The Sage Handbook of the Sociology of Religion*. London: Sage.

Bell, Catherine (1990) 'The Ritual Body and the Dynamics of Ritual Power', *Journal of Ritual Studies* 4(2): 299–313.

Bell, Daniel (1974) *The Coming of Post-Industrial Society*. New York: Basic Books.

(1976) *The Cultural Contradictions of Capitalism*. New York: Basic Books.

(1980) *The Winding Passage. Essays and Sociological Journeys 1960–1980*. New York: Basic Books.

Bell, Daniel A. and Chaibong, Hahm (eds.) (2003) *Confucianism for the Modern World*. Cambridge University Press.

Bellah, Robert N. (1957) *Tokugawa Religion. The Values of Pre-Industrial Japan*. New York: Free Press.

(1963) 'Reflections on the Protestant Ethic Analogy in Asia', *Journal of Social Issues* 19(1): 52–61.

(1964) 'Religious Evolution', *American Sociological Review* 29: 358–74.

(1967) 'Civil Religion in America', *Daedalus* 96 (Winter): 1–27.

(1970) *Beyond Belief*. New York: Harper & Row.

(1975) *The Broken Covenant: American Civil Religion in Time of Trial*. New York: Seabury.

(2003) *Imagining Japan. The Japanese Tradition and its Modern Interpretation*. Berkeley: University of California Press.

Bellah, Robert N. and Tipton, S. M (eds.) (2006) *The Robert Bellah Reader*. Durham and London: Duke University Press.

Bender, Courtney (2003) *Heaven's Kitchen, Living Religion at God's Love We Deliver*. University of Chicago Press.

Bendix, R. (1964) *Nation-Building and Citizenship. Studies of Our Changing Social Order*. New York: Wiley.

Benhabib, Seyla (2002) *The Claims of Culture: Equality and Diversity in the Global Era*. Princeton University Press.

Benson, Sue (2000) 'Inscriptions of the Self: Reflections on Tattooing and Piercing in Contemporary Euro-America' in Jane Caplan (ed.) *Written on the Body: The Tattoo in European and American History*. London: Reaktion Books, pp. 234–54.

Benveniste, Émile (1973) *Indo-European Language and Society*. London: Faber & Faber.

Berger, Peter L. (1967) *The Sacred Canopy*. New York: Doubleday.

(1969) *A Rumor of Angels. Modern Society and the Rediscovery of the Supernatural*. New York: Doubleday.

(1980) 'From Secularity to World Religions', *The Christian Century* (January 18): 41–5.

Berger, Peter L. (ed.) (1999) *The Desecularization of the World*. Michigan: William B. Eerdmans Publishing Co.

Berger, Peter L. and Luckmann, Thomas (1967) *The Social Construction of Reality*. New York: Doubleday.

Berlie, Jean A. (2004) *Islam in China. Hui and Uyghurs between Modernization and Sinicization*. Bangkok: White Lotus Co.

Berlinerblau, Jacques (1999) 'Ideology, Pierre Bourdieu and the Hebrew Bible', *Semeia* 87: 193–214.

Betjeman, John (ed.) (1958) *Collins Guide to English Parish Churches*. London: Collins.

Beyer, Peter (1984) 'Introduction' in N. Luhmann, *Religious Dogmatics and the Evolution of Societies*. New York and Toronto: The Edwin Mellen Press, pp. v–xlvii.

(1994) *Religion and Globalization*. London: Sage.

Biale, David (1992) *Eros and the Jews. From Biblical Israel to Contemporary America*. New York: Basic Books.

Birnbaum, Norman and Lenzer, Gerhard (eds.) (1969) *Sociology and Religion. A Book of Readings*. Englewood Cliffs: Prentice Hall.

Blackburn, Robin (2002) *Banking on Death or Investing in Life. The History and Future of Pensions*. London: Verso.

Bock, D. (2004) *Breaking the da Vinci Code*. Nashville: Nelson Books.

Bohman, J. and Lutz-Bachmann, M. (eds.) (1997) *Perpetual Peace. Essays on Kant's Cosmopolitan Ideal*. Cambridge, MA: MIT Press.

Botman, S. (1999) *Engendering Citizenship in Egypt*. New York: Columbia University Press.

Bourdieu, Pierre (1971) 'Une interpretation de la theorie de la religion selon Max Weber', *Archives europeenes de sociologie* XII: 3–21.

(1977) *Outline of a Theory of Practice*. Cambridge University Press.

Bourdieu, Pierre (with Monique de Saint Martin) (1982) 'La sainte famille: L'episcopat francais dans le champ du pouvoir', *Actes de la recherche en sciences socials*, **44/45**: 2–53.

Bourdieu, Pierre (1987a) 'Legitimation and Structured Interests in Weber's Sociology of Religion' in Scott Lash and Sam Whimster (eds.) *Max Weber, Rationality and Modernity*. London: Allen & Unwin, pp. 119–36.

(1987b) 'Sociologues de la croyance et croyance de sociologues', *Archives science sociales des religions*, **63**(1): 155–161.

(1990) *The Logic of Practice*. Cambridge: Polity.

Bourricaud, Francis (1981) *The Sociology of Talcott Parsons*. University of Chicago Press.

Bowen, J. R. (2004) 'Beyond Migration: Islam as a Transnational Public Space', *Journal of Ethnic and Migration Studies* **30**(5): 879–94.

(2003) *Islam, Law and Equality in Indonesia*. Cambridge University Press.

Bowen, Roger (2006) 'Robert Bellah on Religion, Morality and the Politics of Resentment', *Academe* **92**(1): 33–7.

Braun, Willi and McCutcheon, Russel T. (eds.) (2000) *Guide to the Study of Religion*. London and New York: Cassell.

Brenner, Susan (1996) 'Reconstructing the Self and Society: Javanese Women and "the Veil"', *American Ethnologist* **23**(4): 673–97.

Brentano, Clemens ([1833] 1970) *The Dolorous Passion of Our Lord Jesus Christ according to the Meditations of Anne Catherine Emmerich*. Rockford, IL: Tan Books.

Brookhiser, Richard (1996) *Rediscovering George Washington. Founding Father*. New York: Simon & Schuster.

Brooks, Ann (2006) *Gendered Work in Asian Cities. The New Economy and Changing Labour Markets*. Farnham: Ashgate.

Brown, Dan (2003) *The da Vinci Code*. New York: Doubleday.

(2009) *The Lost Symbol*. New York: Doubleday.

Brown, J. R. (ed.) (1955) *The Merchant of Venice*. London: Methuen.

Bruce, Steve (1990) *Pray TV. Televangelism in America*. London and New York: Routledge.

(1999) *Choice and Religion. A Critique of Rational Choice Theory*. Oxford University Press.

(2001) 'The Curious Case of the Unnecessary Recantation: Berger and Secularization' in Linda Woodhead, Paul Heelas and David Martin (eds.) *Peter Berger and the Study of Religion*. London: Routledge, pp. 87–100.

(2003) *Politics & Religion*. Cambridge: Polity Press.

Brudholm, Thomas and Cushman, Thomas (eds.) (2009) *The Religious in Responses to Mass Atrocity. Interdisciplinary Perspectives*. Cambridge University Press.

Bryant, Joseph (2000) 'Cost-Benefit Accounting and the Piety Business. Is *Homo Religiosus* at Bottom *Homo Economicus?*', *Method and Theory in the Study of Religion* **12**: 520–48.

Bullard, A. (2000) 'Paris 1871/New Caldonia 1878: Human Rights and the Managerial State' in J. N. Wasserstrom, L. Hunt and M. B. Young (eds.) *Human Rights and Revolutions*. Lanham: Rowman & Littlefield, pp. 79–98.

Bunt, Gary R. (2009)' Religion and the Internet' in Peter B. Clarke (ed.) *The Oxford Handbook of the Sociology of Religion*. Oxford: Oxford University Press, pp. 705–22.

Burke, E. and Lapidus, I. M. (eds.) (1988) *Islam, Politics and Social Movements*. London: I. B. Tauris.

Burns, Peter (2004) *The Leiden Legacy. Concepts of Law in Indonesia*. Leiden: KITLV Press.

Casanova, José (1994) *Public Religions in the Modern World*. University of Chicago Press.

Case, W. (2002) *Politics in Southeast Asia: Democracy or Less*. London: RoutledgeCurzon.

Castells, Manuel (1996) *The Rise of Network Society*. Oxford: Blackwell.

Chatelain, Daniele and Slusser, George (2005) 'Balzacs's Centenarian and French Science Fiction' in *The Centarian or the Two Beringhelds*. Middletown: Wesleyan University Press, pp. xxi–lvi.

Chesnut, R. Andrew (2003) *Competitive Spirits. Latin America's New Religious Economy*. Oxford University Press.

Cimino, R. and Lattin, D. (1998) *Shopping for Faith: American Religion in the New Millennium*. San Francisco: Jossey-Bass.

Clark, K. and Parsons, T. (eds.) (1966) *The Negro American*. Boston: Houghton Mifflin.

Clarke, John (1976) 'The Skinheads and the Magical Recovery of Community' in Stuart Hall and Tony Jefferson (eds.) *Resistance through Rituals: Youth Subcultures in Post-War Britain*. London: Harper Collins, pp. 99–102.

Clarke, Peter B. (2006) *New Religions in Global Perspective*. London: Routledge.

Clarke, Peter B. (ed.) (2009) *The Oxford Handbook of the Sociology of Religion*. Oxford University Press.

Coakley, S. (ed.) (1997) *Religion and the Body*. Cambridge University Press.

Cohen, Lizabeth (2003) *A Consumers' Republic. The Politics of Mass Consumption in Postwar America*. New York: Alfred A. Knopf.

Coleman, Simon (2000) *The Globalization of Charismatic Christianity. Spreading the Gospel of Prosperity*. Cambridge University Press.

Comaroff, J. and Comaroff, J. L. (1999) 'Occult Economies and the Violence of Abstraction: Notes from the South African Postcolony', *American Ethnologist* **26**(3): 279–301.

(2000) 'Millennial Capitalism: First Thoughts on a Second Coming', *Public Culture* **12**(2): 291–343.

Connolly, William E. (1995) *The Ethos of Pluralization*. Minneapolis: University of Minnesota Press.

Cooper, R. L. (1993) *Heidegger and Whitehead. A Phenomenological Examination into the Intelligibility of Experience*. Athens: Ohio University Press.

Corrigan, Philip and Sayer, Derek (1985) *The Great Arch: English State Formation as Cultural Revolution*. Oxford: Blackwell.

Cox, Harvey (1965) *The Secular City. Secularization and Urbanization in Theological Perspective*. London: SCM Press.

(2003) 'Christianity' in Mark Juergensmeyer (ed.) *Global Religions. An Introduction*. Oxford University Press.

Croce, P. J. (1995) *Science and Religion in the Era of William James. Eclipse of Certainty 1820–1880*. Chapel Hill and London: University of North Carolina Press.

Crosby, D. A. (1983) 'Religion and Solitariness' in L. S. Ford and G. L. Kline (eds.) *Explorations in Whitehead's Philosophy*. New York: Fordham University Press, pp. 149–69.

Dackson, Wendy (1999) 'Richard Hooker and American Religious Liberty', *Journal of Church and State* **41**(1): 117–34.

Dahrendorf, Ralf (1959) *Class and Class Conflict in Industrial Society*. London: Routledge and Kegan Paul.

(1967) *Society and Democracy in Germany*. New York: Doubleday.

(1979) *Life Chances. Approaches to Social and Political Theory*. University of Chicago Press.

Dallmyer, F. (1999) 'Nationalism East and West', paper presented at the IPSA Conference, Malaga, Spain.

Damrosch, Leo (2005) *Jean-Jacques Rousseau. Restless Genius*. Boston: Houghton Mifflin.

Daniel, Wallace L. and Holladay, Meredith (2008) 'Church, State and the Presidential Campaign of 2008', *Journal of Church and State* **50** (Winter): 5–22.

Davie, Grace (1994) *Religion in Britain since 1945. Believing Without Belonging*. Oxford: Blackwell.

(2006) 'Religion in Europe in the 21st century: The Factors to Take into Account' *Archives européennes de sociologie*, **XLVII**(2), 271–96.

(2010) 'Resacralization' in Bryan S. Turner (ed.) *The New Blackwell Companion to the Sociology of Religion*. Oxford: Wiley-Blackwell, pp. 160–78.

Davis, Kingsley (1940) *Human Society*. London: Macmillan.

Davis, M. (1992) *Beyond Blade Runner. Urban Control – the Ecology of Fear*. Westfield: Open Magazine Pamphlet Series.

Dawson, Lorne L. (2003) *Cults and New Religious Movements. A Reader.* New York: Oxford University Press.

(2009) 'Church-sect-cult. Constructing Typologies of Religious Groups' in Peter B. Clarke (ed.) *The Oxford Handbook of the Sociology of Religion.* Oxford University Press, pp. 525–44.

De Barry, W. T. (1998) *Asian Values and Human Rights. A Confucian Communitarian Perspective.* Cambridge, MA: Harvard University Press.

de Roover, R. (1967) *San Bernardino of Siena and Sant'Antonio of Florence. The Two Great Economic Thinkers of the Middle Ages.* Boston: Harvard Graduate School of Business Administration.

Debord, Guy (1967) *The Society of the Spectacle.* New York: Zone Books.

Delanty, Gerard (2009) *The Cosmopolitan Imagination. The Renewal of Critical Social Theory.* Cambridge University Press.

Demerath III, N. J. (2007) 'Secularization and Sacralization Deconstructed and Reconstructed' in James A. Beckford and N. J. Demerath III (eds.) *The Sage Handbook of the Sociology of Religion.* London: Sage, pp. 57–80.

Derrida, Jacques (1998) 'Faith and Knowledge' in Jacques Derrida and Gianni Vattimo (eds.) *Religion.* Cambridge: Polity.

(2001) *On Cosmopolitanism and Forgiveness.* London: Routledge.

Derrida, Jacques and Vattimo, Gianni (eds.) (1998) *Religion.* Cambridge: Polity.

Dewey, John (1963) *Freedom and Culture.* New York: Capricorn.

(1981) *The Later Works 1925–1953,* 17 vols. Carbondale: Southern Illinois University Press.

Dickstein, M. (1998) *The Revival of Pragmatism. New Essays on Social Thought. Law and Culture.* Durham: Duke University Press.

Dieterich, Albrecht (1905) *Mutter Erde. Ein Versuch uber Volksreligion.*

Dillon, Michele (2001) 'Pierre Bourdieu, Religion and Cultural Production', *Cultural Studies. Critical Methodologies,* 1, 411–29.

Douglas, Mary (1963) *The Lele of the Kasai.* London: Oxford University Press.

(1966) *Purity and Danger: An Analysis of Concepts of Pollution and Taboo.* New York: Praeger.

(1973) *Natural Symbols: Explorations in Cosmology,* 2nd edn. New York: Random House.

(1980) *Edward Evans-Pritchard.* London: Fontana.

Douglas, Mary and Isherwood, Baron (1978) *The World of Goods. Towards an Anthropology of Consumption.* London: Allen Lane.

Drompp, Michael R. (2005) *Tang China and the Collapse of the Uighar Empire.* Leiden: Brill.

Dror, Olga (2007) *Cult, Culture and Authority. Princess Lieu Hanh in Vietnamese History.* Honolulu: University of Hawai'i Press.

Dunn, John (ed.) (1995) *Contemporary Crisis of the Nation State*. Oxford: Blackwell.

Durkheim, Émile ([1893] 1960) *The Division of Labor in Society*. Glencoe: Free Press.

([1895] 1958) *The Rules of Sociological Method*. Glencoe: Free Press.

([1897] 1951) *Suicide. A Study in Sociology*. Glencoe: Free Press.

([1912] 2001) *The Elementary Forms of Religious Life*. Oxford University Press.

([1928] 1958) *Socialism and Saint Simon*. Yellow Springs: Antioch Press.

(1992) *Professional Ethics and Civic Morals*. London: Routledge.

Durkheim, Émile and Mauss, Marcel ([1903] 1997) *Primitive Classification*. University of Chicago Press.

Eastwood, J. (2007) 'Bourdieu, Flaubert and the Sociology of Literature', *Sociological Theory* 25(2): 149–69.

Eden, Robert (1983) *Political Leadership & Nihilism. A Study of Weber & Nietzsche*. Tampa: University of South Florida Press.

Edmunds, June and Turner, Bryan S. (eds.) (2002) *Generational Consciousness. Narrative and Politics*. Lanham: Rowman and Littlefield.

Eisenstadt, Shmuel N. (1982) 'The Axial Age: The Emergence of Transcendental Visions and the Rise of Clerics', *European Journal of Sociology* 23(2): 294–314.

(1985) 'This-Worldly Transcendentalism and the Structuring of the World: Weber's *Religion of China* and the Format of Chinese History and Civilization', *Journal of Developing Societies* 1–2: 168–86.

(2000) 'The Reconstruction of Religious Arenas in the Framework of "Multiple Modernities"', *Millennium. Journal of International Studies* 29(3): 591–611.

(2002) *Multiple Modernities*. New York: Transaction Books.

(2004) *Comparative Civilizations and Multiple Modernities. A Collection of Essays*. Leiden: E. J. Brill.

Eliade, Mircea (1961) *The Sacred and Profane. The Nature of Religion*. New York: Harper.

Elias, Norbert (2000) *The Civilizing Process*, rev. edn. Oxford: Blackwell.

Enayat, H. (1982) *Modern Islamic Political Thought*. London: Palgrave Macmillan.

Engler, Steven (2003) 'Modern Times: Religion, Consecration and the State in Bourdieu', *Cultural Studies* 17(3/4): 445–67.

Fenn, Richard K. (ed.) (2001) *The Blackwell Companion to Sociology of Religion*. Oxford: Blackwell.

Ferguson, Nial (2004) *Colossus. The Rise and Fall of the American Empire*. London: Allen Lane.

Feuerbach, Ludwig (1957) *The Essence of Christianity*. New York: Harper.

Finke, Richard and Stark, Rodney (1992) *The Churching of America 1776– 1990*. New Brunswick: Rutgers University Press.

Fischer, A. M. (2005) *State Growth and Social Exclusion in Tibet. Challenges of Recent Economic Growth*. Copenhagen: IAS Press.

Fisher, Gareth (2008) 'The Spiritual Land Rush: Merit and Morality in New Chinese Buddhist Temple Construction', *Journal of Asian Studies* **67** (1): 143–70.

Flanagan, Kieran (2008) 'Sociology into Theology. The Unacceptable Leap', *Theory, Culture & Society* **25**(7–8): 236–61.

Foucault, Michel (1974) *The Order of Things*. London: Tavistock.

(1991) 'Governmentality' in G. Burchell, C. Gordon and P. Miller (eds.) *The Foucault Effect: Studies in Governmentality*. Hemel Hempstead: Wheatsheaf, pp. 87–104.

(1997) 'Technologies of the Self' in *Ethics, Subjectivity and Truth*. London: Allen Lane, pp. 223–52.

(2003) *Abnormal*. New York: Picador.

(2005) *The Hermeneutics of the Self*. New York: Picador.

Freeman, Christopher (1986) *Regressive Taxation and the Welfare State*. Cambridge University Press.

Frykholm, Amy Johnson (2004) *Rapture Culture. Left Behind in Evangelical America*. New York: Oxford University Press.

Fukuyama, Francis (2002) *Our Posthuman Future. Consequences of the Biotechnological Revolution*. New York: Farrar, Straus and Giroux.

Fuller, L. (1969) *The Meaning of Law*. New Haven: Yale University Press.

Fuller, R. C. (2001) *Spiritual But Not Religious: Understanding Unchurched Americans*. New York: Oxford University Press.

Furseth, Inger (2009) 'Religion in the Works of Habermas, Bourdieu and Foucault' in Peter B. Clarke (ed.) *The Oxford Handbook of the Sociology of Religion*. Oxford University Press, pp. 89–115.

Garrad, John and Garrad, Carol (2009) *Russian Orthodoxy Resurgent. Faith and Power in the New Russia*. Princeton University Press.

Geary, Patrick (1986) 'Sacred Commodities: The Circulation of Medieval Relics' in Arjun Appadurai (ed.) *The Social Life of Things. Commodities in Cultural Perspective*. Cambridge University Press, pp. 169–91.

Geertz, Clifford (1983) *Local Knowledge. Further Essays in Interpretive Anthropology*. New York: Basic Books.

Gehlen, Arnold (1988) *Man: His Nature and Place in the World*. New York: Columbia University Press.

Gellner, Ernest (1992) *Postmodernism, Reason and Religion*. London: Routledge.

George, Cherian (1993) 'Malay youths joining gangs worrying, says Maidin', *Straits Times*, 4 April.

Gerhardt, Utah (ed.) (1993) *Talcott Parsons on National Socialism*. New York: Aldine de Gruyter.

Gerth, Hans H, and Mills, C. Wright (eds.) (2009) *From Max Weber. Essays in Sociology*. London: Routledge.

Gibson, William (1984) *Neuromancer*. London: Gollanz.

Giddens, Anthony (1992) *The Transformation of Intimacy. Sexuality, Love and Society in the late Modern Age*. Cambridge: Polity Press.

Gill, Anthony (2008) *The Political Origins of Religious Liberty*. Cambridge University Press.

Gilligan, E. (2005) *Defending Human Rights in Russia. Sergei Kovalyov, Dissident and Human Rights Commissioner 1969–2003*. London: Routledge Curzon.

Gilsenan, Michael (1990) *Recognizing Islam. Religion and Society in the Modern Middle East*. London: I. B.Tauris.

Glazer, Nathan (1997) *We are All Multicultural Now*. Cambridge, MA: Harvard University Press.

Glock, Charles Y. and Stark, Rodney (1965) *Religion and Society in Tension*. University of Chicago Press.

Gneuss, Christian and Kocka, Jurgen (1988) *Max Weber. Ein Symposium*. Munchen: Deutscher Taschenbuch.

Goldman, Harvey (1992) *Politics, Death and the Devil. Self and Power in Max Weber and Thomas Mann*. Berkeley: University of California Press.

Goldman, Merle (2005) *From Comrade to Citizen. The Struggle for Political Rights in China*. Cambridge, MA: Harvard University Press.

Goldman, Merle and Perry, Elizabeth J. (eds.) (2002) *Changing Meanings of Citizenship in Modern China*. Cambridge, MA: Harvard University Press.

Goldmann, Lucien ([1956] 1964) *The Hidden God. A Study of Tragic Vision in the Pensées of Pascal and Tragedies of Racine*. London: Routledge and Kegan Paul.

Göle, Nilufur (1996) *The Forbidden Modern. Civilization and Veiling*. Ann Arbor: University of Michigan Press.

Goody, Jack (2003) 'The "Civilizing Process" in Ghana', *European Journal of Sociology* **44**(1): 61–76.

Goossaert, Vincent (2005) 'The Concept of Religion in China and the West', *Diogenes* **52**(1): 13–20.

Goudsblom, Johanes (1992) *Fire and Civilization*. London: Allen Lane.

Gouldner, Alvin W. (1970) *The Coming Crisis of Western Sociology*. New York: Basic Books.

Govenar, Alan (2000) 'The Changing Image of Tattooing in American Culture, 1846–1966' in Jane Caplan (ed.) *Written on the Body:*

The Tattoo in European and American History. London: Reaktion Books, pp. 234–54.

Greengrass, M. (2003) 'The French Pastorate: Confessional Identity and Confessionalization in the Huguenot Minority, 1559–1685' in C. Scott Dixon and L. Schorn-Schutte (eds.) *The Protestant Clergy of Early Modern Europe*. Houndmills: Palgrave, pp. 176–95.

Gurko, Leo (1947) *The Angry Decade*. New York: Dodd Mead.

Habermas, Jürgen (1984) *The Theory of Communicative Action*. Boston: Beacon Press.

(2001) *The Postnational Constellation*. Cambridge, MA: MIT Press.

(2002) *Religion and Rationality. Essays on Reason, God and Modernity*. Cambridge, MA: MIT Press.

(2006) 'Religion in the Public Sphere', *European Journal of Philosophy* **14**(1): 1–25.

(2008) *Between Naturalism and Religion*. Cambridge: Polity Press.

Habermas, Jürgen and Mendieta, E. (2002) *Religion and Rationality. Essays on Reason, God, and Modernity*. Cambridge, MA: MIT Press.

Habermas, Jürgen and Ratzinger, Joseph (2006) *The Dialectics of Secularization. On Reason and Religion*. San Francisco: Ignatius.

Hadden, Jeffrey K. and Cowan, Douglas (eds.) (2000) *Religion Online. Finding Faith on the Internet. Research Prospects and Promises*. New York: JAI.

Haeri, Shahla (1989) *Law of Desire. Temporary Marriage in Shi'i Iran*. New York: Syracuse University Press.

(1993) 'Obedience Versus Autonomy: Women and Fundamentalism in Iran and Pakistan' in M. E. Marty and R. S. Appleby (eds.) *Fundamentalisms and Society*. University of Chicago Press, pp. 181–213.

Halliday, Fred (2002) *Two Hours That Shook the World: September 11, 2001*. London: Saqi Books.

(2003) *Islam and the Myth of Confrontation*. London: J. B. Taurus.

Hamberg, Eva M. (2009) 'Unchurched Spirituality' in Peter B. Clarke (ed.) *The Oxford Companion to the Sociology of Religion*. Oxford University Press, pp. 742–57.

Hamilton, Malcolm (2009) 'Rational Choice Theory. A Critique' in Peter B. Clarke (ed.) *The Oxford Companion to the Sociology of Religion*. Oxford University Press, pp. 116–33.

Haraway, Donna ([1985] 1991) 'A Cyborg Manifesto–Science, Technology and Socialism' *Socialist Review* [*reprinted in Simians, Cyborgs and Women. The Reinvention of Nature*]. New York: Routledge, pp. 149–81.

Hardin, R. (2001) 'Conceptions and Explanations of Trust' in K. S. Cook (ed.) *Trust in Society*. New York: Russell Sage Foundation, pp. 3–39.

Hardy, Henry (ed.) (2002) *Freedom and its Betrayal. Six Enemies of Human Liberty*. Princeton University Press.

Hart, William D. (2000) *Edward Said and the Religious Effects of Culture.* Cambridge University Press.

Hartmann, D. and Gerteis, J. (2005) 'Dealing with Diversity: Mapping Multiculturalism in Sociological Terms', *Sociological Theory* 23(2): 218–40.

Harvey, David (2000) *The Spaces of Hope.* Berkeley: University of California Press.

(2006) *Spaces of Global Development.* London: Verso.

Hassan, Riaz (2002) *Faithlines. Muslim Conceptions of Islam and Society.* Oxford University Press.

(2008) *Inside Muslim Minds.* Melbourne University Press.

Hawthorne, Sian (2009) 'Religion and Gender' in Peter B. Clarke (ed.) *The Oxford Handbook of the Sociology of Religion.* Oxford University Press, pp. 134–51.

Hebdige, Dick (1981) *Subculture: The Meaning of Style.* London and New York: Routledge.

Heelas, Paul (1996) *The New Age Movement.* Cambridge: Blackwell.

(2009) 'Spiritualities of Life' in Peter Clarke (ed.) *The Oxford Handbook of the Sociology of Religion.* Oxford University Press, pp. 758–82.

Heidegger, Martin ([1927] 1962) *Being and Time.* New York: Harper and Row.

(1977) *The Question Concerning Technology and Other Essays.* New York: Harper.

Held, D., McGrew, A., Goldblatt, D. and Perraton, J. (1999) *Global Transformations.* Cambridge: Polity Press.

Henkin, L. (1998) 'The Universal Declaration and the US Constitution', *Political Science* 31(3): 512–15.

Hennis, Wilhelm (1988) *Max Weber. Essays in Reconstruction.* London: Allen & Unwin.

Herberg, Will (1955) *Protestant–Catholic–Jew.* New York: Doubleday.

Hertz, Robert (1960) *Death and the Right Hand.* New York: Free Press.

Hervieu-Léger, Danièle (2000) *Religion as a Chain of Memory.* Cambridge: Polity.

Hobbes, Thomas ([1651] 1962) *Leviathan.* Glasgow: Fontana.

Hodgson, Marshall G. S. (1960) 'A Comparison of Islam and Christianity as Frameworks for Religious Life', *Diogenes* 32: 49–74.

(1974) *The Venture of Islam. Conscience and History in World Civilization*, 3 vols. University of Chicago Press.

(1993) *Rethinking World History. Essays on Europe, Islam, and World History.* Cambridge University Press.

Hoffman, Stanley (1993) 'Judith Shklar as Political Thinker', *Political Theory*, 21(2): 172–80.

Holton, Robert J. (2009) *Cosmopolitans. New Thinking and New Directions*. Basingstoke: Palgrave Macmillan.

Holton, Robert J. and Turner, Bryan S. (1986) *Talcott Parsons on Economy and Society*. London: Routledge.

Howell, Brian M. (2008) *Christianity in the Local Context. Southern Baptists in the Philippines*. New York: Palgrave Macmillan.

Howell, Julia Day (2001) 'Sufism and the Indonesian Islamic Revival', *The Journal of Asian Studies* 60(3): 701–29.

Huff, Toby and Schluchter, Wolfgang (eds.) (1999) *Max Weber & Islam*. New Brunswick: Transaction.

Hulsether, M. D. (2000) 'Like a Sermon: Popular Religion in Madonna Videos' in B. D. Forbes and J. H. Mahan (eds.) *Religion and Popular Culture*. Berkeley: University of California Press, pp. 77–100.

Hunt, Stephen (2005) *Religion and Everyday Life*. London: Routledge.

Huntington, Samuel P. (1993) 'The Clash of Civilizations', *Foreign Affairs* 72(3): 22–48.

 (1997) *The Clash of Civilizations. Remaking of World Order*. New York: Touchstone.

Iannaccone, L. R. (1994) 'Why Strict Churches are Strong', *American Journal of Sociology* 99(5): 1180–211.

Ikels, Charlotte (ed.) (2004) *Filial Piety. Practices and Discourse in Contemporary East Asia*. Stanford University Press.

Illouz, Eva (1997) *Consuming the Romantic Utopia. Love and the Cultural Contradictions of Capitalism*. Berkeley: University of California Press.

 (2003) *Oprah Winfrey and the Glamour of Misery. An Essay on Popular Culture*. New York: Columbia University Press.

 (2007) *Cold Intimacies. The Making of Emotional Capitalism*. Cambridge: Polity.

Ingham, Geoffrey (2004) *The Nature of Money*. Cambridge: Polity Press.

Iqtidar, Humeira (2010) 'Muslim Cosmopolitanism: Contemporary Practices and Social Theory' in Bryan S. Turner (ed.) *The Routledge International Handbook of Globalization Studies*. London: Routledge, pp. 622–34.

Isin, Engin and Turner, Bryan S. (eds.) (2002) *Handbook of Citizenship Studies*. London: Sage.

James, William ([1902] 1963) *The Varieties of Religious Experience. A Study of Human Nature*. New York: University Books.

Jenkins, Tim (2006) 'Bourdieu's Bearmais Ethnography', *Theory, Culture & Society* 23(6): 45–72.

John, Arul (2007) 'Malay Youths Want to Erase Gang Past', New Paper, 4 June.

Joppke, Christiaan (2004) 'The Retreat from Multiculturalism in the Liberal State: Theory and Policy', *British Journal of Sociology* 55(2): 237–57.

(2008) 'Transformation of Citizenship: Realizing the Potential' in Engin F. Isin, Peter Nyers and Bryan S. Turner (eds.) *Citizenship Between Past and Future*. London: Routledge, pp. 36–47.

(2009) *Veil. Mirror of Identity*. Cambridge: Polity.

Juergensmeyer, Mark (2000) *Terror on the Mind of God. The Global Rise of Religious Violence*. Berkeley: University of California Press.

Juergensmeyer, Mark (ed.) (2006) *The Oxford Handbook of Global Religions*. New York: Oxford University Press.

Juergensmeyer, Mark (2008) *Global Rebellion. Religious Challenges to the Secular State*. Berkeley: University of California Press.

Kamali, M. (1998) *Revolutionary Islam. Civil Society and State in the Modernization Process*. Aldershot: Ashgate.

(2001) 'Civil Society and Islam: A Sociological Perspective', *European Journal of Social Theory* 4(2): 131–52.

Kamaludeen, Mohamed Nasir and Aljunied, Syed Muhd Khairudin (2009) *Muslims as Minorities: History and Social Realities of Muslims in Singapore*. Bangi: National University of Malaysia Press.

Kamaludeen, Mohamed Nasir, Pereira, Alexius A. and Turner, Bryan S. (2009) *Muslims in Singapore. Piety, Politics and Policies*. London: Routledge.

Kant, Immanuel ([1763] 1998) *Religion Within the Boundaries of Mere Reason*. Cambridge University Press.

Kapstein, Matthew K. (2005) 'The Buddhist Refusal of Theism', *Diogenes* 52(1): 13–20.

Kelley, D. (1977) *Why Conservative Churches Are Growing*. New York: Harper and Row.

Kennedy, Paul (1990) *The Rise and Fall of the Great Powers*. London: Unwin Hyman.

Kepel, Giles (2002) *Jihad. The Trail of Political Islam*. London: I. B.Taurus.

(2004a) *The War for Muslim Minds*. Cambridge, MA: Belknap Press.

(2004b) *The Revenge of God. The Resurgence of Islam, Christianity and Judaism in the Modern World*. Cambridge: Polity Press.

King, Richard (1999) *Orientalism and Religion. Post-Colonial Theory, India and the Mystic East*. New York: Routledge.

Kitiarsa, Pattana (2008a) 'Buddha Phanit: Thailand's Prosperity Religion and its Commodifying Tactics' in Pattana Kitiarsa (ed.) *Religious Commodifications in Asia. Marketing Gods*. London: Routledge, pp. 120–43.

Kitiarsa, Pattana (ed.) (2008b) *Religious Commodifications in Asia. Marketing Gods*. London and New York: Routledge.

Kitzinger, Ernst and Senior, Elizabeth (1940) *Portraits of Christ*. London: Penguin.

Knight, J. (2001) 'Social Norms and the Rule of Law: Fostering Trust in a Socially Diverse Society' in K. S. Cook (ed.) *Trust in Society*. New York: Russell Sage Foundation, pp. 354–73.

Kohn, H. (1944) *The Idea of Nationalism*. New York: Macmillan.

Kolakowski, L. (2001) *Religion If There is No God*. South Bend: St Augustine Press.

Kolas, I. and Thowsen, M. P. (2005) *On the Margins of Tibet. Cultural Survival on the Sino-Tibetan Frontier*. Seattle: University of Washington Press.

Krugman, Paul ([1994] 1997) *The Age of Diminished Expectations. US Economic Policy in the 1990s*, 3rd edn. Cambridge, MA: MIT Press.

Kukathas, C. (1992) 'Are There Any Cultural Rights?', *Political Theory* **29**: 105–39.

Kwon, Heonik (2009) *Ghosts of War in Vietnam*. Cambridge University Press.

Kymlicka, Will (1995) *Multicultural Citizenship. A Liberal Theory of Minority Rights*. Oxford University Press.

(2009) 'The Multicultural Welfare State?' in Peter Hall and Michele Lamont (eds.) *Successful Societies. How Institutions and Culture Affect Health*. Cambridge University Press, pp. 226–53.

Lambeck, M. (ed.) 2002 *A Reader in the Anthropology of Religion*. Malden: Blackwell.

Lane, Jeremy F. (2000) *Pierre Bourdieu. A Critical Introduction*. London: Pluto Press.

Lanternari, V. (1965) *The Religions of the Oppressed. A Study of Modern Messianic Cults*. New York.

Laski, H. J. (1949) *The American Democracy. A Commentary and an Interpretation*. London: George Allen and Unwin.

Laurence, Jonathan and Vaisse, Justin (2006) *Integrating Islam*. Washington, DC: Brookings Institution Press.

Lazreg, Marnia (2009) *Questioning the Veil. Open Letters to Muslim Women*. Princeton University Press.

Le Roux, P. and Sellato, B. (eds.) (2006) *Les Messengers divins. Aspects esthetiques et symboliques des oisseaux en Asie et Sud-Est*. Paris: IRASEC.

Lechner, Frank J. (1985) 'Fundamentalism and Sociocultural Revitalization in America: A Sociological Interpretation', *Sociological Analysis* **46**(3), 243–59.

(1993) 'Global Fundamentalism' in W. S. Swatos (ed.) *A Future for Religion*. London: Sage, pp. 27–32.

(2007) 'Rational Choice and Religious Economics' in James A. Beckford and N. J. Demerath III (eds.) *The Sage Handbook of the Sociology of Religion*. London: Sage pp. 81–97.

Lechner, Frank and Boli, John (eds.) (2004) *The Globalization Reader.* Oxford: Blackwell.

Ledgerwood, Judy and Un, Kheang (2003) 'Global Concepts and Local Meanings. Human Rights and Budhhism in Cambodia', *Journal of Human Rights* 2(4): 531–49.

Lehmann, David (1996) *Struggle for the Spirit. Religious Transformation and Popular Culture in Brazil and Latin America.* Cambridge: Polity Press.

(2002) 'Religion and Globalization' in Linda Woodhead, Paul Fletcher, Hiroko Kawanami and David Smith (eds.) *Religions in the Modern World.* London: Routledge, pp. 299–315.

Lehmann, Hartmut and Ouedraogo, Jean Martin (eds.) (2003) *Max Webers Religionssoziologie in interkultureller Perspektive.* Gottingen: Vandenhoeck & Ruprecht.

Leibniz, Gottfried Wilhelm ([1686] 1992) *Discourse on Metaphysics and the Monadology.* New York: Prometheus Books.

Leshkowich, Ann Marie (2008) 'Wandering Ghosts of Late Socialism: Conflict, Metaphor, and Memory in a Southern Vietnamese Marketplace', *Journal of Asian Studies* 67(1): 5–42.

Levy, J. (2000) *The Multiculturalism of Fear.* Oxford University Press.

Lewis, Bernard (1993) *Islam and the West.* Oxford University Press.

Ling, Trevor O. (1966) *Buddha, Marx and God.* London: Macmillan.

(1968) *A History of Religion East and West. An Introduction and Interpretation.* London: Macmillan.

(1973) *The Buddha. Buddhist Civilization in India and Ceylon.* New York: Charles Scribner's Sons.

(1980) *Karl Marx and Religion in Europe and India.* London: Macmillan.

Lipset, Seymour Martin (1963) *The First New Nation. The United States in Comparative and Historical Perspective.* New York: W. W. Norton.

Littell, Jonathan (2009) 'Chechnya, Year III', *London Review of Books* 31 (22): 3–10.

Lockwood, David (1992) *Solidarity and Schism: 'The Problem of Order' in Durkheimian and Marxist Sociology.* Oxford: Clarendon Press.

Longmore, Paul K. (1989) *The Invention of George Washington.* Berkeley: University of California Press.

Lopez, Donald S. (2002) *Modern Buddhism. Readings for the Unenlightened.* London: Penguin.

Löwith, Karl ([1932] 1993) *Max Weber and Karl Marx.* London: Routledge.

Loyal, Steven (2009) 'The French in Algeria, Algerians in France: Bourdieu, Colonialism and Migration', *Sociological Review* 57(3): 406–27.

Luckmann, Thomas (1967) *The Invisible Religion. The Problem of Religion in Modern Society.* London: Macmillan.

(1988) 'Religion and Modern Consciousness', *Zen Buddhism Today* 6: 11–22.

(1990) 'Shrinking Transcendence, Expanding Religion', *Sociological Analysis* 50(2): 127–38.

Luhmann, Niklas (1984) *Religious Dogmatics and the Evolution of Societies*. New York and Toronto: The Edwin Mellen Press.

(1986) *Love as Passion*. Cambridge: Polity Press.

(1995) *Social Systems*. Stanford University Press.

Lukes, Steven (1973) *Émile Durkheim. His Life and Work. A Historical and Critical Study*. London: Allen Lane.

(1991) 'The Rationality of Norms', *Archives Européennes de Sociologie* 32: 142–9.

Lyotard, Jean-Francois ([1979] 1984) *The Postmodern Condition. A Report on Knowledge*. University of Manchester Press.

MacCullogh, Darmaid (2003) *The Reformation*. New York: Viking.

Macintosh, H. R. (1937) *Types of Modern Theology. Schleiermacher to Barth*. London: James Nisbet.

MacIntyre, Alasdair (1953) *Marxism – An Interpretation*. London: SCM Press.

(1967) *Secularization and Moral Change*. London: Oxford University Press.

(1984) *After Virtue. A Study in Moral Theory*. London: Duckworth.

(1995) *Marxism and Christianity*. London: SCM Press.

(1998) *A Short History of Ethics. A History of Moral Philosophy from the Homeric Age to the Twentieth Century*. London: Routledge & Kegan Paul.

MacIntyre, Alasdair and Ricoeur, Paul (1969) *The Religious Significance of Atheism*. New York: Columbia University Press.

Macken, J. (1990) *The Autonomy Theme in the Church Dogmatics*. Cambridge University Press.

Maffesoli, Michael (1996) *The Time of the Tribes: The Decline of Individualism in Mass Society*, trans. Don Smith. Thousand Oaks and London: Sage.

Mahmood, Saba (2005) *The Politics of Piety. The Islamic Revival and the Feminist Subject*. Princeton University Press.

Maimonides, Moses (1956) *The Guide to the Perplexed*. New York: Dover.

Majid, Anouar (2000) *Unveiling Traditions*. Durham: Duke University Press.

Manby, Bronwen (2009) *Struggles for Citizenship in Africa*. London: Zed Books.

Mandaville, Peter (2001) *Transnational Muslim Politics. Reimagining the Umma*. London and New York: Routledge.

Mann, M. (1987) 'Ruling Class Strategies and Citizenship', *Sociology* **21**(3): 339–54.

Marcotte, Roxanne D. (2010) 'Gender and Sexuality Online on Australian Muslim Forums', *Contemporary Islam* **4**(1): 117–38.

Marcuse, Herbert (1964) *One-Dimensional Man: Studies in the Ideology of Advanced Industrial Society.* London: Routledge & Kegan Paul.

Maresco, P. A. (2004) 'Mel Gibson's *The Passion of the Christ*: Market Segmentation, Mass Marketing and Promotion, and the Internet', *Journal of Religion and Popular Culture* 8(3): 1–10.

Marius, Richard (1999) *Martin Luther. The Christian between God and Death.* Cambridge, MA: Belknap Press.

Marlow, Louise (1997) *Hierarchy and Egalitarianism in Islamic Thought.* Cambridge University Press.

Marranci, Gabriele (2010) 'Sociology and Anthropology of Islam: A Critical Debate' in Bryan S. Turner (ed.) *The New Blackwell Companion to the Sociology of Religion.* Oxford: Wiley-Blackwell, 364–87.

Marsden, George M. (1980) *Fundamentalism and American Culture. The Shaping of Twentieth-century Evangelicalism.* New York: Oxford University Press.

Marshall, T. H. (1950) *Citizenship and Social Class and Other Essays.* Cambridge University Press.

  (1964) *Class, Citizenship and Social Development.* University of Chicago Press.

Martin, David (1978) *A General Theory of Secularization.* Oxford: Blackwell.

  (1990) *Tongues of Fire. The Explosion of Pentecostalism in Latin America.* Oxford: Blackwell.

  (2002) *Pentecostalism: The World their Parish.* Oxford: Blackwell.

Marty, Martin E. (1970) *Righteous Empire. The Protestant Experience in America.* New York: The Dial Press.

Marty, Martin E. and Appleby, R. Scott (eds.) (1991) *The Fundamentalist Project 1. Fundamentalism Observed.* University of Chicago Press.

Marx, Karl ([1844] 1967) 'The Jewish Question' in Lloyd David Easton and Kurt Guddat (eds.) *Writings of the Young Marx on Philosophy and Society.* New York: Anchor Doubleday.

  ([1867] 1974) *Capital,* 3 vols. London: Lawrence and Wishart.

Matar, N. (1998) *Islam in Britain 1558–1685.* Cambridge University Press.

Mauss, Marcel (1979) 'Body Techniques' in *Sociology and Psychology.* London: Routledge, pp. 95–139.

Mazower, Mark (1998) *Dark Continent. Europe's Twentieth Century.* London: Penguin Books.

McCormack, B. L. (1995) *Karl Barth's Critically Realistic Dialectical Theology. Its Genesis and Development 1909–1936.* Oxford: Clarendon.

McGrath, Alister E. (2003) *A Brief History of Heaven,* Oxford: Blackwell.

McLuhan, Marshall (1964) *Understanding the Media. The Extension of Man*. Toronto: McGraw-Hill.

McMylor, Peter (1994) *Alasdair MacIntyre. Critic of Modernity*. London: Routledge.

Mennell, Stephen (2007) *The American Civilizing Process*. Cambridge: Polity Press.

Mernissi, Fatima (2003) *Beyond the Veil. Male–Female Dynamics in Muslim Society*. London: Saqi Press.

Merry, S. E. (2004) 'Colonial and Postcolonial Law' in A. Sarat (ed.) *The Blackwell Companion to Law and Society*. Oxford: Blackwell, pp. 569–88.

Meskell, L. M. and Joyce, R. A. (2003) *Embodied Lives: Figuring Ancient Maya and Egyptian Experience*. London: Routledge.

Mestrovic, S. G. (1997) *Postemotional Society*. London: Sage.

Milbank, John (1990) *Theology and Social Theory. Beyond Secular Reason*. Oxford: Blackwell.

Milbank, John, Pickstock, C. and Ward, G. (eds.) (1999) *Radical Orthodoxy. A New Theology*. London and New York: Routledge.

Mills, C. Wright (1959) *The Power Elite*. New York: Oxford University Press.

Mitzman, Arthur (1971) *The Iron Cage. An Historical Interpretation of Max Weber*. New York: Universal Library.

Modood, Tariq (2008) 'Multiculturalism, Citizenship and National Identity' in Engin F. Isin, Peter Nyers and Bryan S. Turner (eds.) *Citizenship Between Past and Future*. London: Routledge, pp. 113–22.

Montaigne, Michel de ([1580] 2003) *The Complete Essays*. London: Penguin.

Moore, Barrington Jr. (1970) *Reflections on the Causes of Human Misery and upon Certain Proposals to Eliminate Them*. London: Allen Lane.

Nafisi, Azar (2008) *Reading Lolita in Tehran. A Memoir in Books*. New York: Random House.

Nancy, Jean-Luc (2005) *The Ground of the Image*. New York: Fordham University Press.

Navaro-Yashin, Yael (2002) 'The Market for Identities: Secularism, Islamism and Commodities' in Deniz Kandiyoti and Ayse Saktanber (eds.) *Fragments of Culture. The Everyday of Modern Turkey*. London: I. B.Taurus, pp. 221–53.

Nelson, D. D. (1998) *National Manhood. Capitalist Citizenship and the Imagined Fraternity of White Men*. Durham and London: Duke University Press.

Newell, Catherine (2010) 'Approaches to the Study of Buddhism' in Bryan S. Turner (ed.) *The New Blackwell Companion to the Sociology of Religion*. Oxford: Blackwell-Wiley, pp. 388–406.

Nicholson, R. A. (2000) *The Mystics of Islam*. London: Routledge.

Niebuhr, H. R. (1957) *The Social Sources of Denominationalism*. New York: Henry Holt and Co.

Nietzsche, Friedrich (1979) *Ecce Homo*. Harmondsworth: Penguin.

Niezen, R. (2005) *A World beyond Difference. Cultural Identity in an Age of Globalization*. Oxford: Blackwell.

Norton, Robert E. (2002) *Stefan George and his Circle*. Ithaca and London: Cornell University Press.

O'Connor, June (1989) 'Rereading, Reconceiving and Reconstructing Traditions: Feminist Research in Religion', *Women's Studies* 17: 101–23.

Obeyesekere, G. (2003) 'Buddhism' in Mark Juergensmeyer (ed.) *Global Religions. An Introduction*. Oxford University Press, pp. 63–77.

Offe, Claus (2005) *Reflections on America. Tocqueville, Weber and Adorno*. Cambridge: Polity Press.

Oldstone-Moore, Jennifer (2005) 'Confucianism' in Michael D. Coogan (ed.) *Eastern Religions*. London: Duncan Baird, pp. 314–415.

Othman, N. (1999) 'Grounding Human Rights Arguments in Non-Western Culture: *Shari'a* and the Citizenship Rights of Women in a Modern Islamic State' in J. R. Bauer and D. A. Bell (eds.) *The East Asian Challenge for Human Rights*. Cambridge University Press, pp. 169–92.

Otto, Rudolf ([1923] 2003) *The Idea of the Holy*. Oxford University Press.

Ould Mohamedou, M. M. (2005) 'Non-Linearity of Engagement: Transnational Armed Groups, International Law, and the Conflict Between al-Qaeda and the United States', policy brief, Program on Humanitarian Policy and Conflict Research, Harvard University.

Parsons, Talcott (1937) *The Structure of Social Action*. New York: McGraw-Hill.

(1942) 'Democracy and the Social Structure of Pre-Nazi Germany', *Journal of Legal and Political Sociology* 1: 96–114.

(1951) *The Social System*. London: Routledge and Kegan Paul.

(1963) 'Christianity and Modern Industrial Society' in E. A. Tiryakian (ed.) *Sociological Theory, Values and Sociocultural Change: Essays in Honor of Pitrim A. Sorokin*. New York: Free Press, pp. 33–70.

(1964) *Social Structure and Personality*. New York: Free Press.

(1966) 'Introduction' in Max Weber (1966) *The Sociology of Religion*. London: Methuen, pp. xix–lxvii.

(1968a) 'The Distribution of Power in American Society' in G. William Domhoff and Hoyt B. Ballard (eds.) *C. Wright Mills and the Power Elite*. Boston: Beacon Press, pp. 60–87.

(1968b) 'Christianity' in David L. Sills (ed.) *International Encyclopedia of the Social Sciences*, vol. 2. New York: Crowell, Collier and MacMillian, pp. 425–47.

(1971) *The System of Modern Societies*. Englewood Cliffs: Prentice Hall.

(1974) 'Religion in Postindustrial America: The Problem of Secularization', *Social Research* 51(1–2): 193–225.

(1977) *Social Systems and the Evolution of Action Theory*. New York: Free Press.

(1978) *Action Theory and the Human Condition*. New York: Free Press.

(1979) 'Religion and Economic Symbolism in the Western World', *Sociological Inquiry* **49**: 1–48.

(1999) 'Belief, Unbelief and Disbelief' in Bryan S. Turner (ed.) *The Talcott Parsons Reader*. Oxford: Blackwell, pp. 51–79.

(2007) *American Society. A Theory of the Societal Community*. Boulder: Paradigm.

Parsons, Talcott, Bales, R. F., Olds, J., Zelditch, M. and Slater, P. E. (1955) *Family, Socialization and Interaction Process*. New York: Free Press.

Parsons, Talcott, Fox, R. C. and Lidz, V. M. (1972) 'The "Gift of Life" and Its Reciprocation', *Social Research* **39**(3): 367–415.

Parsons, Talcott and Platt, Gerald M. (1973) *The American University*. Cambridge, MA: Harvard University Press.

Parsons, Talcott and Smelser, Neil (1956) *Economy and Society*. London: Routledge.

Paul, Diana Y. (1985) *Women in Buddhism. Images of the Feminine in the Mahayana Tradition*, 2nd edn. Berkeley: University of California Press.

Pecora, Ferdinand (1939) *Wall Street under Oath*. New York: Simon and Schuster.

Peletz, Michael G. (2002) *Islamic Modern: Religious Courts and Cultural Politics in Malaysia*. Princeton University Press.

(2003) *Reinscribing 'Asian (Family) Values': Nation Building, Subject Making, and Judicial Process in Malaysia's Islamic Courts*. Notre Dame, IN: Occasional Papers of the Erasmus Institute.

(2007) *Gender, Sexuality and Body Politics in Modern Asia*. Ann Arbor: Association for Asian Studies.

Perkins, Franklin (2004) *Leibniz and China. A Commerce of Light*. Cambridge University Press.

Pew Research Center (2007) *Muslim Americans. Middle Class and Mostly Mainstream*. Washington, DC: Pew Research Center.

Phillips, Kevin (2008) *Bad Money. Reckless Finance, Failed Politics, and the Global Crisis of American Capitalism*. Melbourne: Scribe.

Pieterse, J. N. (1995) 'Globalization as Hybridization' in M. Featherstone, S. Lash and R. Robertson (eds.) *Global Modernities*. London: Sage, pp. 45–68.

Pope, Liston (1942) *Millhands and Preachers*. New Haven: Yale University Press.

Putnam, R. D. (2000) *Bowling Alone. The Collapse and Revival of American Community*. New York: Simon & Schuster.

Quint, D. (1998) *Montaigne and the Quality of Mercy. Ethical and Political Themes in the Essais*. Princeton University Press.

Radkau, Joachim (2009) *Max Weber. A Biography*. Cambridge: Polity Press.

Ramadan, T. (2004) *Western Muslims and the Future of Islam*. New York: Oxford University Press.

Rasmussen, Barry G. (2002) 'Richard Hooker's Trinitarian Hermeneutics of Grace', *Anglican Theological Review* 84(4): 929–41.

Rawls, John (1993) *Political Liberalism*. New York: Columbia University Press.

(1999) *The Law of Peoples*. Cambridge, MA: Harvard University Press.

Redding, Gordon (1993) *The Spirit of Chinese Capitalism*. Berlin: De Gruyter.

Reid, Anthony (1988) *Southeast Asia in the Age of Commerce 1450–1680*. Yale University Press.

Reid, Anthony and Gilsenan, Michael (eds.) (2007) *Islamic Legitimacy in a Plural Asia*. London and New York: Routledge.

Rey, Terry (2004) 'Marketing the Goods of Salvation: Bourdieu on Religion', *Religion* 34: 331–43.

(2007) *Bourdieu on Religion: Imposing Faith and Legitimacy*. London: Equinox Publishing.

Richman, Michele H. (2002) *Sacred Revolutions. Durkheim and the College de Sociologie*. Minneapolis: University of Minnesota Press.

Rieff, P. (1966) *Triumph of the Therapeutic: Uses of Faith after Freud*. University of Chicago Press.

(2006) *My Life among the Deathworks*. Charlottesville and London: University of Virginia Press.

Rinaldo, Rachel (2010) 'Women and Piety Movements' in Bryan S. Turner (ed.) *The New Blackwell Companion to the Sociology of Religion*. Oxford: Wiley-Blackwell, pp. 584–605.

Robertson, Alexander (2001) *Greed. Gut Feelings, Growth and History*. Cambridge: Polity.

Robertson, Roland (ed.) (1969) *Sociology of Religion. Selected Readings*. Harmondsworth: Penguin Books.

Robertson, Roland (1970) *The Sociological Interpretation of Religion*. Oxford: Basil Blackwell.

(1978) *Meaning and Change. Explorations in the Cultural Sociology of Modern Societies*. Oxford: Basil Blackwell.

(1992a) *Globalization. Social Theory and Global Culture*. London: Sage.

(1992b) 'The Economization of Religion? Reflections on the Promise and Limitations of the Economic Approach', *Social Compass* 39(1): 147–57.

Robertson, Roland and Turner, Bryan S. (eds.) (1991) *Talcott Parsons: Theorist of Modernity*. London: Sage.

Rodinson, Maxime ([1966] 1978) *Islam and Capitalism*. Austin: University of Texas Press.

Roof, Wade C. (1993) *A Generation of Seekers: The Spiritual Journeys of the Baby Boom Generation*. San Francisco: Harper.

(1999) *Spiritual Marketplace. Baby Boomers and the Remaking of American Religion*. Princeton University Press.

Rorty, Richard (1979) *Philosophy and the Mirror of Nature*. Princeton University Press.

(1989) *Contingency, Irony and Solidarity*. Cambridge University Press.

(1998) 'Pragmatism as Romantic Polytheism' in M. Dickstein (ed.) *The Revival of Pragmatism. New Essays on Social Thought, Law and Culture*. Durham and London: Duke University Press, pp. 21–36.

Rosati, Massimo (2009) *Ritual and the Sacred. A Neo-Durkheimian Analysis of Politics, Religion and the Self*. Farnham: Ashgate.

Rosenman, Samuel J. (1938) *Public Papers and Addresses of Franklin D. Roosevelt*. New York: Random House.

Rousseau, Jean-Jacques ([1762] 1979) *Emile or On Education*. New York: Basic Books.

(1973) *The Social Contract and Other Discourses*. London: Dent and Sons.

Roy, Olivier (1994) *The Failure of Political Islam*. Cambridge, MA: Harvard University Press.

(2004) *Globalized Islam: The Search for a New Ummah*. New York: Columbia University Press.

Royle, Edward (1974) *Victorian Infidels. The Origins of the British Secularist Movement 1791–1866*. Manchester University Press.

Rubin, Miri (2009) *Mother of God. A History of the Virgin Mary*. New Haven and London: Yale University Press.

Russell, S. (1996) *Jewish Identity and Civilizing Processes*. London: Macmillan.

Sadiki, Larbi (2004) *The Search for Arab Democracy. Discourses and Counter-Discourses*. New York: Columbia University Press.

Saharso, S. (2000) 'Female Autonomy and Cultural Imperative: Two Hearts Beating Together' in W. Kymlicka and W. Norman (eds.) *Citizenship in Diverse Societies*. Oxford University Press, pp. 224–42.

Said, Edward W. (1978) *Orientalism*. Harmondsworth: Penguin.

(1984) *The World, the Text and the Critic*. London: Faber & Faber.

(1993) *Culture and Imperialism*. New York: Alfred A. Knopf.

Saikal, Amin (2003) *Islam and the West. Conflict or Cooperation?* Basingstoke: Palgrave Macmillan.

Salemink, Oscar (2008) 'Spirits of Consumption and the Capitalist Ethic in Vietnam' in Pattana Kitiarsa (ed.) *Religious Commodifications in Asia. Marketing Gods*. London: Routledge, pp. 147–68.

Sanders, Clifton (1987) Marks of Mischief: Becoming and Being Tattooed. *Journal of Contemporary Ethnography* 16(4): 395–432.

Santos, B. de S. (1995) *Towards a New Common Sense. Law, Science and Politics in Paradigmatic Transition*. London: Routledge.

Sarkozy, N. (2004) *La République, les religions, l'espérance*. Paris: Éditions du Cerf.

Sassen, Saskia (2007) *A Sociology of Globalization*. New York: Norton.

Savage, Mike and Williams, Karel (eds.) (2008) *Remembering Elites*. Oxford: Blackwell.

Scaff, Lawrence A. (2005) 'Remnants of Romanticism. Max Weber in Oklahoma and Indian Territory', *Journal of Classical Sociology* 5(1): 54–72.

Scharf, B. R. (1970) 'Durkheimian and Freudian Theories of Religion: The Case for Judaism', *British Journal of Sociology* 21: 151–63.

Scheff, T. J (2004) 'Elias, Freud and Goffman: Shame as the Master Emotion' in S. Loyal and S. Quilley (eds.) *The Sociology of Norbert Elias*. Cambridge: Polity, pp. 229–42.

Schleiermacher, F. (1996) *On Religion: Speeches to its Cultured Despisers*. Cambridge University Press.

Schluchter, Wolfgang (ed.) (1983) *Max Webers Studie uber das Konfuzianismus und Taoismus. Interpretation und Kritik*. Frankfurt: Suhrkamp.
(1987) *Max Webers Sicht des Islams. Interpretation und Kritik*. Frankfurt: Suhrkamp.

Schmitt, Carl (1976) *The Concept of the Political*. University of Chicago Press.
([1934] 1985) *Political Theology*. Cambridge, MA: MIT Press.

Schneider, L. (ed.) (1964) *Religion, Culture and Society. A Reader in the Sociology of Religion*. New York: John Wiley & Sons.

Scholem, Gershom (1997) *On the Mystical Shape of the Godhead. Basic Concepts in the Kabbalah*. New York: Knopf.

Schopen, Gregory (1997) *Bones, Stones and Buddhist Monks. Collected Papers on the Archaeology, Epigraphy and Texts of Monastic Buddhism in India*. Honolulu: University of Hawaii Press.

Schrag, C. O. (1970) *Existence and Freedom. Towards an Ontology of Human Finitude*. Evanston: Northwestern University Press.

Schultheis, Franz and Pfeuffer, Andreas (2009) 'Mit Weber genen Weber: Pierre Bourdieu im Gesprach' in *Pierre Bourdieu Religion: Schriften zur Kuktursoziologie*, vol. 5. Constance: Constance University Press, pp. 111–29.

Schwab, Raymond ([1950] 1984) *The Oriental Renaissance. Europe's Discovery of India and the East 1680–1880*. New York: Columbia University Press.

Seigel, J. (2005) *The Idea of the Self. Thought and Experience in Western Europe since the Seventeenth Century*. Cambridge University Press.

Sen, Amartya (2009) *The Idea of Justice*. Cambridge, MA: Harvard University Press.

Shankland, D. (1999) *Islam and Society in Turkey*. Huntingdon: The Eothen Press.

Sharot, S. (2001) *A Comparative Sociology of World Religions. Virtuosos, Priest and Popular Religion*. New York University Press.

Shklar, Judith H. (1991) *American Citizenship. The Quest for Inclusion*. Cambridge, MA: Harvard University Press.

Sica, Alan and Turner, Stephen (eds.) (2006) *The Disobedient Generation. Social Theorists in the Sixties*. Chicago University Press.

Silber, I. F. (1995) *Virtuosity, Charisma and Social Order*. Cambridge University Press.

Simmel, George (1997) *Essays on Religion*. New Haven and London: Yale University Press.

Skidelsky, Robert (2009) *Keynes. The Return of the Master*. New York: Public Affairs.

Small Wars Journal. Available at http://smallwarsjournal.com/blog/journal/docs-temp/181-sullivan.pdf, accessed June 2009.

Smart, Ninian (1989) *The World's Religions. Old Traditions and Modern Transformations*. Cambridge University Press.

Smith, Graeme (2008) *A Short History of Secularism*. London: I. B. Tauris.

Smith, Warren W. (2008) *China's Tibet? Autonomy or Assimilation*. Lanham: Rowman and Littlefield.

Smith, Wilfred Cantwell (1962) *The Meaning and End of Religion*. New York: Mentor Books.

Smith, William Robertson ([1889] 1997) *Lectures on the Religion of the Semites*. London: Routledge.

Snyder, F. (2004) 'Economic Globalization and the Law in the Twenty-first Century' in A. Sarat (ed.) *The Blackwell Companion to Law and Society*. Oxford: Blackwell, pp. 624–40.

Sombart, Werner (1915) *The Quintessence of Capitalism*. London: T. Fisher Unwin Ltd.

Somers, Margaret R. (2008) *Genealogies of Citizenship. Markets, Statelessness and the Right to Have Rights*. Cambridge University Press.

Soroush, Abdolkarim (2000) *Reason, Freedom and Democracy. Essential Writings of Abdolkarim Soroush*. Oxford University Press.

Soysal, Y. N. (1997) 'Changing Parameters of Citizenship and Claims-making: Organised Islam in European Public Spheres', *Theory and Society* 26(4): 509–527.

Spencer, B. and Gillén, F. J. ([1904] 1997) *The Northern Tribes of Central Australia*. London: Routledge/Thoemmes Press.

Spinner-Halevy, Jeff (2005) 'Hinduism, Christianity and Liberal Religious Tolerance', *Political Theory* 33(1): 28–57.

Sprenkel, O. B. van der (1964) 'Max Weber on China', *History and Theory* 3(3): 348–70.

Stanlis, P. J. (1958) *Edmund Burke and the Natural Law*. University of Michigan Press.

Stark, Rodney and Finke, R. (2000) *Acts of Faith. Explaining the Human Side of Religion*. Berkeley: University of California Press.

Stauth, Georg and Turner, Bryan S. (1986) 'Nietzsche in Weber oder die Geburt des modernen Genius im professionellen Menschen', *Zeitschrift für Soziologie* 15(2): 81–94.

   (1988) *Nietzsche's Dance: Resentment, Reciprocity and Resistance in Social Life*. Oxford: Basil Blackwell.

Stiglitz, Joseph (2002) *Globalization and its Discontents*. New York: W. W. Norton.

Stolow, Jeremy (2010) 'Religion, Media and Globalization' in Bryan S. Turner (ed.) *The New Blackwell Companion to the Sociology of Religion*. Oxford: Wiley-Blackwell, pp. 544–62.

Stone, A. R. (1991) 'Will the Real Body Please Stand Up? Boundary Stories about Virtual Cultures' in M. Benedikt (ed.) *Cyberspace: First Steps*. London: MIT Press.

Strauss, Leo (1950) *Natural Right and History*. University of Chicago Press.

Strenski, I. (1997) *Durkheim and the Jews of France*. University of Chicago Press.

   (2003) 'Sacrifice, Gift and the Social Logic of Muslim "Human Bombers"', *Terrorism and Political Violence* 15(3): 1–34.

Sullivan, John, P. and Elkus, Adam (2009) 'Postcard from Mumbai: Modern Urban Siege', *Small Wars Journal*.

Swartz, David (1996) 'Bridging the Study of Culture and Religion. Pierre Bourdieu's Political Economy of Symbolic Power', *Sociology of Religion* 57: 71–85.

Swedberg, Richard (1986) 'Introduction' in Talcott Parsons *The Marshall Lectures*. Uppsala: Uppsala University Department of Sociology Research Reports, vol. 4: i–xxxiv.

Tamney, Joseph B. (2002) *The Resilience of Conservative Religion. The Case of Popular, Conservative Protestant Congregations*. Cambridge University Press.

Tanner, J. R. (1960) *English Constitutional Conflicts of the Seventeenth Century 1603–1689*. Cambridge University Press.

Tappert, Theodore G. (ed.) (1967) *Selected Writings of Martin Luther 1523–1526*. Philadelphia: Fortress Press.

Taubes, Jacob (2004) *The Political Theology of Paul*. Stanford University Press.

Tawney, R. H. (1926) *Religion and the Rise of Capitalism. A Historical Study*. London: John Murray.

Taylor, Charles (2002) *Varieties of Religion Today*. Cambridge, MA: Harvard University Press.

(2007) *A Secular Age*. Cambridge, MA: Belknap Press.

Taylor, Philip (2004) *Goddess on the Rise. Pilgrimage and Popular Religion in Vietnam*. Honolulu: University of Hawai'i Press.

Taylor, Philip (ed.) (2007) *Modernity and Re-enchantment*. Singapore: ISEAS.

Tehranian, M. (1993) 'Islamic Fundamentalism in Iran and the Discourse of Development' in M. E. Marty and R. S. Appleby (eds.) *Fundamentalisms and Society*. University of Chicago Press, pp. 341–73.

Tenbruck, Freidrich (1975) 'Das Werk. Max Webers', *Kölner Zeitschrift für Soziologie und Sozialpsychologie* **27**: 663–702.

(1980) 'The Problem of Thematic Unity in the Works of Max Weber', *British Journal of Sociology* **31**(3): 316–51.

Thompson, Edward Palmer (1963) *The Making of the English Working Class*, 2nd edn. London: Victor Gollancz.

Thysell, C. (2000) *The Pleasure of Discernment. Marguerite de Navarre as Theologian*. Oxford University Press.

Tibi, Basam (1995) 'Culture and Knowledge. The Politics of Islamization of Knowledge as a Postmodern Project? The Fundamentalist Claim to De-westernization', *Theory Culture & Society* **12**(1): 1–24.

Tocqueville, Alexis de ([1835/1840] 2003) *Democracy in America*. London: Penguin Books.

([1856] 1955) *The Old Regime and the French Revolution*. New York: Doubleday.

Tong, Joy Kooi-Chin and Turner, Bryan S. (2008) 'Women, Piety and Practice: A Study of Women and Religious Practice in Malaya', *Contemporary Islam* **2**: 41–59.

Torpey, John (2010) 'American Exceptionalism' in Bryan S. Turner (ed.) *The New Blackwell Companion to the Sociology of Religion*. Oxford: Wiley-Blackwell, pp. 141–59.

Tribe, Keith (ed.) (1989) *Reading Weber*. London and New York: Routledge.

Trocki, Carl A. (2006) *Singapore. Wealth, Power and the Culture of Control*. London: Routledge.

Troeltsch, Ernst (1931) *The Social Teachings of the Christian Churches*. London: George Allen & Unwin.

Tu Wei-Ming (1985) *Confucian Thought. Selfhood as Creative Transformation*. State University of New York Press.

Turner, Bryan S. ([1974] 1998) *Weber and Islam. A Critical Study*, 2nd edn. London: Routledge & Kegan Paul.

(1978) *Marx and the End of Orientalism*. London: Allen & Unwin.

(1986) *Citizenship and Capitalism. The Debate over Reformism*. London: Allen & Unwin.

(1987) 'A Note on Nostalgia', *Theory, Culture and Society* 4(1): 147–56.

(1991) *Religion and Social Theory*, 2nd edn. London: Sage.

(1992) *Regulating Bodies. Essay in Medical Sociology*. London: Routledge.

Turner, Bryan S. (ed.) (1993a) *Citizenship and Social Theory*. London: Sage.

Turner, Bryan S. (1993b) 'Preface' in K. Löwith *Max Weber and Karl Marx*. London: Routledge, pp. 1–32.

(1994) *Orientalism, Postmodernism and Globalism*. London: Routledge.

(1996) *For Weber. Essays on the Sociology of Fate*. London: Routledge.

(1997) 'The Body in Western Society: Social Theory and its Perspectives' in Sarah Coakley (ed.) *Religion and the Body*. Cambridge University Press, pp. 15–41.

(1999a) *Classical Sociology*. London: Sage.

(1999b) 'The Possibility of Primitiveness: Towards a Sociology of Body Marks in Cool Societies', *Body & Society* 5(2–3): 39–50.

(2001a) 'The End(s) of Humanity: Vulnerability and the Metaphors of Membership', *The Hedgehog Review* 3(2): 7–32.

(2001b) 'The Erosion of Citizenship', *British Journal of Sociology* 52(2): 189–209.

(2002) 'Cosmopolitan Virtue, Globalization and Patriotism', *Theory Culture & Society* 19(1–2): 45–63.

(2004) 'Weber and Elias on Religion and Violence: Warrior Charisma and the Civilizing Process' in S. Loyal and S. Quilley (eds.) *The Sociology of Norbert Elias*. Cambridge: Polity, pp. 245–64.

(2005) 'Talcott Parsons's Sociology of Religion and the Expressive Revolution. The Problem of Western Individualism', *Journal of Classical Sociology*, 5(3): 303–18.

(2006) *Vulnerability and Human Rights*. Pennsylvania State University Press.

(2007a) 'The Enclave Society: Towards a Sociology of Immobility', *European Journal of Social Theory* 10(2): 287–303.

(2007b) 'Managing Religions: State Responses to Religious Diversity', *Contemporary Islam* 1(2): 123–37.

(2008a) *The Body and Society*. London: Sage.

(2008b) 'Does Anthropology Still Exist?', *Society* 45: 260–6.

Turner, Bryan S. (ed.) (2008c) *Religious Diversity and Civil Society. A Comparative Analysis*. Oxford: Bardwell Press.

Turner, Bryan S. (2009a) 'Reshaping the Sociology of Religion: Globalization, Spirituality and the Erosion of the Social', *The Sociological Review* 57(1): 186–200.

(2009b) 'Max Weber on Islam and Confucianism: The Kantian Theory of Secularization' in Peter B. Clarke (ed.) *The Oxford Handbook of the Sociology of Religion.* Oxford University Press, pp. 79–97.

(2009c) 'Religious Speech. The Ineffable Nature of Religious Communication in the Information Age', *Theory, Culture & Society* 25(7–8): 219–35.

(2009d) 'Goods not Gods: New Spiritualities, Consumerism and Religious Markets' in Ian Rees Jones, Paul Higgs and David J. Erkerdt (eds.) *Consumption and Generational Change. The Rise of Consumer Lifestyles.* New Brunswick: Transaction Publishers, pp. 37–62.

(2009e) 'The Sociology of the Body' in Bryan S. Turner (ed.) *The New Blackwell Companion to Social Theory.* Oxford: Wiley-Blackwell, pp. 513–32.

(2009f) *Can We Live Forever? A Sociological and Moral Inquiry.* London: Anthem.

Turner, Bryan S. (ed.) (2009g) *The New Blackwell Companion to Social Theory.* Oxford: Wiley-Blackwell.

Turner, Bryan S. (2010) 'Revisiting Weber and Islam', *British Journal of Sociology,* January: 161–6.

Turner, Bryan S. and Khondker, Habibul Haque (2010) *Globalization East and West.* London: Sage.

Turner, Bryan S. and Rojek, Chris (2002) *Society and Culture. Principles of Scarcity and Solidarity.* London: Sage.

Twersky, Isadore (ed.) (1972) *A Maimonides Reader.* New York: Behrman House.

Twining, W. (2000) *Globalisation and Legal Theory.* London: Butterworths.

Ullmann, Walter (1977) *Medieval Foundations of Renaissance Humanism.* London: Paul Elek.

Urry, John (2000) *Sociology Beyond Societies. Mobilities for the Twenty-first Century.* London: Routledge.

(2007) *Mobilities.* Cambridge: Polity.

Van der Veer, Peter (1994) *Religious Nationalism: Hindus and Muslims in India.* Berkeley: University of California Press.

van Wichelen, Sonja (2010) 'Formations of Public Piety: Discourses of Veiling and the Making of Middle Class Bodies in Contemporary Indonesia' in Bryan S. Turner and Zheng Yangwen (eds.) *The Body in Asia.* New York: Berghahn Books, pp. 75–94.

Varisco, Daniel Marton (2010) 'Muslims and the Media in the Blogosphere', *Contemporary Islam* 4(1): 157–77.

Vasquez, Manuel A. and Marquardt, Marie Friedmann (2003) *Globalizing the Sacred. Religion across the Americas.* New Brunswick: Rutgers University Press.

Veblen, Thorstein (1918) *The Higher Learning in America. A Memorandum on the Conduct of Universities by Business Men.* New York: B. W. Huebsch.

(1994) *The Theory of the Leisure Class.* Harmondsworth: Penguin.

Verter, Bradford (2003) 'Spiritual Capital: Theorizing Religion with Bourdieu against Bourdieu', *Sociological Theory* 21(2): 150–74.

Voeglin, Eric (1952) *The New Science of Politics.* University of Chicago Press.

Voll, J. O. (1982) *Islam: Continuity and Change in the Modern World.* Boulder: Westview Press.

Vollenhoven, Cornelis van (1909) *Miskenningen van het adatrecht.Vier voordrachten ann de Nederlandsch-Indische Bestuursacademie.* Leiden: Brill.

Volpi, Fredric (2006) 'Strategies for Regional Cooperation in the Mediterranean: Rethinking the Parameters of the Debate' in F. Volpi (ed.) *Transnational Islam and Regional Security.* London: Routledge, pp. vii–xxiii.

Volpi, Fredric and Turner, Bryan S. (2007) 'Making Islamic Authority Matter', *Theory Culture & Society* 24(2): 1–19.

Vries, Henk de (2002) *Religion and Violence. Philosophical Perspectives from Kant to Derrida.* Baltimore and London: Johns Hopkins University Press.

Vries, Henk de and Sullivan, Lawrence (eds.) (2006) *Political Theologies. Public Religions in a Post-Secular World.* New York: Fordham University Press.

Wagner, Peter (1999) 'After *Justification.* Repertoires of Evaluation and the Sociology of Modernity', *European Journal of Social Theory* 2(3): 341–57.

Waley, Arthur (1988) *The Analects of Confucius.* London: Unwin Hyman.

Ward, Graham (2006) 'The Future of Religion', *Journal of the American Academy of Religions* 74(1): 179–86.

Ward, Humphrey (1914) *Robert Elsmere.* London: John Murray.

Warne, Randi (2001) '(En)gendering Religious Studies' in Darlene Juschka (ed.) *Feminism in the Study of Religions. A Reader.* London and New York: Continuum, pp. 147–56.

Warner, M. (1983) *Alone of All Her Sex. The Myth and Cult of the Virgin Mary.* New York: Vintage Books.

Warner, R. S. (2004) 'Enlisting Smelser's Theory of Ambivalence to Maintaining Progress in Sociology of Religion's New Paradigm' in J. C. Alexander, G. T. Marx and C. L. Williams (eds.) *Self, Social Structure and Beliefs. Explorations in Sociology.* Berkeley: University of California Press, pp. 103–21.

Wartofsky, Marx W. (1977) *Feuerbach.* Cambridge University Press.

Watt, William Montgomery (1953) *Muhammed at Mecca*. Oxford University Press.

(1991) *Muslim–Christian Encounters. Perceptions and Misperceptions*. London and New York: Routledge.

(1999) *Islamic Political Thought*. Edinburgh University Press.

Watters, Ethan (2003) *Urban Tribes: A Generation Redefines Friendship, Family, and Commitment*. New York: Bloomsbury.

Weber, Marianne (1907) *Ehefrau und Mutter in der Rechtsentwicklung*. Tubingen: J. C. Mohr:

Weber, Max (1921) *Gesammelte Aufsätze zur Religions soziologie*. Tübingen: J. C. B. Mohr.

([1921] 1952) *Ancient Judaism*. Glencoe: Free Press.

(1951) *The Religion of China. Confucianism and Taoism*. New York: Macmillan.

(1958a) *The Religion of India*. New York: Free Press.

(1958b) *The City*. New York: Free Press.

(1966) *The Sociology of Religion*. London: Methuen.

(1978) *Economy and Society. Outline of Interpretative Sociology*, 2 vols. Berkeley: University of California Press.

(1989) 'The National State and Economic Policy' in Keith Tribe (ed.) *Reading Weber*. London and New York: Routledge, pp. 188–209.

(1991) 'Science as a Vocation' in *From Max Weber. Essays in Sociology*. London: Routledge, pp. 129–56.

(2002) *The Protestant Ethic and the 'Spirit' of Capitalism and Other Writings*. New York: Penguin.

(2009) 'Religious Rejections of the World and their Directions' in Hans H. Gerth and C. Wright Mills (eds.) (2009) *From Max Weber. Essays in Sociology*. London: Routledge, pp. 323–59.

Weiss, Raymond L. and Butterworth, Charles E. (eds.) (1975) *Laws Concerning Character Traits*. New York: Dover.

Wernick, Andrew (2001) *Auguste Comte and the Religion of Humanity. The Post-Theistic Program of French Social Theory*. Cambridge University Press.

Whitehead, A. N. ([1925] 1967) *Science and the Modern World*. New York: Macmillan.

(1926) *Religion in the Making*. Cambridge University Press.

([1929] 1978) *Process and Reality. An Essay in Cosmology*. New York: Free Press.

Wilkinson, Ian (2005) *Suffering. A Sociological Introduction*. Cambridge: Polity.

William, Gibson (1984) *Neuromancer*. London: Gollancz.

Williams, G. (1956) 'The Controversy Concerning the Word "Law"' in P. Laslett (ed.) *Philosophy, Politics and Society*. Oxford: Basil Blackwell, pp. 134–56.

Williams, R. M. (1965) *American Society. A Sociological Interpretation.* New York: Alfred A. Knopf.

Williams, R. R (1997) *Hegel's Ethics of Recognition.* Berkeley: University of California Press.

Wilson, Bryan (1959) 'An Analysis of Sect Development', *American Sociological Review* 24: 3–15.

(1966) *Religion in Secular Society. A Sociological Comment.* London: C. A. Watts & Co.

(1967) *Patterns of Sectarianism. Organization and Ideology in Social and Religious Movements.* London: Heinemann Educational Books.

(1970) *Religious Sects. A Sociological Study.* London: Weidenfeld & Nicolson.

(1976) *Contemporary Transformations of Religion.* London: Oxford University Press.

Wilson, Sherryl (2003) *Oprah, Celebrity and Formations of Self.* Basingstoke: Palgrave Macmillan.

Wittgenstein, Ludwig (1969) *On Certainty.* Oxford: Basil Blackwell.

(1979) *Remarks on Frazer's Golden Bough.* Retford: Brynmill.

Wolin, Richard (1994) *Walter Benjamin. An Aesthetic of Redemption.* Berkeley: University of California Press.

Woodhead, Linda and Heelas, Paul (eds.) (2000) *Religion in Modern Times. An Interpretive Anthology.* Oxford: Blackwell.

Woolf, R. (1968) *The English Religious Lyric in the Middle Ages.* Oxford: Clarendon Press.

Yang, Fenggang (2006) 'The Red, Black, and Gray Markets of Religion in China', *Sociological Quarterly* 47: 93–122.

(2007) 'Oligopoly Dynamics: Official Religions in China' in James A. Beckford and N. J. Demerath III (eds.) *The Sage Handbook of the Sociology of Religion.* London: Sage, pp. 635–53.

(2010) 'Religious Awakening in China under Communist Rule: A Political Economy Approach' in Bryan S. Turner (ed.) *The New Blackwell Companion to the Sociology of Religion.* Oxford: Wiley-Blackwell, pp. 431–55.

Yang, Fenggang and Tamney, Joseph (eds.) (2005) *State, Market and Religions in Chinese Societies.* Leiden: Brill.

Yinger, J. Milton (1967) 'Pluralism, Religion and Secularism', *Journal for the Scientific Study of Religion,* 5(1): 17–28.

Zabala, Santiago (ed.) (2005) *The Future of Religion.* New York: Columbia University Press.

Zaret, D. (2000) *Origins of Democratic Culture. Printing, Petitions and the Public Sphere in Early-modern England.* Princeton University Press.

Zelizer, Barbie (1993) *Covering the Body. The Kennedy Assassination, the Media and the Shaping of Collective Memory.* University of Chicago Press.

Zubrzycki, Geneviève (2006) *The Crosses of Auschwitz. Nationalism and Religion in Post-Communist Poland.* University of Chicago Press.

(2010) 'Religion and Nationalism: A Critical Re-examination' in Bryan S. Turner (ed.) *The New Blackwell Companion to the Sociology of Religion.* Oxford: Wiley-Blackwell, pp. 606–26.

Index

Note: Islamic topics, except *Shari'a*, are grouped under Islam